Praise for Edward F. Murphy's
Dak To

"Excellent . . . honest and realistic . . . Edward Murphy's meticulous research is unflawed and his writing style novel-like."
—*San Antonio Express-News*

"Unique insight . . . a no-holds-barred account . . . highly recommended."
—*Military magazine*

"Masterful . . . The author is to be congratulated on a superb, exciting historical work . . . Should be required reading throughout the army's school system."
—*Infantry magazine*

"Fast-paced . . . an impressive immediacy . . . one of the best recent accounts of the ground war in Vietnam."
—*Publishers Weekly*

"Well detailed . . . recommended."
—*Library Journal*

"Does honor to the men who served there by painstakingly chronicling their complex movements and actions."
—*The VVA Veteran magazine*

"Must reading . . . The value of this book is in the experiences of the men."
—*Army magazine*

Dak To

America's Sky Soldiers
in South Vietnam's Central Highlands

Edward F. Murphy

BALLANTINE BOOKS • NEW YORK

2007 Presidio Press Mass Market Edition

Published in the United States by Presidio Press, an imprint of The Random House Publishing Group, a division of Random House, Inc., New York.

PRESIDIO PRESS and colophon are trademarks of Random House, Inc.

Originally published in slightly different form in the United States in hardcover by Presidio Press in 1993.

All photographs not otherwise credited are from the author's collection or from *Vietnam: The Third Year—173d Airborne Brigade* by Maj. Robert R. Brewer and Sp5 Roger E. Hester (Japan, 1968), as indicated.

ISBN 978-0-8914-1910-5

Cover design: Derek Walls
Cover photograph: © Bettmann/Corbis

Printed in the United States of America

www.presidiopress.com

OPM 9   8   7   6   5

To the Sky Soldiers on The Wall

CONTENTS

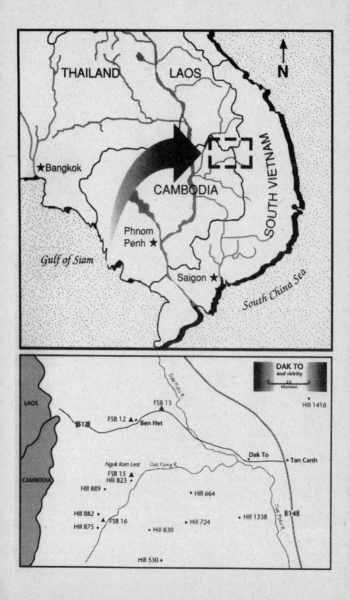

INTRODUCTION

America's ten-year involvement in the ground war in South Vietnam began with a sea battle. Just past noon on 31 July 1964, the destroyer USS *Maddox* steamed into the Gulf of Tonkin, east of North Vietnam, on an electronic spy mission. Under the code name Desoto, the *Maddox*, bristling with electronic intelligence gear, would plot the location of enemy radar and radio installations by homing in on the signals emitted by the North Vietnamese stations tracking her. Meanwhile, skilled technicians would monitor North Vietnamese radio traffic, while others upgraded navigational charts by noting various landmarks.

Earlier that morning, while the *Maddox* sailed toward its location to the southeast of Thanh Hoa, her crewmen spotted four American-made Swift torpedo boats on the horizon. The aluminum-hulled PT boats were headed south toward Da Nang, South Vietnam, after conducting the first in a planned series of covert raids on North Vietnamese coastal military installations.

Though manned by South Vietnamese commandos, the Swift boats actually operated under the direction of the Studies and Observation Group (SOG), a top-secret counterinsurgency force reporting directly to the U.S. Military Assistance Command, Vietnam. Trained by U.S. Special Forces soldiers and Central Intelligence Agency (CIA) operatives, the commandos had been practicing for their mission since March. At a closely guarded base south of Saigon the commandos repeatedly rehearsed their tactics for seaborne infiltration and coastal bombardment. By the end of July the SOG operators decided their charges were ready for their first mission. On 31 July the raiders would strike radar and radio installations on Hon Me and Hon Ngu, two islands about 120 miles north of the demilitarized zone (DMZ) dividing the two embattled countries. If that mission went well the Swift boats would return three days later to shell a mainland radar station at Cape Vinh Son, south of Vinh, North Vietnam.

In their first attack the Swift boats were met by heavy defensive fire as they neared the enemy islands and were unable to land the commando teams. Instead, they fired several dozen rounds from their 40mm cannons at the North Vietnamese positions. The boats then turned for the open sea and set a course for home.

Aboard the *Maddox* the electronic eavesdroppers intercepted a flurry of radio messages about the raid. It was obvious the North Vietnamese were highly agitated by this, the first shelling of North Vietnam by sea. The *Maddox* had been briefed about the so-called A-34 raids but had paid scant attention to them; after all, they had no part in the covert operations.

But then the radio interceptors noted the increasing frequency of the use of the *Maddox*'s hull number—DD-731—in the North Vietnamese messages. Obviously, the North Vietnamese were speculating about the destroyer's role in the raids. Seemingly unconcerned, the *Maddox*'s skipper, Comdr. Herbert L. Ogier, simply ordered a heightened state of watchfulness and continued his mission.

Two days later, 2 August, the *Maddox* cruised past Hon Me. The ship's lookouts spotted three North Vietnamese torpedo boats lingering near the island. A few minutes later the eavesdroppers picked up a message ordering the torpedo boats to attack the *Maddox*. Ogier ordered his ship seaward at full speed.

A short time later the *Maddox*'s radar picked up the three torpedo boats leaving Hon Me. With a top speed of fifty knots they would close on the destroyer in less than an hour. Ogier ordered his guns to fire when the boats closed to ten thousand yards.

At 1508 the ship's five-inch guns fired a salvo across the torpedo boats' bows. They kept coming. A few minutes later, with the boats approaching torpedo range, the *Maddox* let loose again. Still the boats came.

For the next twenty minutes the *Maddox* fired furiously at the three boats, sending great plumes of seawater skyward but scoring no hits. From twenty-seven hundred yards the North Vietnamese launched their first torpedo. Ogier turned sharply to port, averting the seaborne missile. Another torpedo cut through the water. *Maddox* dodged that one, too. Then, one of *Maddox*'s shells finally hit a torpedo boat. It stopped dead in the water. Seconds later, another torpedo boat slowed as if hit. The third boat turned to assist the other two.

A few minutes later four F-8 Crusaders from the carrier *Ticonderoga* arrived on the scene. They strafed the North Vietnamese boats for five minutes, then departed. About that time Ogier received a message from his superiors ordering him to depart the area. He did.

News of the North Vietnamese torpedo attack electrified official Washington. After consulting with his key advisers, President Lyndon B. Johnson held a press conference. He announced to the world that he had ordered the patrols in the Gulf of Tonkin continued. Further, a second destroyer had been added to the patrols. The ship's commanders were ordered to retaliate against any force that attacked them.

On 3 August the *Maddox*, trailed by the *Turner Joy*, returned to the Gulf of Tonkin. Although that day passed uneventfully, the North Vietnamese kept up a constant stream of radio traffic reporting on the ships' progress. That same night SOG's Swift boats launched their second covert attack on North Vietnamese shore installations, shelling a mainland radar site for thirty minutes before withdrawing.

All day 4 August the electronic technicians aboard the *Maddox* listened to a frenzy of North Vietnamese radio traffic about the A-34 raids. Again, it quickly became apparent that the North Vietnamese believed the destroyers controlled the raiders. Several of the intercepted messages contained orders to torpedo boats to prepare for an attack.

By nightfall, as the pair of destroyers turned away from the North Vietnamese coast to the open sea, a heavy squall line had moved into the area. Thick rain clouds, punctured by bright flashes of lightning, covered the area. High winds drove the sea into steep, frothy waves.

As the ships sailed east their radar began picking up blips. Ogier thought enemy torpedo boats might be lying in wait for them. Nerves in the ship's combat information centers tightened as the blips on the radar screen appeared and disappeared. At 2130 some of the blips began closing on the destroyers at high speed. About the same time the *Maddox*'s sonarman cried out, "Torpedo!" Several lookouts also reported seeing a torpedo in the water.

The *Turner Joy* opened fire on one of the blips. It disappeared from the screen. The *Maddox* opened fire, too. The pitch-black night was soon filled with the repeated flashes of five-inch guns. Continuing reports of torpedoes in the water forced the ships into violent evasive maneuvers. At one point the *Maddox*'s sonarman reported hearing twenty-two torpedoes in the water. Eight Crusaders from the *Ticonderoga* arrived overhead. Directed to the location of the North Vietnamese torpedo boats, as represented by the blips on the *Maddox*'s radar, the planes zoomed in for the kill. They flew back and forth across the sea but found no evidence of an enemy presence.

As suddenly as it had begun the engagement ended. The noise of the torpedoes disappeared from the sonarman's headset. The blips vanished from the radar screens. The destroyers turned and fled south at full speed.

When news of this second attack reached President Johnson he did not hesitate long before ordering a retaliatory air strike—code-named Pierce Arrow—against North Vietnamese torpedo boat bases. He also had his aides update a previously written congressional resolution approving of his actions.

In the meantime, the commanders of the *Maddox* and *Turner Joy* had carefully reviewed the engagement. They concluded that most, if not all, of the radar contacts had actually been phantoms caused by radar signals bouncing off the low clouds. The sonar contacts with torpedoes had probably been caused by erroneous readings of the ship's own propeller noises. The commanders hurriedly sent a message to their superiors stating that "many reported contacts and torpedoes fired appear doubtful."

Despite the dubiousness of the attack, President Johnson and his secretary of defense, Robert McNamara, ordered the Pierce Arrow strikes to go. At 2243 on 4 August (Washington time), the first jets roared down the deck of the *Ticonderoga*. Incredibly, less than an hour later, at 2337, President Johnson went on national television to announce the launching of the air strikes.

Armed with that advance warning, the North Vietnamese were ready when the first Crusaders appeared overhead. The planes hit their targets, destroying an estimated twenty-five torpedo boats. The North Vietnamese gunners hit four of the thirty-five U.S. planes, downing two.

On 7 August 1964, the U.S. Senate, with only two dissenting votes, approved a resolution to allow "the president . . . to take all necessary measures to repel any armed attack against the forces of the United States and prevent further aggression" in South Vietnam.

Though armed with this Tonkin Gulf Resolution, President Johnson, because of the approaching election, declined further retaliation despite increased insurgent Viet Cong (VC) aggression against South Vietnamese and American troops in South Vietnam. Even when the VC attacked the large U.S. air base at Bien Hoa, fifteen miles northeast of Saigon, on 31 October, killing four Americans and destroying or damaging thirteen U.S. bombers, Johnson offered no reprisals.

Three days later Johnson was elected president of the United States with the largest plurality ever accorded a candidate. Sixty-one percent of those voting cast their ballot for the man who had pledged to refuse "to allow American boys to do the fighting of Asian boys."

During the month of November Johnson kept his key advisers busy reviewing U.S. policy for South Vietnam. On 1 December he selected the option that essentially extended the current policy. The United States would continue its support to South Vietnam, with bombing reprisals against North Vietnam for incidents such as the "attacks" in the Gulf of Tonkin or at the Bien Hoa air base.

Yet when, on Christmas Eve, the Viet Cong exploded a truck bomb under a downtown Saigon hotel used by the Americans as a residence for officers, causing more than a hundred casualties, President Johnson refused to retaliate. Not until the VC attacked two American army support bases near Pleiku in the early morning hours of 7 February 1965, killing seven GIs and wounding one hundred, did President Johnson order reprisal air strikes against North Vietnam. Within twelve hours of the VC attack U.S. aircraft carriers in the Gulf of Tonkin, in an operation dubbed Flaming Dart, launched planes bound for targets in North Vietnam. The next day future premier Nguyen Cao Ky led planes of the South Vietnamese Air Force in a strike on North Vietnamese communications centers just above the DMZ.

The reprisal air attacks did not stop the VC. On the evening of 10 February they attacked an American enlisted man's barracks in Qui Nhon, a coastal city in central Binh Dinh Province. Twenty-one GIs died and another twenty-two were wounded when their building was blown up. Even as rescuers were pulling broken American bodies from the smoldering wreckage, planes from Flaming Dart II were streaking across the Southeast Asian sky toward North Vietnam.

Based on these continued attacks against purely American targets, President Johnson decided on 13 February to "execute a program of measured and limited air action" against North Vietnam. The air attacks would be scheduled once or twice weekly. The sustained bombing operation would be called Rolling Thunder.

Due to adverse weather the first Rolling Thunder raid did not occur until 2 March. A fleet of 104 U.S. Air Force jets—B-52s, F-100s, and F-105s—dropped 120 tons of bombs at Xom Bang, ten miles north of the DMZ. Enemy response was tough: Six U.S. aircraft were downed.

Since most of the participating air force planes were based at the air base at Da Nang, its security was vital to the success of the continuing Rolling Thunder raids. Though it was guarded by units of the Army of the Republic of Vietnam, MACV commander Gen. William C. Westmoreland seriously doubted their ability to adequately protect the sprawling complex. On 22 February Westmoreland's deputy, Lt. Gen. John L. Throckmorton, recommended that the defense of Da Nang be turned over to the U.S. Marines. Not only would they provide better security, he argued, but their presence would release ARVN troops for offensive operations against the VC.

Westmoreland, against the advice of U.S. Ambassador Maxwell D. Taylor, concurred in the recommendation. Accordingly, that same day he made the request for two marine battalions. Four days later Washington cabled its approval of Westmoreland's request.

At 0900 on 8 March 1965, marines of the 3d Battalion, 9th Marines, began an amphibious landing across the beaches of Da Nang. That afternoon C-130 transport planes brought in the 1st Battalion, 3d Marines, from Okinawa. An American ground presence in South Vietnam was a reality.

Over the next several weeks the role of the marines expanded from static defense to aggressive patrolling within several miles of Da Nang. At the same time, U.S. Army chief of staff Gen. Harold K. Johnson began arguing for an increased U.S. presence in South Vietnam. Only the United States, he insisted to the Joint Chiefs of Staff, was capable of applying sufficient pressure to North Vietnam to force it to halt its support of the Viet Cong.

General Johnson's arguments were enhanced when the Viet Cong exploded a car bomb in front of the U.S. embassy on 29 March. Two Americans and 18 Vietnamese were killed in the thunderous explosion, and another 160 people were injured; the embassy was effectively destroyed.

Westmoreland asked for, and received, nine more American infantry maneuver battalions. Some he would use to establish American bases at Qui Nhon and Nha Trang, others would go to the Chu Lai area south of Da Nang. For protection of the big American air base at Bien Hoa, and the strategically vital base at Vung Tau, at the mouth of the Saigon River, Westmoreland specifically requested the deployment of the elite 173d Airborne Brigade from Okinawa.

CHAPTER 1

TO VIETNAM

The transport plane carrying Brig. Gen. Ellis W. Williamson, commander of the 173d Airborne Brigade (Separate), touched down at Tan Son Nhut airport outside of Saigon early on the morning of 25 April 1965. Williamson's arrival in South Vietnam's capital was in response to a top-secret message he'd received the previous day at his headquarters on Okinawa. In concurring with General Westmoreland's request for the deployment of the 173d to South Vietnam, the Department of the Army ordered Williamson's unit to prepare for the movement.

Accompanied by his S-3, S-4, and his aide, Williamson was escorted to Westmoreland's office at MACV headquarters in downtown Saigon. After a perfunctory greeting, Westmoreland demanded of Williamson, "What are you doing in uniform?"

"I wear one all the time," Williamson answered, somewhat surprised.

"My message specifically said to wear civilian clothes," Westmoreland pointed out.

"I do have slacks and a shirt with me," Williamson offered.

"Put them on before you leave the building," Westmoreland ordered. "I don't want the Viet Cong, or the press, to know you're here."

General Williamson was perplexed at the exchange. Although he was aware of the war that the South Vietnamese government had been waging against the North Vietnamese-backed Viet Cong insurgents, Williamson's own demanding duties had kept him from being completely cognizant of all the factors affecting the United States' role in the Southeast Asian country. He was not sure what was wanted of him or his unit.

As Williamson listened intently, Westmoreland outlined the role he planned for the 173d. With the Rolling Thunder air raids expanding, Westmoreland explained, he was becoming increasingly concerned about the ability of the ARVN to provide adequate security to the U.S. Air Force bases supporting the raids. In addition, the introduction of U.S. Army units to guard the bases would free those ARVN units currently performing that mission for offensive operations against the VC.

General Westmoreland revealed to General Williamson that several U.S. divisions were scheduled to arrive in South Vietnam within months. The 173d would also have the mission of clearing the incoming units' proposed base camp sites of the enemy. The brigade's deployment to South Vietnam, then, would be a temporary one, Westmoreland said, probably not lasting more than sixty days. After discussing a few more details of the brigade's deployment and its mission, the two general officers concluded their meeting.

The next three days were hectic ones for General Williamson and his entourage. They visited the air bases that the brigade would be guarding, met with a variety of American military advisers, as well as key ARVN commanders, and began formulating specific plans for the deployment of the airborne unit. There was a tremendous amount of work to be done to prepare the 173d for its mission in South Vietnam, but General Williamson was a master at overcoming difficult obstacles.

Ellis W. Williamson was born and raised in Raleigh, North Carolina. As a teenager, he had but one goal: to play the trombone in a swing band. In order to gain some practical experience, Williamson joined the North Carolina National Guard in 1935 as a bandsman. Although he expected to stay in the National Guard for only one year, after which he'd be ready to audition with a major band, he ended up spending ten years with his parent regiment. In that decade he advanced from a private in the band to a lieutenant colonel commanding the regiment.

After his first hitch ended, Williamson realized that he had not only improved his trombone-playing skills but grown immensely fond of the people who made up his unit. The men who served with him were the finest he'd ever known. They provided friendship, comradeship, and an opportunity for personal growth that he had not experienced before. Williamson signed on for another hitch.

Before that enlistment was up, Williamson's unit was called to active duty as part of the massive U.S. military buildup in the days just before World War II. On 16 September 1940 the unit became part of the 120th Infantry Regiment, 30th Infantry Division.

To a rapidly expanding army in desperate need of qualified leaders, Williamson was a godsend. His natural talents and uncanny ability to motivate others quickly identified him as officer material. His superiors recommended him for a direct commission. In early 1941 Williamson proudly pinned the gold bars of a second lieutenant on his uniform.

The 30th Infantry Division spent the next three years in training before sailing to England in February 1944. Earmarked for service on the European continent, the division entered France via Omaha Beach in Normandy on 10 June 1944. The still-visible carnage of the D-day invasion just four days earlier was a rude awakening to the horrible realities of war for Lieutenant Williamson and the rest of the 120th Infantry. The novice combat infantrymen stoically gritted their teeth and pushed inland toward the fighting.

Williamson's unit received its baptism of fire during the bitter struggle to capture the strategically important French crossroads town of St.-Lô. From there they participated in Operation Cobra, the massive Allied breakout from the Normandy beachhead. They next chased the fleeing Nazi army across France, entering Belgium in early September. If Williamson, by then a captain and commanding a rifle company, had thought his previous battles were difficult, they paled next to the bloody struggle to capture Aachen, the German town anchoring the formidable West Wall defensive barrier along the Belgian border. From mid-September through mid-October the war-weary men of the 30th Infantry Division battled the fanatical German troops defending Aachen.

Once Aachen finally fell on 16 October 1944, Williamson and the 120th Infantry pushed into Germany, remaining on that front until mid-December. When Hitler launched his desperate offensive into the Ardennes Forest of Belgium on 16 December 1944, the 30th Infantry Division was sent to plug the weak American line. From 17 December 1944 to 26 January 1945, they fought to clear the area around Malmédy-Stavelot of German invaders.

By the time the Battle of the Bulge ended in an Allied victory, Williamson sported the gold oak leaves of a major and was the executive officer of the 120th Infantry Regiment. He held that position as the 30th Infantry Division joined in the crossing of the Roer River in February 1945. The division then charged across north central Germany, eager participants in the race to reach Berlin. They captured the fabled city of Hameln on 7 April 1945 and, a week later, took up positions along the Elbe River, just forty miles from the German capital.

When political considerations snatched the prize of Berlin from the Americans and gave it to the Russians, Major Williamson and the rest of the massive American army remained on the west bank of the Elbe. They were still there when victory was declared on 8 May 1945.

Soon after the war ended, Williamson received a well-deserved promotion to lieutenant colonel and took command of the regiment he had joined ten years earlier as an eighteen-year-old private. He and his division had repeatedly proved themselves in some of the toughest combat experienced in the war. The 30th Infantry Division suffered nearly 17,000 casualties, of whom 3,516 made the ultimate sacrifice.

Out of that terrible experience Colonel Williamson recognized that he had found his calling in life. Always a keen believer in the human factor in any of life's equations, he felt he could make the most out of the rest of his career by staying in the army and working with the finest, most talented group of people he thought the world had ever known. Williamson applied for a regular army commission and received it.

Williamson saw further combat during the Korean War. He made the Inchon landing in September 1950 as the assistant G-3 of Gen. Douglas MacArthur's famed X Corps. Following the successful recapture of the South Korean capital of Seoul, the X Corps moved to the east coast of the Korean peninsula for the drive to the Yalu River and the anticipated end of the war.

The surprise appearance of Chinese Communist forces in the war in November 1950 quickly ended that optimistic attitude. Before the American and South Korean forces really knew what had hit them, they were in full retreat out of North Korea.

This was an entirely new venture for Williamson. His entire career had been built on attacking the enemy and moving forward. Now he had to plan the retrograde movement of a full corps, while under attack.

Williamson performed brilliantly. As a result of his superior planning, the X Corps extracted itself from a near-hopeless situation. With a minimum number of casualties and a minimal loss of equipment, the X Corps removed itself from North Korea intact and ready to resume the offensive.

Williamson's role in this massive effort did not escape the notice of his superiors. Based on his superior performance under difficult conditions, Williamson was selected for promotion to full colonel and was marked for general's stars.

A tour at the Pentagon followed Williamson's service in Korea. While there he became deeply involved in a special study that would drastically overhaul how the U.S. Army went to war and greatly affect Williamson's career.

As early as 1952 army visionaries recognized how rotary-winged aircraft could be used to give ground combat units a flexibility and mobility never before thought possible. Over the next few years these few men championed their new concept to the leaders of the army. Eventually, but reluctantly, senior army commanders decided to further evaluate this new concept of airmobility.

On 15 January 1960 the army chief of staff established a special board to review the army's aviation requirements. Among its recommendations to further explore the necessity of aviation assets in army units, the board proposed an in-depth study to determine whether the idea of air fighting units was practical. As a result of this board's overall recommendations, the army began a cautious enhancement of its aviation assets.

In late September 1961 Secretary of Defense McNamara reviewed the army's aviation plans. Essentially, he concluded that the army was moving too slowly. In April 1962 he charged the army with directions to take a "bold new look" at land warfare mobility. He urged the full use of field tests and exercises to properly assess cost and transport effectiveness. McNamara's zeal for this new concept was so great that he took the unprecedented step of making direct recommendations regarding the personnel to manage the army's effort.

McNamara summed up the emphasis he placed on the army's study of tactical mobility with this statement: "I shall be disappointed if the army's reexamination merely produces logistically-oriented recommendations to procure more of the same, rather than a plan for employment of fresh and perhaps unorthodox concepts which will give us a significant increase in mobility."

Within a week of McNamara's pointed recommendation, Lt. Gen. Hamilton H. Howze, commander of the XVIII Airborne Corps, was appointed president of the U.S. Army Tactical Mobility Requirements Board.

Given unprecedented latitude, the Howze board immediately went to work. The most significant major activity of the board throughout its deliberations was the investigation, testing, and evaluation of the organizational and operational concepts of airmobility. Much effort was devoted to actual field exercises conducted for the purpose of comparing a conventionally equipped force with one made airmobile by adding aircraft.

Over the next four months the board conducted forty tests using assets of the 82d Airborne Division. The tests ranged in magnitude from fairly elaborate live-fire exercises to auxiliary tests of new equipment. By early August 1962 the Howze board had completed its task and submitted its list of recommendations.

The principal tactical innovation to derive from the board's test was for the creation of an experimental air assault division. Instead of the 100 aircraft normally employed in a standard division, the air assault division would have 459 organic aircraft. Airmobility would be achieved by a drastic reduction in ground vehicles—from 3,452 to 1,100. Thus, the aircraft would be able to lift one-third of the division's assault elements at one time.

The Howze board also recommended the creation of an air cavalry brigade. Its function would be a classic one for cavalry—to screen, reconnoiter, and wage delaying actions. Unlike the air assault division, which was designed to join battle on the ground, all members of the air cavalry brigade were to be airborne qualified.

General Howze concluded his report with a terse, emphatic statement: "Adoption by the army of the airmobile concept—however imperfectly it may be described and justified in this report—is necessary and desirable. In some respects the transition is inevitable, just as was that from animal mobility to motor."

Accordingly, the army created the 11th Air Assault Division, quartered at Fort Benning, Georgia. For the next two years the test division put to practical evaluation any and all advancements of the airmobile concept. A key member of the Pentagon staff during the planning stages of the new airmobile concept was Col. Ellis W. Williamson. An early proponent of the new airmobile division, Williamson devoted himself to making the concept work. He knew that the only way the airmobile tests would prove successful was if the right people were in the right positions. He used all his skills and contacts to ensure that the army's brightest young officers were involved in the various tests.

Results proved the prescience of the Howze board. So

well did the new concept work that just two years later the 11th Air Assault Division was redesignated the 1st Cavalry Division (Airmobile). It was hastily refitted for overseas deployment and, in August 1965, shipped out to counter a worsening situation in South Vietnam. The 1st Cavalry Division (Airmobile) repeatedly proved the worth of the airmobile concept in its six years in South Vietnam, amassing an enviable record of combat excellence.

The army made several alterations to the Howze board's recommendation to create a separate air cavalry brigade. It recognized that there not only existed a need for such a test unit, but also for an airborne unit in the Pacific to fulfill the mission of a theater quick-reaction force. This dual mission was unique to the army and would require both a special unit to perform the various tasks entrusted to it and a special commander to mold the fledgling unit into a cohesive battle force.

Fortunately, the army had both the man and the unit for the new mission. It was a measure of his success in the development of the airmobile concept that Colonel Williamson, who qualified as a paratrooper in 1960, was unanimously selected to command the new airborne brigade.

Command of the new unit elevated Williamson to the rank of brigadier general. At the promotion ceremony at the Pentagon in June 1963, Secretary of the Army Elvis J. Stahr, Jr., remarked, as he pinned the star on Williamson's epaulet, "The army's promoting men to general officer a lot sooner than they used to."

"Yes, sir," quipped Williamson. "This is my second promotion in nineteen years."

General Williamson's new unit, the 173d Airborne Brigade (Separate), was activated on 25 June 1963. The 173d Brigade had first come into existence during World War I as part of the 87th Infantry Division. After the war the 173d was transferred to the Organized Reserve. During World War II the brigade evolved into the 87th Reconnaissance Troop and saw action in Europe. The 87th Recon was deactivated in September 1945. On 26 March 1963 the unit was reactivated and redesignated Headquarters and Headquarters Company, 173d Airborne Brigade (Separate).

When the entire brigade was activated in June 1963, it assumed the assets of the 2d Airborne Battle Group, then stationed on Okinawa, Ryukyu Islands, just south of Japan. Organic units to the 173d were the 1st and 2d battalions, 503d Infantry Regiment (Airborne); Company D, 16th Armor; 3d Battalion, 319th Artillery; 173d Engineer Company; 173d Support Company; and Troop E, 17th Cavalry. Authorized strength for the new brigade was 133 officers, 3 warrant officers, and 3,394 enlisted personnel.

The tasks facing General Williamson were formidable. He not only had to whip into shape the main Pacific theater reaction force, but he also had to constantly test new ideas in warfare. Fortunately, Williamson was granted several concessions.

First, the 173d would be based on Okinawa. There it would be free to test its ideas without constant interference from Pentagon staffers.

Then, upon assuming his command, Williamson was asked by General Johnson what he most needed to do the job right. Williamson replied with the one word that had been his key throughout his long and distinguished career: "People." If he had the opportunity to select the best people, he could accomplish his mission and have all the flexibility his brigade needed. Johnson immediately agreed.

Williamson went to work. He had his pick of the West Point classes of 1962 and 1963. The top officers and enlisted men of the 82d and 101st Airborne divisions, as well as the top graduates of the Infantry School at Fort Benning, were recruited for the 173d. In a matter of weeks Williamson had put together a team of officers and senior noncommissioned officers whose combined talent and enthusiasm exceeded that found in any full division.

Once Williamson had assembled his key officers, they began the hard job of putting together the various tests and exercises that were fundamental to the 173d's existence. Though based on Okinawa, the brigade actually spent little time there. Most of its time was spent on the circular island of Oromote.

Located three hundred miles south of Okinawa, Oromote

was ideal for the brigade's training operations. Only about fifteen miles across and heavily wooded, Oromote allowed the brigade's various tests to be conducted under realistic field conditions. Units ranging in size from platoon to full battalion could be deployed to the island to operate without any direct control from brigade headquarters, permitting the unit leaders to make their own decisions.

In accordance with General Williamson's desire to give his paratroopers as much opportunity as possible to develop as individuals, any soldier under his command was free to offer up ideas for testing. Because Williamson had the final say in whether or not a particular idea was put to a field test, many more of these new ideas were actually tested. Free from the watchful eyes of his superiors, Williamson had carte blanche in evaluating these suggestions. In effect, he established an "idea center" in his headquarters to ensure that any idea, however bold or radical, would receive careful and detailed consideration. The only real limiting factor was human safety.

As a result of Williamson's farsightedness, the 173d initiated many ideas that were eventually adopted army-wide. Among the successes achieved by the 173d were the use of helicopters for night artillery adjustment, using permanently mounted machine guns on troop-carrying helicopters, using helicopters to pick up and deliver floating-bridge sections, and eagle flights—small, self-contained, highly trained heliborne forces. Eagle flights could be used tactically to locate and engage an enemy unit or to pursue and attack a fleeing enemy. An eagle flight would be a force ready for immediate commitment either alone or in conjunction with other units.

In addition to its role as a test organization, the 173d Airborne Brigade also had to fulfill its mission as the army's quick-reaction force in the Pacific. Consequently, it spent a considerable amount of time on airborne exercises throughout the Pacific. The brigade trained in Taiwan, Korea, and Thailand, honing its airborne, guerrilla, and jungle-warfare skills to a keen edge. In the first six months of its existence, the 173d Airborne Brigade participated in six major field training exercises and its members made a total of 10,719 parachute jumps.

It was because of its many parachute exercises on Taiwan that the members of the 173d earned the respect and admiration of the Nationalist Chinese soldiers. So impressed with the paratroopers of 173d were the Chinese that they nicknamed the men of the brigade *Tien Bing,* or Sky Soldiers. The sobriquet stuck and was proudly adopted by General Williamson.

As a result of General Williamson's tireless efforts, the 173d Airborne Brigade quickly established itself as one of the premier units in the U.S. Army. Morale was so high that the brigade often experienced a 100 percent reenlistment rate, an unheard-of achievement. Officers tapped to attend career-enhancing courses at stateside installations sometimes turned them down in order to remain in the brigade. This practice became so prevalent that General Williamson had to promise the transferred officers he would somehow make room for them in the brigade upon completion of their courses.

The brigade began 1964 with its individual units fully trained, tested, and operationally ready. For the balance of the year the brigade conducted varied and diversified training, most of it based on contingency plans formulated to meet any conceivable emergency in the theater. The Sky Soldiers continually proved that they were "airborne all the way," conducting 26,339 individual parachute jumps that year. In addition to pure airborne training, the brigade constantly improved its airmobile tactics, developing the concept of vertical envelopment to a high degree.

It was this high state of combat preparedness that made the 173d Airborne Brigade the logical choice, really the only choice, for deployment to South Vietnam. Guarding key air force bases and clearing jungle areas of Viet Cong for incoming U.S. divisions were, in General Williamson's view, ideal roles for his fast-moving, hard-hitting unit. Because of its unique capabilities, and the fact that General Westmoreland advised him that his unit's time in South Vietnam would be limited to sixty days, Williamson felt confident the 173d could still fulfill its mission as the Pacific theater's quick-reaction force.

After three days in Saigon reviewing his new area of operations, General Williamson returned to Okinawa, his keen mind already filled with the changes and reorganization that his brigade would require in its new mission. The most significant change would involve the reduction of the brigade's heavier equipment. Williamson had instantly recognized that the terrain in South Vietnam would limit the need for trucks. He knocked half of them off the brigade's table of equipment. The brigade, though parachute-qualified, would depend upon the helicopter for mobility in South Vietnam. Thus, the tanks of the 16th Armor would be superfluous. Williamson dropped them, too. Instead, he requisitioned armored personnel carriers (APCs). Equipped with .50-caliber machine guns and capable of carrying both men and supplies, the APCs would combine mobility with firepower.

In order to maintain the secrecy required about the move, Williamson withheld announcement of the deployment until 3 May 1965. On that date he sent a commander's note to his paratroopers that they were going to South Vietnam in three days. After nearly two years of tough, intensive training, the brigade was finally going to be put to the ultimate test. In the seventy-two hours the brigade had before the deployment began, a feverish pitch of activity gripped the paratroopers. There were a million tasks to be performed, and everyone was kept busy nearly twenty-four hours a day getting ready. The Sky Soldiers were going to war, and they wanted to be as prepared as possible.

Despite the frantic pace, General Williamson maintained a calm attitude. His main objective as brigade commander had been the development of personnel able to handle with a minimum of supervision any task assigned to them. In essence, he stood back and let his men do exactly what he'd trained them to do.

Because the tour of duty of the 173d was to be a temporary one, General Williamson continued his normal routine. On the evening of 4 May 1965, he and his wife attended a formal dinner given in honor of the Okinawa army commander, Gen. Al Watson. It was a festive evening, until 2200 when the Williamsons made their gracious exit. They returned to their quarters, where the general changed from his formal uniform to combat fatigues. He picked up his bag, kissed his wife good-bye, and left for the airport. Neither knew that his sixty-day mission would last ten months.

In the dark early morning hours of 5 May 1965, the C-130 transport planes carrying the advance elements of the 173d Airborne Brigade began touching down at Bien Hoa Air Force Base. Plane after plane roared down out of the night sky, dropped off their loads of eager but apprehensive paratroopers, then took off to return to Okinawa to pick up another load of men.

The deployment of the 173d to South Vietnam was no longer a secret. Correspondents were at the air base to record the arrival of the first U.S. Army ground combat unit in South Vietnam. General Westmoreland was there to greet General Williamson and his paratroopers. Westmoreland assured the assembled newspeople that the brigade was there temporarily, charged only with providing security to the two key Rolling Thunder bases.

Over the next two days the balance of the brigade arrived at Bien Hoa. The paratroopers quickly went about establishing their base camps and becoming acclimated to the oppressive heat and humidity of South Vietnam. They also began patrolling around the air base, keeping the immediate area clear of insurgent forces. And they continued their training.

General Williamson accepted the fact that his brigade, though fully parachute-qualified, would be almost totally dependent upon the helicopter for movement throughout its area of operations. Aviation requirements for the brigade would be supplied by the 145th Aviation Battalion on an as-needed basis.

Williamson recognized that the airmobile training exercises his brigade had conducted over the past two years were beneficial but not the real thing. He immediately began airmobile exercises under actual combat conditions.

Within two weeks of the unit's arrival in South Vietnam, Williamson was able to note: "We have started our airmobile training. At first we are just practicing 'getting in and getting out' techniques. As far as the individual is concerned, this is a critical operation. Get in quickly and get out quickly and move as rapidly as possible from the landing zone in the right direction into the woodlines. This movement must be made behind a blast of fire from our own hand-carried weapons."

The reality of a shooting war hit home hard for the brigade soon after its arrival in South Vietnam. On 22 May 1965, at 1500, a squad of Sky Soldiers moved through the jungle on a routine patrol within sight of the Bien Hoa air base. Suddenly, one of them tripped a Viet Cong–planted booby trap. The resulting explosion drove shrapnel into the neck of one of the paratroopers. He achieved the dubious distinction of becoming the brigade's first casualty in the Vietnam War.

Later that same afternoon another paratrooper from the 1/503d was wounded when a round from his own M79 grenade launcher exploded too close to him.

These two young paratroopers joined a long and distinguished line of airborne infantrymen who had spilled their blood for their country while serving with the 503d Infantry Regiment (Airborne) and its antecedents.*

---

*The appendix describes the achievements of the 503d in World War II.

CHAPTER 2

VIETNAM—THE EARLY YEARS

General Williamson used the balance of May 1965 to acclimate his brigade to South Vietnam. Though the Sky Soldiers had spent the previous two years training in a wide variety of climates throughout the western and southwestern Pacific, nothing could have prepared them for South Vietnam. The country's weather ranged, as one wag said, "from hot and humid to hotter and more humid." Daytime temperatures hovered in the upper nineties, with humidity levels in excess of 90 percent—when it wasn't raining during one of the two monsoon seasons.

The terrain in which the 173d Airborne Brigade operated around Bien Hoa was a combination of rice paddies and thick jungles. In some areas the paddies stretched for miles, cut only by occasional stands of trees matted with tangled undergrowth. In other areas, the jungle was so thick as to be all but impenetrable. Visibility in these areas was limited to a matter of meters; the jungle made an excellent ambush site for the Viet Cong.

Throughout May the squads, platoons, and companies of the 173d pushed their patrols farther and farther into the jungles surrounding the air bases. The training they'd received in recent years was invaluable, but nothing compared with experience in actual combat conditions. Now, mistakes would cost lives. The men of the infantry units wanted to make as few mistakes as possible.

For the most part, the squad leaders and riflemen of the 173d were in their late teens. They had volunteered for the rugged three weeks of airborne training at Fort Benning for a variety of personal reasons, but most would admit that at the core of their motivation was a strong sense of adventure and a desire to serve with the best.

The senior enlisted men, the noncommissioned officers, at the platoon and company level were career paratroopers who, as much as the youths in their charge, wanted to be where the action was. Many of the senior NCOs had seen combat either in World War II or Korea. These are the men, most in their late twenties to early forties, who provide the backbone of a military unit. Their leadership abilities combined with their military savvy give a unit character and flavor. Those who served with the 173d were some of the best career enlisted men the army had to offer.

The junior officers, those at platoon and company level, were among the sharpest in the army. Physically fit, intelligent, well educated, and proud to be airborne, the lieutenants and captains, most of whom were only a few years older than the enlisted men they commanded, offered the 173d a level of leadership excellence rarely seen in a combat unit. Competition for the privilege of leading a rifle platoon or company was so fierce that most junior officers were limited to just six months' command time.

(Though conceived with good intentions, this policy, which included commanders at the battalion level, would produce many problems. Combined with MACV's policy of rotating personnel back to the United States after just twelve months' service in South Vietnam [assuming, of course, that the individual was not evacuated earlier due to serious wounds or injuries], the six-month command policy meant that a given unit rarely had an officer with any more than six months' field command time. By the time an officer had spent enough time in command to be experienced and effective, he rotated out. Then a new officer arrived, bringing with him inexperience and his own philosophy of command. Changes would be implemented that many times upset what the enlisted men had practiced for the previous six months. These same problems plagued the staffs of units in South Vietnam. By the time a staff officer was truly doing a good job, he was gone. At every level of command, from rifle team leader to brigade commander, valuable combat lessons would have to be learned over and over, unnecessarily spilling American blood in the process.)

The field-grade officers of the 173d, majors and lieutenant colonels, were also outstanding officers. Dedicated to the airborne, in their careers these men had repeatedly proven themselves to be not only consummate leaders of men, but excellent staff officers.

Once General Williamson felt that his brigade was ready, he launched his first large operation. Though tasked with providing security for the air bases, a defensive role, he was not content to sit and wait for the Viet Cong to attack him. Williamson, with General Westmoreland's full support, went on the offensive. He reasoned that if he could keep the enemy off balance they'd be less likely to attack.

On the last day of May, Williamson initiated a four-day operation. Three different objectives were hit by heliborne paratroopers. Their casualties were few against light resistance. Though the paratroopers experienced no heavy fighting, the operation, the first U.S. offensive action in South Vietnam, greatly contributed to the confidence of the Sky Soldiers.

To augment the 173d's firepower, and to give it a third maneuver battalion, General Westmoreland attached to it the 1st Battalion, Royal Australian Regiment (1/RAR), when that unit arrived in-country on 10 June 1965. Composed largely of veterans of the fighting in Malaysia, the 1/RAR brought its own engineers, APCs, helicopters, and artillery. The addition of the Australians would give Williamson the extra punch he needed to really go after the VC.

Along with two battalions of ARVN paratroopers and one of ARVN infantry, the 173d air-assaulted into the notorious War Zone D in late June. This was the first time in more than a year that allied forces ventured into this VC-contaminated area just north of Saigon. Almost from the moment their helicopters touched down, the paratroopers experienced near-steady contact with the VC. During the day the Sky Soldiers patrolled aggressively, uncovering numerous caches of enemy supplies. At night the VC would probe the paratroopers' perimeters.

In early July the brigade worked the south end of War Zone D. While the ARVN 48th Infantry Regiment held blocking positions, the 173d pushed into the area from the north. The paratroopers began engaging VC in numbers previously unexperienced. Entire companies of uniformed VC defended their base areas, fighting stiffly until the overwhelming firepower of the Americans forced them to withdraw.

The four-day operation saw the 1/503d overrun a vast VC base camp, one capable of housing more than twelve hundred men. The camp was so sophisticated it even contained mess halls and classrooms. The Sky Soldiers captured more than a ton of enemy documents, dozens of weapons, several tons of rice, and twenty-eight prisoners.

In August 1965 the 173d made its first foray out of the Bien Hoa area. In Kontum Province, some two hundred miles north of Saigon and adjacent to the junction of the Cambodian and Laotian borders, the U.S. Special Forces had established a series of isolated camps. Manned by contingents of indigenous personnel commanded by a handful of Green Berets, these camps served as early warning sites to detect infiltrating Viet Cong and North Vietnamese Army regular forces moving down the Ho Chi Minh Trail. The Special Forces and their Civilian Irregular Defense Groups (CIDG) had been doing a very good job in the Central Highlands area of Kontum Province—so good, in fact, that the enemy increased its pressure on a number of the camps.

One of these desolate camps, Duc Co, west of Pleiku, had been especially hard hit. Reinforcements in the form of an ARVN regiment were dispatched there. This ARVN unit became heavily engaged with NVA forces before it could reach Duc Co. The ARVN high command wanted to send more troops but knew they, too, would be lost unless a key withdrawal route through strategic Thanh Binh Pass could be held.

The 173d was given the mission of holding the vital pass. Most of the brigade headed north in early August. For the first week of the operation, 10–17 August, the Sky Soldiers conducted a large number of heliborne assaults designed to deny key terrain features to the enemy. Once the ARVN had completed their retrograde movement, the 173d moved to Pleiku. It spent the rest of the month conducting search-and-destroy missions in that area.

Upon its return to Bien Hoa, the brigade had only a short rest before going back into War Zone D. MACV's intelligence network had pinpointed several enemy battalions operating in the area, but actual contact was sporadic. Despite this, the operation was judged a success. In their sweeps the Sky Soldiers uncovered a large quantity of valuable documents, weapons, and supplies. One company alone, Charlie, 1/503d, found sixty-two telescope-equipped sniper rifles, forty-five hundred grenades, and three dozen radios.

Next on the 173d's agenda was the formidable, almost mysterious Iron Triangle. Situated thirty kilometers northwest of Saigon, the Iron Triangle sat just west of Ben Cat astride Highway 13. The brigade's mission was to sweep the area adjacent to the future home of the 1st Infantry Division free of any enemy presence prior to the arrival of that unit from the United States.

The brigade had been assigned a nearly impossible task. The Iron Triangle had been solid VC territory for years. In that time the insurgents had turned the thickly jungled fifty-square-kilometer area into a stronghold nearly unsurpassed in all of South Vietnam. Though the dense jungle prevented the Viet Cong from constructing major permanent camps, they did honeycomb the Iron Triangle with a sophisticated complex of tunnels. These underground networks provided the VC with facilities for aid stations, training rooms, supply depots, and administrative offices. To prevent the ARVN or U.S. forces from overrunning the Iron Triangle, the VC sowed the ground with thousands of mines and booby traps. So frightening was the Iron Triangle's reputation that no ARVN units had dared venture into the area for more than three years.

The 173d's foray into the Iron Triangle began on 8 October 1965. Following massive artillery bombardment, B-52 bomber attacks, and jet fighter air strikes, the brigade's elements air-assaulted into the Iron Triangle. The 1/RAR went into landing zones (LZs) on the north side of the Iron Triangle, midway between Ben Cat and Ben Suc, about eight miles to the west along the Saigon River. They pushed south, joining up with both the 1/503d and 2/503d, which had gone into LZs just south of Ben Suc. The three infantry battalions then maneuvered south and east, sweeping the VC in front of them and clearing them out of the Iron Triangle.

The brigade spent six days tromping through the jungle. They uncovered a number of supply caches and had a few brisk firefights with the VC. However, most of the enemy either fled the area or hid in the tunnels. They had no desire to tangle with the airborne troopers. They'd fight on their own terms at a later date.

Unaware of the Viet Cong's tactics, MACV naturally considered this first venture into the Iron Triangle an unqualified success. General Williamson reported: "The Iron Triangle is no more. The Iron Triangle . . . has now been destroyed. One more enemy bulwark has been completely marked off the situation."

In view of what his brigade had experienced in the weeklong offensive, Williamson was completely justified in his remarks. Unfortunately, he was wrong. The truth was that the Iron Triangle would remain a thorn in the side of the allies for the duration of the war. Operation after operation would be centered on the Iron Triangle; none would neutralize it. It would remain a Viet Cong bastion.

The 173d Airborne Brigade was attached to the newly arrived 1st Infantry Division on 1 November 1965. Together the two units conducted yet another operation in War Zone D. Designated Operation Hump, for the term that soldiers in South Vietnam had adopted to describe their patrols under the blazing sun, the brigade operated north of the Dong Nai River, about twenty-five kilometers north of Bien Hoa. It would result in the brigade's largest and costliest engagement in its five months in South Vietnam.

Operation Hump began on 5 November. Almost immediately it was apparent to the Sky Soldiers this operation would be different. The VC stood and fought on several occasions; there was little attempt on their part to avoid contact.

As the result of one such firefight, it was determined that

a major enemy force sat less than two miles west of where the 1/503d had established its CP. Local patrolling confirmed the presence of the enemy. On the morning of 8 November Charlie Company, 1/503d, moved west from its night laager site. Behind it came Bravo Company; Alpha Company and the battalion's headquarters remained at the bivouac site.

Charlie Company was moving along the edge of Hill 65 (on contour maps specific hill masses are identified by a number representing the height above mean sea level in meters) when, without warning, a fusillade of automatic-weapons fire tore into its lead platoon. While paratroopers screamed in pain from the horrible impact of enemy machine-gun bullets, the uninjured dove for any available cover. The other two rifle platoons moved forward as far as they could to aid the decimated lead platoon. Weapons Platoon set up its 60mm mortars, but the dense overhead cover rendered them useless. Instead, its members established a protected site to care for the casualties.

Once Charlie Company was pinned down, the VC began executing a tactical maneuver that, while basic in its concept, served the enemy well then and throughout the war; they began flanking the isolated company in an attempt to surround it and cut it off from reinforcements.

The enemy's plan might have worked except for the quick reaction of the 1/503d commander, Lt. Col. John Tyler. He immediately dispatched Bravo Company to the aid of Charlie. Their timely arrival prevented the enemy from encircling Charlie. Soon though, Bravo, too, found itself embroiled in a fierce fight.

To prevent U.S. air strikes and artillery from decimating its ranks, the enemy "hugged" the Sky Soldiers, closing to within ten to twenty meters of their perimeter. From that close range they poured a deadly hail of fire on the pinned-down paratroopers.

Within a short time both airborne companies found themselves fighting hand-to-hand with the enemy. Grenades were thrown at close range. Combatants hacked at each other with machetes. M16 rifles and M60 machine guns were fired until their barrels overheated and warped. It was a brutal fight in heavy jungle with neither side giving any quarter.

Colonel Tyler was forced to commit Alpha Company to try to stave off defeat of his other two companies. Throughout the day the two forces battled. The enemy clung so close to the paratroopers that the supporting fire from the 3/319th Artillery was placed behind them. It was hoped this would trap the foe between the artillery and the riflemen. In assault after assault the enemy charged directly at the Sky Soldiers' perimeter, only to be met by heavy fire from a determined force of screaming paratroopers. In the brief lulls in the fighting, the airborne soldiers repositioned themselves, collected ammo from the dead, and moved the wounded to the aid station.

Not until late afternoon did the fighting slacken. Though the paratroopers had fought valiantly, the contact was broken only because the VC withdrew from the battlefield. Sporadic fire harassed the paratroopers throughout the night, but the enemy was pulling out.

At first light chain saws were dropped by helicopter to the anxious rifle companies. Trees up to 215 feet in height and 6 feet thick were felled until a one-ship LZ was completed. The first chopper in was General Williamson's. He remained on the ground, overseeing the evacuation of the casualties, then walked out with the survivors the next day.

General Williamson later told correspondents the enemy corpses he'd seen were dressed in gray uniforms with green sweatshirts, steel helmets, and rucksacks. He said the enemy were in "well-fortified jungle positions. The enemy remained in position and kept firing. We have had a real close-at-hand jungle-type fight. There is no question but that this was a main force unit."

Williamson was right. Subsequent information identified the 173d's opponent as a North Vietnamese Army unit, the Q-761 Regiment. This was one of the first times the NVA had fought in South Vietnam. It would not be the last.

The NVA left 110 of their soldiers lying around Hill 65. Fifty Sky Soldiers died in the firefight; another 82 were wounded. The 173d had been hit and hit hard, but it had acquitted itself extremely well.

Operations in War Zone D continued for the rest of the year. On 22 December 1965 the brigade returned to Bien Hoa for the first of its six Christmases in South Vietnam.

On New Year's Day 1966 the 173d set out again in pursuit of the enemy. This time they headed south and west of Bien Hoa into the Mekong River delta and the marshy area adjacent to Cambodia known as the Plain of Reeds. They had no trouble finding the VC. Almost from the moment the Sky Soldiers jumped from their Huey helicopters, they were in contact. Most of the time the action was light, but on several occasions fierce firefights developed. The VC used the same tactics the NVA had in the November fighting: They flanked isolated units and, when U.S. air strikes and artillery were called in, hugged the paratroopers' perimeter, reducing the effectiveness of the superior firepower.

In the week-long foray, the 173d mauled the 267th VC Battalion and overran the headquarters of the 506th VC Battalion. The brigade also earned the distinction of being the first American unit to fight in three different corps areas in South Vietnam.

Almost immediately upon their return to Bien Hoa, the Sky Soldiers were tapped for another operation. This time they went after the headquarters of the Viet Cong Military Region Four in Ho Bo Woods in Binh Duong Province. Once again under command of the 1st Infantry Division, the 173d sent all three of its battalions on airmobile assaults. The three LZs were hot. Enemy contact was near-continuous from then on. The rifle companies fanned out through the thickly forested area. The paratroopers found an extensive bunker and tunnel system permeating the entire area.

The tunnels were searched by special volunteers dubbed tunnel rats. Armed with a pistol and a flashlight, these brave men would probe the tunnels looking for the enemy. When they were done, explosive charges collapsed the tunnels.

By the time the paratroopers departed Ho Bo Woods on 14 January, they'd captured more than a hundred weapons, including a number of 12.7mm antiaircraft guns.

For the rest of January and February the brigade conducted platoon and company search-and-destroy missions in the vicinity of Bien Hoa. At the end of February a major command change took place in the brigade. General Williamson, the founder and original commanding general of the 173d Airborne Brigade, reluctantly relinquished command. During his tenure Williamson had built the brigade from a raw, incohesive unit into one of the U.S. Army's most effective ones. But his time was up. He had the second star of a major general awaiting him as the post commander at Fort Polk, Louisiana.

Williamson's replacement was Brig. Gen. Paul F. Smith. A paratrooper since the early days of World War II, Smith had jumped into Normandy on D day and made the airdrop across the Rhine in March 1945 with the 507th Parachute Infantry Regiment. Among his postwar assignments was command of the airborne school at Fort Benning and the 504th Airborne Battle Group in Germany.

General Smith took command just as the 173d was getting ready for another sweep into War Zone D. It began with the three battalions going into adjacent LZs, then setting out on predesignated routes. During the first four days, the Sky Soldiers regularly bumped into small groups of VC. Sometimes there would be an exchange of gunfire; other times the VC would melt back into the jungle without firing on the paratroopers. The 2/503d had experienced little contact during the operation when it established a defensive perimeter late on the afternoon of 15 March 1966. Listening posts (LPs) were sent out to warn of any enemy activity.

The night passed quietly. The next morning, as the LPs reentered the perimeter, a platoon from Bravo, 2/503d, set out on a routine clearing patrol, looking for any evidence of the enemy's presence before the battalion began its daily move. At the same time a resupply chopper began descending into the perimeter.

As the Huey neared the ground a hail of automatic-weapons fire poured into it from the surrounding jungle. The chopper crashed heavily into the perimeter. Within seconds the vicious enemy fire forced the paratroopers back into their night defensive positions. Bravo's patrol was trapped between the two forces; in a short time most of its members were casualties.

The VC launched a ground attack at Alpha and Charlie companies, a rare occurrence for the guerrillas. The fighting was so fierce that even the wounded were given weapons and put back on the line. After the first attack was repulsed, the paratroopers moved into better fighting positions. Just as they settled back down, the VC swarmed out of the jungle again.

For the rest of the day the fight raged. Friendly artillery pounded the edges of the perimeter, cutting down dozens of VC. But the enemy kept up their attacks, seeking a weak spot; they found none. The paratroopers held. Not until nightfall did the VC pull back, leaving more than a hundred of their comrades dead in the jungle.

Following this foray into War Zone D, the 173d moved to War Zone C for the next few months. During this period some 173d units would go weeks with no contact with the enemy; others seemed to find the VC at nearly every bend of the trail. Some operations required the Sky Soldiers to be in the field for weeks at a time. On other occasions a company or two would board choppers at Bien Hoa at first light, fly out to a predesignated LZ, unload, sweep the area, then return before nightfall to Bien Hoa. There they'd have a hot meal, see a movie, and sleep on a bunk in a wooden barracks. It was like a commuter war.

Because the Australians were nearing the end of their one-year tour in South Vietnam (the Australians rotated entire units in and out of South Vietnam rather than individuals), a replacement for them had to be found. The army looked no farther than Fort Campbell, Kentucky.

This sprawling base astride the Kentucky-Tennessee border was home to the famed 101st Airborne Division. One of its brigades was already serving in Vietnam, having arrived soon after the 173d. Since the army's only other airborne division, the 82d at Fort Bragg, was its sole worldwide reserve, the 101st was tapped to send one of its battalions to South Vietnam to join the 173d.

The 1st Battalion, 501st Infantry (Airborne), received the

nod on 1 April 1966. An intensified training program was immediately implemented to prepare the battalion for duty in the war zone. Small-unit tactics were stressed, with special emphasis put on the training and development of junior officers. Already the army had realized that the war in South Vietnam was being fought mainly by companies and platoons; the days of large-scale maneuvers of battalions and regiments were long gone. Any lieutenant or captain who did not measure up to the rigorous standards of the 1/501st's CO, Lt. Col. Michael D. Healey (the legendary "Iron Mike" Healey who would later command the 5th Special Forces in South Vietnam), was immediately replaced. Healey combed the 101st for the best qualified officers and senior NCOs. He had no dearth of volunteers to join his battalion.

The 1/501st was redesignated the 4/503d before the battalion left Kentucky. In May 1966 the paratroopers boarded troopships bound for South Vietnam. They officially arrived at Bien Hoa on 25 June 1966.

The 173d Airborne Brigade they joined was far different from the unit that had departed Okinawa thirteen months earlier. Although it was still a tough, proud unit, few of the brigade's original members remained. Those who had survived their one-year tour of duty had rotated out of the war zone. The lessons they had learned in a brutal twelve months of combat were rarely passed on to the new troops, or "cherries." The incoming paratroopers would have to learn them all over again.

Throughout the summer and early fall of 1966 the brigade continued its operations in and around the Bien Hoa area. Its next major operation came in November when the 1/503d and 2/503d (4/503d would spend October and November around Da Nang working with the marines) joined the 1st Infantry Division, the 3d Brigade of the 4th Infantry Division, and the 196th Light Infantry Brigade in Operation Attleboro. Originally, the 196th had commenced the operation in September as a search-and-destroy operation in a VC-infested area east and north of Tay Ninh. As VC resistance increased, more troops were fed into the fight.

By November twenty thousand allied troops, a record

number, were committed to the fighting. Enemy troops were identified as the 9th VC Division and the 101st NVA Regiment, both well-regarded units. They were protecting what U.S. intelligence had identified as the main Viet Cong command center for insurgent activities in South Vietnam and the central office for the VC's political arm, the National Liberation Front.

Though the allied forces claimed eleven hundred enemy dead in Attleboro (already the accuracy of enemy body counts was being questioned at certain civilian and military levels), they did not achieve their stated objectives. The enemy still controlled the area. Consequently, MACV planned a major operation for right after the first of the new year to locate and destroy these enemy political offices.

In November 1966 another change occurred in the 173d, a change that strengthened the unit and made it an even more formidable force. Though trained as paratroopers and schooled in the tactics of airborne assault, the 173d had become increasingly reliant on airmobile tactics. The terrain of South Vietnam, combined with the elusiveness of a crafty foe, rendered airborne assaults all but extinct and made air-mobile assaults the leading edge of modern combat technique.

Since arriving in the war zone the Sky Soldiers had relied on the independent 145th Aviation Battalion for aviation support. The chopper pilots of the 145th were some of the most daring and courageous air jockeys in South Vietnam. They always did their absolute best to support the 173d in every way possible. Still, there was concern about the need to make the 173d a totally independent unit, able to respond to emergency deployments as rapidly as possible and to be completely self-sustaining in the field. The only way to satisfy this requirement was to provide the brigade with an organic helicopter unit.

Consequently, when the 335th Assault Helicopter Company arrived in South Vietnam in November 1966 from Fort Bragg, it was assigned to the 173d Airborne Brigade. From the moment it arrived at Bien Hoa, the 335th (the Cowboys) formed a special bond with the Sky Soldiers. The Cowboys provided not only transportation in the form of lightly armed troop-carrying Hueys (slicks), but also heavily armed Huey gunships for fire suppression missions, as well as choppers for medical evacuations and the routine resupply missions a rifle company in the field required.

No LZ ever seemed too hot, every injured Sky Soldier was of paramount importance, and no mission was too trivial for the Cowboys. They'd routinely go where other chopper pilots refused to venture. The intrepidity of the pilots and crewmen of the 335th Assault Helicopter Company saved the lives of hundreds of Sky Soldiers in the years they worked together.

Three days after Christmas the leadership of the 173d changed for the third time since the brigade had arrived in South Vietnam. General Smith received his second star in November 1966. Since command of the 173d was a brigadier general's slot, Smith was brought to MACV headquarters. To replace him Westmoreland brought in the assistant division commander of the 1st Infantry Division, Brig. Gen. John R. Deane, Jr.

General Deane had enlisted in the army on 1 July 1937. Within a year he had earned an appointment to West Point, graduating as a second lieutenant of infantry in June 1942. During World War II he saw combat action with the 104th Infantry Division in the European theater. He rose from second lieutenant to lieutenant colonel in less than three years.

When Deane first arrived in South Vietnam in February 1966, he assumed the duties of deputy commander and chief of staff of I Field Force. Headquartered at Nha Trang, I Field Force, essentially a corps-level command, exercised operational control over U.S. and allied forces in the II Corps tactical zone, including the Central Highlands. Deane became assistant division commander of the 1st Infantry Division in July 1966. During its operations in the second half of the year, Deane continued to build his reputation as a resourceful and fearless leader. His gallant actions during Operation Attleboro earned him a DSC.

While General Deane was assuming command of the 173d, plans were under way at higher headquarters for the largest operation yet conducted in South Vietnam. The Sky Soldiers would play a key role in that offensive.

In an effort to destroy what it believed was the Viet Cong's main nerve center in South Vietnam, the Central Office of South Vietnam (COSVN), MACV conceived Operation Junction City. Although there was no direct evidence of COSVN's existence, MACV, perhaps because of its own complicated infrastructure, believed the insurgents had to have a similar command structure. The American high command believed COSVN existed somewhere in War Zone C, north and west of Saigon. If COSVN were destroyed, its loss would seriously hamper the Viet Cong's efforts to overthrow South Vietnam's government.

As planned, the operation to destroy COSVN called for five U.S. brigades to form a horseshoe cordon in the western half of War Zone C, with the open end of the horseshoe pointing south. The 173d would form a section of the northeastern portion of the horseshoe. Once the horseshoe was in place, other allied units would attack north, driving any NVA or VC forces into the horseshoe and blocking their escape routes into Cambodia. In essence, it was a classic hammer-and-anvil maneuver, but on a grand scale.

Since the 173d had arrived in South Vietnam, General Westmoreland had sought an opportunity to utilize its airborne capabilities. Although several operations were considered, not until Junction City would an airborne operation become a reality.

The overall plans called for one battalion of the 173d, the 2/503d commanded by Lt. Col. Robert H. Sigholtz, to make a parachute jump into a clearing near Katum, a hamlet just south of the Cambodian border and about forty miles north of Tay Ninh. Once the 2/503d was on the ground, the 1/503d and 4/503d would make airmobile landings north and south of the 2/503d, sealing off the brigade's section of the horseshoe.

While the plans for Junction City were being finalized, the brigade participated in yet another operation into the Iron Triangle. Once again under the operational control of the 1st Infantry Division, the 173d launched Operation Cedar Falls on 8 January 1967. For the next two weeks they swept the Iron Triangle. Though MACV proclaimed Cedar Falls a success, the Viet Cong retained their firm grip on the Iron Triangle.

Once they had returned to Bien Hoa the paratroopers scheduled to make the drop busied themselves rigging their parachutes. Besides 2/503d there were Battery A, 3/319th Field Artillery, an engineer squad, a military police squad, a radio research team, elements of brigade headquarters, and portions of the 173d Support Battalion—845 men in all. These Sky Soldiers were about to make the first combat parachute assault since the Korean War, and they were all keenly aware of the attention that would be focused on them; to a man they wanted the drop to proceed perfectly.

D day, 22 February 1967, saw the 2/503d paratroopers loaded aboard a fleet of sixteen C-130s just after dawn. The lead plane took off at 0825. Soon the other fifteen were airborne and headed west. Within a few minutes they were approaching their jump zone. Helicopter gunships were just finishing their strafing runs when the C-130s appeared on the horizon. A FAC tossed out a smoke grenade to mark the wind direction and speed.

Aboard the C-130s the paratroopers were ordered to their feet: "Stand up! Hook up!" The Sky Soldiers secured their static lines to the anchor cables running the length of the fuselage above their heads. They then checked the equipment of the man in front of them. All was finally ready.

The jumpmaster shouted, "Stand in the door!" The lead paratrooper at each door positioned himself at the ready, his eyes focused on the red light in the door frame. When it went off and a green light below it went on, he'd throw himself out the door.

At precisely 0900 the green light in the lead plane went on. General Deane hurled himself out the right-hand door. At the same time Colonel Sigholtz exited the aircraft's left door. Behind them other paratroopers jumped into the morning air. By 0920 all the Sky Soldiers were on the ground.

The jump had gone off without a hitch. There had been no enemy fire. Only eleven men received minor injuries in the drop. As the paratroopers gathered their equipment, formed up into units, and pushed out to secure the drop zone, they were overwhelmed with a tremendous sense of pride. They had just accomplished what no other unit had in fifteen years.

And though they couldn't have known it at the time, they had just completed what would be the only combat jump during the war in South Vietnam.

Within an hour of the 2/503d's jump, choppers bearing the 1/503d and 4/503d poured out of the skies. They went into four LZs north and south of the 2/503d's jump zone. They, too, received no enemy fire. The northeast corner of the inverted horseshoe was now in place. Patrols from all three battalions moved out to search the area. Elsewhere other units moved into position along the horseshoe. By 1500 all blocking units were ready.

The next morning the attack elements, consisting of the 11th Armored Cavalry Regiment and the 3d Brigade of the 25th Infantry Division, began their drives north. Almost immediately they began uncovering supply caches. But they found no enemy soldiers.

That first sweep established the pattern of Junction City. The enemy, with a few exceptions, elected not to fight. Fleeing in front of the attacking forces from the south, they managed to elude the blocking forces. Instead of fighting enemy forces, the U.S. troops captured tons of their abandoned equipment and supplies. The 173d captured a major VC public information office. In addition to dozens of propaganda films and thousands of still photos, a large quantity of still- and motion-picture cameras, projectors, and developing equipment was uncovered. To distribute the war booty fairly, the brigade later held an auction limited to enlisted men in the rank of sergeant and below.

A company of Sky Soldiers did make contact with the enemy on 3 March, resulting in a vicious firefight that raged for thirty minutes in the jungle east of Katum. When the enemy quit the battlefield he left behind thirty-nine dead; the Sky Soldiers had twenty killed and twenty-eight wounded.

The forces of Junction City never did find COSVN. If it did exist it had evaded the Americans and sought sanctuary in Cambodia. Junction City ended at midnight on 17 March. The U.S. forces claimed more than eight hundred dead VC, plus hundreds of weapons and hundreds of tons of supplies captured.

Operation Junction City II began on 18 March. Designed as a natural continuation of Junction City, Junction City II focused on the portion of War Zone C east of Katum. The 173d was not initially included among the forces to participate in this operation. However, the 1st Infantry Division asked II Field Force command for another brigade, and the 173d was again attached to the Big Red One.

The brigade's mission was to secure the area around Minh Thanh, south and east of Katum. Following an airmobile assault into cold LZs around Minh Thanh on 20 March, the Sky Soldiers moved ten kilometers northwest to establish FSB Parry on 23 March. From 23 March to 13 April, the 173d conducted a series of airmobile assaults on LZs around FSB Parry. Hardly a day passed without one of the rifle companies making contact with the VC. Most of the enemy actions were brief but violent fights in the dark, misty jungle. Rarely did the enemy forces number more than thirty to forty men.

A typical day for a 173d rifle company in Junction City II, as in earlier operations, began before dawn. The paratroopers would be up, silently preparing for the day ahead. As the sky lightened, squad-sized clearing patrols would fan out from the laager site looking for any signs that the enemy had been in the area.

Once the clearing patrols had safely returned, the laager site was cleaned, fighting holes were filled, garbage was buried, and the area was policed of any items that might benefit the enemy. Usually the unit commander had briefed his platoon leaders the night before on the next day's objective. The CO specified the route of march, the pace, and the next laager site.

The platoons rotated the point position each day. Within the platoons the squads rotated the point, also. Most often, because of the thick jungle growth, it was necessary to cut a path through the foliage. Each man carried a machete to hack through thick vines and bushes. In the humid jungles few men could last on point more than an hour or two. Then a new squad would move forward to take their turn at the enervating task.

The hump proceeded as the infantrymen forced their way forward to their day's objective. Rarely did they see any sign of the enemy. If contact was made, the enemy almost always initiated it. Two or three sharp reports would suddenly fill the air. The cries of those hit by the enemy's bullets sent shivers up the backs of nearby paratroopers. As a medic worked his way toward the casualties, the other Sky Soldiers hit the dirt, triggering off magazines of M16 rounds toward suspected enemy positions.

After two to three minutes of firing, the paratroopers would cease fire. All would be quiet. Clearing patrols cautiously left the perimeter, seeking the enemy. A medevac chopper was called to retrieve the casualties. By the time an LZ had been cut out of the jungle, the patrols were back. Most of the time they reported the same thing: "No sign of Charlie, sir." Then the chopper came in, picked up the casualties, and departed. The paratroopers organized back into their squads and continued on.

The rifle companies of the 173d spent weeks at a time in the field. They had few of the amenities other soldiers in South Vietnam experienced. Though the Bien Hoa Air Force Base had a well-stocked two-story PX, few Sky Soldiers ever spent more than a few minutes in it. Rarely did the paratroopers receive a cold beer, a warm shower, three hot meals in a row, a candy bar, or a newspaper.

They wore their boots and uniforms for weeks at a time; frequently their clothes rotted in the damp jungle before a resupply of fatigues was choppered out to them. Whereas rear-echelon troops had six to eight sets of starched fatigues with neatly sewn name tags, chevrons, and badges hanging in their wall lockers, a field Sky Soldier rarely had more than what he wore on his back. Maybe once a month a resupply chopper would drop off some fresh fatigues to the paratroopers in the field. The platoon sergeants would divvy up the unadorned fatigues to those needing them the most.

When a rifle company did get a rare trip back to their Bien Hoa base camp for a few days' stand-down, the paratroopers partied hard. They'd finish their official duties and then head for the string of bars and whorehouses sitting outside the base's gates. For a few hours the war, with its pain, death, and suffering, could be forgotten. Then it was back to the field for four to five more weeks of humping.

While the Sky Soldiers slogged through the jungle of War Zone C, events farther north in the Central Highlands north of Pleiku were about to permanently change the lives of these paratroopers. Their war would take on a violence, a fury, an intensity few of them suspected could exist.

CHAPTER 3

NORTH TO DAK TO

The 4th Infantry Division arrived in South Vietnam in September 1966. In anticipation of its movement to the war zone, the 4th had spent the previous year in intense combat training in the pine forests surrounding its home at Fort Lewis, Washington. Because its ranks had been badly depleted by the demands of a growing U.S. military commitment in South Vietnam, as soon as its deployment was ordered, the 4th had received eight thousand fresh recruits—enlistees and draftees. The recruits received their basic and advanced infantry training with the division. Though this was a drastic departure from the norm, this program did provide a cohesiveness and familiarization within the units that most other divisions dispatched to South Vietnam lacked.

Upon its arrival at Nha Trang the 1st Brigade of the 4th was sent to Tuy Hoa in coastal Phu Yen Province in the II Corps area. There it operated in the lowlands and rice paddies until February 1967. The division's 3d Brigade was sent to the III Corps area around Saigon to operate with the 25th Infantry Division.

When the 25th first arrived in South Vietnam in December 1965, two of its brigades had been sent to Cu Chi, west of Saigon, in the III Corps area. Its 3d Brigade had gone to Pleiku, in the Central Highlands, to serve in the II Corps. The 4th Infantry Division's 3d Brigade went to the 25th Infantry Division simply because it was logistically easier to do that than move both brigades. The 4th's 2d Brigade went to Pleiku to work with the 3d Brigade of the 25th Infantry Division.

Consisting of Kontum, Pleiku, and Darlac provinces, the

Central Highlands abutted the border junction of Laos and Cambodia. Composed of uncountable rugged mountain peaks covered by a thick tangle of triple-canopy jungle, the Central Highlands not only served as an end to North Vietnam's main infiltration route into the south, the infamous Ho Chi Minh Trail, but it also allowed the NVA to stage massive forces in a secluded, nearly impenetrable region. From there they posed a serious threat to the stability of South Vietnam. If the NVA were allowed to control the Central Highlands they could strike eastward, reach the coast, and cut South Vietnam in half. MACV could not allow that.

To monitor the infiltration of NVA units into the Central Highlands, MACV had established a string of Special Forces camps along the border manned by small teams of Green Berets in charge of bands of CIDG. Varying greatly in effectiveness, the CIDG patrolled the vast, trackless area, searching for signs of the enemy. If enemy forces were located, the CIDG avoided direct contact whenever possible. Instead, B-52 bomber strikes would be called in, or ARVN or American reaction forces would be flown in to engage the enemy.

The Special Forces camps were remote in every sense. They were totally dependent upon helicopters, not only for resupply but for reinforcements if attacked. Until reinforcements did arrive, the Green Berets and their mountain tribesmen were on their own, supported only by their own small-bore mortars. Many times the isolated camps were overrun before reaction forces could arrive.

To bolster the Special Forces operations, MACV had originally deployed the 3d Brigade, 25th Infantry Division, to Pleiku. In addition, the 1st Cavalry Division (Airmobile) and the 1st Brigade, 101st Airborne Division, were sent on forays into the Central Highlands to counter specific threats.

When the 4th Infantry Division's 2d Brigade went to the Central Highlands, it established a camp sixteen kilometers south of Pleiku, later named Camp Enari. Within a month of its arrival the 2d Brigade, backed by the 3d Brigade of the 25th, launched an operation along the Cambodian border. The sweeps produced no major enemy contact.

More search-and-destroy operations were conducted in northern Pleiku and southern Kontum provinces for the balance of the year. Humping across the razor-backed ridges and through the snake-infested rain forests, the 2d Brigade began finding the NVA. In a series of sharp clashes the infantrymen learned the hard way that they faced a formidable foe. The NVA were well trained and well equipped. More than 80 percent of the time they initiated the contact. Whenever it appeared they had the upper hand, they pressed the attack. If it seemed the Americans were stronger than anticipated, the NVA broke contact, disappearing into the thick jungle or crossing the border into the sanctuaries of Cambodia or Laos.

In January 1967, Maj. Gen. William R. ("Ray") Peers took command of the 4th Infantry Division. Experienced at fighting the Japanese in Burma during World War II, Peers quickly recognized that his division faced a somewhat conventional jungle war. Accordingly, he instituted procedures designed to meet the challenge of the NVA. He ordered his maneuver battalions to patrol the border areas aggressively and engage the NVA, not waiting for them to attack. He insisted that at least two of each battalion's three rifle companies be in the field at all times. He organized long-range reconnaissance patrols, usually four- to six-man teams, to move clandestinely through the jungle looking for the enemy. Once the LRRPs spotted an enemy formation, they could call in an air strike, artillery, or infantry units.

He also implemented guidelines to prevent his units from being surprised and overrun. Peers's major rule was that rifle companies in the field should not operate more than one kilometer or one hour's march, whichever was less, from one another. In case of contact the engaged company could quickly be reinforced. Peers believed the NVA's intent was to "get some outfit separated and then try to isolate it and go to work on it. So we always had it so another unit could get in to it right away." Peers's vigilance paid dividends, but the crafty NVA were still able on occasion to cut off American units and annihilate them.

Beginning in early February the 4th Infantry Division,

now joined by its 1st Brigade from Tuy Hoa and still operating with the 25th's 3d Brigade, launched a series of aggressive search-and-destroy operations. Operation Sam Houston took the 4th into the southwestern portion of Kontum Province. In mid-February the division had no less than eleven major engagements with the NVA. By March the NVA had had enough and began retreating back into Cambodia to lick its wounds. On 5 April 1967 Sam Houston ended. The 4th claimed 733 enemy KIA against 169 of its own dead.

The 4th Infantry Division moved back to Camp Enari to take up screening positions prior to the coming summer monsoon season. Along east-west Highway 19 the 1st Brigade established a base camp at Le Thanh, northeast of Duc Co, the site of a Special Forces camp. From this base camp, dubbed Jackson Hole, the brigade set up a string of smaller camps ranging from Plei Djereng, another Special Forces camp astride another east-west road, Highway 509 north of Highway 19, to the Ia Drang Valley south of Highway 19. From these positions, the brigade could monitor the NVA's traditional infiltration route along Highway 19 and the Ia Drang Valley.

East of the 1st Brigade's eastern boundary—Highway 14B, which connected Highways 509 and 19—the 2d Brigade established its base at Thanh An (the Oasis). From there the 2d Brigade could conduct search-and-destroy operations behind the screen, monitor the upper Ia Drang Valley, and support the 1st Brigade. Peers called the new operation Francis Marion.

While the 4th's 1st and 2d brigades took up their respective positions, the division's third maneuver element was taken from it. The 3d Brigade, 25th Infantry Division, left the Central Highlands on 12 April 1967. It went north to the I Corps area in Quang Ngai and Quang Tin provinces. There it joined the 1st Brigade, 101st Airborne Division, and the 196th Infantry Brigade to form Task Force Oregon. Under the capable command of Maj. Gen. William B. Rosson, Task Force Oregon was a provisional division organized to allow the two Marine Corps divisions that operated in I Corps to move closer to the DMZ to counter NVA pressure in that area.

With his two brigades deployed, Peers began Francis Marion on 6 April 1967. The rifle companies dispersed into the hostile terrain seeking the NVA. For the first two weeks the infantrymen had only sporadic contact with small forces of NVA, though they found numerous signs of the enemy. In particular, the division's LRRP teams spotted small concentrations of NVA who appeared to be advance parties for a larger force. Intelligence determined that the NVA, having infiltrated the Ia Drang Valley before the screen was in place, were preparing for attacks on the Special Forces camps at Duc Co and Plei Djereng.

The 4th Division's rifle companies began experiencing heavier contact with larger NVA units as April closed. On 30 April Alpha Company, 2/8th Infantry, fought a pitched battle with the NVA just a few kilometers southwest of the Oasis. The next day, while pursuing the NVA, they stumbled across a large enemy base camp. Also on 1 May, the 1st Brigade's Alpha, 3/12th, was attacked by an NVA company while patrolling in the Chu Goungot mountains west of Highway 14B and north of Duc Co.

As a result of this contact the 1st Brigade's 1/8th established a fire support base west of Duc Co and north of Highway 19. Based on LRRP reports, B-52 bombers had unleashed bombing raids hoping to catch the NVA in the area between the Chu Goungot mountains and the Cambodian border. The 1/8th's rifle companies began moving to the northwest on a bomb-assessment operation.

On 18 May Bravo Company, 1/8th, ran into a well-executed NVA ambush. Beginning at 1230 and lasting for seven hours, the company fought desperately for its life. One of its platoons was cut off and quickly surrounded by the NVA. By 1500 twenty-one of the platoon's twenty-nine members were dead, many executed by the NVA as they swarmed over the battlefield; only one member of the platoon survived unscathed. Not until the next day was a relieving company, Alpha, 1/8th, able to fight its way to Bravo.

The very next night, 20 May, all three rifle companies of

1/8th were laagered in a night defensive position about a thousand meters northwest of Bravo's 18 May battle site. At 2119 the NVA hit the battalion with a heavy ground attack supported by an intense mortar barrage and automatic-weapons fire. Three separate attacks were repulsed that long night before the NVA withdrew. They left thirty-seven dead on the jungle hillside. The 1/8th lost sixteen killed and sixty-six wounded.

Sent to reinforce 1/8th, the 3/12th was hit by a ground attack as it moved out of its night laager site on the morning of 22 May. The fighting raged for four hours, the NVA pulling out only after being hit hard by air strikes and artillery. This fight cost the 4th Infantry Division ten dead and seventy-seven wounded. The body count for the NVA numbered sixty-one.

In the first two months of Francis Marion, the 4th Infantry Division had been badly mauled. The division had incurred more than three hundred casualties, of whom more than sixty were killed in action. In countering the enemy's movements through his area of operations, Peers had moved both of his brigades into the vicinity of the Chu Goungot mountains. As a result, his southern flank was weakened. Without a third maneuver brigade in his division to cover that area, the 4th was dangerously exposed. Peers appealed to his boss for help.

Lieutenant General Stanley R. ("Swede") Larsen commanded the I Field Force headquartered at Nha Trang. General Larsen was a World War II veteran who had risen from platoon leader to regimental commander fighting the Japanese on a succession of jungle-clad islands across the Pacific. As a result, he had a better understanding of the uniqueness of the warfare in the Central Highlands than did other senior commanders in South Vietnam. He knew that Peers's division, although in no immediate danger, was being sorely pressed. Peers badly needed a third brigade.

Operating in coastal Binh Dinh Province, directly east of Pleiku, was the 1st Cavalry Division (Airmobile). Larsen wanted to send one of the Cav's brigades to Pleiku. He called General Westmoreland in Saigon on 21 May to explain the situation. "I have to send another brigade into the highlands," Larsen stated. "I'm going to send a Cav brigade."

"No," responded Westmoreland. "Don't do that. Just keep an eye on things. We'll see what happens."

Two days later, after the 4th had been hit hard once again, Larsen again called Westmoreland. "I've got no choice," he said this time. "I've got to send Ray some help. I have to send him the Cav brigade."

"No," said Westmoreland. "I want the Cav intact in Binh Dinh. I'll send Ray the 173d."

General Larsen was not overly excited about the deployment of the 173d Airborne Brigade to his region. To the best of his knowledge the Sky Soldiers had been relatively inactive for the last several months, fighting only small bands of VC. He had wanted a unit more recently experienced against the NVA, but he'd take the 173d.

General Larsen was correct in his assessment of the 173d's combat readiness. Beginning on 1 May 1967 General Deane, who had served as Larsen's chief of staff for five months in early 1966, had taken his brigade into Long Khanh Province, east of Bien Hoa, on Operation Fort Wayne. Enemy contact was light and casualties were accordingly minimal.

After returning to Bien Hoa on 4 May, Deane was ordered to take his brigade into Phuoc Tuy Province, south of Long Khanh, to search for the VC 274th and 275th Main Force regiments. Deane deployed the 1/503d and 2/503d to Phuoc Tuy late on 5 May. Over the next twelve days the brigade elements maintained sporadic contact with the enemy. These engagements were primarily meeting engagements involving small bands of VC harassing the paratroopers. No major engagements occurred, though the Sky Soldiers did find a large number of abandoned base camps and scattered bunkers throughout their AO. On 17 May the operation ended. The brigade returned to Bien Hoa.

Back at their main camp the 173d began routine patrolling around the air force base to discourage VC ground, mortar, or rocket attacks. On the afternoon of 23 May, General Deane was summoned to the II Field Force headquarters at Bien Hoa. There Deane was told by Lt. Gen. Jonathan O. Seaman that he was taking his brigade north. The 4th Infantry Division would have operational control of the 173d; Deane would report to General Peers. Deane would establish a base camp south of Pleiku and act as Peers's reserve force. He could expect to be up north for three months. After the briefing Deane hurried back to his headquarters.

Deane huddled with his S-3, Maj. James R. Steverson, and together the two wrote an operational plan. At 0500 the next morning an advance party headed by Steverson would depart for Pleiku. By noon the brigade would begin the airlift north. Deane called in his battalion commanders, advised them of the move, and issued a string of orders. The battalion commanders passed the word down and soon a flurry of activity engulfed the company areas.

The enlisted men hurriedly packed their rucksacks, cleaned their weapons, and loaded ammo magazines. The typical Sky Soldier carried a tremendous load on his back when he went into the field. Most soldiers carried between one thousand and twelve hundred rounds of ammo for their M16s in magazines or quick-load stripper clips. Although the magazine for the M16 held twenty rounds, most men loaded them with only seventeen or eighteen rounds; any more seemed to overload the magazine's internal spring, causing the weapon to jam after a few rounds.

Hanging from various places on a paratrooper's web gear, or in a canvas bag, were twelve to fifteen fragmentation grenades and two to four smoke grenades. Each man also toted two Claymore antipersonnel mines. Draped across his chest hung one hundred to two hundred belted rounds of ammo for his squad's M60 machine gun. Every infantryman was also required to carry one or more rounds for his company's mortars. A shovel for digging fighting positions rotated between the men of a rifle squad on a daily basis. Sometimes the men had to carry chain saws to cut trees to make LZs.

In addition, the men had to find room for their personal gear. Besides letters from home, writing material, cameras, books, portable radios, mess gear, canteens, and rations, they carried their personal hygiene gear. Even in the field the 173d maintained a high standard of cleanliness. Each man was expected to shave every day, whether in the field or at the base camp.

Depending on a man's personal gear, his load ranged in weight from seventy-five to ninety pounds, most of it carried on his back in a rucksack. No wonder the sound the men made as they hoisted their packs on their backs resulted in their nickname: grunts.

After a frantic night of packing and repacking their gear, the brigade members reported to the Bien Hoa airstrip early on 24 May 1967. Reflecting the "hurry up and wait" attitude of all military organizations, the first paratrooper-laden C-130 didn't get airborne until after noon. For the next three days the air force flew 208 C-130 sorties, ferrying 2,239 men and 2,700 tons of equipment to Pleiku. Since everyone expected to return to Bien Hoa in ninety days, the brigade retained its base camp at Bien Hoa staffed by its rear-echelon personnel. They had no way of knowing the brigade would never return south.

When the paratroopers learned they were going to help the 4th Infantry Division, most of them adopted a superior, almost derisive attitude toward the nonairborne, or "leg," infantry. The 173d possessed great morale. All its men were volunteers for airborne training and most had volunteered for South Vietnam. Many of the paratroopers figured they'd go up north, kick the NVA's ass, then return to Bien Hoa. They'd show the 4th how to fight this war.

Aware of their attitude, Col. James B. Adamson, commander of the 4th Infantry Division's 2d Brigade, spent time with General Deane and his staff trying to explain about the war in the Central Highlands. "This is a different war than what you've been used to in the south," he told them. "First, you must realize that up here in the highlands you are fighting the NVA, not the VC. They're professionals who know how to fight. Second, don't let a company get out by itself where it will be easy pickings for the NVA. They'll wipe it out."

Despite his admonitions, Adamson felt the 173d still retained their superior attitude.

That same attitude infected the 173d's S-3, Major Steverson. Once he brought his advance party to Pleiku, Steverson met with the 4th's G-3, Lt. Col. James R. Lay. In the briefing Colonel Lay essentially told Major Steverson he wanted to help the paratroopers become accustomed to warfare in the Central Highlands and learn how the 4th operated in its dense jungles.

Steverson rejected the advice. He reminded Lay the 173d was the first army ground combat unit in South Vietnam and had been fighting the enemy for two years. As far as Steverson and most of the brigade's command structure was concerned, there wasn't anything the 4th could tell the 173d about fighting in South Vietnam.

Steverson was justified in feeling proud of the 173d's record in the war. It had fought battle after battle with the enemy and continually emerged victorious. There was only one fatal flaw in Steverson's logic: Most of the brigade's fights had been against irregular Viet Cong forces. Very few of the Sky Soldiers in the 173d in spring 1967 had any combat experience against the NVA.

The 173d set up camp at Catecka, about twelve kilometers south of Pleiku. Those who were there remember Catecka as a sea of red mud awash in the torrential downpours of the monsoon season. From 27 May through 30 May the brigade improved its camp at Catecka and the road net in the immediate area. It was difficult work made worse by the thick mud and miserable weather conditions.

Beginning on 1 June General Deane deployed his forces south and southwest of Catecka into the upper Ia Drang Valley. Deane dispatched both the 1/503d and 2/503d into the field, holding 4/503d at Catecka as base security and a reaction force.

The brigade's line companies found few signs of the enemy in its AO. General Deane, though hampered by heavy morning fog and low ceilings in the afternoon, spent as much time as he could in his command-and-control chopper flying over his AO. He saw plenty of old positions from the 1st Cavalry's and the 101st Airborne Division's brigade's operations in the previous year, but no evidence of an NVA presence.

While the 173d searched furtively for the NVA through the rainsoaked hills of southwestern Pleiku Province, events were unfolding to the north in neighboring Kontum Province that would have a deadly impact on the Sky Soldiers.

On the night of 15–16 June 1967, a ten-man element consisting of two Americans and eight CIDG from the Dak To Special Forces camp was destroyed by the NVA 24th Regiment about fourteen hundred meters southwest of their camp. Early in the morning of 17 June, the Dak To camp was pounded by a heavy mortar barrage. At the same time the headquarters of the ARVN 42d Regiment east of Dak To at Tan Canh was hit by mortars and 122mm rockets.

Since it was obvious the NVA were preparing for a major attack on the Dak To camp, its commander asked for protection. General Larsen knew the 173d had had no contact while on Francis Marion, so he ordered General Peers to release two battalions of the 173d for duty at Dak To.

General Deane ordered his deputy brigade commander, Col. Claude M. McQuarrie, to take the 1/503d, 2/503d, Bravo Battery, 3/319th, and various supporting units to Dak To, eighty kilometers to the north. This operation was named Greeley.

Task Force McQuarrie got moving early in the morning of 17 June. The 2/503d, under thirty-seven-year-old Lt. Col. Edward A. Partain, led the way to Dak To aboard C-130s. Colonel Partain was a native of Arkansas who had graduated from West Point in 1951. He then spent a year in Korea as a rifle platoon leader and company commander in the 25th Infantry Division. He attended jump school in 1953, completion of which eventually drew him an assignment to the 7th Special Forces in Germany.

Because of that duty, Partain went to South Vietnam in 1964 as chief of airborne operations for MACV's supersecret Studies and Observation Group. When he finished that one-year tour, he attended the Armed Forces Staff College and had a tour of duty in the Pentagon before returning to South Vietnam in March 1967. He took command of 2/503d upon his arrival.

While the rifle companies moved by air, Partain's very capable S-3, Capt. Kenneth Smith, organized and led the truck convoy carrying the brigade's heavy equipment and gear to Dak To. A twenty-six-year-old native of Des Moines, Iowa, and a former seminarian, Smith was a Distinguished Military Graduate of Creighton University's ROTC program. He had served in the 2/503d since March 1967, first as the assistant S-2, then, beginning in late April, as its S-3.

The fifty-vehicle convoy left Catecka at midmorning on 17 June. It threaded its way up Highway 14, through Pleiku, Kontum, and then into Dak To, arriving just after 1700. The crews established a CP just to the south of Dak To's airstrip.

On 18 June, 1/503d made the move with Colonel McQuarrie's headquarters group to Dak To. They set up CPs adjacent to Colonel Partain's headquarters. That same day the 2/503d began sending its companies into the area almost due south of Dak To. Their main objective was Hill 1338, the dominant hill mass south of the camp. Control of this high ground would deny the NVA a key observation point from which they could direct fire on Dak To.

Charlie Company, 1/503d, received the mission of locating the missing Special Forces and CIDG from the 15–16 June incident. On 20 June Charlie, under Capt. Kirby Smith, found the missing men. It was a horrifying discovery. All of the men had been brutally tortured and their bodies mutilated.

Captain Joseph X. Grosso, the battalion surgeon, had the unpleasant task of identifying the Americans' remains. The twenty-seven-year-old Philadelphian, who had served his internship at Jefferson Medical School, had volunteered for the army when he didn't qualify for a government program that would have delayed his military service until after his residency. He volunteered for airborne training when he learned that officers earned an extra $110 per month for jumping out of airplanes; he was deeply in debt from medical school and an extra hundred bucks every thirty days would be a godsend.

Captain Grosso arrived in South Vietnam and joined the 173d in April 1967. Since then he'd seen a lot of death. But nothing prepared him for the two Green Berets. Their bodies had been cleaved lengthwise, cut wide open from groin to head. Their insides were as clearly exposed as a cross-section drawing in an anatomy textbook. Grosso wondered just what kind of an enemy they were facing in the Central Highlands.

At the same time Captain Grosso was doing his post-mortem, the grunts of Alpha, 2/503d, were wondering if there were any NVA in the Dak To area. The company had been choppered out to an LZ north of Hill 1338 on 18 June. For the next two days they humped across the north side of the huge hill looking for the NVA. They did find a well-developed trail on the hillside and set up ambushes along it, but no NVA moved down the trail.

On 20 June Charlie, 2/503d, made the move onto Hill 1338. They passed through Alpha and headed south, farther up Hill 1338.

After setting up his night defensive position on 21 June about halfway up Hill 1338 and about fifty-five hundred yards south of Dak To, Capt. David H. Milton had his men of Alpha, 2/503d, cut an LZ for the evening resupply chopper. Milton was a twenty-eight-year-old with more than eleven years' service in the army. Born in Boston but raised in Dallas, Milton quit school two months after his seventeenth birthday to join the army. He served as an enlisted man until 1964, when he was accepted at officer candidate school (OCS). He received his commission in December 1964. As a member of the 82d Airborne Division, Milton experienced his baptism of fire during the Dominican Republic revolution in the spring of 1966. His personal gallantry in action during that campaign earned him a Silver Star.

Milton went to South Vietnam in March 1967, joining Alpha upon his arrival. Originally a platoon leader, Milton took over Alpha when its commander was badly wounded and evacuated in May. A short time later Milton received his promotion to captain.

Captain Milton did not inspire the same confidence in his troops as did his predecessor, Captain Kerns. Kerns was charismatic, comfortable with the men, and protective of them in every way he could be. Some of the grunts considered Milton tentative and indecisive. He seemed to lack confidence in himself. Some thought he was not comfortable being a line officer, but he was their CO and they'd do what he told them to do.

🔊 At about 1700 Milton received a radio message from Capt. Ken Smith. Milton was to return with his company to Dak To the next day, planning his route to arrive there no later than 1500. Once back at Dak To, Alpha would take over from Bravo, 2/503d, as security for the battalion headquarters group; the paratroopers called it palace guard duty. The men welcomed the change. Even after just four days they had had it with the mountains and jungles of Dak To. It had rained nearly every day, turning the jungle floor into a morass. The dense clumps of bamboo and towering trees rose to heights exceeding two hundred feet. The dreary weather and dense foliage cast an eerie gloom in the jungle, keeping it in a permanent twilight. The thick undergrowth helped reduce ground-level visibility to just ten to fifteen yards. It was spooky in the jungle, and the grunts were ready to leave it.

Soon after the message from Smith came in, the night resupply chopper descended into the LZ. Besides the regular cargo of rations, mail, and one or two men returning from R and R, the Huey brought in two fifty-five-gallon drums of CS crystals. After vacating their laager site and LZ the next morning, Alpha was to sow the ground with the CS, denying the area to the NVA.

Milton made one more decision the night of 21 June. One of the brigade's Catholic chaplains, Maj. Charles J. Watters, had been humping with Alpha since the company had come into the field four days earlier. Milton didn't think it made any sense for the forty-year-old priest to make the three-mile-plus hump back to Dak To. He suggested that Father Watters go back on the night chopper.

If there was any one man who was universally loved in the 173d, it was Chaplain Watters. A New Jersey native and a graduate of Immaculate Conception Seminary in Darlington,

New Jersey, Chaplain Watters was ordained in 1953, becoming a parish priest. Always the adventuresome type, Watters learned to fly in the late 1950s, eventually earning both his commercial pilot's license and an instrument rating. Still yearning for adventure, he joined the air force reserve at McGuire Air Force Base in 1962. He spent four years as a reserve chaplain and then, with the Vietnam War heating up, decided he wanted a role in the war. He transferred to the army in August 1965, went on active duty, completed paratrooper training, and joined the 173d in South Vietnam in June 1966.

Father Watters quickly earned a reputation among the young paratroopers as a true field chaplain. He felt his place was in the boonies with the combat soldier. That's where he went. Whenever possible, he was with the troops, humping right beside them. He not only took care of their spiritual needs but listened to their bitches, helped them with their personal problems, and gave them general guidance.

Father Watters made the jump at Junction City, one of only three chaplains to do so. When his one-year tour in South Vietnam ended in early June 1967, he extended for another full tour. "His boys" needed him, he felt, and he couldn't let them down.

Although he spent as much time in the field as he could, Father Watters told a reporter in a May 1967 interview that he never carried a weapon. "I'm the peaceful kind. All I shoot is my camera. If they start shooting at me," he joked, "I'd just yell 'Tourist!' Seriously, a weapon weighs too much, and after all, a priest's job is in taking care of the boys. But if we ever get overrun, I guess there'll be plenty of weapons lying around waiting to be picked up."

When Father Watters heard Captain Milton's suggestion that he return to Dak To on the night chopper, he agreed with him. If he went back in that night he'd be able to say Mass for the Catholics in Bravo Company before they headed out. He gathered up his Mass kit and personal gear; then, after wishing the Alpha grunts good luck on their hump the next day, he hopped aboard the chopper.

After the Huey departed, Milton made the rounds of his

company's perimeter. Of his three rifle platoon leaders, two were brand-new. Milton wanted to make sure that they had set their platoons into proper position.

First Lieutenants Richard E. Hood, Jr., and Donald R. Judd had both graduated from West Point with the class of 1966. Along with more than a dozen of their classmates, they had joined the 173d within the previous month and, after completing the brigade's week-long jungle school, had gone out to their rifle company. Hood, a twenty-two-year-old Floridan, had joined Alpha Company about a week before his friend Judd, a twenty-four-year-old native of New York, did on 19 June.

Though new, Judd and Hood had carefully and properly selected their platoon's night positions. Milton was pleased. He thought they knew what they were doing and, with a little more bush time, they would make excellent rifle platoon leaders. Maybe they would be as good as his third platoon leader.

First Lieutenant Jeffrey R. Sexton was a former enlisted member of Alpha. During his first tour he had so impressed his superiors with his intelligence and leadership ability that they highly recommended him for OCS. The Phoenix, Arizona, resident agreed to attend the school at Fort Benning on one condition: Upon commissioning he wanted a platoon in Alpha Company. Strings were pulled and arrangements were made. Sexton went off to Georgia and returned to South Vietnam four months later having swapped his specialist 4th class chevron for the gold bar of a second lieutenant. He'd been back for a few months when Milton took over Alpha. Sexton was an outstanding junior officer whom Milton frequently turned to for advice about operating in the field.

Once satisfied that his company was properly positioned, Milton returned to his CP, a shelter half stretched over a shallow hole. He, like his men, was eagerly anticipating palace guard duty. He'd have a chance to sleep in a dry spot for several days rather than on the rainsoaked jungle floor.

About fifteen hundred meters farther up Hill 1338, Charlie, 2/503d, was moving into its night position. Captain

Ronald R. Leonard had taken command of Charlie in early June. The previous commander, Capt. Thomas Carney, had led Charlie during the jump on Junction City and through all its subsequent campaigns before the move to Pleiku. Carney was a company commander who was truly loved by his men—so much so that the platoon leaders rustled up some liquor while at Pleiku and threw a rousing going-away party for Carney. Charlie Company sorely missed Carney. Such admiration meant that Captain Leonard had a very difficult act to follow.

Ron Leonard grew up in Kansas where he spent a great deal of his time in the outdoors. A premed student at Fort Hays State College, he graduated with a degree in biology in 1959. He taught high-school science and chemistry before accepting a direct commission with the air force in 1963. Unhappy with his assignment, he requested a direct transfer to the army. He got it in the spring of 1966.

Upon switching his air force blues for army greens, Leonard volunteered for infantry and airborne training. When he completed those courses, he went to Fort Hood, Texas. In September 1966 he was promoted to captain. In December he received his orders for South Vietnam. To ensure that he was as prepared as possible for his combat tour, Leonard requested immediate orders for Ranger school. He completed the rugged course in April 1967 and then headed for South Vietnam.

Soon after taking over Charlie Company, Captain Leonard was attending a routine evening briefing at battalion headquarters. While there the company commanders were told the names of the replacement officers being assigned to them. Charlie was to get Lieutenant Judd; Alpha would get 1st Lt. Matthew C. Harrison.

Leonard interrupted. He'd known Harrison at Fort Hood, he said. Would anyone mind if Harrison came to his company and Judd went to Alpha? No one did, so the necessary orders were cut.

Matt Harrison was a very likable twenty-two-year-old 1966 graduate of West Point who had been born there while his father served as an instructor. While still a cadet, Harrison had volunteered for South Vietnam and the 173d Airborne Brigade. His earlier research had proven to him that the 173d was an elite unit. Full of vigor for the new war in South Vietnam, he wanted to serve with the best.

After Harrison completed the brigade's jungle school, a C-130 took him to Dak To. Later that day a resupply Huey carried him out to Charlie's position on Hill 1338. It was 20 June.

Harrison couldn't believe what he saw when he jumped off the chopper. Huge trees disappeared skyward. Massive stands of bamboo were everywhere. Nearly every square foot of ground was covered by vegetation. The company's laager site was visible for only a few meters before the jungle swallowed it up. Sharp drop-offs extended downward on both sides of the ridge finger where Charlie was camped. Welcome to the war, Harrison told himself.

The next day, 21 June, Charlie continued its trek into the higher reaches of Hill 1338. The going was extremely difficult. The thickly matted undergrowth slowed forward progress to a hundred meters per hour or less. The point squad was forced to hack its way through vines and branches with machetes. The high heat and humidity made the task doubly difficult. Men on the machetes had to be rotated every fifteen minutes lest they collapse from the exertion.

Traveling with Charlie was a platoon of CIDG from the Dak To Special Forces camp. They not only provided additional manpower but were supposed to be guides to the area. Captain Leonard thought they were of dubious quality. Their lieutenant spoke English, so communication with them was fairly easy. The lieutenant made it clear he felt there were enemy in the area. He also made it obvious that neither he nor his men wanted to be there.

Leading Charlie Company up Hill 1338 was 1st Lt. Phillip Bodine's 2d Platoon. Bodine grew up in Rock Island, Illinois, where he enlisted in the army in January 1965, just before his nineteenth birthday. He was soon selected for OCS, receiving his commission in December 1966. Bodine had deployed to South Vietnam in March 1967 with an aviation battalion from Fort Bragg. He was not happy with his assignment, so he asked his CO for a transfer to the infantry. A few weeks later he was checking in with the 173d at Bien Hoa.

By midafternoon on 21 June, Captain Leonard started looking for a night laager site. He selected a location adjacent to their line of march. As the men moved into position and began digging their night fighting positions, Lieutenants Harrison and Bodine ordered their squad leaders to organize the LPs for the night. The three- or four-man teams would take up positions thirty to fifty meters outside the perimeter to give advance warning of any enemy attack.

One of the two LPs Lieutenant Bodine prepared consisted of two paratroopers and three of the CIDG. He wanted this LP to backtrack along their day's path to watch for any NVA shadowing them. Bodine accompanied the small patrol so he could place them in position.

As they were leaving the perimeter, one of the CIDG motioned to Bodine. "*Beaucoup* [many] VC here," the man said. "No go."

"You'll go," Bodine said as he pushed the man forward. Behind him the rest of the company was busy preparing for the night.

Bodine's little patrol moved about forty meters downhill. Bodine brought up the rear to prevent the CIDG from returning to the camp. The jungle was so thick with bamboo clumps and vegetation that Bodine could not see his point man only ten meters ahead.

When an exchange of gunfire shattered the evening stillness, Bodine instantly hit the dirt. A minute of silence passed. He snaked forward, keeping low.

When Bodine reached his point man, the excited youngster hurriedly explained that he'd stumbled upon an enemy soldier just five feet away. Before the paratrooper could fire, the enemy soldier got off a burst, missing the Sky Soldier but hitting one of the CIDG; the Montagnard's corpse lay sprawled nearby. The American had returned fire. By then, though, the NVA soldier had disappeared.

Bodine radioed the information to Leonard. Leonard called Bodine's patrol back and then set about tightening up his company's defense. He fully expected an attack that night.

The dead CIDG was placed in the center of the perimeter. If weather permitted, a chopper would pick up the body the next morning. For most of the Americans this was the first casualty of war they had seen. For many it was the first dead person they'd ever seen. Lieutenant Harrison had never seen a corpse, never even been to a funeral. For him, seeing the dead Montagnard brought home the stark reality of a shooting war more effectively than any training class ever could. He now knew for sure this war was for real.

The paratroopers of Charlie spent a nervous night. Sentries continually reported hearing movement near them. Captain Leonard refused to let them fire their weapons; he didn't want them to give away their position. Few of Charlie's members got much rest.

Below them Captain Milton's Alpha Company passed a more restful night. They were returning to base camp the next day. They'd been out in the field for four days, seen no enemy, and most importantly, suffered no casualties. It had been a good patrol.

Both groups of men were as isolated from one another as they could be. The fifteen hundred meters that separated them might as well have been fifteen hundred miles. Each company lived in its own world, cut off from knowledge about the other and the outside world.

Probably not more than a dozen men in the two companies knew that Israel had invaded Egypt in a blitzkrieg-type attack just a few weeks earlier. All would have been surprised to learn that our Israeli allies had attacked a U.S. Navy spy ship in the eastern Mediterranean on the second day of the war, killing and wounding dozens of innocent U.S. sailors.

A few of the newer arrivals might have known that Jefferson Airplane's *White Rabbit* topped the popular music charts back in the States. None knew that the female half of the popular singing duo Sonny and Cher had just announced she was pregnant with her first child. If they had known of it, almost every one of the Sky Soldiers would have applauded the recent conviction of world heavyweight boxer Cassius Clay for refusing induction.

The fact that President Lyndon B. Johnson that very day

had met with Russian premier Aleksey Kosygin in Glassboro, New Jersey, to discuss peace plans for the Middle East would have had little effect on the Sky Soldiers.

There were really only two things that mattered to the paratroopers that June day: They were still alive, and they had one less day to serve in their 365-day tour in Vietnam.

CHAPTER 4

BATTLE OF THE SLOPES

Dawn on 22 June 1967 brought thick fog and low clouds to the Dak To area. None of the 173d's choppers would be flying until the morning sun burned off the fog.

On Hill 1338 the two companies of 2/503d were stirring. The triple-canopy jungle cut the morning light to a gray shadow, reducing visibility to mere meters. That had deadly consequences for one man in Charlie Company.

An FNG, Pfc. Jimmy Lee Cook, stepped outside the company's perimeter to take a leak. He didn't tell anyone he was going. When he finished and started back into the perimeter a nervous sentry spotted his shadowy movement amidst the dense vegetation. The sentry triggered a burst from his M16, thinking he'd seen a marauding NVA. When the sentry and his squad leader moved forward to inspect the kill, they saw their terrible mistake.

Captain Leonard was not happy with the death of one of his men or with the carelessness that caused it. And now he had a second corpse to deal with. He had no idea how long it would be before a chopper could get in and retrieve the bodies. Leonard got on the radio and reported his situation to the TOC. Then he started preparing his company for the day's patrol.

At Alpha's bivouac site, Sgt. William Nichols, a twenty-one-year-old from Long Island, New York, awoke that morning filled with dread. A tough veteran who'd been in South Vietnam since February, Nichols had made the jump during Junction City with Alpha and had come with them to Dak To. For the past few months he'd been an FO with 2d Platoon for Alpha's 81mm mortars. The previous evening the Weapons Platoon's platoon sergeant told Nichols to return to the Weapons Platoon; he'd been with 2d Platoon long enough and it was time for a change.

Nichols's morning jitters were noticed by one of his buddies. "What's the matter, Sarge?" the man asked.

"I don't know. I just feel something's not right."

"Calm down," the man advised. "You're too jumpy. You've been with the line platoons too long."

Nichols returned to getting his gear ready, trying to keep his nervousness under control.

A short distance away another member of Weapons Platoon packed his rucksack, too. Private 1st Class John Steer was a rowdy nineteen-year-old from Minneapolis. As a youngster he'd been in and out of trouble, running away from school and home at fifteen, settling in California. He worked odd jobs there for a while before returning home. Eventually, he got into trouble again, but this time he faced jail. The judge in the case offered to drop the charges if Steer enlisted. He agreed. He'd been in South Vietnam and with Alpha since March 1967.

Some of the other members of Weapons Platoon considered Steer a smart aleck, and he was. He didn't like mortars. He wanted to be in a rifle platoon and let everyone know it every chance he had.

The night before, when told they'd be returning to Dak To via the same trail they'd been monitoring for the past few days, Steer couldn't believe it. It was gospel among the grunts to avoid repeat use of trails. The crafty enemy frequently booby-trapped them or set up ambushes along their length. Steer and his buddies spent that night bitching about the next day's hump.

Actually, Captain Milton had little choice in his company's route of march. The ridge finger they were on had such steep sides, covered with the typical dense jungle growth, that any other route would have taken several days to traverse.

Milton assigned Lieutenant Judd's 2d Platoon to the point position. Next came 3d Platoon led by Lieutenant Hood. Milton's CP group would follow, and behind them would come Weapons Platoon. Lieutenant Sexton's 1st Platoon was given the task of spreading the CS crystals over the LZ and laager site before falling in at the column's rear.

At 0625 Lieutenant Judd started off. As the tail end of his platoon disappeared downhill into the jungle, Hood started his platoon forward. The Weapons Platoon members, all eighteen of them, squatted along the trail waiting their turn to move. Lieutenant Sexton's platoon had donned their gas masks and were spreading the tear gas around the LZ.

Sergeant Nichols had just stood up when the sharp crack of rifle fire broke the morning calm. The firing continued for ten seconds or so, then died down. It was 0658.

Captain Milton radioed Judd. The young lieutenant reported that his point squad had walked smack into ten to fifteen NVA coming toward them on the same trail. The NVA had opened up first, hitting some of Judd's men. He didn't know how many, or how badly. Judd had put his remaining men into a defensive perimeter.

Private 1st Class Steer heard someone say that the firing was just 2d Platoon reconning by fire. "Bullshit," he retorted. "That's AK-47 fire." With that the distinct crack of M16s could be heard. It was 2d Platoon fighting back.

After getting off the radio with Judd, Milton radioed the battalion TOC. He reported the contact to Capt. Ken Smith. Colonel Partain and his executive officer, Maj. H. Glenn Watson, were also present in the TOC. While Partain and Smith plotted the coordinates in order to bring in supporting artillery fire, Watson stayed on the radio with Milton.

Major Watson was not overly concerned. Alpha seemed to have the situation under control. He advised Captain Milton to "develop the fight and keep us informed."

Back on Hill 1338 Captain Milton turned to his senior medic, Sp5 Richard E. Patterson. "Doc, they need a medic down there," he said.

Patterson started to send one of the other medics but thought better of it. Oh, hell, he told himself, I'll go.

Patterson started down the slippery trail. Although only eighteen, he had been in the army nearly two years. Born in a poor Boston neighborhood, he saw the army as an opportunity to improve his lot. Just after his seventeenth birthday in September 1965, he enlisted for four years, expecting to learn a trade that would carry over to civilian life.

Now he was dodging down a muddy jungle path, heading toward the sound of battle. He soon stumbled across one of the other medics, lying along the trail, shot in both arms. Another Sky Soldier tended to the medic so Patterson hurried on.

Meanwhile, Lieutenant Judd had pulled back up the trail about seventy-five meters to a small clearing where he joined up with Lieutenant Hood. Together, they formed a V-shaped perimeter, Judd's men on the left, Hood's on the right. The paratroopers sought cover where they could, firing back at the invisible enemy.

Patterson burst in on the position, which reached only about fifteen meters across. Men were scattered everywhere, some firing, the others frantically scanning the jungle walls in front of them for any sign of the approaching NVA.

Just then a horrible, bloodcurdling scream erupted from down the trail. Patterson froze. Seconds later a weaponless, panicked paratrooper came running into the clearing, a look of sheer terror in his eyes. Tears rolled down his face and he was screaming as he moved toward Lieutenant Hood.

"I'll kill you, you motherfucker!" he yelled. "I'll fucking kill you!"

Hood stood still, unsure of what to do. Then, one of the NCOs grabbed the crazed youngster and wrestled him to the ground.

What the hell is going on? Patterson wondered. Before he could learn what had caused the man's outburst, the crash of grenades and the roar of small-arms fire filled the little clearing. Patterson and the others still standing hit the dirt.

A short distance away a paratrooper was hit in the stomach, his intestines spilling onto the ground in a steaming tangle. Patterson and another medic crawled to the casualty. The two knelt on either side of the man, desperately trying to pack the intestines back into place and bandage the wound.

The small-arms fire grew heavier, AK-47 rounds snapping past the heads of the two medics. Patterson leaned forward to speak when the other medic suddenly jerked. Patterson met his friend's gaze as a stream of blood eighteen to twenty-four inches long spurted from the man's neck. An AK-47 round had hit the medic in the throat. As Patterson watched, shocked, the medic slowly slumped forward, gushing blood across the jungle floor as he died. Pushing the body aside, Patterson returned to saving his patient.

Back at the company CP, Milton was relaying the coordinates of his pinned-down platoons to the TOC. He wanted artillery brought down in front of his platoons, and he wanted it now. Within minutes shells from the 105mm howitzers of the 3/319th were on their way.

Artillery can be ineffective in the jungle. Not only is it nearly impossible to accurately adjust the fire by visual reference, but the shells have a tendency to burst in the tops of tall trees, scattering shrapnel harmlessly about.

Also, the NVA knew the cannoneers would not fire too close to their own infantrymen. They took advantage of this caution by moving as close to the paratroopers as they could, hugging the perimeter. The American artillery crashed ineffectively behind them.

At the first sound of contact, Lieutenant Sexton had moved his platoon to Milton's position. With the firing downhill building in volume, Milton ordered Sexton to send one of his squads forward, carrying extra ammo. Sexton sent four men and an M60 gunner. They didn't return.

In the clearing Specialist Patterson had his hands full with casualties. Only he and one other medic were still functioning. They both crawled along, hugging the jungle floor as close as they could, moving from casualty to casualty. The plaintive cries of "Medic!" carried over the incredible roar of M16s, AK-47s, and exploding artillery shells.

To flatten himself as much as possible, Patterson pushed his medical bag in front of him as he moved. A sudden burning pain on the back of his right hand stopped his movement. An enemy round had ripped open his hand, exposing the bones.

He barely had time to accept that when there was a sudden roar behind him. A grenade had exploded near his right foot, sending red-hot shards of jagged metal into his right ankle and tearing his Achilles tendon. He felt as if his foot had been blown off. He lay still, wracked with pain.

At the battalion TOC, the reports from Milton were causing increasing concern among the staff. The rapid buildup of enemy fire had finally convinced Partain and Watson that this was no ordinary contact. The faint sound of the firing could already be heard at the TOC. Something big was definitely up.

Colonel Partain grabbed Captain Smith and Sgt. Maj. Vincent Rogiers and headed for the chopper pad. He wanted to get above the action as soon as the weather permitted and coordinate the artillery and upcoming air strikes. Major Watson stayed at the TOC, on the radio.

Back on Hill 1338, the two pinned-down platoons were still holding on. Enemy fire had slackened a bit, giving the paratroopers a little rest. Then, at about 0810, Specialist Patterson heard someone up front holler, "Here they come!"

With that the firing picked up in earnest.

The enemy came straight up the hill at the perimeter in a full frontal attack. The heavy jungle prevented the Sky Soldiers from getting more than a fleeting glimpse of the attackers, but the muzzle blasts of the AK-47s were clearly visible. M16s and M60s pounded out a furious hail of return fire.

The paratroopers held off the attackers, estimated by Hood to Captain Milton as being platoon-sized. The assaults were renewed periodically for the next thirty minutes.

Colonel Partain and his command entourage had now arrived above the battle site. Within seconds of his arrival Partain learned one of the realities of fighting in the highlands: The triple-canopy jungle prevented the airborne commander from seeing anything on the ground. He had no idea where Milton's men were or where the NVA were. He could depend only on the coordinates relayed by Captain Milton, which came from either Judd or Hood.

Based on the information he had, Partain called in an air strike. In order to bring in the jets, or fast movers, the artillery had to be shifted while the planes were in the area. Not everyone thought air strikes should be used. Because air strikes were less accurate than artillery, the NVA knew that the closer they moved to an allied unit, the safer they were.

Major Watson knew this, too. When the order for use of the fast movers came to him, he thought it was a mistake. "Negative," he responded to the order to shift the artillery.

General Deane, who had arrived in the area, came up on the battalion net. "Shift the artillery," Deane ordered, over-riding Watson.

From 0820 to 0825 the jets dropped their bombs along the east side of the ridge. Ten minutes later Huey gunships arrived on the scene. To help mark their platoons' perimeter for the close-in support from the gunships' weapons systems, Lieutenants Judd and Hood had their men toss out smoke grenades, or "pop smoke" in the grunts' jargon.

Another reality about fighting in the highlands became apparent: The thick jungle dispersed the smoke so widely that the gunships couldn't get an accurate fix on the paratroopers' location.

On the ground the effects were disastrous. The rising columns of smoke told the NVA right where the Americans were. Specialist Patterson noticed the increase in small-arms fire immediately. Seconds later NVA mortar rounds began crashing into the perimeter, tearing American flesh. Amid the renewed cries of "Medic!" Patterson heard paratroopers yelling, "No more smoke. No more smoke." But it was too late. The NVA now had an accurate fix on their positions.

Even while the gunships were firing blindly into the jungle around them, the NVA were massing for another ground attack. About this time Lieutenant Judd radioed back to Milton, "Six, we're bracing for an all-out attack. We're laid out well. About a hundred gooks are getting ready to hit us."

Before Milton could respond the roar of M16 fire filled the handset. He was starting to wonder if the two platoons would make it. They had been in contact for almost two hours and there was no end in sight. If anything the enemy appeared to be stronger. Milton had to do something.

He turned to Lieutenant Sexton, squatting down nearby.

"Jeff, gather up all the ammo you can and get down the hill. You've got to help them hold."

Lieutenant Sexton nodded grimly, then passed the word to his platoon sergeant. Shortly the platoon disappeared down the trail.

A few minutes later Sexton's platoon reached the trapped men. The fresh troops moved forward quickly, handing out ammo and canteens. No sooner had they gotten into position than the enemy fire began anew.

The pain from his wounds kept Specialist Patterson from moving about as he had earlier. Instead, he tossed bandages and other medical supplies to those farther away from him. Some of the casualties crawled to Patterson so he could treat them.

One paratrooper came to Patterson in hysterics. He'd been shot in the left cheek. The enemy round had shattered the cheekbone, leaving the man's eye dangling free. Patterson patched him as best he could, then told him to head up the hill. From time to time casualties escaped from the beleaguered perimeter and started uphill toward Milton's position. Members of the Weapons Platoon came downhill to help them.

Private 1st Class Steer made several such trips. On one he slung a wounded man over his shoulder and started uphill. Before he'd made it halfway back, an enemy sniper fired at them. The wounded man screamed sharply, then fell limp. Steer carried the corpse to Milton's CP and headed downhill once again.

First Sergeant Michael Deeb grabbed Sergeant Nichols and another man and headed downhill. They'd moved only a couple of dozen meters when they found a casualty slumped along the trail. Deeb told Nichols, "Cover us," as he and the other man lifted the casualty. As they struggled uphill, slipping and sliding in the mud, Nichols walked backward behind them, M16 at the hip, his eyes searching for any sign of the enemy. They made it safely to Milton's CP.

On the next trip Sergeant Nichols was again covering Deeb and another man as they carried an unconscious paratrooper to safety. Suddenly he spotted three armed Asian men smiling at him from a nearby opening in the jungle. Because he knew there were CIDG working in the area, Nichols didn't fire at them.

"Hey, Top," he called to Deeb, "we got any friendly gooks in the area?"

"No," came the reply.

"Shit," Nichols swore. He spun back to the opening. The enemy soldiers were gone. Nichols's spine tingled with fear. Below him the firing built into a steady roar.

Captain Leonard's Charlie Company was also up at dawn that day. Besides breaking camp, eating, and preparing for the day's march, they had to wrap the two corpses in ponchos. The overhead jungle was too thick to permit a medevac, so they'd have to carry the bodies until they found a suitable extraction site.

At about 0700 the crackle of gunfire was heard. Leonard heard it; so did Lieutenants Bodine and Harrison. They all switched their PRC-25 radios to the battalion net so they could monitor the situation.

A short time later Colonel Partain radioed Captain Leonard. "Charlie Six, hold your present position," Partain ordered. "Be prepared to move to the assistance of Alpha."

Leonard acknowledged the change of orders and then passed the word to his platoon leaders. All continued monitoring the radio transmissions.

At the TOC, the weather had finally cleared enough to allow Partain and the others to board the chopper. As Partain left he told Major Watson to get Charlie Company moving to help Milton. It was about 0900.

Watson radioed Milton. "Charlie Six. Get down to Alpha, now. They've got a hell of a fight on their hands and they need help."

Captain Leonard prepared his company for the move. Based on the contact the night before and the situation with Alpha, Leonard believed the NVA were in the area in significant numbers. He sensed that they were setting a trap for any relieving company. He wasn't going to fall into that trap and have his company destroyed.

In his instructions to his platoon leaders, Leonard told them to proceed cautiously. The point squads conducting the cloverleaf sweeps would clear fifty to sixty meters in front of the company. Once they had circled back and reported the terrain clear, the rest of the company would advance. Then the cloverleafing would start again. In this way Charlie Company would leapfrog its way downhill.

Lieutenant Peter Kretso took the point with his 3d Platoon. Lieutenant Harrison followed. Then came the Weapons Platoon and Leonard's CP group. Because his platoon had had the point the previous day, Lieutenant Bodine's 2d Platoon brought up the rear.

Bodine wasn't happy about that. He felt that since he was the most experienced platoon leader and the one who knew the terrain best because he'd led the previous day's hump, he should be on point. But Leonard wasn't going to take the time to realign his platoons.

Charlie Company started downhill at about 0930. If there were enemy in the area they had undoubtedly either laid booby traps or were waiting in ambush, so Leonard wouldn't let his company follow the same track they'd used the day before. Instead, the cloverleafing squads busted a new trail. They moved slowly, cautiously, leery of any waiting NVA. It was slow, but it was safe.

Several times on the move, the point man reported noise or movement on his flanks. Leonard personally crept forward to investigate. A couple of times he requested artillery strikes in suspicious areas. Most of the time he dismissed the sounds as insignificant.

Because the jungle undergrowth was so thick, it was necessary to rotate the point squads and cloverleafers frequently lest the troops become tired and inattentive. Leonard had no desire to be ambushed because of a tired private 1st class. When Kretso's men had had enough, he pushed Matt Harrison's platoon through them to take the point.

The lack of significant forward progress on Charlie Company's part agitated Major Watson. He didn't think Captain Leonard was moving fast enough. He got on the radio. "Charlie Six, you've got to move faster! Get down that hill!"

Leonard acknowledged the command, but he wouldn't be pushed. In fact, he couldn't move that much faster. The terrain was simply too difficult. Rather than risk exhausting his men or running headlong into an ambush, he elected to continue at the more cautious pace.

Watson continued to prod Leonard to pick up the pace. "Goddamn it, Charlie Six," he radioed. "I need you down there now. Get moving!"

Leonard would radio back that he was moving as fast as he could. The terrain, the dead weight of the two corpses his Weapons Platoon was struggling with, and the very real threat of an ambush, he told Watson, prevented him from moving any faster.

Colonel Partain overheard the exchanges. He broke in on the frequency. "Charlie Six, I need you down here immediately! Get moving!"

Captain Leonard continued his cautious advance.

At the battle site, Specialist Patterson could hear Partain's chopper overhead. At least they weren't forgotten, he thought. Several times he caught glimpses of the chopper through holes in the treetops.

Unfortunately, if Patterson could see Partain's chopper, so could the NVA. The Huey started taking fire. The pilot yelled, "We're hit!" He turned back to Dak To, his chopper trailing smoke.

At the airstrip Colonel Partain and Sergeant Major Rogiers raced to another chopper while Captain Smith headed to the battalion TOC; having seen the terrain, he could help coordinate the supporting fire.

The situation had not improved for Alpha Company on Hill 1338. The arrival of Lieutenant Sexton's platoon at the battlefield had not prevented the NVA from continuing their attacks. In fact, Specialist Patterson thought it had intensified them.

A few minutes before 1000, Lieutenant Sexton radioed Milton. "Six, they're getting ready to hit us again. I think we can hold out."

Milton radioed back encouragement. There was nothing else he could do.

A mortar barrage preceded the renewed NVA assault. Patterson had been lying next to a platoon sergeant when a mortar round went off behind them. Its shrapnel ripped into the medic's backside, tearing a huge hole in his right thigh. A second blast tore flesh from his left buttock. The wounds stunned the youngster, but he didn't even know he'd been hit until he reached around to find out why his backside was all wet. His hand came back covered with blood.

A determined NVA ground assault came next. All Patterson could hear was the roar of weapons and the screams of the wounded. He didn't know yet that Lieutenants Hood, Judd, and Sexton were all killed or badly wounded.

At his CP Milton listened to the firing build. As the fighting progressed, wounded continued to come back to his CP. Milton ordered Sergeant Nichols and another man to move uphill a little way with chain saws and start cutting an LZ for medevacs.

Nichols and his buddy had felled only a few trees before they became aware that enemy bullets were smacking into the trees around them. Nichols thought the NVA snipers were probably firing more at the noise of the chain saws than at him specifically, but that was enough. He and the other man tossed aside the saws, grabbed their M16s, and took up firing positions around the CP.

Back downhill Specialist Patterson watched in horror as an M60 gunner changed his weapon's warped, glowing barrel with his bare hands. The man was so frantic that he barely noticed his blistering skin.

Patterson still was able to patch up the wounded who crawled to him, but he noticed that there were fewer paratroopers moving around. About this time he heard men cry out, "Ammo. We need ammo." He stripped ammo packs off corpses and threw them to the riflemen.

Colonel Partain was back overhead by now. He was still calling in air strikes and coordinating the gunships' runs. Suddenly, his chopper shuddered from a burst of machine-gun fire. One round passed right between Partain's legs, went through his canvas seat, and hit Sergeant Major Rogiers, wounding him slightly before exiting the open door.

The pilot called back that he'd lost hydraulic pressure. They were going in. Partain braced for the crash.

Somehow the young warrant officer pilot nursed his wounded bird back to Dak To. Despite the pilot's skill the Huey crashed heavily at the airstrip. Everyone walked away, but Colonel Partain had badly jolted his jaw; the injury bothered him for months, finally forcing his evacuation in December.

Once out of the chopper Partain ignored his sharp pain and hurried to the TOC. About the time he arrived there, at approximately 1035, Captain Milton reported that he'd lost contact with his three platoon leaders. Frantic at the news, Major Watson and Captain Smith took turns yelling at Captain Leonard to ignore the movement on his flanks and hurry to Alpha's location.

General Deane had arrived at the brigade TOC by this time. Based on reports from Milton and from Partain's aerial observation, General Deane correctly surmised that Alpha Company had not fallen into a prepared ambush but had stumbled into a moving NVA column of indeterminate size. Deane figured the main body of the NVA unit would continue its movement while holding Alpha at bay. He pored over his maps, identifying likely routes of movement, and then barked off the coordinates to the artillery liaison officer. The latter relayed those figures to 3/319th's fire direction center. The 105mms poured howitzer shells into those areas, hoping to catch the fleeing NVA.

Colonel Partain reported his findings to General Deane. When Deane learned that Partain had had two choppers shot out from underneath him, he gave Partain his own chopper and crew and sent him back into the air. Before Partain departed, he ordered his remaining company, Bravo, to vacate its base security positions and chopper into an LZ north of where Alpha's three platoons were fighting for their lives.

Captain Roger Willoughby wasted no time in saddling up his Bravo Company. He, too, had been monitoring the radio transmissions. Willoughby, a quick, decisive man with close-cropped blond hair who always seemed to have a cigar jammed in his mouth, already had his men ready to go. They were traveling light, carrying only weapons, ammo, water, and a few rations. When Partain ordered him to go, Willoughby had Bravo at the chopper pad in minutes.

Lieutenant C. Allen McDevitt watched his platoon board the choppers. A twenty-four-year-old graduate of Arizona State University, McDevitt had had experience as an enlisted man in a Special Forces reserve unit in his hometown of Wilmington, North Carolina, before going to Arizona. An ROTC instructor at ASU had encouraged him to seek a commission. McDevitt did and found himself headed to South Vietnam in May 1967.

On the plane over, his seat partner was Don Judd. They hit it off instantly, and both were pleased when they were assigned to the same battalion. They planned to take their R and R together. Now as his chopper headed south, McDevitt wondered how his friend was doing.

The troop-laden choppers set down in a one-ship LZ about twelve hundred meters north of Alpha's forwardmost position. McDevitt's platoon was the first in. He moved his men into the thick stands of bamboo, unable to see more than a few meters. He hadn't progressed very far when NVA small-arms fire drove his platoon to the ground. The enemy firing was soon so heavy that they couldn't advance.

Behind him, a smoke grenade used to mark wind direction on the LZ had set the elephant grass on fire. The arrival of the rest of the company was thus delayed. McDevitt started calling artillery into the area in front of him. Bravo's rescue attempt stopped cold.

Back at the battle site Specialist Patterson was growing weaker from loss of blood. He was dimly aware that one of the platoon sergeants, though wounded himself, was crawling among the survivors. "We're low on ammo," he told each man. "The gooks are coming back. Those that can, pull out and get back to the CP."

Patterson was shocked. That meant the wounded, including himself, would be abandoned. He couldn't believe it. For the first time Patterson felt he would die. He'd never again see his wife, pregnant with their first child.

Around him those able to move were already crawling into the surrounding jungle. Patterson decided to go with them; he wanted to see his first child.

He snaked his way toward the protection of the jungle and joined up with the platoon sergeant who'd told the others to pull out. Just as he reached him a burst of fire ripped over the two men. One bullet plowed into Patterson's right hip. Most of the rest of the burst hit the sergeant. He slumped forward heavily.

"Come on, Sarge," Patterson urged. "We've made it this far; we can get out."

"I can't go any farther," the sergeant gasped. "I've had it. I quit."

Patterson pleaded with him, but the sergeant stayed put. Patterson crawled on alone.

Bullets were smacking into the ground around him and cracking sharply overhead. Ahead of him he could hear other paratroopers breaking through the foliage as they made good their escape. Patterson was frantically pulling himself along using both hands. As he entered the jungle he glanced over his shoulder. For the first time that day he saw the NVA. They were emerging from the jungle on the other side of the perimeter, AK-47s held at the hip. Patterson pulled himself all the way into the underbrush.

A short time later Patterson realized he could not go any farther. He lay there hopelessly. Then a sergeant went past him, crawling on all fours. Patterson called to him for help. The sergeant stopped, turned, and stared at Patterson for a long time. Then he called to two nearby paratroopers to help Patterson. They tried to help him to his feet, but his right leg kept collapsing. Only then did Patterson realize his right hip was shattered.

Finally, one of the paratroopers threw Patterson over his shoulder and started uphill. Behind him, Patterson could hear the wounded screaming for mercy as the NVA walked among them, executing those paratroopers still alive.

The little band had almost made it up the hill when the NVA took them under fire. Patterson was dropped to the ground while the others dove for cover. One of the men with

Patterson turned and started firing his M16 downhill. The man took a burst of AK-47 fire in the groin, losing a testicle.

While that man writhed in pain, four men from the CP suddenly appeared above them. Patterson pleaded for help. "Please don't leave me here. I can't take another hit. I'll die if I do."

One of the paratroopers, Sp4 William L. Reynolds, slid down to Patterson while the others went to aid the other man. Reynolds threw himself between Patterson and the NVA. "I'll get you out of here," he said, then jerked as he took an AK-47 round in the hip. Amazingly, the slug embedded itself in the Bible that Reynolds carried in his hip pocket. He had a huge bruise and a sore leg from the impact, but lost no blood.

Above them someone obtained a rope. One end was thrown down to Reynolds. He tied it under Patterson's arms. Patterson was then pulled to the top. He felt no pain, only relief at making it out of the killing zone. Someone carried him to Milton's CP area, where he was placed with the other wounded.

Sergeant Nichols and Private 1st Class Steer were busy helping the wounded and the stragglers. No one kept an accurate count of who made it out of the battle site. Most estimates place the number at between twelve and fifteen.

About this time Captain Milton told Sergeant Nichols to take some people and move downhill. Nichols looked around him. He and another fifteen paratroopers were still uninjured. About thirty-five wounded, most ambulatory, lay around the CP area, moaning from their pain. "There's no one left to send," Nichols told Milton. Milton nodded, then moved slowly back to his radio telephone operator (RTO).

It was now about 1130. Ten minutes later Captain Milton ordered an artillery strike to his northwest. Under its cover Milton had what remained of his company move uphill about fifty to seventy-five meters. A small knoll there offered a better defensive position. There was also a small clearing, which could be easily expanded into a one-ship LZ. While the Weapons Platoon members started their work,

Milton radioed to Partain the question uppermost in his, and others', mind: Where was Charlie Company?

Captain Leonard's company was still cautiously making its way downhill. Although Colonel Partain, Major Watson, and Captain Smith had all implored Leonard to ignore the movement to his flanks and move rapidly to Alpha's aid, Leonard refused to be prodded into a foolhardy move. He kept his cloverleafing squads on their mission. Leonard still believed the NVA were lying in wait for him.

As the company proceeded downhill, Lieutenant Bodine noted the point platoon had missed the ridge finger that they'd come up the previous day.

"Six," Bodine radioed Leonard, "we missed the finger that'll take us right down to Alpha. Do you want me to take the point from here?"

Leonard said no. He didn't want to reverse the order of his platoons. He consulted his map. "We'll take the next finger," he advised Bodine. "It leads us there, too."

Bodine wasn't happy. He felt they were moving too slowly. Already the gunfire below them had faded.

In the meantime, all of Captain Willoughby's Bravo Company had finally made it into their LZ. They started uphill. As before, NVA smallarms fire erupted around them before they'd covered much ground. This time Willoughby also detected the NVA moving around his left, or east, flank. He called for an air strike.

From 1335 to 1440 A-1E Skyraiders dropped five-hundred-pound bombs and napalm in a protective arc around Bravo. Still they couldn't advance.

At about the same time the air strikes began for Bravo, Charlie Company reached Alpha's earlier LZ. The CS crystals sown by Sexton's platoon had a disastrous effect on Leonard's paratroopers. They donned their gas masks, but most found the mask's filters had become wet in all the downpours and were no good. Soon, half the company were on their knees, retching and with snot running from their noses and tears pouring from their eyes.

Then the CIDG balked. They wanted no part of walking

through the contaminated area. Captain Leonard wanted to leave them there but couldn't. Instead, he had one of the CIDG jump on his back piggyback-style and carried the man across the area this way. Other paratroopers did the same. In a short while all the CIDG had passed through the tear gas.

In the resulting confusion Bodine's platoon took over the point. Guided by some soldiers sent uphill by Milton, Bodine was the first to reach Alpha Company's position. Bodine thought Captain Milton, whom he'd known at Fort Bragg, was very uptight. He seemed in control, but his eyes belied his demeanor: They were filled with fear. Bodine started putting his platoon members into protective positions around what was left of Milton's 130-man company. The linkup occurred at 1420.

A few minutes later Captain Leonard and the rest of Charlie Company arrived. Leonard immediately put his medics to work on Milton's wounded and sent others to expand the LZ while he conferred with Milton. When Leonard learned what had occurred, he decided to reach the isolated elements of Alpha Company.

A squad from Lieutenant Bodine's platoon was selected to move downhill. Bodine felt that it was his duty to accompany them, but Leonard nixed the idea.

The squad started downhill. Soon they were out of sight. A few minutes later the squad leader radioed back that he'd come across a dead American. Leonard told him to continue. More dead bodies were found. About then the squad received a flurry of small-arms fire. Leonard ordered them to return. It was too late in the day to get involved with an enemy force of unknown size.

At the battalion TOC the staff officers were immensely relieved that Charlie Company had finally arrived. Colonel Partain ordered medevac choppers in to pull out Milton's wounded. One of the first dusted off was Specialist Patterson.

After the wounded were evacuated, Partain ordered Chinooks in to remove the rest of Milton's company. Lieutenant Harrison was surprised that Milton left. So was Lieutenant Bodine. Captain Leonard thought it very unusual that Milton would allow himself to be removed from the battlefield while more than half of his company was missing, but Milton departed. While the evacuation proceeded, Leonard had his platoon leaders prepare strong defensive positions. He thought the NVA would attack them that night.

Back at Dak To Sergeant Nichols was surprised when he jumped off the chopper. Instead of a helping hand, everyone at the base went about their business as if nothing was wrong. As Nichols stood there an NCO came by and assigned him to a guard detail for the night. Nichols didn't want that; he wanted a hot meal, then he wanted to go back to Hill 1338. Those were his buddies out there. He belonged out there. But it was not to be.

Private 1st Class Steer ignored the order to serve on guard duty. Instead, he found some liquor and got drunk. He desperately wanted to forget all that had happened.

Captain Leonard had visitors on Hill 1338 that afternoon. Colonel Partain had dispatched Major Watson and Sergeant Major Rogiers to the LZ. Watson was still fuming about Leonard's apparent slowness in reaching Alpha.

When Watson's chopper touched down, that was the first time he'd actually been in the jungles surrounding Dak To. He could not believe how thick and tangled the vegetation was, what a rugged obstacle the terrain presented. He began to understand more clearly what Leonard had faced. Still, he proceeded to chew out Leonard with a vengeance. He told Leonard in no uncertain terms that he thought he'd moved too slowly.

When Major Watson was done with him, Captain Leonard noticed the sergeant major was chewing out his first sergeant. Leonard wouldn't stand for that. Any decisions that had been made were his alone, and he carried the full responsibility. He ordered Sergeant Major Rogiers to leave his first sergeant alone.

A short time later Watson and Rogiers left. After they had an opportunity to conduct interviews with Captain Milton and survivors in his company, and review all the available information relating to the contact, they both concluded they had been too harsh in their judgment of Captain Leonard.

Neither man had fully appreciated the environment that Leonard had been forced to operate in. Also, all the evidence indicated that Alpha's battle was essentially over by 1030. Charlie Company could not have gotten there by then, regardless. Nothing Leonard could have done would have changed the outcome.

Charlie Company spent a restless night on Hill 1338. They had a protective ring of artillery dropping around them all night. Several thousand meters below them Bravo Company also spent a noisy night. They, too, had artillery ringing them.

At 0700 the next morning, 23 June 1967, Captain Willoughby started Bravo moving south. The undergrowth was a hopeless tangle, slowing progress to just meters per hour. Willoughby's movement was also hampered by occasional small-arms fire from NVA stay-behind teams. They didn't hit anyone, but they sure slowed down Bravo.

Captain Leonard selected his most experienced platoon leader, Lieutenant Bodine, to lead the advance downhill to search for any survivors of Alpha's desperate fight. Bodine was ready to move out at 0800. He put his best man on point, then gave the signal to move out.

Bodine's men moved cautiously, carefully examining every possible ambush position. Bodine wanted no surprises. He was particularly concerned about the massive clumps of towering bamboo that lined his path. "Watch the bamboo," he warned his men repeatedly. He was also concerned about a neighboring ridgeline to his right. If there were NVA on it they'd have an excellent flank view of his advancing platoon.

Nothing happened.

As they drew closer to Alpha's battle site they began coming across the debris of war. Helmets, rucksacks, canteens, ammo magazines, and an occasional M16 littered the area. Bodine's nerves tightened. Off the trail's sides he could see a crumpled body or two.

Next Bodine came to a relatively clear area. Twenty meters across rose a large stand of trees. Bodine thought it was a perfect spot for an ambush. He radioed Leonard. "Six," he said, "I want to recon this by fire."

Leonard agreed.

Bodine put a couple of squads on line, then had each man fire a full magazine into the area. The air vibrated with the sharp reports.

As the magazines emptied, Bodine heard someone screaming, "Rawhide! Rawhide!"

A bedraggled paratrooper came stumbling out of the trees at the far side of the clearing. The man had been wounded in the previous day's action but had evaded the NVA. As a medic treated his wounds Bodine asked him where the rest of Alpha was.

"Just a little ways down the trail," the youngster said in a quivering voice.

Bodine took his platoon forward. A short distance beyond the clump of trees he spotted the mass of bodies. Bodine, ignoring the carnage, moved beyond the site and set up a protective line. Then he radioed to Captain Leonard to come forward.

A few minutes later Captain Leonard brought the rest of the company down.

No one could comprehend the horrible scene. Dozens upon dozens of American bodies lay sprawled in death's grotesque grip. A heavy veil of black flies swarmed over the swollen corpses and the thick pools of blood and gore. The smell of death hung so heavily in the jungle that many of Charlie's paratroopers were unable to control their stomachs. They staggered behind trees to vomit.

It was immediately apparent to Lieutenant Harrison that many of Alpha's men had been executed; a large number of the bodies bore ghastly exit wounds in their faces. Other corpses had been mutilated, their features destroyed, ring fingers cut off, and ears removed.

The scene was almost too much for Harrison to handle. He'd never expected to encounter something like this on his third day in the field. He couldn't deal with it on a human scale. His mind and body began functioning solely on their five years of extensive military training. Oblivious to the carnage, Harrison started searching for his classmates, Judd and Hood. He found their bodies within minutes.

Helicopters brought in stacks of body bags. Charlie Company's grunts began the gruesome task of filling the rubberized green canvas bags with the remains of their comrades.

Three members of Alpha's decimated platoons had miraculously survived the slaughter. One was the man Specialist Patterson had witnessed changing his M60 barrel with his bare hands. Another man had been shot three times in the back but lived. Lieutenant Harrison found a man who, while he played dead, had had his ring finger cut off by a machete-wielding NVA. After the NVA left the battlefield, the man, in his delirium, tried to reattach the severed digit to its stump with the tape that wraps around a smoke grenade's cardboard canister. Then he stuck his injured hand in an abandoned canteen cover.

Bravo Company finally arrived at the site at about 1500. They immediately pitched in to finish policing up the ground. Within minutes of his arrival, Lieutenant McDevitt heard the news about his friend Don Judd. It didn't seem possible; just two weeks earlier they'd been making plans for R and R. How could Judd be dead?

Back at Dak To, Captain Milton began the grim task of positively identifying the dead. The NVA had been known to switch dog tags on American corpses, causing untold agony for family members when the deception was uncovered. Assisted by 1st Sergeant Deeb and Sergeant Nichols, who knew the members of 2d Platoon, Milton spent the next two days properly identifying his men.

The final toll for Alpha Company was shocking. Out of 137 men in Alpha on 22 June 1967, 76 were killed. Another 23 were wounded. Of the dead, 43 suffered fatal, close-range head wounds.

Captain Grosso, the brigade surgeon, signed all the death certificates. Those for the executed Sky Soldiers listed the cause of death as "fragmentation wounds to the head." A few weeks after the incident Grosso was given a statement, prepared by an unknown source at brigade headquarters, which confirmed the executions. However, Grosso never read it. He was so disgusted by the brutal realities of war he simply scrawled his signature on the document.

Bravo and Charlie companies spent several days patrolling the area looking for evidence of NVA casualties. Lieutenant McDevitt's platoon of Bravo found no NVA corpses. In another of Bravo's platoons Pfc. Steven F. Varoli, a tough nineteen-year-old from Deerfield Beach, Florida, helped dig up several graves containing fresh NVA corpses. Lieutenant Bodine's men uncovered a dozen or so dead NVA; Lieutenant Harrison's platoon discovered a few more. That wasn't much to show for the devastation that had befallen Alpha.

As was his practice after a tough fight, General Westmoreland flew in to talk with survivors. At Dak To, on 23 June 1967, he stood on a jeep's hood in front of Alpha's two dozen remaining members. He motioned the men to gather informally around him. Sergeant Nichols looked around and remarked to a buddy, "Ain't many of us left, are there?"

Westmoreland began his remarks by praising the men for their courage. Then he said, "You took on a tough NVA unit and whipped their asses!"

Sergeant Nichols knew Westmoreland had a responsibility to build morale, but this bordered on the absurd. Alpha had been whipped, not the NVA. Nichols leaned over to his friend. "Wonder what he's been smoking," he asked rhetorically.

Westmoreland continued his pep talk for several more minutes and then went to be briefed by Generals Larsen, Peers, and Deane.

From evidence gathered from the NVA dead, intelligence determined that Alpha had had a meeting engagement with a battalion of the NVA 24th Infantry Regiment. The 24th was believed to have been responsible for most of the activity around Dak To during the past several weeks. Undoubtedly, they had been transitting the Hill 1338 area en route to Cambodia for refitting. That explained why they had not stayed to fight after chewing up Alpha Company.

MACV withheld announcement of the Thursday fight

until the following Monday. Incredible as it seems, the reason MACV gave for the delay was that they wanted to prevent the enemy from learning that contact between the two forces had been broken.

In reality, the 173d was piecing together information on the enemy dead. The yardstick for measuring American battlefield successes in South Vietnam was the enemy body count. Even in 1967 the system was subject to abuse because military commanders had a habit of reporting enemy casualties that enhanced their own, and their unit's, image. In the case of the Battle of the Slopes, as the paratroopers were calling the fight, the reported enemy casualty figures even shocked the survivors.

MACV press releases credited Alpha Company with destroying more than 475 NVA. The 173d's combat after-action report stated 513 NVA had been killed. The report claimed 106 NVA dead as the result of an actual body count. The other 407 were credited to the artillery fire General Deane had called in on likely avenues of movement, even though not one body had been found in these areas.

The men who had been on Hill 1338 were shocked when they heard the figures. Based on the remains they had pulled from shallow graves, their best estimate of NVA killed in action varied between fifty and seventy-five.

Even General Larsen expressed surprise at the high body count. He called General Westmoreland in Saigon and asked him to hold up release of the figures. Westmoreland told Larsen, "Too late. They've already gone out."

Alpha Company was rebuilt over the next few days, absorbing one hundred new men in less than a week. Then it headed back into the field. The veterans were very leery of being in the field with a company composed mostly of new officers and men. Sergeant Nichols and several others finally went to Captain Milton with a request. They wanted to form a special point squad, consisting of themselves. They just didn't want to trust their lives to the FNGs. Milton agreed. The permanent point squad became a reality.

On 9 July 1967 Alpha, 2/503d, was preparing its night

position. They were near the top of a large hill mass over-looking the Dak Klong River valley about sixteen kilometers southwest of Dak To. As Captain Milton brought in his nightly defensive artillery registration rounds, something went wrong. A 105mm round came in short, hitting the trees above Alpha and spraying the men with shrapnel. Three soldiers died, six were wounded.

One of the wounded was Captain Milton himself. He took a load of shrapnel in his stomach, causing wounds so severe that they eventually forced his retirement from the army.

At Dak To that night, Capt. Ken Smith was sitting beside the airstrip waiting to hop a flight to Bien Hoa. Since a major had recently arrived in 2d Battalion and claimed the S-3's slot, Smith was going to the rear to assume command of the brigade's administrative Headquarters Company.

Suddenly, a jeep braked hard in front of Smith. The enlisted driver told Smith to return to battalion headquarters immediately. There Colonel Partain informed him of Milton's misfortune. Smith was to chopper out and take over Alpha right then. He did.

The army could not have one of its companies suffer the losses Alpha, 2/503d, did without holding someone responsible. The blame was not focused on the brigade or battalion commanders for sending companies into hostile areas by themselves. This despite the fact that a very upset Colonel Adamson recommended to General Peers that General Deane bore the responsibility and should be relieved. Nor was the finger pointed at Capt. David Milton for feeding his forces into the fight in piecemeal fashion. Instead, the brass fixed their anger on Charlie Company and its commander, Capt. Ron Leonard.

Partain thought Leonard was indecisive and had deliberately moved too slowly on 22 June 1967. As a result, he held Leonard responsible for the disaster. Partain decided Leonard had to go.

By the end of July Captain Leonard had been transferred to the 4/503d. Lieutenant Harrison was angry when he learned Leonard had lost his company. He thought it totally unwarranted and unfair. He went so far as to voice his concerns directly to Colonel Partain, an unheard-of act for a lieutenant. His efforts were futile.

Besides Harrison, others were also surprised at the removal of Leonard. Sergeant Major Rogiers was very skeptical about Leonard's transfer. Even Major Watson thought Leonard got a raw deal. Both men had developed a greater appreciation for the difficulties Leonard faced on 22 June once they'd visited the battle site. Colonel Partain had never been on Hill 1338 and did not realize how difficult the terrain was.

After Leonard went, further steps were taken to purge Charlie of any officers who'd participated in the events of 22 June. Lieutenant Harrison moved to Alpha Company. Lieutenant Bodine went to Bravo Company. Lieutenant Kretso was given a job at battalion.

When Captain Leonard arrived at the 4/503d headquarters, he met with Lt. Col. James Johnson, the newly arrived battalion commander. Johnson asked why Leonard had come to his battalion. Leonard explained the circumstances. Colonel Johnson conducted a discreet inquiry into the events of 22 June. He, too, became convinced that Captain Leonard had been made a scapegoat. He kept Leonard in his battalion, making him the S-2.

CHAPTER 5

HILL 830

In reaction to the destruction of Alpha Company, 2/503d, General Westmoreland gave General Larsen the additional maneuver battalions he had been requesting. On 23 June 1967 the 1st Battalion, 12th Cavalry, from the 1st Cavalry Division's 1st Brigade, arrived at Dak To, where it fell under General Deane's command. Deane sent the 1/12th about fifteen kilometers south of Dak To, where it initiated search-and-destroy operations.

The next day the ARVN 1st Airborne Task Force and the 3d Brigade, U.S. 1st Cavalry Division, arrived in Kontum from Saigon and Binh Dinh Province, respectively. These units were sent to the north and northeast of Kontum, where they conducted systematic search-and-destroy missions.

Deane sent his own battalions about twenty kilometers to the west and southwest of Dak To. If the NVA 24th Infantry Regiment was still in the area, he wanted his paratroopers to find them.

Lieutenant Colonel Lawrence Jackley's 4/503d set up Fire Support Base 4 for Battery B, 3/319th Artillery, on 4 July. The FSB sat atop Hill 664, eleven kilometers west and south of Dak To. Security for the cannoneers was rotated among the rifle companies.

Colonel Jackley, a tall, thin native of Des Moines, Iowa, where he was born on 27 March 1928, graduated from West Point in 1950. Four years later he qualified as a parachutist and then attended the Special Warfare School at Fort Bragg. Just before he went to South Vietnam in August 1966 he'd been a battalion executive officer in the 82d Airborne Division at Fort Bragg. Jackley spent six months as a staff officer with the I Field Force at Nha Trang before taking command of 4/503d from "Iron Mike" Healey in February 1967.

Jackley was a strong, innovative commander. Among his early changes in the battalion was the creation of a fourth line company. He used the battalion's Antitank and Recon platoons to form the nucleus of Dog Company. Then he had each of the other three companies transfer a number of NCOs and enlisted men to Dog, warning them not to use this as an excuse to rid their companies of malingerers, malcontents, and troublemakers. Dog Company never mustered more than sixty-five to seventy men organized in just two rifle platoons, but it did give Jackley a much-needed fourth maneuver element.

Another of Jackley's ideas was what he called LZ commandos. After several of his companies had been ambushed during Operations Junction City and Junction City II on what had been thought to be cold LZs, Jackley came up with this idea. The LZ commandos, volunteers all, would be the first troops into an LZ. Backed by several gunships, the LZ commandos would clear the LZ of any enemy troops and then call in the slicks carrying the riflemen. Once Jackley instituted the LZ commandos, he never lost another man due to an ambush on an LZ.

Jackley was backed by four experienced, tough company commanders, three of whom were West Point graduates. Captain Alan Phillips, a tall, dark-haired, twenty-nine-year-old, was the son of a career naval officer. He graduated from West Point in 1959, selecting infantry as his branch. Captain Phillips had first served in South Vietnam in 1963 as an adviser to an ARVN airborne battalion at Bien Hoa. He returned to South Vietnam in November 1966 to take command of the 173d's LRRP platoon. He held that position until late May 1967, when he assumed command of Alpha.

The commander of Bravo Company was twenty-five-year-old Capt. Daniel Severson. A thick-necked, athletically built graduate of the University of Maine, Severson had entered the army via the ROTC program. He had originally come to South Vietnam as the executive officer of Charlie, 4/503d, when Colonel Healey brought the battalion over from

Fort Campbell in June 1966. Transferred to Bravo as its XO, Severson was badly wounded in a fight with VC near Ben Cat on 16 January 1967. On that day he took over a platoon after its leader had been injured in a VC ambush. Severson, despite several painful wounds, attacked and destroyed an enemy emplacement. For this he received the DSC.

When his one-year tour of duty was completed, Severson voluntarily extended for six months. He felt he knew what he was doing in the field and could thus be more effective than a new officer. With all the new men in the company due to MACV's one-year rotation policy, he considered it foolhardy to send them into combat under an inexperienced officer.

Many of Severson's men thought he was a little reckless. He was seen by them as a pusher, intent on attaining the day's objective regardless of obstacles. He liked to be where the action was, closing with the enemy.

Both Charlie and Dog companies were commanded by graduates of West Point's class of 1965. Lieutenants William J. Connolly and John M. ("Mike") Deems had come to South Vietnam with the 4/503d in June 1966 as platoon leaders. When their tours were ending Colonel Jackley promised them companies if they extended. The opportunity to command a rifle company in combat just two years out of West Point was too great a temptation for the two twenty-four-year-olds; they both said yes.

The young officers went home on thirty-day leaves, Connolly to Boston and Deems to Nevada. When they returned to South Vietnam both reported to Colonel Jackley. The two young lieutenants were concerned that Jackley might go back on his word; both were aware there were plenty of captains throughout the brigade who had not yet commanded companies. But despite pressure from brigade, Colonel Jackley was as good as his word. The meeting was short and sweet. "Connolly gets Charlie and Deems gets Dog. Do a good job. Don't let me down. You're dismissed."

Connolly, an easygoing, unflappable man with a thick Boston accent, was quickly accepted by the men of Charlie Company. Secure in his ability to command men in combat, he quickly turned Charlie into one of the better companies in the brigade.

Deems, like Connolly, was viewed by his men as an officer greatly concerned with their welfare. He never asked them to do anything he wouldn't do himself. As far as they were concerned, if anyone could get them safely through their 365 days, it was Deems.

After leaving Bravo at FSB 4 for security, Alpha, Charlie, and Dog established a battalion perimeter several kilometers to the south. They spent the next three days conducting extensive patrols and holding live-fire battle exercises to train the new members of the companies.

On 7 July Charlie Company rotated back to FSB security duty while Captain Severson's Bravo Company came out to the field. That same day the battalion received a specific mission. They were to move approximately twenty-five hundred meters to the southwest to locate, block, or engage an NVA regiment suspected of operating in that vicinity.

As far as Captain Phillips knew, the mission was a reaction to radio-intercept intelligence. This information was originally gathered from various highly classified sources. Then it was disseminated to brigade staff officers who further analyzed it. Any useful information was used to plan specific daily assignments for the battalions. Upon being given such a mission, the battalion's staff would prepare an operational order. These orders were then passed down to the involved companies.

Captain Phillips, along with nearly everyone else at the company or lower levels, never felt he received enough information regarding a particular mission. Each night the company's communications sergeant would receive a coded message. Decoded, it revealed the next day's marching orders. Rarely was anyone told why they were headed toward a specific objective or what they would find when they got there. It was a very frustrating way to fight a war.

In an unusual move, Colonel Jackley informed the company commanders that the battalion S-3 would be accompanying them on this move. Major Walter D. ("Doug") Williams would not only establish a forward TAC CP but would be the ground commander. Major Williams was a very likable officer from Maryland who had graduated from West Point with the class of 1956. New to South Vietnam and the 4/503d, Major Williams asked Colonel Jackley if he could accompany this three-company operation. As the battalion operations officer, Williams felt his participation in a ground operation would be good experience. Jackley reluctantly agreed.

Major Williams and a small entourage choppered out to the battalion laager site at 1725 on 7 July. A short time later choppers carrying eleven CIDG from the Dak To Special Forces camp arrived. The CIDG were to be used during the operation as trackers and trail guides.

The three companies began heading south at 0640 on 8 July. The first day's trek was a relatively easy hike through a river valley. Jungle-covered hills on each side of the valley made Dog Company's Lt. Robert Allen nervous. A twenty-one-year-old from Oklahoma City, Allen had joined Dog just a few weeks earlier. Though he'd been on a couple of operations around Pleiku, the attack on Alpha, 2/503d, made him particularly wary and alert. His eyes kept sweeping the surrounding hills. He was sure the NVA were up there, watching their every move.

The first day's hump covered slightly more than a thousand meters—good progress considering the incessant rain that caused much slipping and sliding in the mud, resulting in one broken ankle, which required a medevac. At about 1500 the three companies established a battalion-sized defensive perimeter. LPs were sent out while the other men dug fighting holes.

In Bravo Company's sector its 2d Platoon RTO worked feverishly to dig his hole. Though the ground was heavy with rainwater, the thick tangles of underground roots made the work very hard. Specialist 4th Class Phillip Owens, from Arlington Heights, Illinois, had arrived in South Vietnam in February 1967, three months before he turned nineteen. Originally assigned to a rifle platoon, Owens had displayed his courage during a vicious firefight in War Zone C on 7 April 1967 when he ignored heavy enemy fire to pull his wounded platoon leader out of the line of fire. Owens was decorated for that act, and a short time later he switched over to carrying the radio for his platoon commander.

Owens liked carrying the radio, despite its extra twenty-five pounds, because it provided him with a little more information about what was going on. The average EM humping the ridges had no idea where they were or where they were going. Extra knowledge about their operations helped Owens understand his role in the war.

When Owens had dug his fighting hole about four feet deep and six feet long, he stopped, satisfied with his effort. He put some overhead cover in place and went to check in with his platoon leader.

Leading 2d Platoon was 1st Lt. Peyton Ligon, another member of West Point's class of 1966. Born in Pleasant Hill, Tennessee, and raised in Raleigh, North Carolina, Ligon completed Ranger training and qualified as a parachutist before heading to South Vietnam. He was part of the large contingent of the class of 1966 that arrived in-country in June. He celebrated his twenty-fourth birthday on 23 June while processing into the 173d. Although he'd been in Bravo just three weeks, Ligon had already earned the respect of his platoon for his cool, professional manner.

Rain continued to pour down on the Sky Soldiers on the second day of the patrol. Since the three companies were deep within the triple-canopy-jungle–covered mountains, the rain made the footing very treacherous. Sometimes ropes had to be used to pull paratroopers up the steep slopes. And the moisture brought out mosquitoes and leeches. Everyone kept their shirt cuffs and collars buttoned, but the parasites still found access to the paratroopers' flesh. Few men were fortunate enough to find their skin free of the leeches at the end of the day.

Major Williams had spent most of the day marching with Bravo and Dog, while Alpha had the point. Being on point was taxing. Captain Phillips was tired from the day's efforts, but Major Williams came to him wanting to discuss the next day's operations. Phillips invited Williams to stay for a C-ration supper. The two men didn't know each other well but had a long, pleasant conversation that damp evening on an unmarked hilltop miles from anywhere. Phillips learned that Williams had been a friend of his brother-in-law at West Point. They also spoke about Williams's tour as an exchange officer with the Indian army. While there he had learned to combat-load elephants. Since they were deep in elephant country, both officers wished they had some of the beasts to help carry their gear.

Finally, Major Williams left to sleep at Captain Severson's CP. Captain Phillips pulled his poncho over his tired frame, hoping he could get a decent night's sleep. He did.

Just before the companies were to move out on 10 July, Major Williams received instructions from Colonel Jackley to move to Objective 49. No reason was given for the change in plans. The men of 4/503d were simply told to go there. To them, Objective 49 was simply a spot on the map about a thousand meters northwest of where they had spent the night. The column headed out with Captain Severson's Bravo Company on the point.

The hump on 10 July was tiring in the continued downpour, but it was uneventful. As Bravo approached Objective 49 from the southeast, at approximately 1320 Colonel Jackley came up on Major Williams's radio. Brigade S-2 had just passed on the latest intel. The NVA were now supposed to be on Hill 830, about eight hundred meters to the southwest. That's where Jackley wanted his three companies to head now.

Major Williams halted the column to issue the necessary orders; no one objected to the unexpected break. For simplicity's sake, Williams ordered the three companies to turn around and reverse the order of march; Alpha would now be on point with Bravo in the trail position. Williams and his entourage marched in front of Bravo and just behind Dog.

It rained intermittently as the column headed southwest. The overcast sky plunged the jungle into an even deeper gloom. The thickly matted vegetation and dense, towering stands of bamboo reduced the visibility to a dozen or so meters; the man at the rear of a platoon column rarely saw the man at the head of the column.

By 1530 Captain Phillips was starting to think about a night laager site. To organize three company perimeters, coordinate fire plans, and get all the mortars and LPs in position before nightfall would take two to three hours. It would be dark around 1830; Phillips wanted to be in position by then. He radioed back to Major Williams, communicated his ideas, and received Williams's approval to find a night laager site on Hill 830.

At this time Alpha Company was ascending the northeast slope of Hill 830. Leading the way was 1st Platoon, followed by 2d Platoon, Phillips's command group, and finally 3d Platoon. Right behind them, Lieutenant Deems's Dog Company had one platoon in a shallow saddle, while his second platoon was descending the southwest slope of a hill slightly northeast of Hill 830. Behind them, Major Williams's command group marched, and then came Bravo Company.

Captain Phillips radioed his 1st Platoon leader, Lt. Daniel Jordan, a very likable twenty-three-year-old Notre Dame graduate, to start looking for a bivouac area. Seconds later Jordan radioed back, "Six, I've just hit a trail. It looks like it was recently used. And I mean recently."

From fifty meters back Phillips responded, "Put your squads on line. Move up the hill slowly. Keep your eyes open."

Jordan did as ordered. A few minutes later he gave the hand signal for his platoon to move out.

Back in Bravo's column Lieutenant Severson halted momentarily to consult his map. "Goddamnit," he remarked to his RTO and FO, "here we are. Where are the gooks? They're supposed to be here. This is just typical S-2 bullshit."

With that, the crackling of NVA small-arms and machine-gun fire erupted with a roar from Alpha's direction. Severson and his men hit the dirt.

As Lieutenant Jordan's platoon reached the military crest of Hill 830, the jungle in front of them exploded with enemy fire. At least two light machine guns and numerous AK-47s sent hot lead flying downhill into the thirty-man platoon.

Jordan and his men dove for cover. Within seconds they were sending M16 and M60 fire back up the hill.

Captain Phillips was on the ground barking orders into the radio. He told Jordan to have his platoon advance by fire and movement. He directed 2d Platoon, under Lt. David Alligood, to move off to the left, where a slightly higher ridge offered good cover as it led to the crest of Hill 830 above Jordan's platoon.

Under a shower of leaves and branches brought down by the heavy volume of enemy fire, Phillips tried to reach his 3d Platoon leader, Lt. Warren Denny, by radio but couldn't. He turned to his runner, a cherry.

"Go back to Lieutenant Denny," Phillips told the visibly shaken youngster. "Tell him to move up on the right. He's got to take pressure off Jordan."

The private took off. He was back in minutes. "I can't find Lieutenant Denny, sir," he said.

Phillips knew the soldier was rattled and probably hadn't moved more than a few meters. He sternly ordered the youngster to try again.

Up front Jordan had his hands full. Under his courageous leadership and bold initiative, his platoon had moved forward about ten meters, to within twenty meters of the NVA's camouflaged bunkers. He bravely moved from man to man, urging them forward. Inspired by Jordan's fearlessness, they tried, but the enemy fire was too strong. They were soon pinned down.

While waiting to hear from Lieutenant Denny, Captain Phillips and his first sergeant, Owen Schroeder, moved about the battlefield, positioning the men, directing their fire, and calming them by their presence.

Phillips crawled up to one M60 gunner who he thought was firing indiscriminately. "Slow down your fire, trooper," Phillips said. "You're wasting ammo."

"Shit, sir," replied the gunner. "All that firing you hear is incoming."

Phillips gulped and moved off. A few minutes later he watched in shock as another gunner was killed. Without hesitation the assistant gunner grabbed the weapon. Seconds later he, too, fell. A nearby rifleman crawled over to the weapon. Soon, he had the M60's heavy slugs flying uphill. Phillips couldn't believe the courage he was witnessing. He was incredibly proud of his paratroopers.

By this time Lieutenant Denny had crawled forward. Phillips sent him off to the right in an attempt to flank the NVA positions. Since the ground was steeper in that area, Phillips felt the NVA would be too preoccupied by Jordan's and Alligood's movements to detect Denny.

Denny hurriedly got his men on line and started uphill. Within minutes he was reporting to Phillips that he'd stumbled on numerous empty bunkers. One of Denny's men tossed a grenade into what he thought was a sandbagged bunker. A shower of foul fecal matter proved it was an NVA latrine.

While Phillips's platoons were maneuvering, Lieutenant Deems's 2d Platoon, in the lead of Dog Company, closed up behind Alpha to take up supporting firing positions. Deems was in front of 1st Platoon, about halfway down the slope of the rearmost hill, when the firing broke out. He and the others immediately set up a defensive perimeter. Enemy rounds were cracking through the bamboo and trees around them, but Deems correctly decided that this was overfire from the NVA firing at Alpha rather than fire directed specifically at them.

A little behind Deems, Lieutenant Allen, under fire for the first time, was hugging the ground, impressed by the noise. The firing, from both sides, was much louder than he'd ever anticipated. The roaring filled his ears. Enemy rounds were cracking overhead without letup.

The excitement filled Allen's veins with adrenaline. Here he was, lying on a muddy trail, while not more than a hundred meters away men were fighting for their lives. He turned to his platoon sergeant and said, "I'm itching to get into this."

The sergeant, a veteran near the end of his tour, calmly said, "You don't want to do that, sir."

Undaunted by the words of caution, Allen got up and started running down the trail. Within a few meters he tripped on a vine. He sprawled full length in the mud. Behind him he could hear the sergeant laughing. He sheepishly returned to his platoon.

As the fighting around Alpha continued unabated, Allen grew concerned that the NVA would surround them as they had Alpha, 2/503d. He nervously radioed Deems several times about his concern. Finally, Deems told him to calm down.

Another of Deems's paratroopers was experiencing his first combat, too. Specialist 4th Class James R. ("Jake") Duffy, a twenty-year-old from Scituate, Massachusetts, had arrived in South Vietnam in May 1967. A mortarman, he was assigned as the RTO for one of the battalion's 4.2-inch mortar FOs. His FO team rotated among the line companies as needed.

When the firing started, Duffy hugged the ground behind his FO. He was supposed to radio back to the mortar crews the adjustments given to him by the FO. Duffy found he was so scared he couldn't function. It had never dawned on him that combat could be this frightening. Finally the FO, a cool veteran, grabbed the radio from Duffy and called in his own corrections. Duffy lay there wondering how he could possibly survive ten more months of this.

With his three platoons and one of Dog's heavily engaged with the dug-in NVA, Phillips called for gunships, air strikes, and artillery. Within minutes artillery rounds were crashing into the jungle uphill from Alpha.

Soon the gunships and fast movers were on station overhead. But they proved to be useless. The thick overhead canopy would not allow them to fire with any accuracy.

Colonel Jackley, too, was overhead in his C-and-C chopper. Any help from him, though, was out of the question. The jungle was just too thick for him to see anything. Phillips could hear his chopper overhead but couldn't see him, either. Phillips reported his situation periodically but was too busy to give more than perfunctory reports to Jackley.

At the sound of firing, Captain Severson had immediately ordered his company to fall back a few dozen meters to a more easily defended small knob protruding from the ridge.

The heavy chatter of enemy machine guns made Severson, too, think of Alpha, 2/503d; he didn't want his company surrounded and chopped up as they had been. Bravo went into a defensive perimeter while Severson monitored the fight on his radio. It was all very confusing, but Severson could tell that Alpha was in a difficult situation.

A few minutes later Major Williams, still with Dog Company, radioed Severson. In an excited voice he said, "Take your company around to the right. I want you to hit that hill from the northwest. The gooks are hitting Alpha from there, too, and we need to stop that firing."

While Severson planned his movement, word of the attack spread among the company, most of whose members were relatively new and experiencing their first action. They started to panic. Severson quickly calmed them. By then he'd decided the movement was too risky without supporting artillery fire. And he couldn't call in artillery because he didn't know exactly where Alpha was positioned.

Just then Major Williams came into Bravo's perimeter with his two RTOs and the artillery FO team. "I want you moving to the right," Williams asserted.

"I don't think that's a good idea, sir," Severson said. He and Williams had disagreed before over other tactics, and Severson didn't particularly like Williams.

"The gooks are hard to flank," Severson continued. "Besides, where's our supporting fire?"

Williams admitted he'd been unable to maintain radio contact with Jackley. Either something was wrong with Jackley's radio or the terrain and damp weather were preventing the radio's signal from being received. There would be no supporting fire.

"If we attack now," Williams insisted, "we'll catch 'em by surprise. We'll get the fire later."

"I want to talk to the six," Severson said.

Severson had no luck reaching Jackley either. Severson and Williams continued arguing for several more minutes. Then Williams asked, "Are you afraid, Captain?"

"Where will you be, sir?" Severson responded defiantly.

"I'll be right with you."

"Okay. Let's go."

Severson took three platoons and began a hasty move to the right. He left his fourth platoon and his first sergeant in position to cut an LZ. The platoon sergeant, MSgt. Lawrence Okendo, quickly put some of the men in defensive positions while he had the rest begin hacking away at the trees and bamboo with machetes.

Sergeant Okendo was a pugnacious little career soldier fighting his third war. He had the unique distinction of being the only current member of the 173d to have fought with the 503d Parachute Infantry in World War II. Born in Hawaii in 1922, Okendo had experienced a troubled youth. He bounced in and out of several reform schools before a judge gave him the option of going to jail or enlisting. Okendo enlisted.

Because of his toughness Okendo volunteered for the paratroopers. He joined the 503d in time to make the jump in New Guinea. He fought throughout that campaign, emerging unscathed. He was not so lucky on Noemfoor. He spent several months in the hospital recovering from his wounds. Okendo then joined the 7th Infantry Division for the vicious campaign on Okinawa. He saw further combat in the Korean War with the famed 187th Airborne Regimental Combat Team, commanded by Col. William C. Westmoreland, and later, the 7th Infantry Division. He'd joined Bravo, 4/503d, in May 1967.

While Okendo's platoon worked on the LZ, NVA sniper fire continuously cracked overhead. Most of it smacked into the surrounding bamboo, making a terrific racket. One round struck a paratrooper in the right hand, slightly wounding him. Another man had his arm laid open by a mishandled machete. Okendo had Specialist 5th Class Jackson, the platoon medic, tend them.

Master Sergeant Okendo was with one of the riflemen when they heard a crashing in the jungle in front of them. Since they couldn't see anything in the thick brush they held their fire, thinking it was one of Severson's party returning with a message. Then one of the CIDG from Alpha came staggering out of the jungle, a wounded grunt on his back and six M16s cradled in his arms. Okendo quickly relieved the little fellow of his burden. Specialist Jackson began treating the casualty while the Montagnard disappeared back into the jungle, going for another of Phillips's casualties.

Captain Severson, his three platoons, and Major Williams didn't have to advance very far before beginning their attack. About a hundred meters from Okendo's reserve position they descended into a shallow saddle. Before them the side of Hill 830 rose steeply, covered by a confusion of bamboo, trees, and thick underbrush.

Severson paused briefly to put his platoons on line. Lieutenant Ligon was on the right with his RTO, Specialist Owens, at his side. The paratroopers started up the slope. It was so steep they were forced to half-crawl as they climbed hand over hand.

Halfway up, Severson ordered Ligon to echelon to the left. By the time he had done so the center platoon, in the lead, had made it to within thirty meters of the slope's summit. Then the NVA opened up.

The sudden onslaught of small-arms and machine-gun fire stunned Bravo. They went to ground, unable to fire back. Private 1st Class Jerald Lytle, a Native American from South Dakota, was so jolted he dropped his rifle and fled. In his scramble downhill he lost a precious pack of love letters from his girlfriend. He made it nearly to the base of the hill before he gained control of his panic and started back uphill.

Only a few of Bravo's paratroopers were firing back; Severson screamed at the others to shoot. A sergeant near him suddenly collapsed, his body riddled with bullets. Severson continued yelling at his men to open up. Slowly, as the new combatants responded to their training and survival instincts, they began returning the enemy's fire.

From his position Severson could see that the NVA were in well-emplaced bunkers near the top of the slope. He estimated their strength at between two platoons and a full company. Their firing was heavy, sweeping the hillside, pinning the paratroopers down.

Lieutenant Ligon was crouched down behind a tree trunk. The opening blast of fire had caught him by surprise. He reached to flip off his rifle's safety and accidentally released its magazine. He hastily slipped another into the weapon and fired uphill. Around him many of his men were shocked into inactivity. He, too, yelled at them to open fire. He pointed out targets to his men by firing his rifle at bunkers. Soon his platoon was sending out a heavy volume of fire.

Private 1st Class Lytle, meanwhile, had picked up a casualty's weapon and climbed back up the hill. He felt he would die for sure, so he braced himself for the bullet he knew was going to hit him. Moving from cover to cover, he triggered short bursts from the M16. He didn't have any targets; he just fired uphill whenever he could see muzzle blasts from the NVA's weapons. He dropped behind a wide tree, firing and reloading, firing and reloading.

Lieutenant Ligon, followed closely by Specialist Owens, continued to move about, defying the hail of enemy fire to urge his platoon forward. It was a tough job. Any movement resulted in a heavy volume of fire. Casualties mounted. Owens saw a buddy, Pfc. Frazier D. Huggins, go running downhill, badly wounded; he would die later that night. Owens saw another friend, medic Sp4 Joel Sabel, go down as he moved toward a casualty.

Captain Severson had taken a slight wound in his left arm. The tear in his flesh angered him more than it hurt. "Looks like another Purple Heart," he noted to his RTO.

After being bandaged by a medic he started working his way to his left, toward Lieutenant Ligon. He knew he had to get the platoons moving uphill or they'd be wiped out. He couldn't pull back; that would just expose his men to more enemy fire. His training and natural aggressiveness told him he had to attack.

Severson hadn't moved more than ten meters when a deep explosion erupted near him. Mortars! NVA 60mm and 82mm mortar rounds began crashing up and down the slope. Paratroopers screamed in agony as red-hot shrapnel tore their flesh. Severson kept going. He'd moved about five meters past Major Williams's position when a mortar exploded right between them.

The blast slammed into Severson's right side, gravely

wounding him. He bellowed, "Medic! Medic!" as he recovered from the shock. He frantically looked for the medic. Then he saw him sitting in a daze, holding his footless leg. Behind him Severson could see the crumpled forms of Major Williams and several others. Severson resumed crawling toward Lieutenant Ligon.

The first mortar blasts had startled Ligon. He thought they were short rounds from a friendly artillery battery. He grabbed the PRC-25's microphone from Specialist Owens and screamed at the FDC, "Check fire! Check fire!" Seconds later he realized they were enemy mortars.

As the powerful shells exploded up and down the line of cowering paratroopers, Ligon sought out Severson. He found him covered with blood. In pain-wracked gasps, Severson told Ligon to pull the troopers into a perimeter and call the reserve platoon forward.

While Owens bandaged a plastic map case into place over Severson's gaping stomach wound, Ligon radioed back to the reserve platoon.

Master Sergeant Okendo overheard the radio conversation and readied the men for the advance. Then his platoon leader called to him. "Where are you going, Sergeant?"

"To help Lieutenant Ligon, sir. He's getting hit hard."

From the hole the lieutenant occupied with the first sergeant he yelled to Okendo, "Get back into position. You're not going anywhere unless I order it."

Fuming, Okendo put his men back into a defensive perimeter.

A short time later Ligon radioed back again. "I'm in command of the forward elements," he told the reluctant lieutenant. "We need your help up here."

"I'm the senior lieutenant and I'll take command," came the response.

Ligon was incredulous. "Listen, you son of a bitch, if you want the command, come up here and take it," he retorted.

But the lieutenant and the first sergeant still refused to come out of their hole.

Lieutenant Ligon was the only Bravo officer still functioning; one of the other platoon leaders had been killed and the other had run off into the jungle, screaming incoherently, after taking a round in the back.

While Ligon argued with the unwilling lieutenant, Severson managed to raise Colonel Jackley on the radio. He briefly explained Bravo's situation and asked for immediate medevacs. Jackley had to tell him he couldn't order in the dustoffs until the area was secure.

In his C-and-C chopper circling above the nearly impenetrable jungle canopy, Jackley seethed with rage at his inability to do anything to help his decimated companies. He had no idea of their exact locations, so he could not coordinate air strikes and artillery. With only sporadic radio contact, Jackley wasn't even sure how many of his command were still alive. He knew, though, that with night falling and no hope of any reinforcements getting in, his options were limited. Jackley started radioing to Captain Phillips.

On the slopes of Hill 830 Captain Phillips was bogged down too. North Vietnamese Army mortars had crashed down on Alpha also, causing numerous casualties. Lieutenant Jordan was dead, his body riddled by enemy machine-gun bullets while he urged his platoon up the hill. Phillips knew that Bravo had been chopped up and that the approaching nightfall would prevent any reinforcements from reaching him.

About this time Colonel Jackley finally succeeded in reaching Phillips. He ordered Phillips to break contact, make his way to Bravo, set up a joint perimeter, and hold through the night. Defensive artillery would ring them all night, providing some protection.

Colonel Jackley next radioed Lieutenant Deems to tell him to advance to Bravo's position. Deems immediately complied, moving with Lieutenant Allen's platoon since his other one was still intermingled with Alpha.

By the time Allen got his platoon on the way, a steady rain had started falling. The men kept low, moving slowly but steadily. On point was nineteen-year-old Sp4 Class Morrell J. Woods. Woods had grown up in the small northern Arkansas town of Norfolk, where he spent much of his youth in the region's deep woods, hunting, fishing, and camping. He felt at home in the jungle, and many of the paratroopers thought he was the best point man in the battalion.

With Dog moving toward Bravo, and Alpha breaking off its fight, Lieutenant Ligon noticed a visible reduction of enemy fire in his area. He surmised the NVA had used the mortar barrage to cover their withdrawal. Either they thought the American force was stronger than it was, or they had just meant to fight a delaying action. Regardless, Ligon was grateful for the respite.

Owens's PRC-25 suddenly crackled with Colonel Jackley's voice calling, "Bravo Six. Bravo Six."

Severson had lapsed into unconsciousness from loss of blood, so Ligon responded, "This is the new Bravo Six."

When Ligon informed Colonel Jackley that the situation had stabilized, Jackley told him to hold his position. Dog Company was on the way. Ligon couldn't move anyway, burdened as he was with dead and wounded.

At his position, Master Sergeant Okendo had been monitoring the radio traffic, keeping abreast of the situation. His platoon leader and the company first sergeant still cowered in their hole, refusing to allow Okendo to move to Ligon. So Okendo had concentrated on hacking an LZ out of the jungle. But it was too much work for too few men.

As the decrease in firing from the NVA allowed, Ligon evacuated some of his wounded back to Okendo's position, thinking that he had cleared an LZ. Private 1st Class Lytle hoisted onto his back a man with a severe stomach wound and joined a few others taking casualties back to Okendo.

About this time the lead elements of Lieutenant Allen's platoon arrived at Bravo's forwardmost position. The first thing Specialist Woods saw when he came upon Bravo were the rain-darkened forms of fallen paratroopers. There were so many he didn't think anyone in Bravo was still alive. Then he noticed a few men clustered behind what was left of a thick clump of bamboo; the NVA fire had cut the bamboo down to within a few feet of the ground.

Sporadic enemy rifle fire, mingled with occasional bursts of machine-gun fire, kept most of the men under cover.

Woods spotted Major Williams nearby and crawled to him. "Sure is a motherfucker," he said. Williams didn't respond. Then Woods looked closer and saw that most of the major's right side was gone. Woods moved away, taking up a position behind the root clump of a fallen tree.

The first evidence Lieutenant Allen saw of Bravo's fight was the corpse of a gut-shot sergeant lying in his path. Rainwater mixed with the man's blood, washing it into the mud. Allen pushed aside the body and continued snaking forward.

Allen next came upon two paratroopers manning an M60. Both were crying. "Thank God you're here," they sobbed. Allen calmed them down and continued on. He soon came upon Lieutenant Ligon, spoke briefly with him, and then joined Lieutenant Deems in putting their Sky Soldiers into a half-circle defensive position facing uphill.

Allen could hear Colonel Jackley's chopper flying overhead. Several of Allen's men were angry because Jackley wasn't on the ground with them. One said to Allen, "If I get a clear shot at that motherfucker, I'll blow him out of the sky." Allen said nothing.

About this time, around 1730, Lieutenant Deems radioed Captain Phillips. Deems expressed his concerns about Phillips's chances of making it safely to his position due to the rugged terrain and rapidly approaching darkness. Colonel Jackley overheard this exchange. He concurred with Deems. He ordered Phillips to make his way to Okendo's closer position instead.

Master Sergeant Okendo, still monitoring the radio, realized Captain Phillips probably didn't know his exact location. Acting on his own initiative, Okendo, accompanied by Specialist Jackson to help with Phillips's wounded, set out to find Alpha and guide them safely into his perimeter.

Okendo and Jackson worked their way down the hill. After a short time they met up with Phillips. Okendo spotted the tall captain, his poncho draped over him to ward off the rain, a bamboo walking stick in hand, moving up the trail. They conferred briefly, and then Okendo led the way back to his position.

Okendo's LZ was too small to permit choppers to land.

Instead, the medevacs lowered litter baskets on cables. Only the lieutenant who'd been shot in the back made it out before the deteriorating weather forced the cancellation of all flights. Since he'd made his way to Okendo's position, the officer had been babbling hysterically, causing panic among some of the other men. Okendo made sure the lieutenant was pulled out.

When the dustoffs ended, Okendo told Captain Phillips about the performance of the platoon leader and the company first sergeant. Phillips walked to the hole where the two men still huddled.

"Have you checked the perimeter yet?" Phillips demanded of the lieutenant.

"No, sir."

"Get out of that hole now and do your job. Don't come back here. I want you on the line," Phillips ordered.

The lieutenant refused to budge. The first sergeant stayed put too. Phillips walked away, leaving them where they were. He had too many other major problems to deal with to discipline them now.

Lieutenants Deems and Ligon faced problems of their own. Although most of the enemy fire had died down, an occasional sniper's round kept the Sky Soldiers on edge. They, too, had a large number of wounded. Several, including Captain Severson, needed immediate attention or they would not survive the night. Since Ligon had more wounded than his medics could handle, he radioed Master Sergeant Okendo to come forward and remove some more of the casualties to his position. Then Ligon guided in the medevac choppers for his most seriously wounded.

Since there was no LZ for these helicopters either, they dropped their litters through the treetops, too. Severson, passing in and out of consciousness, felt himself being strapped into the wire basket. With rain pouring onto his face he was pulled upward. Tree branches scraped his body as he was winched to the chopper. He tried to fend them but finally gave up. Minutes later he lay on the chopper's floor. One of the battalion's doctors started working on him immediately.

Only two or three more of the men from Ligon's position were extracted before the foul weather shut down that operation.

Private 1st Class Lytle made one of the last trips to Ligon's position to bring a wounded Sky Soldier back to Okendo's perimeter. By the time he started back, leading a blinded man, it was dark. The normal fifteen-minute trip stretched into an hour as Lytle stumbled through the featureless night jungle. He fought back his panic, not wanting to upset his charge. Finally, he heard voices. American voices. Filled with relief, he staggered into the laager site.

Later that night, while helping tend the wounded, Lytle happened upon a friend from his days at Fort Benning, Sgt. Orville Smith. Smith, who had been an avid fan of the popular World War II television series *Combat,* now lay quietly on the wet jungle floor smoking a cigarette, his legs mangled. "Smitty, you don't smoke," Lytle observed.

"I do now," came the reply.

Lytle then sat fascinated as his friend calmly described watching the line of NVA machine-gun fire stitch across the ground toward him before the bullets tore into his limbs.

"Man," said Sergeant Smith with incredulity, "it was just like *Combat*."

Lytle couldn't believe it.

Lieutenant Allen set up his CP about ten meters behind a large stand of bamboo. He placed Sgt. William Dunston's squad in front of the bamboo as an LP. Allen fully expected an enemy attack that night. Fortunately, none materialized.

The shattered remnants of 4/503d spent a miserable night. Rain fell incessantly; the temperature dropped. Since most of the men had dropped their rucksacks where they had first made contact, few had any ponchos or warmer clothing. Those who did selflessly gave them to the casualties.

No one suffered more than the wounded that night. With limited medical supplies, the medics could not do much to ease their pain. Their moans and anguished screams filled the night, haunting the unscathed. One man screamed, "I want my mother. Mother! Where are you? I want my mom."

Others pleaded for morphine, or called for their wives, or just cried.

At first light on 11 July, Lieutenant Deems radioed Lieutenant Allen, "Get a patrol out and recon the hill."

Allen repeated the order to Sergeant Dunston. Dunston replied almost immediately. "Six, we don't have to recon the hill. I'm right in the middle of the gooks' positions."

It was true. Just meters from where Dunston and his squad had spent a watchful night, the abandoned NVA bunkers began. Allen took his platoon on a sweep to their immediate front. It soon became apparent the two fractured companies had laagered at the edge of a fairly large NVA base camp. The paratroopers counted more than sixty bunkers and foxholes ringing the base camp; many were covered with a two-foot-thick layer of logs and dirt for overhead protection.

As Allen's platoon pushed deeper into the enemy camp, they found more evidence of a large NVA presence. Specialist Duffy came upon numerous cooking areas; a small perimeter of command bunkers sat at the center of the complex. Abandoned equipment and ammo were scattered about. But there were no NVA to be found.

Lieutenant Allen reported his findings to Deems, who relayed them to Captain Phillips. Deems radioed back to Allen to continue to sweep the area and make a map of the hill showing the enemy positions.

As soon as the heavy morning ground fog lifted, helicopters arrived to drop down chain saws. It took more than two hours of hard work, but an adequate LZ was finally hacked out of the jungle. With the dustoffs hovering three to four feet above the tree stumps, the remaining casualties were loaded aboard. The persistently adverse weather caused frequent delays in the medevacs; the last wounded were not lifted out until after 1900.

At midmorning Colonel Jackley made it into Okendo's LZ. With him were Captain Grosso; Maj. Roy V. Peters, a Catholic chaplain; and Sgt. Maj. Ted G. Arthurs. Arthurs was a no-nonsense senior NCO who ran a tight ship. Enlisted men lived in fear of his imposing presence, made all the more menacing by his practice of shaving his head. Arthurs delighted in his nickname, "The Wufman," a sobriquet given to him by a problem soldier whom Arthurs had severely disciplined back at Fort Campbell. Arthurs enjoyed fostering his tough image by howling like a wolf in a loud voice at opportune moments. The battalion's officers had a tremendous amount of respect for Arthurs; the enlisted men knew he really had their best interests at heart in all his actions.

Captain Phillips brought Colonel Jackley up-to-date on his situation. Jackley and Arthurs then moved among the paratroopers, listening to their stories and praising their actions. Jackley had particularly high praise for Lieutenant Ligon. Ligon's cool courage had prevented a rout and kept the casualties from being worse than they were.

Once Jackley and Arthurs completed their tour of the site, Master Sergeant Okendo approached his friend, the sergeant major. Okendo told Arthurs of the cowardice of his platoon leader and the first sergeant. Arthurs, in turn, reported the incident to Colonel Jackley. Once he learned the circumstances, Jackley had the two men put on the next available chopper to the rear. (Although nearly everyone who was on Hill 830 wanted the two men court-martialed, they were not. They were simply transferred out of the brigade.)

Lieutenant Allen had, by this time, completed his survey of the battlefield. He had found three dead NVA and three AK-47s. As he walked back into the perimeter carrying the weapons, he spotted Colonel Jackley. Feeling proud of his accomplishments, Allen strode briskly up to the colonel. "I'm Lieutenant Allen, sir. Here's the map of the NVA positions and three rifles I found," he said.

Jackley looked at him, then, pointing, responded, "You'd better get those weapons on that chopper, Lieutenant, or I'll have your ass."

Allen was stunned at the rebuke. He didn't know what prompted the colonel's anger but felt his caustic attitude was probably because he didn't appreciate what had happened on the ground. He never liked Jackley after that.

*   *   *

On the morning of 11 July Major Peters said Mass; the religious ceremony was very well attended. The rest of that day and the next, the three companies combed the battlefield in search of any overlooked friendly casualties, any enemy dead, and any NVA items of intelligence value. Captain Phillips took a patrol back to the scene of his fight. The company's rucksacks lay untouched where they had been dropped. Near the top of Hill 830, in a small area cleared of vegetation, which Phillips thought might have been a command site, he found the body of one of his troopers. The corpse had been carefully and respectfully laid out under a poncho. Phillips found it a touching tribute to the youngster's gallantry.

Two more base camps were found on the hill. All contained well-prepared positions that showed evidence of having been occupied for some time.

On 12 July Lieutenant Deems's company discovered a wounded North Vietnamese soldier on the southwest side of Hill 830. The badly frightened soldier claimed to be a medic only recently arrived from the north. A special helicopter was called in to take him back to Dak To for medical treatment and interrogation.

As a result of the sweep of the battlefield, a total of nine NVA bodies were found. A small quantity of arms, ammo, and miscellaneous equipment was also found.

Besides Major Williams and his RTO, 4/503d suffered twenty-two dead and sixty-two wounded. (Alpha lost ten KIA, thirty-two WIA; Bravo nine KIA, twenty-four WIA; Dog one KIA, two WIA; and Headquarters Company two KIA and four WIA.)

On the afternoon of 12 July, Bravo was lifted out of the field to be replaced by Lieutenant Connolly's Charlie Company. To replace the casualties Sergeant Major Arthurs put out a call for volunteers from the rear-echelon support troops. The response was excellent. Cooks, MPs, engineers, and clerks all stepped forward to help their airborne brothers in the line companies.

Although Lieutenant Ligon had done an outstanding job leading Bravo on Hill 830, he was far too junior to continue in command. Alpha's XO, Lt. George T. Baldridge, took over Bravo; a short time later Baldridge received a promotion to captain.

On 13 July the three companies headed south from Hill 830, following the trail of the fleeing NVA. The point squads immediately began finding discarded enemy equipment. Occasional blood trails were found and followed. Most did not pan out; a few led to fresh corpses. These were buried where they were found.

The humping through the wild hills continued without letup while the rain poured from the sky. The Sky Soldiers were wet, cold, hungry, and tired, their backs straining under their heavy rucksacks as they struggled on in the boot-grabbing mud. Progress was laboriously slow; daily gains were sometimes measured in just hundreds of meters.

Father Peters had volunteered to stay in the field with the line companies. A native of Sacramento, California, Peters had been a priest since 1948 and a regular army officer since 1960. At forty-two he found the going particularly rugged. Just because he was a chaplain didn't mean he wouldn't be put to work. Indeed, he was loaded down with Claymore mines. The extra weight made it even more difficult for him to walk on the muddy jungle floor, but Father Peters knew his presence comforted the young paratroopers. The priest set an inspiring example; the youngsters wouldn't dare complain about their ordeal as long as Father Peters could take it.

The companies took more casualties; regrettably they were not from enemy action. Just after noon on 15 July a friendly artillery round landed in the midst of Dog Company's lead squad. Two paratroopers died and four were severely wounded.

That same day the 4/503d's companies linked up with two companies from 1/503d about two and a half kilometers southeast of Hill 830. The units sent out patrols, which soon reported back with news of more enemy base camps found. All were unoccupied. One was very large, large enough to support a full battalion.

On 17 July Colonel Jackley ordered his companies to move

to a pickup zone (PZ) for removal to Dak To. The rugged terrain prevented the column from reaching the PZ on time. Not until 0945 on 18 July were the three companies able to close on the PZ. By noon all were back at the airstrip at Dak To.

The 4/503d would spend a week at Dak To before returning to the field. Besides no humping under eighty-pound packs, the week meant refreshing swimming in the Dak Poko River south of the base, hot meals, warm beers, and a few hours of pleasure with the laconic whores at the base's brigade-tolerated whorehouse. For the 173d's other two battalions, the war in the Central Highlands went on.

CHAPTER 6

TUY HOA

While 4/503d absorbed replacements and trained them in live-fire exercises, the 1/503d and 2/503d continued their search for the elusive NVA. The POW taken by Dog Company, 4/503d, told his interrogators he was a member of the K-101D Battalion, Doc Lap Regiment. Based on his information and other sources, American intelligence believed this enemy unit, as well as the NVA 24th Regiment, 174th Regiment, and several smaller VC units, were still operating in the tri-border area and were intent on disrupting the Special Forces camps. General Deane, determined to hunt down the marauding NVA who'd chewed up his unit, sent his rifle companies into the field on search-and-destroy missions. Deane hoped to engage the enemy in a decisive battle that would blunt their efforts to control the tri-border area.

General Deane's grand plans meant little to the average Sky Soldier. All he knew was that he was out in the boonies, humping day after day in the monotonous mountains and valleys of the Central Highlands. The infantryman's existence was made all the more miserable by the near-continuous monsoon rains. Two to three inches of rain fell nearly every day, soaking the paratroopers to the point that their fatigues literally rotted off their bodies. The jungle floor turned into a quagmire, making each step a major effort. Some days the Sky Soldiers slipped and slid so much that their forward progress seemed nonexistent.

Private 1st Class Michael Nale had joined Bravo Company, 2/503d, right after its abortive rescue attempt of its sister company, Alpha, on 22 June. An amiable eighteen-year-old from Florence, Alabama, Nale had received training as both a medic and an infantryman. During his first few months with Bravo, Nale found more opportunity to use his medical skills than his fighting ones. With so many men losing their footing during the humps, it was a rare day when someone did not get hurt.

One day, as Bravo struggled hand over hand up a steep hillside, a paratrooper suddenly fell face forward when his feet lost traction. Before he could catch himself he slid down the hill. His slippery descent ended when he collided with a clump of bamboo. He hit it so hard that a long sliver of bamboo entered his upper arm, embedding itself in the soldier's armpit. Nale removed the splinter, then patched up the Sky Soldier, ministering to him while waiting for a dustoff.

A major source of irritation to the paratroopers was leeches. The ubiquitous creatures infested the jungle. Several times each day every Sky Soldier carefully inspected his body for the hideous annelids. Rare was the Sky Soldier fortunate enough to be free of the bloodsuckers. When found, the leeches could be removed by touching them with the lighted end of a cigarette or dousing them with insect repellent.

Sometimes that was not possible. One paratrooper in Nale's company had to be medevaced after a leech crawled into his penis. Other Sky Soldiers had leeches take up residence in their ears and noses while they slept. These worms were perhaps the most disgusting of the jungle's creatures.

As the Sky Soldiers continued their pursuit of the NVA, they moved farther west, closer to the Cambodian border. In late July Nale's company, still under the command of Captain Willoughby, was on patrol just seven kilometers east of the border. For nearly a week they'd been searching the north side of a large hill mass on the west edge of the Dak Klong River valley. Dominated by Hill 875, the jumble of hills yielded many signs of the NVA's presence. Several times they stumbled on abandoned enemy base camps. Nale saw directional arrows cut into the bark of trees; sometimes the NVA even used actual Montagnard arrows to point the way through the dense jungle.

On the night of 20 July a furious thunderstorm lashed the

area. Deep crashes of thunder punctuated by bright flashes of lightning rolled across the hills all night. In one burst of lightning Nale thought he saw an NVA soldier standing outside the perimeter. He called a warning to his bunker mate, but the next flash revealed nothing. For Nale and the others it was a spooky night.

The next day Bravo was up at dawn and on their way. Lieutenant McDevitt had developed considerable respect for Captain Willoughby in the month he'd been in Bravo. To McDevitt, Willoughby was an aggressive commander unafraid of closing with the enemy.

As Bravo headed north about five hundred meters north of Hill 875, Captain Willoughby prepped the jungle in front of him by keeping a wall of artillery rounds crashing down several hundred meters in advance of his march. As happened so often in the war, a short round landed perilously close to Bravo.

Lieutenant McDevitt and his RTO had just walked past his platoon's first sergeant, a skinny Hispanic named Gonzales, when they heard the unmistakable roar of an approaching howitzer round. Yelling, "Incoming!" McDevitt and the radioman raced for a depression in the ground ahead of them. Before they reached it Sergeant Gonzales went flying past them. He dove into the little hole, McDevitt and the RTO tumbling in on top of him. A split second later the friendly round exploded with an earsplitting crash mere meters away. McDevitt burrowed as low as he could, anticipating the next round.

Willoughby was on the artillery net screaming at the FDC, "Check fire! Check fire! Goddamnit, check fire!"

Someone at the FDC asked Willoughby for a range correction. Willoughby exploded in anger. "Fuck a correction!" he yelled into the handset. "Send another round this way and I'll kill the son of a bitch who fires it."

Willoughby then set about gathering up his scattered company and getting it moving again.

After the noon break Nale's squad took over the point. Still without artillery support, they reconned by fire every few meters, firing their weapons into the jungle ahead of them. Nale was armed with an M79 grenade launcher; while the others fired off bursts of M16 fire, Nale would plop a few explosive rounds ahead of them. They'd done this a few times when suddenly, as they approached a small, jungle-covered knoll, Nale realized that green tracers were zipping past his head. Only the NVA used green tracers.

"Hit the dirt!" someone screamed.

Nale had never been under fire before, so he just lay there waiting for somebody to do something.

That someone proved to be Willoughby. Nale watched in awe as the captain charged forward, yelling through teeth tightly clenched around a cigar butt, "Let's take this fucking hill, men!"

McDevitt also heard Willoughby give the order. He was surprised. "Shit," he said to no one in particular. "If you want the fucking hill so bad, take it yourself." Then he got up and started his platoon forward.

Willoughby led the way, firing his weapon from the hip as his company spread out beside him.

Nale and a buddy, Pfc. Doug Roth, moved forward. B-40 rockets crashed around them. Ignoring the danger, the pair closed on an enemy bunker. While Roth pinned down the defenders with M16 fire, Nale pumped grenades at the bunker. It fell silent.

Around them other paratroopers advanced steadily, startling the enemy with their bold attack. Nale's friend, Private 1st Class Varoli, manned an M60. He cradled the heavy weapon across his left forearm, a belt of ammo trailing behind him, as he moved deliberately forward. The weapon bucked as he put out rounds, oblivious to the fire directed at him and the B-40s crashing nearby.

Varoli had accounted for several NVA bunkers when his luck ran out. A B-40 slammed into the jungle floor just in front of him. The blast sent him sprawling, knocking the M60 from his hands. Scores of jagged metal shards peppered his legs, arms, and hands. Varoli had been in South Vietnam since April and was a veteran of a dozen firefights. He'd survived them all unscathed and had started to feel invincible. The shock of being wounded stunned him. "Look,

I'm hit!" he yelled to his buddies. "Those motherfuckers got me." He crawled off to find a medic.

A short distance away Nale and Roth fought on. To Nale, the action seemed confusing, with explosions going off everywhere, green tracers snapping through the trees and bamboo, and everyone yelling epithets and obscenities. Behind him, he could hear Sfc. Edward Kitchen darting back and forth, trying to keep the men on line.

The NVA bunkers were constructed so that they were very difficult to see in the dark foliage. Nale and Roth jumped right over one, unaware of the danger until a paratrooper behind them yelled a warning. That Sky Soldier killed two NVA in the bunker with rifle shots.

Nale and Roth continued their attack. Suddenly, something whooshed between the two paratroopers. Nale instinctively turned. The blast from the B-40 hit him in the neck and right arm and blew him into a shallow ditch. As he landed, an NVA sniper fired a round that creased his back. Roth lay nearby, bleeding heavily from a deep wound across his forehead.

Nale found his M79, chambered a round, and let it fly. He thought snipers were perched in the tops of bamboo clumps. His grenades shattered the bamboo.

A few minutes later Nale watched in amazement as another paratrooper, a tough former boxer everyone called "Mugsy," took a round directly in the chest. Nale saw the round hit Mugsy, exit his back, and plunk into the dirt. The image was so vivid, yet so unreal, that Nale thought he was watching special effects on television.

As Mugsy fell backward, he searched for the sniper. He spotted him, fired, and killed him, all before he hit the ground. Nale couldn't believe it.

A few minutes later the fight abruptly ended. Captain Willoughby's bold initiative had overwhelmed the NVA. Bravo's paratroopers found thirteen dead NVA. Ten Sky Soldiers were wounded; none were killed.

Based on what he found, Lieutenant McDevitt concluded that the action had involved a platoon or less of NVA acting as stay-behinds while a larger unit made good its escape. As he surveyed the knoll he found several sniper's lairs in the tops of trees and at the tops of bamboo clumps, where the inner stalks were roped together to form a perch. The ingenuity of the enemy impressed McDevitt.

While the 173d Airborne Brigade prowled the jungles southwest of Dak To, the NVA began putting pressure on two isolated Special Forces camps farther north. Almost every night during the last half of July, Dak Seang and Dak Pek, twenty and forty-five kilometers north of Dak To, respectively, were pounded by vicious mortar, rocket, and recoilless-rifle fire. On the morning of 3 August 1967, a CIDG company made contact with two NVA companies one kilometer west of Dak Seang. A relief force also found itself under attack. Not until early afternoon did the fight end.

Because a ground attack on the camp seemed likely, the ARVN 1st Battalion, 42d Infantry Regiment, was hurried into the area. That same day the ARVN 5th and 8th Airborne battalions choppered into Dak Seang. When the 8th Airborne Battalion headed west out of Dak Seang the next morning, they bumped into a strongly entrenched NVA force just outside the camp. That fight lasted several hours before the NVA withdrew.

On the afternoon of 4 August, the 1/42d found the NVA on a hilltop farther west of Dak Seang. That fight raged the rest of the day and into the next. The ARVN 8th Airborne headed to the fight. On 6 August they ran into two companies of NVA dug in on the hill just north of where the ARVN 1/42d was still fighting. The NVA were so determined to halt the South Vietnamese paratroopers they sent six separate ground attacks against the embattled ARVN, the last coming at dawn on 7 August.

The ARVN 8th Airborne withstood and repulsed each ground attack but sustained heavy losses. As a result, the ARVN 5th Airborne passed through them to capture a hill just to the west. There they found an NVA regiment-sized base camp complete with VIP-type bunkers and a large command bunker that contained an elaborate mock-up of the Dak Seang Special Forces camp. Documents left behind by the rapidly retreating enemy indicated that the NVA 174th Regiment had occupied the camp.

The heavy contacts so close to Dak Seang convinced General Peers that the nightly bombardments of Dak Pek were a prelude to a massed ground attack on that Special Forces camp. Accordingly, he lifted the 1/503d out of the jungle near Hill 830 and sent them to Dak Pek; they arrived there late in the afternoon of 4 August. They were joined by the 4/503d on 9 August.

The 4/503d had a new commander when it made the move. Colonel Jackley had been replaced by Lt. Col. James H. Johnson on 4 August. A thirty-eight-year-old native of Washington, D.C., Johnson entered the army through the ROTC program at the University of Maryland, receiving his commission in June 1950. After service in Korea he decided he wanted to make the army his career. While stationed in Berlin in the early 1960s, Johnson served with General Deane. When Johnson received orders to South Vietnam, Deane specifically requested he be assigned to the 173d.

Johnson didn't think much of his new battalion when he took over. He thought the troops were sloppy, their living quarters were dirty, and their discipline was lax. He felt several of the battalion's staff officers had negative attitudes, so he weeded them out as soon as possible. He blamed the problems and the defeatist attitude he thought permeated his new command on the losses suffered in the 10 July fight. He immediately instituted tighter control and adherence to regulations as a method to restore confidence and an aggressive spirit in the troops.

Not all the officers and men of the battalion agreed with Johnson's assessment. Lieutenant Connolly, for example, felt that the new CO's judgments were clouded by his lack of knowledge about the conditions the paratroopers operated under. It was extremely difficult, if not impossible, to maintain decent living conditions in the Central Highlands during the monsoon season.

On 10 August the two airborne battalions commenced search-and-destroy operations to the south and west of Dak Pek. CIDG elements accompanied each company. The allied forces discovered several enemy base camps but no NVA soldiers. They humped the boonies for ten days with no contact of any sort. General Peers concluded that his quick reaction to the threat against Dak Pek had thwarted the NVA's plans. Intelligence information confirmed that the NVA had withdrawn into Laos.

On 20 and 21 August the two airborne battalions were helicoptered back to Dak To. The ARVN battalions also departed the area, returning to their home bases near Saigon.

More patrolling in the mountains around Dak To occupied the 173d's three battalions for the next few weeks. Reacting to intelligence information, the rifle companies continued looking for the enemy. As hard as they searched, though, they found precious little to destroy. To many of the Sky Soldiers it was as if the NVA had completely abandoned the area.

A key element in the search for the NVA was the brigade's LRRPs. These daring volunteers operated in small teams, ranging far in advance of the rifle companies. Their mission was to live clandestinely deep in the jungle, seeking any sign of the enemy. Because they usually functioned in five-man teams, the LRRPs studiously avoided contact with the enemy. Their job was to find the enemy, not fight them.

Captain Thomas H. Baird ran the LRRPs for most of the summer of 1967. An outstanding soldier, Baird, a member of West Point's class of 1961, had volunteered for Special Forces training in 1964. As soon as he donned the distinctive green beret, he went to South Vietnam. Baird spent the six months from November 1964 to April 1965 as the leader of an A team, the Special Forces element usually in charge of a CIDG force manning an isolated post such as those found in the Central Highlands.

Though married with two children, Baird returned to South Vietnam in March 1967. He requested assignment to the 173d because the unit had an excellent reputation. He spent three months as the 173d Support Battalion's S-3, then the LRRP leader's slot opened when Capt. Alan Phillips took over Alpha 4/503d.

Baird's Special Forces background made him an ideal

LRRP commander. He understood how to operate stealthily, living off the land, keeping the enemy under observation without revealing himself. Though Baird's job was to assign his teams to specific AOs in response to the S-2's directives and to oversee their operations, he occasionally found it necessary to personally lead a team in the field. His troops loved him for it. Baird was extremely protective of his men. He would not allow them to be used on foolhardy operations or as regular infantry. To ensure that only the highest quality men served with the LRRPs, Baird personally interviewed each applicant for a spot with his LRRPs. Only those who measured up to his exacting standards were accepted.

One who did was Sp4 Irvin Moran. Moran grew up in Princeton, New Jersey, where he starred on his high school's baseball team. When he graduated in June 1965, he immediately enlisted in the army. Moran received training as an MP before joining the 82d Airborne Division at Fort Bragg. After a year of putting up with the petty harassment that abounded at the stateside post, Moran volunteered for service in South Vietnam.

Moran arrived in the war zone in February 1967. He was assigned to the 173d's MP platoon. Most of his time was spent either escorting truck convoys or on guard duty, which didn't allow him to feel he was doing his part in the war. When he heard about an opening in the LRRPs, he applied. After a tough interview with Captain Baird, Moran was accepted. He transferred to the LRRPs in July 1967.

A typical mission for Moran and his four teammates had them boarding a slick at the Dak To airstrip before dawn. Accompanied by two more slicks and two gunships, they'd set off for their assigned AO. After several false insertions to confuse the enemy, the LRRPs would jump out.

From the moment they left the chopper the team operated as a well-oiled machine. Communicating via hand signals, the team kept off any trails, moving overland, constantly alert for any sign of the enemy. They moved slowly, avoiding any noise, not wanting to reveal their presence to the NVA.

If they spotted an NVA force, the LRRPs could call in an air strike or an artillery barrage. Because they assumed their presence was compromised after such a fire mission, the LRRP team immediately moved to an extraction site. After a few days' rest at their base camp they'd depart on the next mission.

Targets were rare in the summer and early fall of 1967. Moran and his team were on several dozen missions and, other than an occasional sign of the NVA, they found nothing significant. One other team did spot hundreds of NVA moving through the jungle near the Cambodian border one day. They called in an air strike, but by the time the fast movers arrived on station the enemy column had crossed the border.

In a contact on 19 August about twenty kilometers northeast of Dak To, a LRRP team spotted two dozen NVA moving through the jungle. The team leader, SSgt. Charles J. Holland, called in an artillery mission and then ordered his team to head for an extraction site. As they moved to the PZ they came under fire from a previously undetected force of NVA. A hail of small-arms fire followed the team in its race to the PZ. Once there Sergeant Holland realized that the team's radio had inadvertently been left behind. Unwilling to leave the radio in the hands of the NVA, Holland went back up the trail alone. He never returned. When the extraction chopper arrived, the rest of the team had no choice but to board it.

Holland's body was found the next day. He'd made it back to the radio and strapped it to his back. He'd covered only a short distance back toward his team when the enemy cut him down.

On 23 August 1967 General Deane turned over command of the 173d Airborne Brigade to Brig. Gen. Leo H. Schweiter. Schweiter came to the 173d from Fort Campbell, where he'd been the assistant division commander of the 101st Airborne Division. He had experienced his first taste of combat with the Screaming Eagles when he'd jumped with them into Normandy, France, in the predawn hours of D day, 6 June 1944. He was captured that day, later escaping. He made the jump into Holland that September and fought in the Battle of the Bulge at Bastogne, Belgium, in December. A man possessing great personal courage, Schweiter earned a Silver Star at Bastogne for attacking and destroying a Nazi tank.

As a member of the 7th Infantry Division during the Korean War, Schweiter participated in the dramatic amphibious landing at Inchon in September 1950. When the 7th landed on North Korea's east coast a few weeks later, Schweiter was with them. He fought in the frenzied withdrawal from North Korea in November, earning a second Silver Star for his heroism. He then took command of the 7th's 32d Infantry Regiment.

In the years after Korea Schweiter carved a niche for himself as an outstanding officer who was an early advocate of airmobility. Just before he received his first star and transferred to Fort Campbell, Schweiter had served with the 5th Special Forces Group in South Vietnam.

An anomaly to many who knew him, General Schweiter had a personality and style of command that made it extremely difficult for him to follow the more affable "Uncle Jack" Deane. Brusque and taciturn, Schweiter was easily irritated whenever things did not go his way. Stolid, self-disciplined, and intolerant of error, he expected his subordinates to adhere to his high standards of performance. When they did not he could fly into a rage. At one briefing a staff officer was unprepared to answer Schweiter's pointed probes. The general's berating and intimidating comments caused the officer so much stress that he passed out cold. Schweiter relieved him on the spot.

Lieutenant Mike Deems left Dog Company, 4/503d, to become Schweiter's aide. He soon found himself in the worst assignment of his career. Whenever anything went wrong for Schweiter, Deems found himself blamed. Even something as innocuous as a radio failure on the general's C-and-C chopper brought Schweiter's full wrath to bear on Deems. As much as Deems had anticipated the positive career move of serving as a general's aide, he grew to hate the job.

Captain Baird thought that Schweiter was reckless. One time, the general, through his S-2, ordered Baird's LRRPs to rappel down ropes through the 150-foot jungle canopy rather than use choppers to enter their AOs. Baird was furious at what he considered an idiotic and dangerous directive. He protested the order; it was suicide for his beloved troops. Fortunately for Baird, Schweiter changed his mind before his protests reached the general's ears.

Colonel Partain considered Schweiter an ill-tempered, tyrannical man. He thought the general lacked confidence in himself and, consequently, could be indecisive. To Partain, Schweiter overly concerned himself with minor details, particularly those perquisites accruing to a general officer. Partain once witnessed Schweiter spend a considerable amount of time worrying about the organization of his general's mess.

Schweiter had idiosyncracies, as do most men, which made being under his command a trying experience for some; but those habits rarely reached the enlisted ranks. Indeed, Schweiter as a general officer had a deep concern for the enlisted men. He went out of his way to provide the paratroopers with whatever amenities he could. He liked to see the Sky Soldiers in the field receive at least one hot meal a day. He forbade his staff officers to partake of certain luxuries, such as a ration of ice cream, unless he was assured that the line companies had their ration.

Three weeks after General Schweiter took command, the bulk of the 173d prepared to depart Dak To. The continued lack of contact convinced General Rosson that the NVA were no longer threatening the Pleiku–Kontum–Dak To area Special Forces camps; he felt that General Peers's 4th Infantry Division, now at full strength with the assimilation of a third infantry brigade, could handle the situation in the Central Highlands. So General Rosson found another mission for the 173d Airborne Brigade.

South and east of Dak To, on South Vietnam's coast, lay Phu Yen Province. With the fall harvest imminent, rice-rich Phu Yen presented an inviting target for local VC units. The 173d would provide protection to the local South Vietnamese peasants during the harvest while driving the VC from the province; the brigade would also provide security for the large air force base at Tuy Hoa, the provincial capital. General Rosson dubbed this new effort Operation Bolling.

Not all of the 173d would be going to Tuy Hoa; Colonel Partain's 2/503d, supported by Battery A, 3/319th Artillery, stayed at Dak To. They would form part of Task Force 77 with the ARVN 3d Airborne Battalion, the ARVN 1/42d Infantry, and a mike force company for an expedition into the Tumuroung Valley north of Dak To.

The rest of the 173d started departing Dak To on 17 September 1967. Air Force C-130s ferried the Sky Soldiers to the Tuy Hoa Air Force Base. After the torrential rains and steep mountains of the Central Highlands, Tuy Hoa was a welcome relief for the paratroopers. Some of the rifle companies held barbecues on Tuy Hoa's white sand beaches, with the paratroopers frolicking in the frothy ocean, no longer combat-hardened infantrymen but, instead, fun-loving youngsters.

Specialist 4th Class Arturo Ortiz, a twenty-three-year-old in Lieutenant Connolly's Charlie, 4/503d, sometimes imagined that the beaches at Tuy Hoa were simply an extension of the beaches he'd grown up on in Venice, California. He also expressed amazement at seeing blue skies day after day rather than a canopy of mountain-hugging clouds.

One of Ortiz's buddies in Charlie was Pfc. Gerhard Tauss. Born in Yugoslavia in 1943 to a German soldier, Tauss immigrated with his family to Los Angeles in the early 1950s. He had been in the process of transferring to a four-year state university from a local junior college in 1966 when his brief nonstudent status caught the attention of his draft board. On the advice of a friend who'd served in the 82d Airborne Division, Tauss volunteered for airborne school after basic training. It was a decision he never regretted. Tauss loved the close camaraderie of the Sky Soldiers. He'd never known a finer group of men, from Lieutenant Connolly on down.

Tauss thought being at Tuy Hoa was like being in Hawaii. Gentle breezes caressed statuesque palm trees while he and his friends romped on the beach playing football and baseball. He almost forgot the army and the war.

What prevented him from completely forgetting was the petty harassment from rear-echelon officers. They were always pestering Tauss and others for minor offenses: Their hair was too long, buttons were unbuttoned, shirts were not tucked into pants. Tauss, and most other enlisted men, adopted a fatalistic attitude. "Fuck it," they'd say. "What are they gonna do, send us to Vietnam?"

Of course, Tuy Hoa was not all fun; there was still a war to be fought, a war far different from that fought in the Central Highlands.

At Tuy Hoa, the enemy were primarily local VC guerrilla forces. Rarely did they function in groups of more than five or six men. They operated mostly at night, when they would move supplies, ambush allied units, or fire a few mortar rounds on allied positions.

As a result, most of the 173d's operations around Tuy Hoa were conducted at the platoon level. The young lieutenants leading the platoons relished the opportunity to function as separate entities, unencumbered by the watchful eye of a company commander. Combat operations in and around Tuy Hoa provided the officers invaluable experience.

One man in particular who benefited from the time at Tuy Hoa was 1st Lt. David S. Holland, a rifle platoon leader in Alpha, 1/503d. A diminutive, bespectacled officer, Holland, a twenty-four-year-old graduate of the University of Virginia, had first come to South Vietnam in August 1966 as an MP officer. He pulled a one-year tour with an MP battalion in Saigon, constantly feeling that he had not done his part in the war. He didn't want to face his grandchildren thirty years in the future and tell them he'd spent his war years processing drunks in and out of jail. So, when his tour of duty ended, Holland requested a branch transfer to the infantry.

In late September Holland reported to Lt. Col. David J. Schumacher, the brigade's former XO, then commanding the 1/503d. Schumacher sent Holland to Alpha, 1/503d. A slick took Holland out to Alpha's field bivouac that afternoon. When he jumped off the bird Holland instantly regretted his decision. He faced the smelliest, dirtiest, grubbiest group of young men imaginable. He did not suspect that in a matter of weeks he'd be just like them.

In the weeks that followed Holland took his twenty-five-man rifle platoon on numerous operations. He developed his skills as a combat leader in dozens of small skirmishes. Though he had once entertained doubts about his ability to handle combat, Holland soon swaggered with confidence.

Combat in the Tuy Hoa area usually consisted of brief contact with small bands of VC. The squads of a rifle platoon would set up ambushes along likely avenues of VC movement. Then they'd wait for someone to walk into the trap.

The 173d's rifle companies spent a great deal of time patrolling in the coastal mountain ranges of Phu Yen. Though not nearly as rugged as Dak To's mountains, these ranges still provided the enemy with plenty of opportunities for concealment. The Sky Soldiers had to go in and root out the VC. Sometimes they were successful, sometimes they weren't.

Charlie Company, 1/503d, had three of its platoons on a sweep one day when they came upon a clearing. Scouts inched forward. They soon hustled back with good news: In the jungle across the clearing was a force of NVA, sound asleep. Charlie's men deployed around the camp. In short order the NVA were wiped out.

First Lieutenant Charles D. Brown led one of Charlie's platoons. Lieutenant Brown, unlike most other officers in the 173d, had no college education. Born in 1944, Brown grew up in Orlando, Florida. Even though his father was a captain in Orlando's police department, Brown was a wild youngster who partied constantly and did poorly in school. In 1964, two years after graduating from high school, he realized he was going nowhere fast. He enlisted in the army to give his life some direction.

After two years as an enlisted man Brown applied for OCS. Accepted, he received his commission in the spring of 1966. A year later he arrived in South Vietnam.

While processing in through Bien Hoa, Brown heard what a good company Charlie, 1/503d, was. So he boarded a chopper and flew out to their bivouac site. He woke Capt. Kirby

Smith from a sound sleep to explain that he wanted to be a member of Charlie. Smith was angry. "You woke me up to tell me that?" he demanded.

Brown assured him it was true.

Despite his anger Captain Smith apparently admired Brown's boldness, because he took him on as the XO. Brown spent several months in that primarily administrative slot before he took over Charlie's 3d Platoon just before it left Dak To.

One day while taking his platoon down a trail in Tuy Hoa's mountains, Brown heard a gong sounding. Upon investigation Brown realized that an elderly man in a nearby village was signaling the presence of his platoon to the VC by banging out a warning on his gong. Fearing an ambush, Brown propped himself against a tree, shouldered his CAR-15, and killed the enemy agent with one shot.

"See," Brown advised the new members of his platoon, "a lot of times you need only one shot. Don't always use automatic. Save ammo and make your shots count."

It was a brutal but necessary lesson on the realities of war.

First Lieutenant Alfred A. Lindseth, Bravo, 4/503d, knew the value of this lesson firsthand. Lindseth, a boyishly handsome, mild-mannered member of West Point's class of 1966, had joined Bravo after its fight on 10 July. Lieutenant Ligon was a good friend from their academy days and, since Lindseth had been running Charlie, 4/503d's, Weapons Platoon and didn't like that, he requested a transfer to Bravo. A twenty-three-year-old off a North Dakota farm, Lindseth felt completely at home as a rifle platoon leader and was, in fact, among the best in the brigade. He instilled a considerable amount of confidence in his men, working and training them constantly to improve their combat skills.

Lindseth had his platoon out one day in the same mountains where Lieutenant Brown had slain the VC agent. Lindseth was proud of his men; they were moving along the ridgeline without a sound. He was just allowing himself the satisfaction of feeling confident in his ability as a small-unit commander when a flurry of automatic-weapons fire shocked him back to reality.

When the gunfire ended, Lindseth hurried forward to his point squad. There he learned that four well-armed NVA had been walking toward his platoon on the same trail, chatting casually. When Lindseth's point squad saw the enemy, the three men opened fire, each paratrooper firing a full magazine from his M16.

Incredibly, only one NVA was killed; the other three escaped. Lindseth was furious. How could three men firing their M16s on automatic miss three out of four targets just meters away? He vowed to conduct more firearms training.

While 1/503d and 4/503d enjoyed the beaches of Tuy Hoa and struggled with the VC trying to extort rice from the local farmers, Task Force 77 poked into the Tumuroung Valley. This wide area north of Dak To was suspected of harboring an NVA regimental headquarters; TF 77 would find out.

Slicks carried 2/503d to the southern mouth of the Tumuroung; Battery A, 3/319th, established a FSB a short distance away while the ARVN units and the mike force moved into blocking positions to the north. The rifle companies of the 2/503d would sweep north, driving any NVA into the ARVN.

For nearly three weeks the 2/503d searched the Tumuroung Valley. As had happened at Dak To, the Sky Soldiers found plenty of signs of the NVA but no enemy soldiers. When it was evident that there was no NVA regimental headquarters in the area, TF 77 was ordered out.

Bravo and Charlie companies, 2/503d, were pulled out by Chinooks. Captain Ken Smith was advised that there weren't any lift ships to get his Alpha Company out; he could either laager at his position another night and be picked up the next day or hump out of the valley to Highway 14 where trucks would pick them up.

Smith didn't like his choices. Both left him vulnerable and exposed. He had no desire to spend a night alone in hostile territory, so Smith opted to hump out of the valley. He requested that a walking wall of artillery fire be laid down in advance of his route of march. Only then did he feel he had a chance of disrupting any NVA attempt to surround his company.

Smith's Sky Soldiers had about twelve kilometers to cover. Even though they had found no evidence of the enemy being active in the area, Smith felt they were there. And if they were, Smith was painfully aware of what had happened to this same company on 22 June 1967 when they'd been caught alone by the NVA.

Everyone in the company was scared when they started off. Tension was high; the entire company was aware of its vulnerability. With the artillery fire churning the ground in front of them, Smith's company advanced, moving parallel to the trail. Nerves were stretched taut as the march proceeded. Suddenly, one of Smith's young paratroopers panicked and leveled his weapon at him. "Goddamnit," he screamed, "you'll kill us all!"

Before Smith could react, his trusted first sergeant, Michael Deeb, dropped the youngster with a rifle butt stroke to the head. The others carried the kid until he came to; then he quietly rejoined the marchers. Smith could have pressed charges but didn't; he understood the youngster's fear.

Alpha made it safely to where the trucks waited for them. The company loaded up and went into Dak To without incident.

Task Force 77 was disbanded on 11 October 1967. The 2/503d and Battery A, 3/319th, boarded C-130s at the Dak To airstrip that same day for movement to Tuy Hoa. With their departure Operation Greeley officially ended.

The rifle companies of 2/503d spent a few days enjoying the beaches of Tuy Hoa before joining their sister companies in the field. As had they, 2/503d soon found itself making regular contact with local VC units. On one typical night in mid-October, Bravo Company, 2/503d, had set up a series of ambushes along a suspected VC trail. Private 1st Class Mike Nale, who along with his friends Privates 1st Class Varoli and Roth had rejoined the company after six weeks in the hospital, waited patiently with his fire team one night for someone to enter the killing zone of their ambush. Nale was on watch when he heard noise. Quickly he awoke the sleeping members of his fire team. "I got movement," he whispered.

All three men could hear the heavy breathing and rustling just feet from their position in the brush along the path. The movement approached them, moved away, then neared again. Nale's throat and mouth were dry as he waited for a clear shot on the moonless night. He wasn't sure how many VC there were, but he knew he'd get a couple of them before they could fire back.

Suddenly, the noise was right in front of him. Nale could hear his heart beating as he gripped his M16. There was a deep grunt, and then Nale saw it: a huge hog. Nale's platoon dined well that night.

Not all ambushes ended so well. On another night one of Nale's buddies was badly wounded; they couldn't cut an LZ where they were, so they had to hump out of the jungle, carrying the casualty to a PZ where medics would meet them.

By the time the ambush patrol arrived at the PZ, Nale's fatigues were soaked with the man's blood. While the medics and a doctor worked on the man, Father Watters administered last rites. Nale had a lot of respect for the chaplain. Father Watters always seemed to be where he was needed.

A short time later the casualty was loaded on the medevac. The helicopter disappeared into the night sky. Nale never did hear if the guy made it or not.

A number of changes occurred to the 173d in late October. Because MACV now planned to keep the Sky Soldiers in the II Corps zone, the brigade's rear echelon left Bien Hoa to establish their headquarters at An Khe in Binh Dinh Province. The move required a massive effort on the part of the 173d Support Battalion and rear detachment personnel. All the brigade's equipment not already up north and all the personal gear of the troops in the forward area had to be containerized and then trucked to Saigon. From there they were taken by sea transport to Qui Nhon. Truck convoys formed up there for the drive to An Khe.

The strength and maneuverability of the 173d Airborne

Brigade increased substantially in late October with the arrival of a fourth infantry battalion, the 3/503d. Formed at Fort Bragg in April 1967, the new battalion had spent the interim six months undergoing extensive training with the 82d Airborne Division. More training at the brigade's jungle school, quickly reestablished at An Khe, began for the new arrivals on 27 October. Once they completed the specialized training they'd join the rest of the Sky Soldiers on Operation Bolling.

The 1st and 2d battalions of the 503d followed the lead of the 4th Battalion by forming a fourth rifle company in October. Each battalion combined the assets of their respective antitank and rifle platoons to form Dog Company. Though the battalions' other three rifle companies were required to transfer men out of their ranks to help flesh out Dog, the new companies rarely mustered more than sixty men formed into two or three platoons.

In the 2d Battalion, Capt. Ken Smith, the senior company commander, was transferred from Alpha Company to form Dog. He reluctantly left Alpha, asking Colonel Partain for one concession: He wanted to have his XO, 1st Lt. Bartholomew O'Leary, and his first sergeant, Michael Deeb, make the move with him. Both men not only possessed considerable combat experience but were outstanding leaders. Also, Smith knew that he'd be transferred to another job after his six months' command time ended, so he wanted to ensure that Dog Company would be left in the capable hands of Lieutenant O'Leary.

Lieutenant Colonel Partain left the 2d Battalion in October to assume the duties of the brigade executive officer. Command of the 2d Battalion passed to Maj. James R. Steverson. Since arriving in the brigade in February, Steverson had functioned primarily as the brigade's S-3. By all accounts he had done an excellent job as the operations officer. With less than four months remaining in South Vietnam, Steverson needed a battalion command to round out his tour.

As the end of October 1967 approached, the 173d found itself fighting the same war it had fought around Bien Hoa.

Most enemy contacts were with small VC units. Platoon-sized operations were the norm, giving the brigade's junior officers a tremendous amount of experience. Squad leaders, too, often conducted their own ambushes and patrols, gaining combat knowledge and enhancing their own leadership talents.

While the young Sky Soldiers slogged through the rice paddies around Tuy Hoa, other young men and women, half a world away, did their best to end the war in South Vietnam. October 1967 saw America's largest antiwar demonstration, when tens of thousands of demonstrators marched on the Pentagon. Supporting antiwar protests were held on dozens of college campuses across the country.

When word of the antiwar movement's activities reached the Sky Soldiers, they reacted with derision. Few of the paratroopers could understand why there was so little support for their sacrifices back in "the World."

A special target of scorn for the American fighting man were the hippies. These long-haired, tie-dye-clothed social rebels who reveled in the world of illicit drugs had reached their zenith in 1967's "Summer of Love." While singer Scott MacKenzie invited the world to "wear some flowers in your hair" when going to San Francisco, the Beatles crooned that "All You Need is Love." Sky Soldiers who saw pictures of the unkempt hippies in stateside magazines couldn't believe it. What was happening to the country that had sent them to war? they wondered.

Not all the news from home was unwelcome, though. Particularly popular among American women that year was the new miniskirt. The grunts loved it, too.

The vast majority of Americans took no role in the growing antiwar movement, nor did they engage in the counter-culture movement. Mostly they did not pay much attention to the war. They simply went about their daily business, enjoying good-paying jobs in an economy booming because of the U.S. military effort in Southeast Asia. Away from work Americans enjoyed movies like *Camelot* and *Cool Hand Luke*. Popular books included William Styron's *Confessions of Nat Turner* and Leon Uris's *Topaz*. With the upcoming holiday season, the attention of the average American began focusing on plans for Thanksgiving and Christmas.

Any pleasant thoughts the Sky Soldiers might have had about the holidays were shattered when they received word on 1 November that they were returning to Dak To.

CHAPTER 7

BATTLE AT NGOK KOM LEAT

North Vietnam's premier military strategist, Gen. Vo Nguyen Giap, adopted a new policy in mid-1967 designed to expel the hated Americans from South Vietnam, overthrow the puppet government in Saigon, and reunite his country. Rather than a tactical defensive strategy, which concentrated on the theory that control of the countryside would strangle South Vietnam's cities, Giap planned a bold new offensive strategy aimed at the country's populated areas.

Giap instigated a series of clashes along South Vietnam's frontiers as the preliminary phase of his 1967–68 winterspring campaign. He carefully planned each of the actions so they seemed to be extensions of his army's normal tactics. His real intentions, however, were to draw American forces away from South Vietnam's populated areas while masking the infiltration of NVA troops into the country. Once he had all his forces in place and had the Americans heavily tasked in the outlying regions, Giap would launch his massive general offensive with large-scale assaults on nearly all of South Vietnam's major cities, military installations, and provincial capitals. Giap was convinced that once South Vietnam's population sensed that a North Vietnamese victory was imminent, they would join his forces in a huge general uprising.

Giap's general offensive/general uprising was scheduled for Vietnam's grandest holiday, the celebration of the lunar new year on 30 January 1968, known in both countries as Tet.

MACV, of course, had no knowledge of Giap's grand plan. What they did know was that NVA forces were reappearing in Kontum Province. Allied intelligence indicated that the NVA were once again preparing to attack and destroy the Special Forces camp at Dak To. In response to this new threat, Major General Peers began sending units of his 4th Infantry Division back into the Dak To area on 28 October 1967.

Peers ordered his 1st Brigade under Col. Richard H. Johnson to move from Jackson Hole near Pleiku to Dak To. The first unit to complete the move was the 3/12th Infantry, commanded by Lt. Col. John P. Vollmer, which arrived at Dak To on 28 October. It was soon joined by the 3/8th Infantry under Lt. Col. Glen D. Belnap. Vollmer sent his companies to the south of Dak To while Belnap's fanned out to the southwest.

Because his division was once again being stretched thin with the advent of this new operation, dubbed MacArthur, Peers turned to General Rosson for reinforcements. Rosson tapped the 173d Airborne for a battalion.

Rosson's directive reached General Schweiter's headquarters late on the morning of 31 October. Schweiter huddled with his S-3, Maj. Bartow D. Daniel, preparing the necessary plans. Schweiter's most experienced battalion commander, Lt. Col. James H. Johnson, would take his 4th Battalion to Dak To, supported by Battery B, 3/319th Artillery. They would depart Tuy Hoa the very next day. Major Daniel cut the required orders.

Colonel Johnson received word of the movement on the afternoon of 31 October. He immediately put his staff to work making the necessary arrangements. His line companies would have precious little time to prepare.

Alpha Company, 4/503d, had made an air assault into an LZ west of Tuy Hoa earlier that morning. They made no contact but found obvious signs of a VC presence. The company commander, Capt. James J. Muldoon, felt he'd make contact before the day was over.

Muldoon had taken command of Alpha just a few weeks earlier when Captain Phillip's replacement had been evacuated. A native of Scranton, Pennsylvania, the twenty-seven-year-old Muldoon had originally come to South Vietnam in May 1967 expecting to receive an assignment to the 5th

Special Forces. Instead, he went to the 173d. He spent five months as the S-3 (Air) for the 4th Battalion before moving to Alpha.

Muldoon was surprised when he received a radio call from Lieutenant Colonel Johnson late on 31 October telling him to move back to his LZ to be picked up for return to Tuy Hoa.

"I'm on a hot trail, Six," Muldoon told Johnson. "I'd like to continue the pursuit."

"Get moving now, Captain. The slicks will be there in an hour."

Muldoon ordered his platoons to about-face and began the retrograde movement.

Charlie Company's commander, newly promoted Capt. William Connolly, received the same order. He was told no more than was Muldoon. Neither was Bravo's CO, Capt. George Baldridge, nor Dog's CO, the former LRRP leader, Capt. Thomas Baird. Not until all had been assembled at Tuy Hoa AFB the next day awaiting C-130s did they learn they were going to Dak To.

Many of the men who'd been there in summer felt immediate apprehension. Connolly didn't like the idea of returning to the rugged mountains of the Central Highlands; he'd had enough humping in that terrain to last a lifetime. Specialist 4th Class Ortiz of Connolly's company felt the same way. But he also feared the NVA. He knew they were very professional soldiers who had no fear of the airborne. In Dog Company, Lieutenant Allen also felt the icy cold fingers of fear. He, too, knew what the NVA were capable of doing in a fight; he'd hoped he'd seen and heard the last of Dak To.

But, of course, what the Sky Soldiers felt made no difference. After being told to remove their 173d insignia so as not to alert any enemy agents to the movement, the men of the 4/503d were crammed into the cargo bays of C-130s. The first C-130 lifted off the Tuy Hoa runway at 1100 on 1 November 1967. The aircraft carried the 4th Battalion to the airstrip at Kontum; trucks moved the Sky Soldiers the rest of the way to Dak To. The movement to Dak To was completed by 1715 on 2 November. The paratroopers then came under control of Col. Richard Johnson's 1st Brigade, 4th Infantry Division.

Lieutenant Colonel James Johnson was ordered to send his battalion west of Dak To about twenty kilometers along Route 512 to Ben Het. There FSB 12 was being constructed. Johnson's battalion would not only provide security for the burgeoning base but would also conduct search-and-destroy operations in the area.

Captain Connolly's company led the way west the afternoon of 2 November. The rest of the battalion and the artillery battery made the short trip on the morning of 3 November.

Fire Support Base 12 fairly buzzed with activity. Dozens of helicopters of all sizes flitted through the sky on a variety of missions. Trucks, tractors, and bulldozers roared across the landscape, carrying cargo, towing artillery pieces, and scraping the earth flat. To the men of the 4th Battalion it was obvious that something big was in the air; several thought they would be invading Laos.

While the Sky Soldiers settled in at FSB 12, the 4th Infantry Division stumbled upon information revealing the NVA's full plans. In the early morning hours of 2 November, at the hamlet of Bak Ri west of Ben Het, an ARVN outpost accepted the surrender of a North Vietnamese NCO. Sergeant Vu Hong claimed to be an artillery specialist with the NVA 66th Regiment. He told his interrogators he'd been in the Dak To area, scouting firing positions for his unit's rockets, mortars, howitzers, and antiaircraft guns, for several weeks. His regiment was one of four infantry regiments and one artillery regiment forming the NVA 1st Division. The 66th Regiment, according to Sergeant Hong, planned to attack Dak To from the southwest; the NVA 32d Regiment took up positions south of Dak To to prevent any counterattacks against the 66th. The NVA 24th Regiment held a position in the hills northeast of Dak To ready to pounce on any allied reinforcements from that direction. The NVA 174th Regiment was northwest of Dak To prepared to act as a reserve or offensive force as the need dictated. The various batteries of the NVA 40th Artillery Regiment supported the infantry regiments.

Hong seemed to know too much for a mere sergeant, but his information confirmed and tied together what the 4th Infantry Division's G-2 shop had already picked up from other sources. With this new intelligence in hand, the 4th Infantry Division's operations staff prepared battle plans to meet the NVA.

The first contact in Operation MacArthur involved 4th Infantry Division units and the NVA 32d Regiment. On 3 November, while patrolling on Hill 1338, Bravo Company, 3/12th, came under heavy fire from well-emplaced enemy forces. Fighting just nine hundred meters south of where Alpha Company, 2/503d, had been massacred on 22 June 1967, Bravo, 3/12th, battled for several hours before the NVA withdrew. Bravo had six wounded; the NVA left behind four dead.

The next day, southwest of Dak To, Alpha Company, 3/8th, clashed with elements of the NVA 32d Regiment at 0950 and again at 1120. Two Americans died in the fights; eight NVA bodies were found. Just before noon that same day Bravo, 3/12th, now reinforced by Alpha, 3/12th, again found the enemy, this time a well-entrenched battalion of the NVA 32d Regiment. Not until air strikes dropped in two dozen thousand-pound bombs with delayed-action fuses did the NVA pull out. Bravo suffered four killed and six wounded; thirteen NVA died.

As evidence mounted that the NVA threat against Dak To was more serious than originally suspected, General Rosson released the rest of the 173d to General Peers. The 1/503d and Battery C, 3/319th, began deploying to Dak To via Kontum starting at 0750 on 5 November. The 2/503d and Battery A, 3/319th, went directly to Dak To from Tuy Hoa on 6 November.

In the meantime, based on the intelligence information provided by defector Sergeant Hong and from other sources, Col. Richard Johnson suspected that the headquarters of the NVA 66th Regiment was located in the valley stretching south of Ben Het. He ordered Lt. Col. James Johnson to find and destroy that enemy headquarters.

Lieutenant Colonel James Johnson decided to keep Bravo

Company to secure FSB 12 while his other three rifle companies moved south and southwest of Ben Het. Dog Company would take the center route while Charlie moved on its right and Alpha on its left. Johnson stressed the need for the companies to stay close to one another; he didn't want a repeat of the 22 June incident.

When Johnson briefed his company commanders on the details of their mission, he mentioned that a LRRP team had found signs of recent digging on several of the ridge fingers south of Ben Het. The companies' objective was to go out there and engage the enemy, Johnson said.

Captain Connolly started to protest. "If they're doing a lot of digging out there, there must be something big going on," he said. He wondered if the three understrength companies could handle an enemy regiment, if that was what they found.

"You'll have air and artillery support. I expect you to go out there and do your jobs," Johnson told the three company commanders.

Connolly's concern, and the other commanders', too, was the small size of his company. His Charlie Company fielded about 125 men, Muldoon's about 110, and Dog only 65.

To bolster their strength, each company was assigned a platoon of CIDG under the command of a South Vietnamese Special Forces NCO. None of the company commanders was happy with this arrangement. All three felt the Montagnards were of dubious quality at best. How they would react under fire was questionable. Captain Baird tried to solve the problem by interspersing the CIDG throughout his two platoons. But the battalion S-3 told Baird to let the CIDG operate as a separate platoon. Baird didn't like it but complied.

The Montagnards were an interesting group. Some were only thirteen or fourteen years old; others looked well past sixty. The older Montagnards had been at war with the North Vietnamese for five years or more. Their Special Forces leaders liked to pretend the CIDG fought the NVA for patriotic reasons, but they were mercenaries, plain and simple.

At first light on 4 November 1967, trucks moved the 4th Battalion companies to their starting point. By 0845 they were on the way. The first day's hump took the three companies south from Ben Het across the Dak Honiang River valley, which lay at the northern end of a tangle of jungle-covered hills known locally as Ngok Kom Leat. None of the three companies saw any sign of the NVA that first day. They laagered that night along the northeastern edge of the hills.

The next morning the companies pushed into the ruggedness of Ngok Kom Leat; Charlie moved along the west flank, with Dog to its east, and Alpha guarded the left flank. Immediately, the Sky Soldiers plunged into the twilight netherworld of the Central Highlands jungle. Because of the rugged terrain, crossed by numerous ridge fingers running off the main hill, the progress of the rifle companies was very slow. In order to proceed south, for example, Captain Baird found he had to first move along east-west–running fingers before being able to turn south.

Just before noon Connolly's company discovered a small abandoned enemy base camp. He reported the find to Johnson, who told him to push on. Less than an hour later, just five hundred meters from the first camp, Charlie stumbled upon another enemy base camp. This one was empty, too, but it contained a large number of bunkers and foxholes.

Captains Baird and Muldoon were monitoring Connolly's calls to Johnson. Although they had found no signs of the NVA, nearly everyone felt they were in the enemy's backyard. Lieutenant Allen of Dog Company could feel the electricity of anticipation charging the jungle air. He felt it was only a matter of when they'd make contact, not whether.

At about 1300 that day, Lieutenant Colonel Johnson ordered Muldoon to send one of his platoons on a thousand-meter sweep to the east. Muldoon didn't like that. He had no desire to put one of his platoons in jeopardy by dangling it seductively in front of the NVA. Reminding Johnson of his orders to keep the units close to one another, Muldoon told him he'd take his entire company on the tangent but wouldn't send a platoon out alone. Johnson concurred.

Muldoon made the sweep to the east. He found nothing.

The second night out all three companies were due for

resupply. It took several hours of hard work to cut the necessary LZs. The hacking of the machetes and the roar of the resupply chopper worried Lieutenant Allen. Any NVA within miles would know right where they were. He thought it was a hell of a way to fight a war.

On the morning of 6 November Lieutenant Colonel Johnson ordered Muldoon to move back west and fall into trail behind Baird's Dog Company. He further ordered all companies to move toward Hill 823 at the southeast edge of Ngok Kom Leat across the Dak Kal River. Hill 823 would be the site of a new fire support base. The three companies would secure the site and prepare it for the howitzer battery.

Because he had to complete his resupply that morning, Muldoon didn't clear his laager site until after 0900. To surprise any NVA who might be shadowing them, Muldoon ordered SSgt. David Terrazas and six men to stay behind and set up an ambush. If he'd made no contact within an hour, Terrazas was to abandon the ambush and rejoin the company.

At Dog's laager site the paratroopers prepared for their day's movement. Those Sky Soldiers who had humped the Highlands during the summer with its torrential downpours were pleased at the pleasant fall weather. The days were warm, with clear blue skies. Nights could be cool, but they were dry.

Lieutenant Allen's 1st Platoon had had the point the day before, so on 6 November the job fell to the 2d Platoon leader. First Lieutenant Michael D. Burton was a 1966 graduate of the Virginia Military Institute. The twenty-three-year-old had arrived in Dog as a replacement after the 10 July fight. A likable young man, Burton had quickly proven himself a capable leader.

Dog Company started out at 0845. Burton's platoon led the way, followed by the CIDG. Baird and his command group came next; Allen's platoon protected the rear. They moved on a compass bearing that would take them to Hill 823. The thick undergrowth and steep terrain forced them to detour frequently in order to avoid the worst of the jungle.

Burton's point squad under Sergeant Wertz had started up a ridge finger. At about 1130 Sp4 Emory L. Jorgenson, on point, suddenly froze. A single strand of gray-clad wire ran along the ground parallel to his path. He quickly cut the wire and reported his find to Burton. He, in turn, relayed the news to Captain Baird. Baird told Burton to follow the wire.

While Baird halted the rest of the company, Burton sent Wertz's squad forward. They moved about two hundred meters before finding a pith helmet. They reported this to Burton.

When Baird received this new information, he pulled his company into a defensive perimeter while he radioed the find to Lieutenant Colonel Johnson. Baird told Johnson he wanted to follow the wire to its terminus. Johnson agreed.

Baird didn't want to be sucked into an NVA trap; he wasn't sure that the commo wire was not bait. To give himself as much protection as possible, Baird ordered cloverleaf sweeps at the front and rear of his unit. After each squad completed its sweep, Baird would move the company to the forward limit of the cloverleaf. He continued to move up the ridge by bounds, alert to any sign of the enemy. It was slow progress, but relatively safe.

At the rear of the company column, Sgt. Morrell Woods conducted one of his platoon's sweeps. His keen senses were alert for any evidence of the NVA. He saw no signs of the enemy but, on his third or fourth cloverleaf sweep, he could hear some NVA talking. The heavy jungle, interspersed with massive stands of dense bamboo, limited his visibility to about twenty meters, so he couldn't pinpoint their location. But he radioed Lieutenant Allen with word of the enemy's presence.

While Dog Company inched its way up the ridge, Lieutenant Colonel Johnson concluded that none of his three companies would make their objective, Hill 823, that day. Consequently, Lieutenant Colonel Johnson radioed Capt. George Baldridge to have his Bravo Company ready to go to Hill 823 immediately. While Baldridge hustled up his paratroopers, Johnson ordered air strikes and artillery to pound Hill 823. He not only wanted to rout any NVA ensconced on the hill but hoped the ordnance would clear away a good portion of the jungle growth for an LZ.

On the slopes of Ngok Kom Leat, Lieutenant Burton, who'd been monitoring Lieutenant Colonel Johnson's transmissions, heard the 105s and 155s whistling toward Hill 823. Soon the heavy crashes from their explosions rolled against the jungle. While he waited near Baird during one of the cloverleaf sweeps, Burton heard the CO ask the company first sergeant, "What do you think, Top?"

First Sergeant William Collins had close to ten months' combat experience in South Vietnam. He possessed the leadership qualities that made him an outstanding field NCO. Baird had a lot of respect for Collins's opinion.

"Skipper," said Collins slowly and solemnly, "I think you can go up the ridge and make contact, you can go down the ridge and make contact, or you can stay here and make contact."

Baird agreed. So did everyone else. They could feel it. The NVA were all around them.

Baird told Burton to move out. He warned the younger man to carefully space his platoon members: Baird didn't want them too bunched up or too far apart.

Burton started his platoon. They were moving up a faint trail that ran along the ridge finger's right, or northern, side. To the right of the trail the ground fell off. As the trail proceeded up the finger and neared the top of the ridge, the ground flattened out and the jungle became a little less dense. Where the trail actually joined the top of the ridge finger, the ground spread out for thirty to forty meters before sloping down on either side.

Shortly before 1300 Burton's point man found fresh, bare footprints in the ground, a bamboo commo-wire spool, and fresh human feces. Burton tensed as he ordered his men onward.

At the point of his platoon Burton had two scouts moving parallel to the trail. They passed through a shallow saddle—actually an elongated dip in the trail—and continued beyond the upward end of the dip to where the ridgeline broadened out. Here Burton sent one of his squads to the far left; another moved to the center of the ridge and the third stayed near the trail. Because of the terrain, the squads in the center and on the right held their positions; Sgt. Jimmie R. Worley's squad on the left advanced.

As Worley's squad inched forward, one of the men in the center squad, Specialist 4th Class Hobbs, happened to glance directly uphill from his position. An NVA stuck his head up in the undergrowth about twenty meters away. Before Hobbs could react the enemy soldier disappeared.

Worley's squad continued to pick their way slowly forward. Private 1st Class Anthony Brangaitis, a nineteen-year-old born and raised in Brooklyn, New York, was so sure the NVA were nearby that he fixed his bayonet to his M16. Brangaitis had joined Dog in July. He'd taken some sniper fire while at Tuy Hoa but had not experienced any real combat. As he licked his suddenly dry lips he knew that was going to change real quick.

Another of Worley's men saw an NVA soldier moving toward him along a trail farther up the ridge. He called softly, "I got a gook." The NVA disappeared before anything could be done.

Seconds later Sp4 Charles E. Moss, also in Worley's squad, spotted another NVA soldier. Rather than call an alarm he triggered a burst from his M16. The enemy soldier was slammed into the jungle by the impact of the shells.

When Burton reported the contact to Baird, the CO ordered him to immediately pull his squads back into a defensive perimeter. Baird thought Burton was a little too aggressive; he didn't want him to get into something he couldn't handle. Once Burton's squads were back, Baird planned to pound the area in front of him with artillery and air strikes.

Burton ordered his squads to fall back to his position. To cover their movement Burton fired a clip from his M16 into the area where Hobbs had seen the NVA.

A heavy fusillade of AK-47 fire unexpectedly answered Burton. The enemy slugs tore into a stand of bamboo to Burton's right, passing through the thick stalks with a heavy thwack, spraying water everywhere. Burton beat a hasty retreat to the low point of the dip in the trail.

Private 1st Class Brangaitis had nearly made it to cover

when the NVA opened up. A man near him fell, his chest badly torn by bullets. Brangaitis hit the dirt. Enemy rounds were snapping overhead with a violent fury. Tree branches and leaves showered down upon him. He could scarcely believe he was still alive; it seemed there were NVA tracers passing within inches of his head.

Over the next few minutes Burton pulled back his platoon. Most of his men were in the lowest part of the saddlelike depression they'd just passed through. Burton instinctively knew that it was a poor position, since the enemy held the high ground to his front, but for the moment it was the best he could do.

Twenty-five meters behind Burton, Captain Baird had also hit the dirt with the rest of his CP when the firing started. Behind him, and on top of the high ground leading down into the elongated dip, Lieutenant Allen instantly reacted to the outbreak of firing by having his platoon form a defensive perimeter. He couldn't raise Baird on the radio. He started crawling forward to the captain.

Burton was also making his way to Baird. He moved through the undergrowth in a crouch, trying not to draw any fire. Baird, in the meantime, had started crawling forward toward a large tree. Right behind him came his artillery FO, 1st Lt. Lawrence L. Clewly, Battery B, 3/319th, another West Pointer. Before they'd covered five meters, Clewly took an enemy round in his buttocks. He screamed painfully that he was going to die. Someone pulled him out of the way. His RTO, Sp4 Ernie L. Fulcher, immediately started calling in rounds in the area directly in front of Burton's platoon.

At about the same time that Baird reached the tall, protective tree, Burton approached him from the other direction. Just then a spray of enemy machine-gun fire swept the area. Burton realized he had inadvertently revealed Baird's CP to an NVA machine gunner who'd been stalking him. Burton hurried back to his platoon.

Baird felt a slug hit an ammo pack on his belt, another slam into his rifle's stock, and a third rip into his left wrist. That bullet tore his radial nerve, sending waves of sharp pain coursing through his body. A medic crawled up, slipped a morphine syrette into Baird's upper arm, and injected the painkiller into the muscle. The wound still hurt like hell, but Baird stayed in command.

The CIDG between Baird and Burton had taken cover at the first shot. Now, as the firing directed at Burton grew in intensity, spilling over into the CIDG's area, they broke. To a man, they got up, raced past Baird's position, and headed for Allen's area.

Specialist 4th Class Jake Duffy saw them streaming rearward. He and his FO, Specialist 5th Class Mattingly, were still working with the 4.2-inch mortars. Duffy had had several more contacts since the 10 July fight and had a better idea of what to expect in a firefight. Although the volume of fire here was much heavier than at Hill 830, he remained calm, coolly relaying Mattingly's instructions to the mortar batteries.

First Sergeant Collins went racing after the CIDG. He knew he had to stop their panicked flight before their fear spread to the paratroopers. Despite his shouted commands for them to halt, they moved all the way back to Lieutenant Allen's position before stopping: There was no place left for them to go. Allen, who'd returned to his platoon after Baird had been hit, sent one of his squads forward to take up positions around the CP. He placed the frightened CIDG among his Sky Soldiers as best he could.

No sooner had Lieutenant Burton returned to his platoon than the enemy firing started anew. The sheer intensity of the massed enemy fire scared Burton. He'd never heard anything like it. Instead of distinctive individual bursts from several weapons, this was a constant roar of small-arms and machine-gun fire. The noise was so loud that Burton could not hear the M16s of the men near him firing back. The bullets crashing noisily through the bamboo, splattering the soldiers with water, added to the din. For the first time Burton started thinking he might not make it out of this fight.

Burton couldn't spend much time worrying about his potential longevity. Several of his forwardmost men had spotted the NVA preparing for an attack and were yelling warnings.

Burton moved among them, pointing out likely avenues of approach in the jungle. Then the NVA were there.

Private 1st Class Brangaitis saw three or four NVA coming at him through the trees and bamboo. He fired quick bursts from his M16. The enemy fell. More appeared. Brangaitis kept shoving magazines into his M16, firing them off.

Staff Sergeant James D. Shafer knelt in the open, firing his M16 at a dozen NVA rushing his position. He got three or four of them before he fell. Staff Sergeant Edward J. Smith took Shafer's place. Soon he was joined by SSgt. Michael A. Plank and Sp4 Leroy W. Rothwell. Together the three men stopped the NVA cold.

Though Specialist Fulcher and Specialist Duffy had done outstanding jobs in relaying firing directions to their respective artillery and mortar batteries, Captain Baird thought that the fire was generally ineffective due to the thick overhead jungle cover. He wanted air strikes.

Baird radioed his request to Lieutenant Colonel Johnson, who was hovering nearby in his C-and-C chopper. Johnson refused the request. The battalion commander, fifteen hundred feet above the jungle, could not fully comprehend the murderous volume of fire directed at Baird's small company. He didn't think what Dog Company faced warranted diverting the F-100s from their mission of clearing Hill 823 for Bravo Company.

Baird couldn't believe it. His company of less than sixty effectives faced annihilation unless he received help. He grabbed the PRC-25's mike from his RTO.

"Goddamnit, Six," he screamed over the din of the gunfire. "You'd better get your fucking head outta your ass. We're in some deep shit down here. If we don't get some air we're gonna get overrun!"

The desperation in Baird's voice convinced Johnson to divert several F-100s from Hill 823. He attributed Baird's unprecedented outburst to the pain of his wound and the side effects of the morphine he'd received. Johnson felt that Baird had lost control, that he was near panic.

But Baird was not panicked. He remained firmly in control. He had just realized that his pinned-down company would be overrun by the superior NVA forces unless he got some help.

Within minutes the first jets were screaming above Ngok Kom Leat at treetop level. On their first run, they dropped 250-pound bombs directly in front of Burton's platoon. Sergeant Smith heard them coming and dropped behind a fallen tree trunk. The bomb blast was so close Smith felt he'd have been killed if he hadn't been behind the log. One bomb landed so close that one of Burton's medics was hit by its fragments as he protectively covered a casualty with his own body.

In spite of the accurate bomb bursts, when the F-100s broke off their attack the NVA immediately came at Burton's platoon again. The uniformed, well-armed enemy soldiers moved right down the hill, firing their weapons. Burton's Sky Soldiers started knocking them down. Enemy snipers also unleashed rounds on the paratroopers. When he had a target Private 1st Class Brangaitis tried to get the snipers, but he had little luck. Somebody did get one, though, for his body dangled head down from a rope tied from his ankle to his perch at the top of a clump of bamboo.

After this ground attack failed, enemy action dropped to sporadic firing. Burton's men held their positions. Those who could, moved about, helping the wounded back to a casualty station established between Baird and Allen. The relative lull lasted about twenty minutes, then the firing built again for five minutes before slackening off again. This pattern continued for the next several hours.

At Lieutenant Allen's position there had been no direct enemy fire for the first ninety minutes of the fight. An occasional enemy round slapped through the trees, but those were simply stray rounds from Burton's fight. Most of Allen's time was spent placing his men in position, calming them, and preparing them for the ground attack he knew was coming.

At about 1500 the volume of fire passing overhead increased noticeably. A few minutes later Allen heard the distinctive crack of AK-47s. They were close. He knew the

NVA were coming for him. He called to his men, urging them to be ready.

Then someone yelled, "Here they come!" M16s and M60s opened fire. The thick foliage prevented most of Allen's men from actually seeing the NVA. They simply fired at any movement or muzzle flashes in front of them. Most of the enemy's fire came from down the ridge. Allen knew that Dog Company was surrounded and being squeezed from both ends. Obviously, the NVA had followed them right up the ridge finger and were just waiting for the right opportunity to overrun the paratroopers.

Sergeant Woods lay on one side of a tree and a fifteen-year-old Montagnard on the other. When enemy rounds started hitting around them, the Montagnard rose up, preparing to flee. Woods pushed him down. He did this several more times before his attention was diverted by movement at the base of a nearby tree. As Woods triggered a burst of M16 fire at the enemy soldier, the Montagnard jumped up. Woods grabbed the youngster by the belt and pulled him to the ground just as a spray of AK-47 slugs tore into the tree where the Montagnard's head had been. "See!" Woods said to the shaken soldier. "Stay down."

Lieutenant Allen was tossing smoke grenades to mark his position for the jets and helicopter gunships. A short distance away, where the wounded lay, Lieutenant Clewly saw the smoke. "Stop that!" he screamed. "You'll give our position away. Stop that! You'll get us all killed!"

Clewly kept up his yelling until Allen told him to shut up or he'd kill him himself. Clewly shrank back down.

Artillery shells were hitting in front of Allen's position, but he didn't know who was directing the fire; there was no FO with him. He hoped whoever was calling in the corrections knew what he was doing. Due to the thick jungle Allen could not see most of the artillery bursts. He didn't know if they were doing any good, but he didn't want them to stop.

The fight around Dog Company continued. An occasional probe was made at the perimeter, but it was easily fended off. Gunships, F-100s, and artillery placed a protective ring around the company, but it still needed help.

*   *   *

When it became apparent to Lieutenant Colonel Johnson that Dog Company could not extricate itself, he ordered both Alpha and Charlie companies to move to its aid.

Earlier that day Captain Muldoon's element of CIDG, on point, had opened fire when the Montagnards claimed they had spotted a dozen or so NVA moving toward them in the jungle. Muldoon instantly put his company into a defensive perimeter. He had the Weapons Platoon leader, Platoon Sgt. Thomas W. Thornton, drop a number of 60mm mortar rounds around the company. Patrols found a blood trail and two AK-47s but no NVA. Muldoon continued his patrol.

At about 1400 Muldoon got the call from Lieutenant Colonel Johnson to go to Baird's aid. Alpha Company was about fifteen hundred meters east of Baird, near Hill 729. Alpha would have to move downhill, cross a small river valley, then move uphill to Baird's position.

To expedite his movement, Muldoon decided to leave the CIDG on point; they'd been doing okay so far. But he didn't completely trust them. He told their NCO, "You guys are supposed to know this area. Get me to Dog and get me there without running into NVA. If you lead me into an ambush you guys will get it first. Now get me there and get me there fast."

The CIDG NCO nodded gravely and moved back to his men.

Muldoon then radioed Sergeant Terrazas to close up. In the ensuing conversation it became readily apparent that Terrazas had absolutely no idea where he was, although he could hear firing. Muldoon told him to move toward the noise; it had to be from Dog Company. Terrazas could join Alpha there. Muldoon gave the order to move out.

Initially, the CIDG moved at a fairly good pace. However, as Alpha Company drew closer to Dog Company's battle site and the noise of the fighting grew louder, the Montagnards began to slow down. Soon, their route began to twist and turn through increasingly thick undergrowth. Before long Alpha Company's progress slowed to a crawl.

Muldoon repeatedly exhorted the CIDG to move faster

but to no avail. Finally, Muldoon angrily ordered the CIDG to step aside. He sent 2d Platoon, under Lieutenant Denny, to take the point. To speed his company's movement Muldoon ordered rucksacks dropped. Then Denny's point squad took off, cutting and hacking their way through the dense jungle as fast as they could.

In the meantime, Sergeant Terrazas and his six men had safely entered Dog Company's lines at about 1530. Lieutenant Allen immediately placed them among his men.

About thirty minutes later F-100s were once again dropping bombs and napalm canisters against suspected NVA positions. The FAC directed one jet to lay some napalm in front of Burton's platoon. Something went wrong. Instead of placing the fire bomb in front of Burton's position at the west end of Dog Company's perimeter, the pilot dropped it just outside of Allen's position at the southeast end of the embattled company.

Lieutenant Allen heard the fast mover screaming in and braced himself for the expected blast a hundred meters away. Instead, on the other side of a huge clump of bamboo only twenty meters away, the boiling red flame and black smoke of the jellied-gasoline bomb suddenly erupted. Since the jungle greatly reduced the spread of the terrifying weapon, Allen was not sure what damage, if any, the napalm had done to the enemy. All he knew was that the strike was awfully close.

First Sergeant Collins got on the radio to Baird. "Jesus, Six," he pleaded, "that was awful fucking close."

Baird didn't know what Collins was talking about.

Captain Connolly had also been ordered by Lieutenant Colonel Johnson to move to Baird's aid. Charlie Company was about a kilometer west of Dog Company, higher up in the jumbled ridges composing Ngok Kom Leat. Connolly was to clear the ground above Baird's embattled perimeter, relieving enemy pressure from the west.

Connolly's most direct route to Baird was up and over an intervening ridgeline. He gave the necessary order and his men started the trek. Near the top of the ridge Connolly's lead element, his CIDG platoon, suddenly came under fire from dug-in NVA. Backed by M60 fire from the following Sky Soldiers, the Montagnards knocked out several NVA bunkers. They started upward again. A second network of NVA bunkers opened fire. This time the CIDG pulled back. Connolly ordered them to return to the firing line. They refused. As far as they were concerned they'd done enough for the day. If the Americans wanted the hill, they could take it.

Connolly was furious. He directed one of his platoons, under twenty-two-year-old 1st Lt. Paul S. Jones, to assault the NVA line. In the resulting fight Jones was wounded and the attack ground to a halt. Connolly had his FO call for artillery but was told that none was available; the tubes were busy supporting Dog Company and Bravo Company, which was now having troubles of its own on Hill 823.

Connolly yelled at the FDC and they finally sent a few rounds his way. But it wasn't enough. Charlie Company would have to go after the NVA without a protective umbrella of artillery. Connolly ordered his men forward. Using fire and maneuver tactics they slowly made their way into the NVA's line, methodically wiping out one bunker after another.

Several kilometers to the east Captain Muldoon's Alpha Company had dropped into the river valley and found the going easier as it entered the foothills of Ngok Kom Leat. Then, through a break in the jungle, the paratroopers on point, Sp4s Herman L. Slaybaugh and Dennis T. Ridders, spotted three NVA walking away from them. The point men began stalking the trio. Behind them, unable to see what was going on, Lieutenant Denny tried radioing Ridders to determine the cause of the slowdown. When they didn't respond, Denny shouted at them.

That alerted the NVA, who ran for cover. Slaybaugh and Ridders immediately opened fire but dropped only one of the soldiers.

Up on the ridge, Lieutenant Allen and Sergeant Terrazas heard Alpha's gunfire. They took a compass azimuth toward the sound and radioed the heading to Muldoon.

With that Muldoon pressed onward. Soon Slaybaugh spotted the gray commo wire. He followed it up the ridge finger. As Alpha neared the site of the fight, its Sky Soldiers began to hear the cries and moans of wounded NVA from deep within the surrounding jungle. Here and there in the jungle small patches of napalm still burned with an oily blackness. Then, just twenty meters from Lieutenant Allen's position, Alpha Company found the remains of fifteen badly burned NVA. The enemy soldiers lay in firing positions holding their charred weapons in blackened hands. The misdirected napalm canister had accidentally saved Lieutenant Allen's platoon from a strong enemy attack.

At 1700 Lieutenant Denny's platoon entered Lieutenant Allen's position. Muldoon halted the rest of his company just outside Allen's lines while he went forward to confer with Baird.

During the afternoon Lieutenant Burton had fought off several more NVA probes. During one attack Specialist 4th Class Jorgenson was killed defending his position. An NCO was badly wounded trying to retrieve his body.

The NVA maneuvered several more machine guns into positions enabling them to fire on Burton's men. Any movement by the Sky Soldiers brought an angry burst of fire from the enemy weapons. Sometimes the machine guns sprayed the area around Burton simply to remind him that they were there. Burton and his men were badly frustrated by their inability to do anything about the guns.

The afternoon hours passed slowly. Burton worried that reinforcements would not reach them during daylight hours. If that happened he was sure the NVA would overrun them in the dark. There was just no way that Burton's twenty or so remaining effectives could hold off the reinforced platoon he estimated faced them.

When Captain Muldoon reached Captain Baird's position, he saw that Dog Company's situation was far worse than he'd imagined. He hurriedly ordered his medics to tend to the numerous wounded. Then he pulled his platoons forward to reinforce Dog Company's lines. As the newcomers moved about the perimeter, occasional bursts of automatic-weapons fire from NVA farther up the ridge sent everyone scrambling for cover.

Another air strike was called in. That seemed to quiet the enemy. Muldoon, who had assumed command of Dog Company from Baird, ordered Lieutenant Denny to move through Burton's position and clear the area of enemy.

As Denny prepared to move out, Burton warned him, "Don't go. There's machine guns up there."

Denny grinned at him before ordering one of Burton's M60 teams to accompany his platoon. Then he gave the order to move out. The men barely made five feet when the NVA machine gun spoke. Burton's M60 gunner was killed instantly and his assistant badly wounded. Burton was angry. Two of his men had been lost through the impetuous actions of another officer.

The two platoons held their positions.

As darkness increased and the enemy fire slackened, Muldoon called in medevacs. Earlier attempts to evacuate the casualties had been beaten back by enemy fire. Now the dustoffs were able to get into an LZ hastily cleared by Alpha Company's Weapons Platoon. From about 1830 to 2200 the critically wounded were pulled out. Captain Baird, at his own insistence, was the last man taken out that night.

Once the medevacs were completed, Muldoon ordered Burton, Allen, and Denny to move in to the center of the perimeter; he wanted as tight a perimeter as possible. Enemy fire harassed the Sky Soldiers throughout the night, with an occasional grenade and some mortar rounds dropping in. Muldoon had Spooky, the minigun-equipped C-47, spray suspected enemy gun locations with its murderous fire on several occasions. He also dropped H and I artillery fire around his two companies as a precaution against any NVA probes.

Charlie Company spent the night about a kilometer from Muldoon's position. After clearing out the last of the NVA, Captain Connolly had realized he could not possibly reach Dog Company before dark. Since he had no desire to be stumbling around at night in enemy-controlled jungle, and since Muldoon had reached Baird, Connolly stopped where he was. His night passed without incident.

With dawn on 7 November it quickly became obvious that the NVA had abandoned the battlefield. Captain Muldoon dispatched several clearing patrols. Their sweeps confirmed the enemy's absence. With that danger removed, Muldoon focused his efforts on the remaining casualties.

However, Lieutenant Colonel Johnson had other plans for Alpha Company. He ordered Muldoon to join up with Charlie Company and then proceed to Hill 823, where Bravo Company had been fighting all night. When it became obvious that the conclusion of the medevac operation and the need for resupply precluded that movement, Lieutenant Colonel Johnson changed the orders: Charlie would move to Alpha and Dog companies. Once that linkup occurred, Alpha would retrieve its rucksacks and then the three companies would move southeast to Hill 823.

While waiting for Charlie Company to arrive, Muldoon sent patrols out to police the battlefield. In front of his platoon's positions Lieutenant Burton found eight dead NVA and a number of weapons. He was impressed by the newness of the enemy's weapons, uniforms, and equipment. It was obvious that he'd fought fresh, well-disciplined troops.

Later, while examining the bodies of the napalm-burned NVA, Burton pulled a pistol from the belt of a dead officer. He turned it over to 1st Sergeant Collins with instructions to forward it to Captain Baird as a souvenir. Collins, in turn, collected money from the troops to have an appropriate tribute to Baird engraved on the pistol. Collins later gave the money and pistol to Sergeant Major Arthurs, who was preparing to leave for Hawaii on R and R. Arthurs would have the pistol engraved and forwarded to Baird's wife.

The survey of the battlefield turned up a total of twenty-eight NVA bodies and thirty-four weapons, including six machine guns and two B-40 rocket launchers. Dog Company lost five killed and eighteen wounded; Alpha Company suffered one killed and two wounded.

As Lieutenants Allen and Burton reviewed the fight, they realized that the NVA had been holding positions along the ridge finger, just waiting for Dog Company to pass through before closing their trap. The NVA certainly knew they were there; all the resupply activity on the evening of 5 November had clearly revealed the presence of the Sky Soldiers to the NVA.

Intelligence data collected from the enemy dead indicated that Dog Company had been moving toward the headquarters of the NVA 66th Regiment's 2d Battalion. Perhaps the NVA thought that Dog Company might not notice their camp and might pass them by. But once the commo wire was found, Dog Company's fate was sealed. While most of the enemy force pulled out, Baird's small company was tightly squeezed in a vise, and a blocking force kept Connolly's company in place.

Allen and Burton were convinced they had been saved by Captain Baird's cautious advance up the trail and his insistence on air strikes once the engagement began. If he had not disrupted the enemy's plans by forcefully insisting that Lieutenant Colonel Johnson release some jets to him when he did, both officers felt the NVA could have rolled over them as easily as they had Alpha Company, 2/503d, in June.

The two young officers also were tremendously proud of their mostly inexperienced paratroopers. The enlisted men obeyed orders instantly and without any hesitation. Under unrelenting blasts of enemy fire they held their positions, never yielding to repeated NVA attacks.

Captain Connolly's Charlie Company arrived at Muldoon's position around noon. While they held the perimeter and helped in the resupply, Alpha Company retraced its route of the previous day to retrieve its rucksacks. Third Platoon had the point, and the CIDG element brought up the rear. As they neared their rucksacks one of the CIDG fired his weapon.

Captain Muldoon immediately halted the company. He brought the offending CIDG rifleman and his sergeant forward. "You two are going on point right now," he heatedly told them. "If that shot was a warning to the gooks, you'll get it first. Now move the fuck out!"

A few minutes later Alpha Company found its rucks where they had dropped them. They were untouched. The company returned to Connolly's position without further incident.

Although Lieutenant Colonel Johnson had planned for all four of his rifle companies to rendezvous on Hill 823 the afternoon of 7 November, it was not to be. A resupply helicopter crashed while taking off from Ngok Kom Leat. The chopper went down right in front of Private 1st Class Brangaitis's position. He thought enemy fire had hit the chopper, so he instantly prepared for an attack. However, it turned out that a mechanical problem caused the Huey to crash.

Since it was necessary to strip the Huey of its radios, machine guns, and other equipment, the paratroopers remained in place one more night while that was done. In the morning, after determining that the helicopter could not be extracted safely, the paratroopers destroyed it.

That afternoon the three companies finally made it to the base of Hill 823. They patrolled around the hill that day; the next day they were pulled back to Ben Het and FSB 12. Lieutenant Colonel Johnson had intended to pursue the NVA to the west, but higher headquarters decided his maneuver elements needed a few days to recuperate and absorb replacements.

CHAPTER 8

FIGHT FOR HILL 823

Colonel Richard H. Johnson, CO, 1st Brigade, 4th Infantry Division, had ordered a fire support base carved out of the top of Hill 823. With troops of his brigade, which included the attached 4/503d, patrolling near the outer reaches of the artillery batteries at FSB 12, Colonel Johnson recognized the need for a new FSB closer to the action. Hill 823 would be designated FSB 15.

As soon as Lt. Col. James Johnson realized his three companies in the field would not be able to reach Hill 823 as planned, he ordered Bravo, 4/503d, to make the combat assault. Release of Bravo, 4/503d, from its protective mission at FSB 12 was made possible by the arrival of the 1/503d from Tuy Hoa. All four of the 1/503d's rifle companies would deploy to FSB 12 as soon as they arrived at Dak To. Lieutenant Colonel Johnson told the Bravo Company commander to be ready to go onto Hill 823 at 0900 on 6 November.

There had been a number of changes in Bravo Company's makeup since its fight at Hill 830 on 10 July 1967. First Lieutenant George T. Baldridge had transferred over from Alpha Company to take command of Bravo on 13 July; two weeks later he received his promotion to captain.

Baldridge was a tall, dark-haired thirty-year-old who'd been in South Vietnam since February 1967. Born in Boise, Idaho, to a career soldier and his wife, Baldridge grew up at a succession of army posts around the world. In 1959 he enlisted in the army, serving in the ranks for six years before going to OCS. After he was commissioned in 1965, he completed airborne and Ranger training.

When he took over Bravo Company many of the men were still jittery after the Hill 830 fight; they felt they had moved too rapidly to join the battle and, as a result, paid a heavy price. Baldridge assured the paratroopers he was not the reckless, bold type. He would run his company cautiously, spend his men's lives sparingly. Over the next few weeks Baldridge confirmed his assurances; he would not take needless risks.

As first sergeant, Bravo Company had thirty-three-year-old MSgt. Jerry M. Babb, a fifteen-year veteran from Memphis, Tennessee. After the debacle with the previous first sergeant, Bravo needed a strong senior NCO whom the younger enlisted men could depend on to provide an inspiring example of leadership and fortitude. Bravo had that and more in Babb.

When Babb arrived in Bravo, Master Sergeant Okendo was filling the role of first sergeant. Okendo reverted to his old position. In October, because of a hearing loss and since he had enough combat time, Okendo was sent to the rear to assist in gathering up slackers avoiding combat with their units.

First Lieutenant Peyton Ligon left Bravo in October to join the battalion staff as S-3 (Air). First Lieutenant Al Lindseth remained with Bravo but had been promoted to XO. Two days after the 4/503d arrived back in Dak To, Lindseth left on a well-deserved R and R.

Lindseth's old platoon, the 2d, was now commanded by 2d Lt. Hugh M. Proffitt. Proffitt, like Baldridge, had grown up in a military family, living on air force bases around the world. When he graduated from high school in 1963, Proffitt was living with his family in Hutchinson, Kansas. He spent several years studying at the local junior college before enlisting in the army's warrant officer candidate program as a helicopter pilot trainee. When that didn't work out, he applied to, and was accepted at, the infantry OCS program. He was commissioned in October 1966.

Proffitt arrived in South Vietnam in early October 1967. He had time to conduct only a few field operations around Tuy Hoa with his platoon before the call came to go to Dak

To. As a result, most of the Sky Soldiers in 2d Platoon were still unsure of their lieutenant. They looked instead to their platoon sergeant, Sfc. Lawrence J. Wiggins, for experienced leadership.

In charge of 1st Platoon was 1st Lt. Larry R. Moore. He, too, was a relative newcomer, having joined Bravo in late September. Moore impressed Babb as the rare type of officer who recognizes he's a rookie and is willing to learn. Moore depended upon his platoon sergeant, Sfc. John L. Ponting, for guidance in combat.

The most experienced platoon leader in Bravo was 1st Lt. Robert H. Darling, in charge of 3d Platoon, and he'd only been in South Vietnam since August. A likable twenty-four-year-old former teacher from Pennsylvania, Darling was intent on earning combat decorations. He frequently told his platoon sergeant, SSgt. Joaquin P. Cabrera, how much he wanted to earn a Silver Star. Master Sergeant Babb felt Darling had the potential to make a fine rifle platoon leader if they could keep him alive for the first few months.

Sergeant Phil Owens now carried Captain Baldridge's radio. After Lieutenant Ligon moved up to the battalion staff, he recommended to Baldridge that he take Owens as his RTO as soon as possible. As far as Ligon was concerned, Owens not only was a good radio operator but knew his job as an RTO. Owens stuck with his officer at all times, not afraid to follow him anywhere.

On the night before the assault, Owens and a few buddies were talking before they bedded down. One of the men casually asked Owens, "If you got hit tomorrow, where would you want to get it?"

The question troubled Owens. Like many combat-wise soldiers, he had avoided thinking about his own mortality and exposure to injury. In the daily struggle for survival that was an infantryman's lot, he had pushed those thoughts from his mind. Instead, he simply adopted a fatalistic attitude: If he bought it, he bought it. He didn't expect to be wounded so he evaded the man's direct question. But the questioner persisted, rattling off various body locations that were likely areas for getting hit. Owens sure didn't want a head or stomach wound, let alone a round in the chest. Like all soldiers he dreaded a hit in the balls. He didn't think he could stand it if he lost a leg or two. He certainly had no desire to give up any of his limbs, but finally, to silence the man, he answered, "My left arm. I guess I could do without my left arm."

The discussion continued for a few minutes before Owens crawled off to his hooch.

Lieutenant Colonel Johnson surveyed Hill 823 from the air on 5 November. He saw a broad hilltop, heavily covered with trees, multiple stands of bamboo, and dense underbrush, which appeared defensible. The south side of the hilltop and most of the east side fell off sharply, denying the enemy an approach from those directions. To Johnson's experienced eye the easiest approaches for an enemy counterattack would be along the wide fingers running from the summit to the west and northwest. Bravo Company would have to carefully secure that area to prevent an NVA attack.

With the combat assault (CA) scheduled to begin at 0900, Johnson had ordered early morning air strikes to blast an LZ onto the top of Hill 823. Because his surveillance flight the previous day had failed to reveal any sign of an NVA presence, Johnson limited the air strikes to five. They should be enough to clear an LZ.

Just before 0900 Johnson again had his C-and-C chopper hover above Hill 823. It was readily apparent the aerial bombs had not sufficiently cleared the summit for an LZ. He ordered up more air strikes with larger ordnance.

While the bombing missions were being organized, Captain Baldridge's men sat patiently alongside the LZ at FSB 12; nearby sat the Cowboys' Hueys, their massive turbines turned off to conserve fuel. For the cynical grunts this was typical army bullshit: Hurry up and wait.

They waited until past noon. When Lieutenant Colonel Johnson again surveyed Hill 823, he saw that the extremely heavy foliage had greatly diminished the impact of the five-hundred-pound bombs. Instead of clearing an area, the blasts had simply leveled the trees and bamboo, scattering them in a tangled pattern across the hill. Johnson was thinking he might have to call in even more air when he spotted a likely LZ. Off the southeast end of the summit, perhaps twenty to thirty meters downhill, enough of the trees had been downed to allow one Huey at a time to get in. Johnson designated it the LZ and ordered Bravo to saddle up.

The first Huey rose from FSB 12 about 1330. The slick carried members of Darling's platoon; Baldridge wanted his senior platoon leader on the ground first so he could cross the crest of the hill and take up defensive positions along the vulnerable western approach. One of the platoon members was a redheaded nineteen-year-old, Sgt. Leo E. Hill. A high-school dropout from Cleveland, Ohio, Hill had been in Bravo since June 1967. Because he was in the rear being interviewed for battalion soldier of the month, Hill missed the 10 July fight at Hill 830. Instead, he was called from the interview room to go to the landing pad near the aid station to help with the dead. Though Hill had seen dead men before, the extent of the casualties from that battle really awakened him to the stark realities of war.

In the intervening months Hill developed a well-deserved reputation as a first-class point man. His innate sixth sense for spotting danger had been honed to a fine edge during his eighteen stateside months with the 82d Airborne Division. Most of that time had been spent on training missions deep in the desolate swamps of rural Georgia. Hill learned a lot about living in the wild during those months.

Now, as his chopper banked over Hill 823, Sergeant Hill glanced out the open door. He saw two enemy soldiers squatting together near the top of the hill. As he watched they jumped up and ran off toward the west.

Minutes later the slick hovered above the LZ while a pair of gunships crossed protectively overhead. The slick couldn't actually land due to the many shattered tree stumps. Instead, Hill and the others dropped about six feet to the ground and moved out to take up defensive positions around the LZ while their chopper withdrew to make room for the next one.

Hill and the half-dozen other Sky Soldiers found their way seriously impeded by the mishmash of fallen vegetation

Brigadier General Ellis W. Williamson and Gen. William C. Westmoreland. *Courtesy Maj. Gen. Williamson, U.S. Army*

Brigadier General John R. Deane. *Courtesy Maj. Robert R. Brewer and Sp5 Roger E. Hester, U.S. Army*

Brigadier General Leo H. Schweiter. *Courtesy Maj. Robert R. Brewer and Sp5 Roger E. Hester, U.S. Army*

Chaplain (Maj.) Charles J. Watters, posthumously awarded the Medal of Honor for his gallantry on Hill 875. *Courtesy U.S. Army*

Specialist 4th Class Irvin W. Moran, LRRP. *Courtesy Irvin Moran, U.S. Army*

Captain David Jesmer, A/1/503d, receives the Silver Star. *Courtesy Dave Jesmer, U.S. Army*

Sergeant Joseph S. Mescan, A/1/503d. *Courtesy Joe Mescan, U.S. Army*

Lieutenant Larry Kennemer being carried into the aid station after he was wounded on Hill 882. *Courtesy U.S. Army*

Captain Thomas McElwain, C/1/503d, after the fight on Hill 889. *Courtesy Brewer and Hester, U.S. Army*

Lieutenant Gerald T. Cecil, C/1/503d. *Courtesy Gerald Cecil, U.S. Army*

Sergeant Robert E. Wooldridge, C/1/503d, in the well-publicized photo taken during his first tour in 1966. *Courtesy Bob Wooldridge, U.S. Army*

Private 1st Class John A. Barnes, C/1/503d, posthumously awarded the Medal of Honor for his bravery on November 11, 1967. *Courtesy U.S. Army*

Captain James P. Rogan, B/2/503d. *Courtesy Allen McDevitt, U.S. Army*

Specialist 4th Class Steven F. Varoli, B/2/503d. *Courtesy Steven Varoli, U.S. Army*

Master Sergeant Enrique Salas, A and B/2/503d. *Courtesy Enrique Salas, U.S. Army*

Lieutentants Paul Gillenwater, left, and Allen McDevitt, B/2/503d. *Courtesy Allen McDevitt, U.S. Army*

Private 1st Class Carlos Lozada, A/2/503d, posthumously awarded the Medal of Honor for his bravery on Hill 875. *Courtesy U.S. Army*

Sergeant Steve Welch, left, and Sp4 Raymond Zaccone, C/2/503d. *Courtesy Steven Welch, U.S. Army*

Lieutenant Colonel James H. Johnson, 4/503d. *Courtesy Maj. Gen. James Johnson, U.S. Army*

Captain George Baldridge, B/4/503d. *Courtesy George Baldridge, U.S. Army*

Lieutenant Alfred
Lindseth, B/4/503d.
*Courtesy Al
Lindseth, U.S. Army*

Lieutenant Peyton Ligon receiving the Bronze Star. *Courtesy
Col. Peyton Ligon, U.S. Army*

Sergeant 1st Class William L. Cates, B/4/503d, killed on Hill 875. *Courtesy Phil Owens, U.S. Army*

Sergeant Major Ted Arthurs, left, 4/503d, and MSgt. Larry Okendo, B/4/503d. *Courtesy Larry Okendo, U.S. Army*

Airborne M60 gunner at the ready. *Courtesy Brewer and Hester, U.S. Army*

Master Sergeant Jerry Babb, left, and Staff Sergeant Johnnie Riley, right, on Hill 823. Unidentified soldier in the background. *Courtesy Phil Owens, U.S. Army*

Sergeant Ray Bull, C/4/503d. *Courtesy Ray Bull, U.S. Army*

Specialist 4th Class James ("Jake") Duffy, mortar forward observer attached to C and D/4/503d. *Courtesy Jake Duffy, U.S. Army*

Captain Thomas H. Baird, D/4/503d. *Courtesy Tom Baird, U.S. Army*

Lieutentant Michael Burton, D/4/503d. *Courtesy Mike Burton, U.S. Army*

Sky Soldiers hustle a casualty to a waiting medevac.
Courtesy Brewer and Hester, U.S. Army

The faces of these Sky Soldiers reflect the weariness of fighting the NVA in the Central Highlands. *Courtesy Brewer and Hester, U.S. Army*

littering the ground. The tangled branches and bamboo stalks littered the landscape like pieces in a giant's game of jackstraws. In some places they were knee-deep, making any movement difficult.

Behind the struggling squad another Huey dropped off its load. It was soon replaced by another, then another, until by 1430 all 120 members of Bravo were on the ground.

Captain Baldridge came in on the third slick. He was surprised at how littered the hill was with the trees and shrubs scattered about by the bombs. He saw that his paratroopers were having a hard time maneuvering the short distance uphill from the LZ to the top of Hill 823. While he waited for the rest of his company to land, Baldridge had Sergeant Owens radio a request for some chain saws to Lieutenant Colonel Johnson. Once he had his troops dug in, Baldridge planned to enlarge the LZ and clear it of debris, making resupply easier.

As Baldridge and Owens made their way to the top of the hill, they were both surprised at the large amount of enemy equipment lying about. Rucksacks, canteens, cooking utensils, and an occasional broken weapon were scattered all over. The two also found several well-prepared bunkers. It was obvious that a large force of NVA had recently been encamped on the hill and had fled before the air strikes. Baldridge worried about where they had fled to and when they'd be coming back.

According to the plan Baldridge had given to his platoon leaders, their platoons were ringed around the top of Hill 823 as follows: Using a clock face with 12:00 pointing north, Darling's platoon held the sector from 8:00 to 12:00; Moore's platoon covered from 12:00 to 4:00; and Proffitt's platoon held the perimeter from 4:00 to 8:00. The Weapons Platoon members, led by SSgt. Johnnie R. Riley, were setting up their 60mm and 81mm mortars in a bomb crater at about the 4:00 position. Their crater sat below the highest point of the hill, defiladed against any enemy fire that might sweep the hilltop.

Captain Baldridge established his CP just to the southeast of the center of Bravo's perimeter. He, Owens, and the rest of the CP group busied themselves preparing their position. When the chopper arrived with the chain saws, Master Sergeant Babb detailed several men from the CP group, including himself and some members from the weapons group, to start working on the LZ. Babb started one of the chain saws and began clearing away a stand of bamboo.

Just before 1500 Captain Baldridge, closely followed by Sergeant Owens, began a tour of the perimeter. All went well until Baldridge stopped at Lieutenant Darling's CP. Baldridge asked Darling to point out his LPs. Darling paused, then hesitantly told Baldridge, "I forgot to send them out, Skipper."

Baldridge was shocked at Darling's carelessness. "You get an LP out and you get it out now, Lieutenant," Baldridge ordered harshly. Then he and Owens returned to their CP.

Darling detailed two men, Sp4 Louis C. Miller and Pfc. Robert J. Bickel, to set up the LP. They moved cautiously down the slope, generally proceeding in a northwest direction.

When they'd advanced about sixty meters outside of the perimeter, a violent fusillade of AK-47 fire suddenly erupted from the trees just in front of them. Miller died instantly; Bickel fell badly wounded.

Darling, instantly taking in the situation, went to his men's rescue. Followed by his RTO, Sp4 James L. Ellis, and Pfc. Clarence A. Miller, Sp4 Linwood C. Corbett, and Pfc. Rufus J. Dowdy, Darling charged headlong down the slope.

The little group made it halfway to Bickel when about thirty NVA, hidden in the heavy jungle to their right, opened fire. All five fell, riddled by enemy slugs.

The rapid outbreak of enemy rifle fire, not ten minutes since he'd given Darling his orders, startled Baldridge. He hit the dirt, Owens on his left side. He radioed to Darling. The response came from a dying Specialist 4th Class Ellis, "November's hit bad," he gasped. Then the radio went silent.

At 3d Platoon's position the Sky Soldiers could hear the NVA laughing and shouting below them. They couldn't see them, however, because of the thick wall of jungle foliage.

They could see Private 1st Class Bickel, though. Badly

wounded but still alive, Bickel was crawling up the slope, screaming frantically for help. "Help me! Please help me! Someone help me! I'm dying!"

Several paratroopers prepared to start down for Bickel. Their plans were halted when a green-clad NVA soldier leaned around a tree and killed Bickel with a single rifle shot in the back.

Enraged, Sgt. Alfred McQuirter, one of Darling's squad leaders, boldly went downhill and killed the enemy soldier.

Baldridge kept calling for information; from his position he couldn't see anything. From Darling's platoon's location, Sergeant Cabrera filled the captain in on what had happened.

Baldridge took immediate action. He detailed Sergeant Ponting of Moore's 1st Platoon to take over 3d Platoon. He next ordered Staff Sergeant Riley to get his mortars into action. Baldridge wanted the 81mms to hit about 250 meters in front of 3d Platoon's position while the 60mms fell about 100 meters out. The captain also ordered Riley to send a few Weapons Platoon members forward to plug the holes in 3d Platoon's line caused by casualties. Baldridge had the artillery FO start dropping shells from the howitzers at FSB 12 in front of the threatened platoon.

Events were developing with incredible rapidity. Only a few minutes had passed since Darling's death, and already NVA small-arms fire was cracking across the top of the hill.

Just meters behind Baldridge's command group Babb and the others still operated their chain saws, the saws' noise drowning out the sounds of the erupting battle.

Baldridge and a few others around him started throwing rocks and clumps of dirt at Babb to alert him to the danger. Finally, a dirt clod struck Babb and he turned around. When he saw the others on the ground his reaction was instant; he threw the saw aside and dove for cover.

Baldridge watched the chain saw sail through the air. He thought Babb surely must have set the world record for chain-saw tossing!

In the area where Proffitt's platoon tied in with 3d Platoon, about fifteen NVA suddenly attacked right up the slope. Proffitt had been inspecting the opposite end of his sector when the firing started. He hit the ground and low-crawled to the point of contact. His platoon had opened fire, driving off the NVA, but not before one of Proffitt's M79 grenadiers was killed and another man slightly wounded.

A brief lull followed, giving Bravo's men a few minutes to collect themselves. In the pause those paratroopers who had not completed their fighting holes when the firing started worked feverishly to finish them. Captain Baldridge watched in amusement as one youngster near him dug a hole so fast his movements seemed a blur.

At about 1515 the NVA attacked up the slope again. This time about thirty of them came rushing out of the bamboo. They were met by a hail of M16, M60, and M79 fire. Other Sky Soldiers threw grenades as fast as they could pull the pins. Riley's 60mm mortar rounds were dropping with incredible accuracy among the NVA. Their bursts, followed by the screams of the injured and dying NVA, did much to calm the nerves of the embattled paratroopers.

Several Sky Soldiers had set up an M60 machine gun and a 90mm recoilless rifle at the forward edge of a bomb crater near the junction of 2d and 3d platoons. From this position they were able to pour devastating fire into the attacking NVA. Reacting to this fire, several NVA snuck up and tossed grenades into the crater. The paratroopers pulled back to the near lip of the crater. From there they tried to dislodge the NVA with their own grenades but were unsuccessful. This grenade duel would continue most of the night.

When the ground attack ended the NVA began pounding the Americans with a succession of mortars, RPGs, and B-40 rockets. Their explosions erupted across the hilltop in a constant roar.

Master Sergeant Babb was doing his best to melt into the ground to escape the shards of jagged metal ripping by just inches above him. He even undid the buckles of his web gear so he could move his ammo pouches off to the side. Lying on them made him feel as if his rear end was draped over a log.

Overhead, Lieutenant Colonel Johnson watched the explosions. His afternoon was not going well. All four of his companies were in the field and, in the last couple of hours, three of them had come into contact with the NVA. All three company commanders called for help, but there just wasn't enough support for them all.

Based on reports from the company commanders, Johnson determined that Captain Baird's Dog Company faced the most serious danger. He began diverting as much of the available support to Ngok Kom Leat as he could.

Captain Baldridge was directing the strafing runs of two F-100 fighter jets. Their 20mm cannon shells tore violent paths around the hilltop. Some struck so close that a few of the paratroopers received minor wounds from the shell fragments.

At approximately 1530 Lieutenant Colonel Johnson watched helplessly as a string of mortar explosions moved toward Baldridge's CP group.

Sergeant Owens lay on Baldridge's left, his M16 clasped in his left hand, the radio mike in his right. He had been relaying messages between Baldridge and Johnson on the battalion net while Baldridge issued orders to his platoon leaders over the company net through another RTO who lay on his right.

Suddenly, Owens heard someone scream, "Short round!" He ducked. The blast was close; the concussion violently rocked Owens. When the dust had settled he raised his head to speak into the mike. After several attempts to reach Johnson failed, Owens suddenly realized his phone cord had been severed. Something else didn't seem quite right but he couldn't put his finger on it. There was a loud ringing in his ears and then the opening throbs of sharp pain. He didn't know what it meant. Then he passed out.

A mortar round had exploded almost in the middle of the command group. Huge chunks of jagged metal zinged through the air. One large piece ripped into Owens's left armpit, mangling the flesh and severing an artery. Red-hot shrapnel tore deeply into Baldridge's left leg; it hit so hard he thought someone had struck him with a baseball bat.

Babb's effort to lower his rear end proved futile: Shards of shrapnel tore into his buttocks. He felt as though he'd been kicked by a mule and then lifted a couple of feet off the ground before being slammed back down. He lay there stunned for a few minutes, waiting for his ears to stop ringing and his head to clear.

When he looked up Sergeant Owens was staring at him. "Top, I lost my arm," Owens said.

Babb could tell Owens was going into shock. He crawled toward him. As he did Owens tried to sit up. Babb reached him just then, pushed him down, and covered him with his body to protect him from the grazing small-arms fire.

Then Babb saw the gaping wound in Owens's left side. The severed artery pumped deep purple blood onto the ground with each beat of Owens's heart. Babb screamed, "Medic! Medic!" but Doc Richardson was busy treating another serious casualty. So Babb slipped his fingers into Owens's wound and pinched off the pulsing artery.

Owens continued to pass in and out of consciousness. During one lucid moment he could hear Johnson's voice crackling over the radio, "Where's Bravo Kilo? What happened to Bravo Kilo?"

Somewhere in the fog of pain Owens heard someone respond, "He's Whiskey," meaning he'd been wounded. Owens found it all very interesting.

Later Owens heard Doc Richardson's voice in the background saying, "He's dying. I'll give him some morphine to make it easier." Owens wondered who the medic was talking about and then passed out again, not feeling the needle slide into his arm.

Captain Baldridge took a quick head count and found that seven besides himself had been wounded by the mortar blast. He radioed Lieutenant Moore, the senior surviving platoon leader, and advised him he'd been hit. "Be prepared to take over command," Baldridge said.

Then Baldridge radioed a damage assessment report to Lieutenant Colonel Johnson. "I'm hit, sir," he said, "and won't be able to stay in command much longer. Lima Six is on standby to take over but I don't think he's ready for that."

Johnson concurred. He sent a message to Ben Het telling his headquarters company commander, Capt. Ron Leonard, to get ready to take over Bravo. Next, he ordered his chopper onto Hill 823's LZ. Three of its occupants jumped off to act as an interim command group. As Maj. Richard M. Scott, 4/503d; XO, Capt. Shirley W. Draper, 3/319th artillery liaison to 4/503d; and Sgt. Maj. Ted Arthurs made their way to the top of the hill under fire, other Sky Soldiers carried several of the more seriously wounded to the waiting bird.

Sergeant Owens was unceremoniously thrown aboard the C-and-C Huey. The cold metal floor against his back felt reassuring. Johnson leaned down and said, "You'll be all right, son." Owens passed out again.

Seconds later, the chopper rose amidst a hail of enemy small-arms and automatic-weapons fire; then it turned and headed for Ben Het.

At the TOC at Ben Het Master Sergeant Okendo had been monitoring the battalion's nets. When he heard that Babb had been wounded he knew what that meant. "Shit," he told himself, "there goes my R and R."

He was right. A few minutes later Lieutenant Colonel Johnson ordered Okendo and Leonard to be ready for an immediate pickup. They were going out to Bravo. Okendo went off to find Leonard.

A few days earlier Captain Leonard had taken command of the battalion's Headquarters Company. Since arriving in 4th Battalion in late July, Leonard had filled the slot as S-2.

Okendo found Leonard in the headquarters tent. "Get your stuff together, sir," he told Leonard. "We're going forward."

Soon the two men were at the landing pad. Once the casualties were removed from Johnson's chopper, Leonard and Okendo boarded. During the short ride out to Hill 823, Johnson briefed Leonard on the situation. The captain nodded grimly as he took in the details.

The firing had subsided when Johnson's chopper touched down again. After Leonard and Okendo hopped out, the remaining casualties, including Baldridge and Babb, were loaded aboard and evacuated.

Captain Leonard found the situation fairly well stabilized. Major Scott had reorganized the platoons, moving additional men from Moore's platoon forward to strengthen the threatened perimeter. Captain Draper had taken over calling in a protective wall of artillery fire.

Together, Sergeant Major Arthurs and Master Sergeant Okendo toured the perimeter. Where necessary they had the paratroopers improve their fortifications. They knew the NVA would be back that night, and they wanted everyone prepared.

Later, Okendo called in a resupply of ammo, including cases of grenades. The chopper brought it in at about 1830. Okendo oversaw the distribution of ammo and supplies, and everyone settled in for the anticipated attack.

Just before 2000 the men on the western perimeter reported hearing movement below them. One Sky Soldier cautiously peeked over the rim of a bomb crater. Not five meters away stood an NVA soldier. The paratrooper raised his M79 and fired. The round hit the enemy in the head, decapitating him.

Seconds later a barrage of enemy grenades and B-40 rockets, accompanied by an occasional mortar round, descended on the hilltop. The NVA harassed the Bravo troops with the missiles throughout the night. The enemy tried many times to get individual Sky Soldiers to reveal their positions, sometimes even throwing dirt clumps at the paratroopers, but the fire discipline among Bravo's members was excellent.

Sergeant Leo Hill had taken up a position with a buddy, Specialist 4th Class Diaz, and an engineer. Several times during the long night Hill could hear the NVA moving furtively on the slope below him. In response, Diaz would point his M79 nearly straight up, then they'd all duck as the missile landed and exploded only fifteen to twenty feet away.

The engineer, whose name Hill never did get, at one point crawled back to the CP to get more grenades. He returned with about fifty. He and Hill used them all before dawn.

Aerial protection for the paratroopers came from Puff the Magic Dragon and its vicious array of miniguns. The C-47 flew fire support missions for Bravo Company as well as Dog. Grunts at both locations took great comfort in the neon light-like streams of tracer rounds that poured out of the miniguns. Thousands of rounds per minute chewed up the ground around the base of Hill 823. Sometimes the rounds came frighteningly close to the Sky Soldiers. Sergeant Hill was pelted with clods of dirt several times as the bullets carved furrows in the ground in front of his bunker. He was terrified that the friendly fire would find him in his hole.

The flare ship Spooky droned overhead throughout the night, too. One-million-candlepower flares were dropped every fifteen minutes, bathing the surrounding landscape in an eerie glow.

As soon as the fighting had started that afternoon, Sergeant Riley's FO, Sgt. John ("Mike") Jeakle, had made his way to the western edge of the perimeter. From that exposed position the twenty-one-year-old from Detroit, who had dropped out of high school to join the paratroopers, had kept a steady pattern of mortar shells dropping among the NVA.

Jeakle stayed in position as night fell. He, too, could hear the enemy moving about on the spur below him. He'd estimate the position of the NVA and then call a fire mission back to Riley. The screams of wounded North Vietnamese would tell him if his aim in the darkness had been true.

One enemy soldier in particular harassed Jeakle. The troops dubbed him "Cowboy" because he'd dash into the open, yell "Yahoo!" throw a grenade uphill, and then disappear into the bamboo. Jeakle tried several times to get him with a 60mm mortar but the pesky enemy soldier always survived. By carefully calculating the distance from the sound of "Cowboy's" voice, Jeakle was finally able to get him with a brace of mortar shells; at least he heard no more "Yahoos" after that.

Throughout the night paratroopers on the firing line kept calling to Jeakle to "bring 'em in closer." He radioed the adjustments to Riley, bringing the shells closer to the line than he should have. Jeakle himself received minor shrapnel wounds from the blasts, but that was necessary to hold the NVA at bay. Riley's superb performance on the mortar tubes coupled with Jeakle's pinpoint accuracy materially contributed to Bravo's survival on Hill 823.

Despite this massive display of protective fire support, some NVA still managed to crawl close enough to attack the paratroopers. At about 0500 ten enemy soldiers emerged from a gully that led straight to the junction of the 1st and 3d platoons. Supported by RPG fire the NVA charged up the hill behind a barrage of hand grenades. They nearly succeeded in breaching the perimeter. Only the calm courage of the Sky Soldiers prevented that. While directing his men in repulsing the attack, Staff Sergeant Cabrera died when an RPG hit directly behind him.

At dawn Captain Leonard had the company mark its positions with smoke grenades. Air force jets soon rocketed in, dropping bombs and making strafing runs to within two hundred meters of the company. Next, other fast movers sprayed flaming napalm farther down the ridge. Then gunships from the Cowboys came in, adding their firepower to the hill's defenses.

While the jets were dropping their bombs, several NVA made their way to the outer edge of the bomb crater on the west end of the hill. Sergeant Okendo had just dropped down next to Private 1st Class Wilbanks on Bravo's side of the inner edge of the crater when the NVA jumped into the crater and tried to attack up the inner end. Okendo boldly leaned over the crater's rim and blasted the lead soldier with his M16. The others fled. Okendo and Wilbanks rushed to the outer edge of the crater, tossing grenades after the enemy.

When the gunships completed their run, Leonard ordered Proffitt to take a patrol down the finger running to the west. They were to secure any weapons and search any enemy bodies they found.

Proffitt led a column of his paratroopers out of the perimeter. Cautiously making their way through the tangle of torn trees and underbrush, they began moving down the slope. Within the first fifty meters they found between fifteen and twenty NVA bodies, many within grenade range of Hill's and Diaz's position. In horrifying testimony to the deadly effect of Staff Sergeant Riley's mortars, most of the corpses were tangled masses of flesh. Some bodies were barely recognizable; most had had their limbs violently torn away from their torsos. Entrails hung from tree limbs; arms and legs were strewn about as if a violent doll maker had gone crazy.

Halfway down the slope the patrol took a burst of enemy small-arms fire. After everyone scrambled for cover Proffitt called for mortar fire. Sergeant Riley expertly dropped fifteen rounds into the area suspected of harboring the NVA. The firing ended. The patrol moved on.

Sergeant Major Arthurs and Master Sergeant Okendo followed Proffitt's patrol out of the perimeter. While the patrol had formed up Okendo had heard the cries of a wounded NVA. If he were still alive Okendo wanted him captured. They found him, but he was more dead than alive. Still, he defiantly raised his weapon at the two NCOs. Before Okendo or Arthurs could respond, a nearby paratrooper shot and killed the NVA.

Okendo unslung the instant camera he always wore around his neck and handed it to the Sky Soldier. "Get a picture," he told the man. Okendo and Arthurs squatted behind the body while the soldier took their picture.

Proffitt's patrol pushed out to the base of the spur and proceeded about a hundred meters into the surrounding bamboo. Near the base of the finger they came upon a tall tree from which a rope ladder hung. Proffitt sent Specialist 4th Class Ramirez up the ladder. When the young man completed his climb he yelled down that he had a perfect view of FSB 12.

Throughout the area the paratroopers found large quantities of new enemy equipment, ranging from weapons to gas masks. The Sky Soldiers marveled at the quality of the equipment. It was obvious the NVA were as well supplied as they were.

Proffitt's patrol moved back up the slope beginning at 0800, carefully sweeping along the sides of the ridge finger. More evidence of the horribly destructive force of American firepower came to light as additional maimed corpses were found.

One of Proffitt's men discovered a large bunker nearly

hidden by extensive overhead cover. In the bunker's recessed entrance lay a dead NVA. Sergeant Wiggins jumped down to check the corpse for any intelligence material. As he landed, another NVA inside the bunker fired a pistol shot at him. Wiggins, unharmed, scrambled for cover. The paratroopers gathered around the bunker yelled for the NVA to *chieu hoi* but only received another pistol shot for an answer.

Okendo called for a white phosphorous grenade. Wiggins handed him one. Okendo threw it in the bunker. As he did so the enemy soldier fired another pistol shot. The ejected cartridge collided with Okendo's downward-moving wrist, embedding itself in his flesh.

As the WP grenade burned up the oxygen in the bunker, the NVA soldier had two choices: suffocate or flee. He fled. He broke from the bunker, wildly firing his pistol. Specialist 4th Class Worrel, an M60 gunner, cut the man down with a short burst from his weapon. Despite having taken five or six of the heavy rounds, the NVA was still alive, gasping in short, tortured breaths. Okendo walked over to him and finished him off with a shot in the head. The enemy soldier proved to be an officer. On his person were a number of documents, which the paratroopers gathered up for intelligence. Sergeant Wiggins got the man's pistol. Someone else took his belt buckle.

Proffitt's patrol finished its sweep without finding any more living enemy. Apparently they had withdrawn, fearful of the superior American aerial firepower. Once Lieutenant Proffitt returned to the perimeter, Captain Leonard met with his officers to plan their next move. At the same time, Master Sergeant Okendo organized parties to police up the enemy dead. In all, more than a hundred NVA bodies were picked up and dumped into the bomb crater at the western end of the hill. By then Bravo's final casualty figures had been calculated. Okendo radioed to the battalion adjutant that Bravo had lost nine killed and twenty-eight wounded.

Small patrols were sent forth from Hill 823 for the rest of the day. A few more enemy bodies were uncovered. Evidence found on the dead indicated that the NVA were part of the 66th Regiment.

Late that morning Lieutenant Colonel Johnson, accompanied by his RTO, Sp4 Stanley Jones, landed on Hill 823. Though an occasional enemy mortar round slammed into the hill, Johnson moved about, talking to his paratroopers, congratulating them on their stand. While waiting for the rest of his battalion to close on Hill 823, Lieutenant Colonel Johnson received reinforcements. General Schweiter attached Charlie Company, 1/503d, to the 4/503d. Slicks started bringing them into Hill 823, now designated FSB 15, at about 1300.

Bravo Company was pulled off Hill 823 on the afternoon of 8 November. Lieutenant Colonel Johnson had intended to continue his pursuit of the enemy, but General Schweiter wanted the battalion to have a few days' rest. While the other companies of the 1/503d moved out to Hill 823, Johnson's battalion took up positions in and around Ben Het. They would spend the next few days conducting road-clearing operations and patrolling to the west and north of FSB 12.

A flurry of high-level visitors flew into Ben Het to be briefed on the recent battles. Among them were South Vietnam's premier, Nguyen Cao Ky, and its president, Nguyen Van Thieu. At one point Lieutenant Colonel Johnson hopped off his chopper at FSB 12 and found MACV's assistant commanding officer, Gen. Creighton W. Abrams, waiting for him.

"Tell me what's happening here, Colonel," Abrams asked Johnson.

"I can't tell you what's going on with the brigade, sir, but I'd be happy to tell you about my battalion," Johnson replied.

Abrams said that would be fine. Johnson took him into his TOC where he and his surprised S-3 conducted an impromptu briefing for the senior commander. A short time later a group of nervous brigade staff officers descended on the TOC and escorted Abrams back to their headquarters.

On the afternoon of 9 November Master Sergeant Okendo received a message from Lieutenant Colonel Johnson to report to the helipad. He had a visitor. Who the hell can be coming to see me? Okendo wondered.

At the helipad Okendo was enthusiastically greeted by Col. William J. Livsey, the G-3 for the 4th Infantry Division, in company with Major General Peers, the 4th Infantry Division commander. Fifteen years earlier, as a brand-new second lieutenant, Livsey had been Okendo's platoon leader in Korea. The two warriors exchanged pleasantries for a few minutes, and then, while General Peers listened, Okendo answered Livsey's probing questions about the fight on Hill 823.

Livsey had transferred into the 4th Infantry Division in late June. He immediately made a careful study of the 4th's operations in the Central Highlands, including the 2/503d's fight on 22 June, and reached several conclusions. Combat in the rugged Central Highlands demanded different tactics. Any units operating in the jungle, including battalions, must stay within easy reinforcing distance of other units. Under no circumstances should small units be sent into the field by themselves; the NVA would quickly isolate, surround, and annihilate them.

Further, he didn't think U.S. ground units should become involved in combat with dug-in NVA forces. They could too quickly lose their fire superiority in the close-quarter fighting. Livsey also concluded that the 173d frequently made poor use of their artillery support. Too often, he thought, artillery fire was checked in order to allow gunships and jets to make their strafing or bombing runs. Too often, air strikes and gunships could not effectively penetrate the thick jungle canopy. Plus, he believed, the cessation of artillery fire allowed the NVA to press closer to the Americans' perimeter, further reducing the effectiveness of artillery, air strikes, or gunship runs.

Livsey preferred to send forth small units of scouts to locate concentrations of NVA. Once they were spotted, huge amounts of artillery and tactical air strikes could be brought to bear until the NVA were destroyed. Then the infantry could be sent in on mopping-up operations.

Livsey communicated his conclusions to the 173d's operations officer, as well as the battalion commanders, several times, but to no avail. They paid little attention to him. He felt the paratroopers did not want a leg telling them how to fight a war.

As the next few weeks passed, Livsey wished the paratroopers had listened to him.

CHAPTER 9

TASK FORCE BLACK

Allied reinforcements were pouring into Dak To. Even after General Rosson released the last two battalions of the 173d (General Schweiter had argued that the 3/503d was too new to send to the highlands, so they continued Operation Bolling around Tuy Hoa), General Peers moved the 1/8th Infantry from his 2d Brigade in Darlac Province to Dak To and attached it to the 1st Brigade. Within the next few days General Rosson would also send Peers two 1st Cavalry Division battalions, the 1/12th Cavalry and the 2/8th Cavalry.

In addition, the ARVN 9th Airborne Battalion was flown into Dak To from Saigon, where they had formed a major portion of South Vietnam's Joint General Reserve. General Peers oriented them to the northeast of Dak To to confront the NVA 24th Regiment. The ARVN 2/42d Regiment provided security for the Dak To command complex, which now contained a 4th Infantry Division forward tactical command post as well as General Schweiter's headquarters. The ARVN 2/42d also patrolled Route 512, which bisected Dak To and Ben Het as it ran westward from Highway 14, at Tan Canh, to Laos.

The ARVN Joint General Staff would soon replace the ARVN 9th Airborne Battalion with the ARVN 3d Airborne Battalion. They were joined by the ARVN 2d Airborne Battalion and the 3/42d Regiment. All these ARVN battalions focused their efforts against the NVA 24th Regiment.

General Rosson authorized the additional maneuver battalions because of the increase in enemy contact. At nearly every turn the forces patrolling around Dak To were colliding with determined NVA units. On 7 November, just three kilometers east of Hill 830, Alpha and Dog companies, 3/8th Infantry, were attacked, losing ten dead and thirty-five wounded. The next day eight more infantrymen from the same companies were wounded during an early morning mortar attack. At 1840 at the same site a savage NVA ground attack against Alpha and Dog raged for more than three hours. When the fighting ended eleven more soldiers lay dead and thirty-eight were wounded.

On the southwest slopes of Hill 1338 Charlie and Dog companies, 3/12th Infantry, found well-prepared enemy positions every fifteen hundred to two thousand meters. A brief firefight would ensue, artillery would pound the NVA, and the grunts would move over the area, counting the enemy dead. Usually there would be a dozen or so dead NVA, and the two rifle companies lost four or five.

A third company, Bravo, joined Alpha and Dog, 3/8th, on 9 November. The next day, while the companies were moving up a ridge toward the summit of Hill 724, the NVA hit them again. A brutal fight lasted into the next day. Only the massive application of artillery and air strikes broke the enemy's attack. The NVA left 92 of their comrades on the battlefield. Eighteen American infantrymen died; nearly 120 were wounded. The huge casualty rates so depleted the companies that one mustered only 44 men, another 59, and the largest counted but 79.

Although it was obvious to Generals Rosson and Peers that the rapid introduction of allied troops into the Dak To area had blunted the NVA's plans to overrun the camp, it was just as obvious that the enemy had no plans to concede the area.

To keep the pressure on the NVA, General Schweiter ordered the reinforcement of the fire support base on Hill 823. Fire Support Base 15 would not only house Charlie Battery, 3/319th, but also the headquarters of the 1/503d as it took over patrolling in the surrounding AO from 4/503d.

Colonel John J. Powers, the deputy brigade commander since 1 November, set up a brigade forward CP at FSB 15. A West Pointer who'd graduated in 1945, the forty-four-year-old Powers had served with the U.S. Army, Vietnam, staff at

Long Binh for six months before replacing Colonel McQuarrie. But he was no stranger to ferocious combat. As a company commander with the 3d Infantry Division in the Korean War, he'd earned the DSC for his personal valor.

General Schweiter ordered Lt. Col. David J. Schumacher's 1/503d to pursue the NVA who had battered Bravo 4/503d on 6 November and to prevent any other NVA units from closing on Dak To.

Colonel Schumacher had less than three months remaining on his tour when he moved his battalion to FSB 15 on 9 November 1967. The first six months of his tour had been spent as the brigade's executive officer, handling mostly administrative details. Despite this innocuous assignment Schumacher had a reputation for being a career-oriented officer, with little concern for or empathy with his subordinates.

As far as Powers was concerned, Schumacher was simply an officer who wanted to get his career ticket punched with battalion combat-command time before rotating back to the United States to a cushy staff job and a promotion to colonel. Schumacher was an adequate battalion commander, to be sure, but he never generated either the support among the subordinate officers in his battalion or the loyalty among his superiors at brigade level that normally existed among the airborne brethren.

To accomplish his assigned mission, Colonel Schumacher created two task forces: TF Black would consist of Charlie Company and two platoons of Dog Company; TF Blue contained Alpha Company and the remaining platoon of Dog. Schumacher's fourth rifle company, Bravo, commanded by Capt. Jerry Draper, would remain at FSB 15 to provide the necessary security forces.

Leading Charlie Company was twenty-six-year-old Capt. Thomas McElwain. Born and raised in Logan, West Virginia, McElwain had dropped out of school on his seventeenth birthday to enlist. He spent the next six years as an enlisted demolitions expert, earning his highschool diploma during his off-duty hours. By 1963 he knew he wanted to make a career out of the army, so he applied for OCS. In October of that year he pinned on the gold bars of a second lieutenant.

McElwain arrived in South Vietnam in August 1967 after a tour as the commander of the United Nations honor guard in South Korea. He took over Charlie Company from Capt. Kirby Smith in September. Because Charlie had had little contact with the enemy in recent months, McElwain wanted to institute some training programs to bring his paratroopers back to a high level of alertness, but he didn't have to. On his first mission as Charlie's commander, the company went into a hot LZ west of Tuy Hoa. VC lead was flying through the air as the Hueys deposited the troops on the ground. In an instant McElwain saw his men revert to acting like the elite combat airborne infantry they were.

Although initially judged by the veterans of Charlie as being too aggressive in his desire to close with the enemy, McElwain soon came to be loved by his men. It became apparent that, because of his years in the ranks, McElwain preferred the company of enlisted men to that of officers. He drank with them, gambled with them, and exchanged stories of sexual prowess. He played a mean guitar and sang like Glen Campbell. The men worshipped him. They'd have followed him to Hanoi if he'd asked.

McElwain was so popular he even had his own batman. Specialist 4th Class Darryl Fitch, Captain Smith's former driver and runner, took over taking care of McElwain. In the field Fitch dug McElwain's bunker, pitched his tent, prepared his meals. The captain had a special fondness for peaches and pound cake, treats rarely found in C rations. Fitch spent a good deal of his time bargaining with the others to get their cans of peaches and pound cakes for the captain. In Fitch's opinion McElwain was not only the best officer, but one of the best men he'd ever known.

Captain McElwain took an instant disliking to Colonel Schumacher. He, too, felt Schumacher epitomized the ticket puncher so prevalent in the army's officer corps. He viewed his battalion commander as an opportunist, far more interested in furthering his career and accumulating combat glory than in caring for his men. After one particular action at Tuy Hoa, for example, Schumacher had ordered his staff to prepare a recommendation awarding him the Silver Star.

McElwain knew the award was a sham and was openly pleased when brigade rejected the recommendation.

McElwain's dislike for Schumacher was no secret to the enlisted men of Charlie Company. Whenever Schumacher would chopper into his CP, McElwain would tell his troops to pop smoke in order to advise the pilot of wind conditions. Invariably, someone would respond, "Fuck the smoke; let's toss a frag." McElwain would laugh.

On 8 November, before pushing off from Hill 823, McElwain, in response to the S-4 officer's radioed request for a list of supplies he needed, asked for water. Schumacher broke into the net and told McElwain, "Water doesn't win wars, Charlie Six. We can't waste valuable chopper space with water. There's a blue line at the base of the hill. Send a patrol down there for a resupply."

Reluctantly, McElwain ordered Lt. Charles Brown to send out a detail. He did and the squad ran into eight NVA. Private 1st Class John M. Kapeluck died in the resulting exchange of gunfire. Kapeluck's tragic, unnecessary death did not endear Schumacher to Charlie Company.

Alpha Company's commander, and the leader of TF Blue, was thirty-one-year-old Capt. David Jesmer. A big man standing six feet two inches tall and weighing two hundred pounds, Jesmer had tried out for the New York Giants and the San Francisco 49ers upon graduation from college in 1959. He didn't make it, so he used his ROTC commission to go on active duty with the army. He ended up being recruited by General Westmoreland at Fort Campbell to play on the 101st Airborne Division's football team. Jesmer did that for two years and then took his discharge to return to his home in Sacramento, California, and a job in a local bank.

Two years later, in January 1965, bored with the banking profession, Jesmer returned to active duty. In May 1967 Jesmer went to South Vietnam. After a stint as the 1/503d's S-3, he took over Alpha in July. In a driving rainstorm a chopper flew Jesmer out to his new command. He joined them on Hill 882, about ten kilometers south of Ben Het.

Jesmer was shocked at what he found. Though his company roster showed many more, only about eighty-five men were in the field. He radioed his XO to get every man not holding an essential job in the rear out to the field immediately. In the next twenty-four hours about fifty more members of Alpha showed up. From that point on Alpha had no more slackers.

Over the next few weeks Jesmer led his company on extensive patrols throughout the area. They found little evidence of the NVA. Occasionally, they'd hear the NVA at night, but they never saw them. One time Jesmer followed a fresh trail up Hill 875 but could not close with the enemy. He had the feeling the NVA had been ordered to avoid the Americans. Not until after the company had moved to Tuy Hoa did Alpha make any contact with the enemy. In a brief encounter several VC were killed.

To prepare his men for the inevitable heavy contact, Jesmer stressed training. His cardinal rule was for the lead platoon, upon contact, to immediately form the base of a horseshoe. The other two rifle platoons would form the legs of the horseshoe, while the weapons platoon covered the rear. The company CP would form in the middle of the perimeter. With this formation Jesmer felt that his company would present a formidable barrier to any NVA attempts to overrun them.

Unlike McElwain, Captain Jesmer got along well with Colonel Schumacher. Jesmer thought Schumacher was a very good battalion commander who gave orders and expected them to be carried out in a professional manner. Jesmer didn't think an army officer could ask for anything more.

Captain Abraham Lincoln Hardy led Dog Company. A big, husky twenty-five-year-old Texan, Hardy had arrived in South Vietnam in February 1967. His most recent assignment had been as the battalion motor officer. When Schumacher formed Dog Company in September, Hardy received the nod to command it.

Colonel Schumacher directed Captain McElwain to take TF Black west from FSB 15 for two kilometers and then turn south toward Hill 889. At the same time TF Blue would depart FSB 15 to the southeast, then turn back to the west, paralleling by about a thousand meters south TF Black's track. The two units would rendezvous on Hill 889.

The task forces left FSB 15 early on the morning of 10 November. Progress was slow due to the thick underbrush intertwined with the ubiquitous stands of bamboo. Burdened by their heavy rucksacks, the paratroopers walked hunched over as they snaked their way down Hill 823's slopes and ventured into the unknown.

In Alpha Company, Lt. David Holland struggled with his pack as he shepherded Weapons Platoon forward. Holland had not been pleased when Captain Jesmer transferred him to Weapons Platoon just before they left Tuy Hoa. The platoon had only fifteen men and one 81mm mortar, so Holland felt more like a squad leader than a platoon leader. In protest, he and some of the men from his new platoon visited one of the bars along the airstrip when they passed through Kontum and got rip-roaring drunk.

When the C-130 deposited him on the Dak To airstrip the next day, Holland suffered from a vicious hangover. He quickly sobered, though, when he saw choppers carrying casualties into Dak To from the south. From across the wide valley he could see Hueys flying out of the dark green hillsides, small black dots suspended beneath the birds. As the choppers drew closer Holland realized the black dots were actually the corpses of grunts killed in action. For the first time, Holland faced the fact of his probable death in combat. It surprised him that this acceptance of his fate calmed him and allowed him to carry out his duties without worry.

As the task forces neared the base of Hill 823, the point men began finding evidence of an enemy presence. A large number of blood trails less than twenty-four hours old attested to the deadly efficiency of the previous night's H and I fire. Task Force Black also found several sets of bamboo-reinforced steps cut into the lower slopes of Hill 823. Abandoned NVA equipment lay scattered throughout the area. Every man in both task forces, veteran and novice alike, knew they were venturing deep into NVA territory. When the fighting started, it would be on the enemy's terms, not the Sky Soldiers'.

Task Force Blue laagered that first night about a thousand meters southwest of Hill 823. Captain Jesmer set up a tight night perimeter, put out his LPs, and registered artillery fire. Though several of the LPs reported hearing movement at various times, the night passed quietly for TF Blue.

Captain McElwain's force had felt throughout the day that they were hot on the trail of the NVA. Every few hundred meters the point came across another sign of them. One time the point man stumbled across commo wire. McElwain had his communications sergeant splice into the wire. In a short time they got a ring-back. The wire was live.

McElwain reported this to the battalion S-3, Capt. Edward Sills. Sills, a twenty-eight-year-old Georgian, cautioned McElwain, "Be careful, Tom. The little people are all over the place."

McElwain agreed.

Task Force Black set up for the night on an unnumbered knoll about two thousand meters west of Hill 823. Captain Hardy placed the platoons into positions around the laager site while McElwain sent out LPs.

Charlie's 1st Platoon leader, Lt. Edward Kelley, took eight of his twenty-three platoon members back down their line of advance to set up an ambush for anyone following them. Like McElwain, Kelley, a twenty-six-year-old from Dothan, Alabama, had first served in the army as an enlisted man. When his three-year hitch ended in 1962, Kelley entered Auburn University, serving not only in the school's ROTC program, but also in the local National Guard Special Forces unit. When he graduated in May 1966 he was commissioned a second lieutenant. A year later he arrived in South Vietnam.

Kelley, considered by his men to be a very businesslike officer, carefully placed his small force into position, then settled in for the night, keeping a 50 percent watch. A short time later it started raining. The heavy downpour not only limited whatever visibility there was in the jungle at night, but muffled any sound. The NVA could have walked within feet of Kelley and his men and they'd never have known. But, as far as he knew, they didn't, and the night passed uneventfully.

*   *   *

Captain Sills, whom all the company commanders considered an outstanding S-3, relayed Colonel Schumacher's orders for 11 November to Captain Jesmer. TF Blue would move west toward TF Black, linking up with them that day or the next. The combined force would then move southwest on parallel ridgelines toward Hill 889. It was expected that the remnants of the NVA 66th Regiment would be found somewhere in the area.

Jesmer had his force ready to go by 0800. A scout dog and its handler moved with the point team. Jesmer had little faith in the dog. The previous day it had alerted every hundred meters or so, greatly slowing his task force's progress. Jesmer had more faith in the instincts of his point men.

Second Lieutenant Ed Robertson led his 2d Platoon out of the laager site first. Behind him came 1st Lt. John Robinson's 1st Platoon, Jesmer's CP group, Lieutenant Holland's Weapons Platoon, and 1st Lt. Larry Kennemer's 3d Platoon. Kennemer was a twenty-two-year-old Texas A and M graduate who'd been in South Vietnam since June 1967. Because there was no platoon leader's slot open then, Kennemer had spent most of his first three months in-country as Colonel Schumacher's gofer. He joined Alpha in September.

Not more than two hundred meters from its starting point, the scout dog alerted. Before Jesmer could respond to what he thought was another false alarm, the jungle in front of Robertson exploded with gunfire. The men reacted instantly, going to ground and seeking cover. The other platoons hastily moved into position, forming the protective horseshoe perimeter that Jesmer had drilled into them. It was 0828.

Jesmer immediately radioed a report of the contact to the TOC. Schumacher was there, unable to get his C-and-C chopper into the air due to morning fog. "I've got about a platoon of them," Jesmer told Schumacher.

Up front, Robertson's men exchanged rifle fire with the enemy. As was normally the case, few NVA were visible in the thick foliage; the Sky Soldiers could only fire back at muzzle blasts and fleeting shadows. Grenades exploded with sharp crashes, driving steel shards into human flesh.

Executing his normal procedure, Jesmer had his platoons make a fighting withdrawal while the artillery and 4.2-inch mortar FOs radioed fire missions into their FDCs. Within minutes of the retrograde movement 105mm shells were pounding the enemy. Closer in, 4.2-inch mortar rounds crashed through the treetops to explode among the NVA positions. Unfortunately, one mortar round fell short, killing one of Jesmer's men and wounding several more.

Lieutenant Holland's Weapons Platoon had not even made it off the laager site when the fight started. Holland immediately set up his mortar. No fire was coming his way, so he just had his men drop rounds directly in front of Robertson's platoon.

Kennemer's platoon, just twenty-two men, were firing their M16s and M60s into the jungle but really had no targets. Most of the firing from the NVA was still concentrated against Robertson's men.

In response to Jesmer's request the fast movers were now on station overhead. An airborne FO relayed Jesmer's instructions for the bombing run. Within minutes the F-100s were screaming overhead, their five-hundred-pound bombs tearing huge holes in the jungle canopy.

By now it was after 1100. When the jets finished their work more artillery pounded the enemy positions. Thirty minutes later Jesmer sent out a squad-sized patrol, accompanied by the scout dog, to survey the area.

The NVA were gone. All that remained were the corpses of those killed by the air and artillery. As Jesmer examined the bodies he was impressed with the newness of the enemy's equipment and weapons. None of it looked as though it had been in the field very long.

Jesmer also thought it strange that the enemy soldiers all wore rucksacks and were not in prepared positions. He concluded that his opponent had been a rear-guard element with orders to delay his movement. And he knew why: From radio conversations he'd monitored over the last few hours between Schumacher and McElwain, it was apparent TF Black was in desperate straits. He had to get his men moving if TF Black was to be saved.

*   *   *

Colonel Schumacher's orders to Captain McElwain for the morning of 11 November were to follow the commo wire. He wasn't to move too far, though, because Schumacher wanted TF Black to remain in that area for another day, searching for the NVA while waiting to link up with TF Blue.

Between them, McElwain and Captain Hardy agreed to send a platoon in each direction following the wire. The other platoons would conduct reconnaissance sweeps of the area.

Lieutenant Brown was tapped to take a squad on a clearing patrol around the laager site. Brown considered the movement routine; Kelley's ambush had returned to the perimeter without finding any sign of the NVA. Brown departed the laager site just after 0800.

Not fifty meters distant, Brown's point man spotted an NVA trail watcher about twenty meters away. The paratrooper fired, wounding the NVA. Brown signaled his patrol to pursue the wounded man while he started to radio a report to McElwain. Before he could, McElwain came up on the net.

"November Six," McElwain said to Brown. "What the hell's going on?"

Brown told him, then added, "We're following a blood trail. I'll pursue."

"No," McElwain ordered. He had just been informed by Schumacher to be prepared to move to Jesmer's assistance. McElwain didn't want a small force out by itself where it would be vulnerable.

"I don't have a lot of time to waste," McElwain snapped. "I'll send someone else out."

Brown argued but to no avail.

Lieutenant Gerald Cecil's 2d Platoon had been chosen to follow the commo wire, so it stood ready to move. The platoon had enjoyed a relatively relaxing morning. Sergeant Philip H. Scharf, a twenty-year-old from Fond du Lac, Wisconsin, even had time after breakfast to write a letter home. Then word came to move out.

Scharf paired up with his buddy, Sgt. Robert E. Wooldridge. Most of the men in Charlie 1/503d called Wooldridge Sergeant Opie for his uncanny resemblance to child star Ronnie Howard of the *Andy Griffith Show*, then popular on stateside TV. Wooldridge, who had just turned twenty in October, was somewhat of a legend in Charlie. He'd first come to the company in May 1966. During that tour a photojournalist had snapped his picture. That shot, showing Wooldridge with a full, combat-loaded rucksack, had been widely circulated back home, bringing him some fame.

When his first tour ended, Wooldridge volunteered for another full year in South Vietnam, with the stipulation he stay with Charlie. Assured that that would be okay, Wooldridge headed off for a thirty-day leave in his hometown of Newton, Iowa. There he met and married a young lady before returning to war.

Now he was serving as an FO for the platoon's 81mm mortars. He joined with Scharf as Cecil's platoon started out.

If Sergeant Opie was a legend in Charlie Company, Lieutenant Cecil was its celebrity. He was one of ten West Pointers to be selected by *Newsweek* magazine for a special article on the 1966 graduating class. Reporters followed the ten men for nearly a year, recording their graduation, marriages, and further training. The resulting article appeared in the 10 July 1967 issue of the magazine, complete with pictures of Cecil as he went through the army's rugged Ranger training. He'd already been in South Vietnam for several months when the article ran, so he received, and accepted with his gracious Kentucky charm, a good deal of ribbing.

Cecil was respected not only by the other officers in Charlie but by his platoon members as well. Aggressive and determined, Cecil constantly taught his men the tricks of jungle fighting he'd learned in Ranger school. As a result, he had a great deal of confidence in the ability of the twenty men in his platoon to perform well in any encounter.

Second Platoon's point man, Pfc. John Rolfe, led the platoon out of the perimeter. Cecil was the third man in the column. They soon passed Brown's small force, which moved back to the company perimeter.

Cecil's platoon proceeded down a fifty-meter-wide finger running generally south from the laager site. As they moved farther downhill the jungle canopy thickened, casting an eerie half-light on the jungle floor. Underbrush grew to nearly chest height. Visibility in the twilight gloom rarely exceeded five meters.

Noiselessly, the platoon inched down the finger. Then Rolfe raised his arm in the signal to halt. As Cecil watched nervously, Rolfe slowly swiveled his head around, an upright index finger to his lips in the classic sign for silence. Then, without a word, he turned and shot another trail watcher.

In the silence that followed, Captain McElwain came down the finger. Together, he and Cecil examined the enemy corpse. "Look at this," Cecil pointed out. "This gook just came south. His uniform's fresh and there's even Cosmoline still on his rifle."

McElwain agreed. He felt a chill run up his back. He could feel eyes hidden in the jungle boring in on him.

"They're out there, Jerry," McElwain said. "I can feel 'em. Be careful."

McElwain returned back uphill to the company CP. Cecil signaled his platoon to move out. As they proceeded down the ridge it narrowed, with the sides starting to slope more sharply. Within another hundred meters the spur's descent increased.

Cecil moved his platoon slowly, sending two-man teams to cloverleaf along the ridge's edges. No one talked; any communications were strictly by hand signals.

Second Platoon reached the low point of the finger where it formed a slight saddle before running uphill to the neighboring ridge. A sixth sense warned Cecil that he was minutes from a fight. He hurriedly signaled his cloverleaf teams back, then formed his squads on line, the line's ends bent slightly back.

"Guys, we're in it," Cecil whispered to those around him. "The gooks are here, I know it. When I signal everyone fire."

A split second later Cecil triggered a burst from his CAR-15.

Before the men around him could open fire too, the jungle in front of them erupted in a cyclone of enemy fire. AK-47s, RPDs, and B-40 rockets streaked out of the jungle toward the Sky Soldiers. The men hit the jungle floor, firing wildly.

Although he didn't know it at the time, Cecil was at the open end of a large horseshoe-shaped ambush. If he'd moved any farther forward he and his platoon would have been cut to ribbons in a vicious cross fire. As it was, they faced a hailstorm of fire from what Cecil estimated to be several squads of NVA.

Toward the rear of Cecil's column Sergeants Wooldridge and Scharf were out of the direct line of fire from the initial NVA outburst. However, as they aggressively moved forward, a soldier five feet from them caught an NVA round in the face. The men watched in horror as the rear of the soldier's head exploded in a red spray.

A few seconds later another Sky Soldier came running back from the head of the column. He'd been shot in the chest. However, the AK-47 bullet must have been defective, because the round only penetrated half its length into the man's sternum. Wooldridge and Scharf instantly nicknamed the soldier Sergeant Ricochet.

The pair hit the dirt and started crawling forward to the center of the fight. Ahead of them the sharp crack of M16s and the angry firing of M60s responded to the bark of AK-47s. The two men could see NVA darting between the trees at the bottom of the ridge finger's side slopes. They fired at the fleeting shadows.

Then both heard the unmistakable thunk of NVA mortars. Wooldridge knew the weapons were close and being fired nearly straight up. "Damnit, Phil," he cried. "We're gonna get hit!"

Sure enough, an NVA mortar round dropped noisily through the overhead foliage to land just five feet in front of the men. It was a dud. Before they could congratulate each other on their luck, another mortar shell exploded with a blinding flash in nearly the same place.

After the blast had rolled over the two, Wooldridge heard Scharf saying, "Opie, you're hit! You're gonna get a medal out of this." Tiny slivers of jagged metal had torn into Wooldridge's right arm.

"Shit!" said Wooldridge. "Talk about me. Look at you." Scharf's forearms had been peppered by fragments of the enemy round, too.

Rather than congratulate each other on their Purple Hearts, the intrepid duo moved closer to the action. Ignoring their wounds, they started pulling casualties out of the line of fire and redistributing ammunition.

Back at the top of the hill, Captain McElwain, acting on reports from Cecil, radioed Colonel Schumacher at the TOC that Cecil was engaged with an NVA squad. This was at about 0950.

A few minutes later, as the firing in front of Cecil continued without letup, McElwain dispatched Lieutenant Brown and his platoon as reinforcements. As Brown headed down the ridge finger, Cecil radioed to McElwain that he felt he was actually facing a full platoon; the firing was just too heavy for a single squad.

Brown's men moved as fast as they could toward Cecil. The roar of the firing increased as they neared the saddle. Soon enemy rounds were snapping past them. They sought cover. Within a dozen or so meters of Cecil's position the heavy volume of fire brought Brown's platoon to a halt.

The two platoon leaders could yell back and forth but couldn't physically link up. Brown reported his situation to McElwain, adding that the enemy force appeared to be a company or greater in strength. McElwain dutifully reported this change to Schumacher.

McElwain decided to move to the scene of the fighting himself. He left Lieutenant Kelley's platoon and Weapons Platoon, under 1st Lt. Ray Flynn, at the laager site and then gathered his CP group and headed for Cecil and Brown.

Once at the site McElwain set up a CP and took command. The viciousness of the fight shocked McElwain. The roar of small-arms and automatic-weapons fire spread a constant drone throughout the jungle. Every few minutes the sharp crash of a hand grenade or B-40 rocket or mortar shell reverberated through the trees. The shrill screams of the wounded added to the confusion. McElwain realized that the situation was more desperate than he had imagined. Clearly the NVA were in greater strength than his company could handle. He had to tighten his perimeter in order to concentrate his fire-power to reduce the chance the enemy could penetrate his line. From a prone position behind a large tree, McElwain radioed Cecil to pull back toward Brown.

Though not more than thirty minutes had passed since the first outburst of fire, Cecil had already lost three killed and had a dozen wounded, several so badly they could barely move. To cover the pullback Cecil had his men plant Claymores in the dirt, crawl backward the length of the detonating cord, and fire the deadly efficient weapon. In this way the remnants of the shattered 2d Platoon moved closer to Brown.

Two of Cecil's men were so badly wounded they could not pull back. Unwilling to order anyone else to risk their lives, Cecil advanced twice under the blaze of enemy fire to carry the casualties to safety.

Few of the paratroopers had yet to actually see the NVA. Later they would learn the enemy soldiers had heavily cam-ouflaged themselves with natural foliage. They were so well hidden that only the muzzle blasts from their weapons gave them away.

Besides the small-arms fire, enemy mortar rounds contin-ued to play havoc with the Sky Soldiers. Just as Sergeant Scharf finished pulling one casualty to safety, a mortar round exploded behind him. A jagged shard of red-hot metal slammed into the rear of his right thigh, tearing a large gash and making Scharf think of how a football must feel on kickoff. No sooner had a medic reached him than another mortar exploded, zinging shrapnel across the area. The medic fell, badly wounded. Scharf took shrapnel in the chest and face, with one piece tearing through his lower lip and knocking out three teeth before burying itself in the back of his tongue. Hot blood filled his throat as his tongue swelled, making breathing difficult. Scharf rolled over onto his chest, rising to his hands and knees, gagging for air. Now I'm in deep shit, he thought.

Soon a second medic reached him, hastily bandaged his
wounds, and moved on. Later someone pulled him to where
the wounded had been collected. A medic wanted to perform
a tracheotomy but Scharf refused. No one was going to slice
open his throat.

The fighting raged on with hardly a letup. When McElwain realized the NVA were moving around him along the
edges of the ridge finger's slopes, he radioed for Lieutenant
Kelley to join them. McElwain also radioed Captain Hardy.

Hardy had taken his two platoons in the opposite direction
that morning, following the commo wire. When McElwain
advised him he was in trouble, Hardy immediately turned
back.

In front of Hardy, Kelley moved his platoon toward the
sound of the battle. Before they'd covered half the distance,
the NVA opened fire; one NVA gunner was so close Kelley
could see the foliage part from his muzzle blast.

Kelley's men had sought cover, but he ordered them to get
up and move. By crouching and darting from cover to cover,
the platoon made it to the battlefield, taking up positions
along the perimeter's exposed flank.

Kelley could not believe the bedlam. There was firing
everywhere; B-40 rockets flew across the battleground; mortar shells exploded with a deafening crash; men were screaming in anguish as their bodies were torn by enemy metal. It
was absolute chaos.

Within minutes several of Kelley's men were hit. His
medic took six rounds in one leg and was immobile. Three
M60 gunners were killed within seconds as the tattoo of an
enemy RPD tore across their position.

Soon after Kelley joined the fight, Captain Hardy brought
his men from Dog Company into the perimeter. At about this
time Lieutenant Flynn reported to McElwain that he was
taking rifle fire at the laager site.

McElwain didn't want the dozen or so men in Weapons
Platoon isolated and annihilated, so he ordered Flynn to bury
the mortars and come to him.

Flynn threw his two mortars into two fighting holes, covered them with ponchos and dirt, and headed downhill, the

NVA hot on his trail. By the time he made it into the perimeter, NVA fire was coming from all four sides. The 170 paratroopers of TF Black were completely surrounded.

The weather had cleared enough by 1030 for Colonel Schumacher to climb into his C-and-C chopper at FSB 15 and circle over the battleground. He faced the same problem Lieutenant Colonel Johnson had with his 4/503d just five days earlier: Three of his four companies were heavily engaged, and the thick jungle prevented him from seeing what was going on.

Based on reports from Jesmer and McElwain, Schumacher quickly determined that TF Blue's situation was the least serious. With artillery and air pounding the enemy positions in front of Jesmer, Schumacher turned his attention to TF Black.

McElwain had been in nearly constant communication with Captain Sills, at the TOC, and Colonel Schumacher. At about 1100, after Captain Hardy and Lieutenant Flynn had linked up with him, McElwain reported to Schumacher he thought he was facing an entire NVA battalion and desperately needed help.

Schumacher fired back, "Charlie Six, you don't know what you're facing. First you report a squad, then a platoon, then a company. Now it's a battalion. Get up and go after those people."

McElwain exploded in rage. "Goddamnit, Six, if you don't get us some fucking help down here you won't have a Charlie Company left. Listen to me, get us some help."

Schumacher yelled back at McElwain, "Don't you swear at me, Captain. I will not tolerate that. Now get hold of yourself."

Eavesdropping on the net at the TOC, Captain Sills could not believe what he heard. He'd been talking to McElwain on and off for more than an hour, listening to the constant crackle of gunfire in the background. This was no small firefight; Sills thought McElwain might be overrun unless he got help. He felt frustrated not only by his own inability to help, but by Schumacher's apparent inability to comprehend the seriousness of McElwain's situation.

Someone, however, did recognize TF Black's dire straits. As Sills listened, General Schweiter broke into the net. "You'd better listen to your man on the ground, Colonel," radioed Schweiter. "If he says he's facing a battalion, he's facing a battalion."

General Schweiter knew Schumacher had run out of options. Jesmer's TF Blue was still stymied with its own firefight, so he couldn't make it to help McElwain. Bravo, 1/503d, was guarding FSB 15; sending them to TF Black would dangerously expose the FSB to an enemy attack during the time necessary to get a replacement company to Hill 823.

Schweiter made up his mind. He radioed Lieutenant Colonel Johnson, 4/503d, at his CP at Ben Het. "Charlie First Batt's in trouble. Get ready to send a reaction force to relieve them," Schweiter said tersely.

Johnson began organizing a rescue party.

After General Schweiter told Captain Sills to locate an LZ for the relieving company, Sills radioed that information to Colonel Schumacher. "I already know that," snapped Schumacher. "Just get on with it."

Then Sills radioed the good news to McElwain. As he did, Schumacher cut in. "I'm running this fight, Captain," he said testily. "Stay off the net."

With that admonition ringing in his ears, Sills ran to the waiting chopper. A short time later he was circling the jungle near TF Black's position, desperately seeking an LZ in the heavy jungle cover.

After a tense fifteen minutes of searching, Sills found what he was looking for. Less than a thousand meters west of McElwain's position was a clearing that could just accommodate one chopper. He marked it on his map, then signaled the pilot to head back to FSB 15. There, he radioed the welcome news to General Schweiter, Colonels Schumacher and Johnson, and Captain McElwain.

Word of the rescue attempt reached McElwain at about 1115. It could not have come at a better time. The fighting had continued without letup. Casualties had been mounting at an alarming rate. The more seriously wounded had been moved toward the rear of the perimeter, where a slight depression offered some protection from the small-arms fire raking the paratroopers' lines. Those less seriously wounded stayed in the fight. TF Black needed every able rifleman on the line.

Among the dozen or more dead was Capt. Abe Hardy. Ever since he'd made it into the perimeter he'd been racing boldly among the embattled paratroopers, shouting directions and encouragement.

At one point he came over to Lieutenant Brown. "How's everything here, Lieutenant?"

Startled to see the captain standing near him, apparently unconcerned about the bullets buzzing by and mortars and rockets crashing in the jungle, Brown replied, "Just fine, sir. Don't you think you ought to get down?"

Hardy just nodded and moved away. Later, McElwain saw Hardy running from cover to cover, firing his rifle, yelling curses at the enemy. When Hardy moved near where McElwain was lying, McElwain called to him, "Slow down, Abe. You can't beat them yourself."

Hardy smiled and moved on. He ended up near Lieutenant Kelley's position.

Exceptionally heavy AK-47 and RPD fire had been slamming into Kelley's platoon. One youngster, unable to take the pressure any longer, jumped up and started yelling obscenities at the NVA. Kelley tackled him and pulled him to cover. He saw another of his platoon members, wounded several times, staggering around in shock. He brought him down, too. Another severely wounded paratrooper lay nearby, hysterically screaming over and over, "I don't wanna die!"

Captain Hardy bounded by Kelley, running to a new position. As Kelley watched, Hardy caught a burst of rifle fire full in the chest. He died instantly. Kelley radioed the news to McElwain. Dog Company's only other officer, Lt. George L. Brown, took over the company.

Lieutenant Cecil was an inspiration to all who witnessed his actions that day. Exercising bold initiative, Cecil moved among his platoon, repositioning the men, distributing ammo, and encouraging the paratroopers by his deeds. Cecil had taken a bad wound in the right hip when an NVA sniper, tied in the upper reaches of a tree, dropped a grenade between him and another man. The painful injury never slowed him. When one of his men's M79 jammed, Cecil passed him his CAR-15 and slipped forward to pick up a dead NVA's AK-47 and ammo. He then used that weapon to kill three enemy soldiers charging his platoon. Later, he mowed down at least six more within ten meters of his position.

Because of the large number of casualties in his platoon—four men were dead and all but one of the remaining were wounded—Cecil crawled back to Lieutenant Brown's position several times to ask for help.

Brown hated to select men to move down to Cecil's battered section of the perimeter, but he had no choice. As he glanced among his platoon members they'd look back at him, their eyes pleading with him to pick someone else. However, when Brown made his selection those Sky Soldiers would instantly pick themselves up from the jungle floor and crawl down to Cecil. Brown was never as proud of being a paratrooper as he was that day.

One of the men Brown sent to Cecil was Pfc. John A. Barnes. A twenty-two-year-old from Dedham, Massachusetts, Barnes had completed a one-year tour in May with the 173d Engineer Company when he volunteered for another tour on one condition: He wanted to man an M60 machine gun in a rifle company. His condition was met.

Lieutenant Brown was happy to have the firepower of another M60 in his platoon, but some of the enlisted men were not. Private 1st Class Don Martindale, an ammo bearer, didn't like it because it meant he had to hump more ammo. Martindale liked Barnes, though he couldn't understand why anyone would volunteer to serve as a grunt. Barnes's eagerness to fight earned him the nickname "Combat."

Barnes was a very likable young man, eager to please and always willing to do more than his share. But he was a pack rat and one of the slowest and sloppiest soldiers in Brown's platoon. No matter how much Brown threatened or cajoled, Barnes could not get his stuff together on time in the morning.

Several times Brown had to leave a fire team behind to guard Barnes as he packed all of his gear into his rucksack. Then they'd all run to catch up with the platoon. Barnes never seemed to have his gear squared away and was the butt of many platoon jokes, but he never lost his cheerfulness and never complained.

And he didn't complain when Brown tapped him to reinforce Cecil's platoon. He just picked up his weapon and snaked off.

At Cecil's position Barnes sent belt after belt of M60 ammo ripping into the enemy's position. His firing proved so effective the NVA soon singled him out as a major threat. Hot lead from several AK-47s literally engulfed his position, shooting him off his M60. Helpful hands pulled the badly wounded former engineer out of the line of fire. Soon Barnes was being tended by a medic at the makeshift aid station.

Another inspiring example of calm under fire that day was the FO from Charlie Battery, 3/319th. Lieutenant Richard A. Elrod, a Texan, moved fearlessly about the perimeter, calmly calling in fire directions to the FDC. He brought the 105mm fire in as close as he dared, hoping to shatter the enemy's line.

In front of Lieutenant Kelley's sector, artillery rounds were tearing up the jungle just twenty-five meters away. Some members of his platoon were hit by the friendly shrapnel, but Kelley knew it couldn't be helped. He realized that many of the NVA were actually between the wall of artillery and his position and thus relatively safe from the shells' destructive force.

At about 1120, soon after Captain Hardy was killed, the enemy fire slackened enough to allow the beleaguered paratroopers some respite. In the lull, the men used knives, bayonets, and helmets to scrape shallow, protective trenches in the soil. Even being lower by just three to four inches contributed immeasurably to their sense of security.

Since most of the paratroopers had left their rucksacks at the laager site in anticipation of spending another night there, and had been putting out rounds at an unbelievable rate for several hours, nearly all of them were running low on ammo. Lieutenant Kelley cautioned his men to "hold your fire unless you've got a sure target."

Ammo and water were collected from the dead; the wounded stripped themselves of extra magazines and passed them out to their buddies. Some adventuresome paratroopers crawled out of the perimeter to collect weapons and ammo from dead NVA.

Just before the lull, Sergeant Wooldridge had killed an enemy soldier who had leaned out from behind a tree only five meters away. Since he'd nearly fired off the five hundred rounds he'd been carrying, Wooldridge used the break in the firing to crawl from his position to claim the enemy's weapon.

Captain McElwain radioed Captain Sills word of the critical ammo shortage. (After being admonished by Schumacher, the two had simply switched to another frequency and continued their communications.) Sills soon had a Huey fitted with a sling load of ammo. Warrant Officer Gary Bass, one of the Cowboys, volunteered to fly the hazardous resupply mission.

At 1120 Bass hovered over the embattled hillside. The dense foliage prevented him from pinpointing the location of TF Black. On the ground McElwain could only catch occasional glimpses of the slick through the treetops. He radioed directions to Bass by sound, but then the NVA opened fire on the chopper.

The paratroopers could hear the rounds slamming into the aluminum-clad chopper. The volume of fire was unbelievable.

The chopper shuddered under the impact, Bass fighting for control of the damaged helicopter. In the rear, the crew chief dropped the ammo as Bass banked for Dak To. Members of TF Black watched helplessly as the crates tumbled down the slopes, out of reach.

Several more ammo resupply attempts were made, but the furious enemy fire drove them off, too.

The arrival of Bass's chopper signaled a renewal of the enemy firing. B-40 rockets roared out of the jungle to crash among the paratroopers. Grenades arched through tree limbs, exploding in the trees to spray the men below. The sharp crack of AK-47s built to an ear-shattering crescendo.

Sergeant Wooldridge had moved toward a dead Sky Soldier to collect his ammo when he heard an AK-47 bark. A sharp pain suddenly engulfed him. Two rounds had passed through his pant leg; a third plowed into his left kneecap. A medic slapped a bandage on the wound and sent Wooldridge off to join the other wounded.

The enemy onslaught raged until nearly 1300. Then it slackened off again. Once again the Sky Soldiers used the lull to improve their positions, move casualties to safety, and wait for help.

Captain William Connolly's Charlie, 4/503d, had returned to FSB 12 from a patrol north of Ben Het at 0700 on 11 November. Connolly spent several hours getting his company fed and resupplied; then he crawled into his bunker for some much needed sleep. He'd barely drifted off when word came that Colonel Johnson wanted to see him. Connolly's company was going to rescue TF Black.

When Charlie's paratroopers learned they were going to the aid of a sister company, an electric charge of excitement bolted through them. After weeks of being hit by the enemy, they now had a chance to strike back and save some fellow Sky Soldiers.

By noon, Connolly's company was lined up at the LZ waiting for the choppers. Not until 1300 did the flight of slicks arrive. Bristling with anticipation, the paratroopers, carrying extra ammo and water for TF Black as well as their own basic load, jumped aboard.

On the first chopper was twenty-one-year-old Sgt. Ray Bull of Yuba City, California. A member of Charlie since July, Bull belonged to a special point team handpicked by Connolly for their stealth in the jungle. When their chopper touched down in the tight clearing, Bull and Sp4 David Atkins leapt out the door. Once assured the LZ was cold, they started through the jungle toward TF Black.

Behind them the choppers carrying the rest of Charlie,

4/503d, settled one at a time, disgorged their occupants, and lifted off.

The enemy renewed their assault on TF Black at 1330. One second all was quiet; then enemy mortars began falling, followed by heavy small-arms fire. McElwain, who'd been wounded in the back by shrapnel from an exploding mortar, crawled from his CP to the most threatened sector of his perimeter. Adding his rifle fire to the fight, he helped drive back a determined attack, killing several NVA.

McElwain had passed the word of the expected relief to his men. At first, the news lifted the spirits of the trapped paratroopers. However, as the fight continued with no sign of the reinforcements, desperation set in.

Lieutenant Kelley was sure he was going to die. With the calm assurance of those who know their end is imminent, Kelley only hoped he wouldn't suffer. He just wanted to go swiftly. To ensure that, he pulled a round out of a magazine and stuck it in his pocket. That way he'd have one left to use on himself when the NVA overran the position.

While they were huddled at the base of a tree Lieutenant Brown's RTO, Pfc. Bruce Linton, turned to him. "Sir, do you think we'll make it out of here?" he asked.

"Do you want me to be honest?"

"Yes."

"No, I don't think we will."

Linton patted his pocket. "I've got a letter to my wife in here. If you make it out and I don't, will you see that she gets it?"

Brown assured him he would.

"Is there anything I can do for you, Lieutenant?"

"No," Brown answered.

"One more thing, sir," Linton said. "Do you mind if I call you Charlie?"

Brown laughed out loud. "No. You can call me Charlie."

Sergeant Wooldridge also thought they'd be overrun. As the wounded continued to pour into the aid station he wondered how many able-bodied men there could be left to hold the perimeter. Casualties were strewn everywhere, some horribly wounded. He saw intestines hanging from torn stomachs,

jaws shot off, and limbs shattered. One medic, Sp5 Ennis El-
liott, had been hit five times; both his arms were broken. But
still he struggled to aid the others.

Ten feet from Wooldridge Private 1st Class Barnes lay with
several other wounded. Suddenly, one of them screamed,
"Grenade!" People scrambled to flee the deadly NVA missile,
but not Combat Barnes. Instead, he pulled himself off the
ground and then flopped back down, covering the grenade
with his body.

The blast threw Barnes five feet. He lay there, a gaping
hole in his middle. He cried, "My God, I'm gonna die! I'm
gonna die! Tell my mommy I love her." Then he died.

Though Wooldridge and several others received minor
wounds from the grenade's shrapnel, Barnes's heroic self-
sacrifice saved them from certain death.

Captain Jesmer's TF Blue had been ordered by Colonel
Schumacher to move with all haste to McElwain's aid. Jesmer pushed his people hard, but the jungle impeded their
advance. Also, the scout dog kept alerting, warning of an enemy presence.

As TF Blue neared the crest of yet another steep, jungle-
covered hill, enemy fire broke out. Jesmer's men instantly
deployed, returning fire.

Jesmer ordered his force to pull back while he called in an
artillery strike. After the shells had pounded the enemy positions, TF Blue crept forward. There was no sign of the NVA.

Soon afterward Colonel Schumacher ordered Jesmer to
set up a laager. Night was approaching. There was no way
that TF Blue could reach McElwain before nightfall, and
Schumacher didn't want Jesmer wandering in the dark. Besides, Captain Connolly was closing in on TF Black.

Captain Connolly's company moved through the heavy
brush as fast as they could. At the point, Sergeant Bull and
Specialist Atkins could hear the firing as they drew closer to
the battle site. They had been using compass headings to
guide their way, but soon the constant crackle of small-arms
fire made that unnecessary.

A short distance back, Sp4 Jake Duffy, now the 4.2-inch mortar FO, and his RTO, Pfc. Darryl Haymes, pushed forward, bent under the weight of the extra ammo they carried for TF Black. They moved on an adrenaline high, the prospect of action and the chance to save American lives filling them with anticipation and excitement. Both men knew they were well beyond the range of their mortars, so they'd be acting as riflemen. They shifted their M16s nervously from hand to hand as they followed Bull and Atkins.

Private 1st Class Gerhard Tauss stayed in constant contact with Captain Sills at the 1/503d TOC. Sills was impressed with Tauss's cool demeanor on the radio. Because Connolly was busy overseeing the movement of his company, Sills relayed information to him through Tauss. Never once did Tauss get nervous or upset. He passed on messages between the two officers with precision and speed.

Sills's operations NCO, Sfc. Thomas A. Kelly, monitored the radios with particular concern. From May until late September Kelly had been a platoon sergeant in Charlie, 1/503d. He knew nearly every man in the company. News of the heavy casualties caused him great concern. If he could have, he would have boarded a helicopter himself and gone to help his buddies. But he couldn't. He was forced to sit helplessly in the TOC, listening with growing frustration to the sounds of the furious battle.

Captain McElwain stayed in constant radio contact with Connolly. As Connolly reported his progress, McElwain relayed the news to his men. The advance cheered the paratroopers. They knew that if Charlie, 4/503d, could break through the ring of NVA surrounding them, they'd survive.

Sergeant Bull and Specialist Atkins were the first to arrive at TF Black's laager site. Just as they entered the area an NVA opened fire from twenty meters away. The two men instantly dropped. Each threw a grenade. They failed to detonate; in their excitement they'd both forgotten to pull the pins.

Before they could throw another grenade, a pair of Chicoms plopped to the ground just meters in front of them. They went off with a roar. Neither man was hit. In response, they sprayed the jungle in front of them with M16 fire.

A short distance away another member of the point squad captured two NVA who were rifling the abandoned rucksacks. Bull saw them a few minutes later. They were very young and very, very scared.

Soon the rest of Connolly's 120-man force had assembled at the laager site. Below them, the sounds of heavy firing attested to the plight of TF Black. Connolly signaled his men to move toward the fight. The paratroopers started down the ridge finger, moving cautiously, darting from tree to tree.

The closer Connolly's company came to TF Black, the heavier the firing became. Several men fell, hit by enemy rounds. Connolly's advance ground to a halt just a hundred meters from McElwain's position.

Several times Connolly's company tried to continue, but each time a flurry of small-arms fire held them back. After repeated attempts to move were stymied, Connolly realized that most of the firing was coming from nervous members of TF Black. He radioed McElwain. Together the two captains coordinated Connolly's advance. McElwain would pass the word for his paratroopers to hold their fire at a certain time. Then Connolly's men would run down the slope into McElwain's perimeter.

When the word came the men of Charlie, 4/503d, jumped up from the ground and ran forward. Yelling and screaming, triggering short bursts from their weapons, they rushed headlong toward their comrades. Cries of "Geronimo! Airborne! First Batt, it's Fourth Batt! Move it! Move, MOVE, MOVE!" filled the air.

Within minutes the two forces had linked up. Joyous shouts of relief came from the trapped men. Sergeant Bull asked the first man he saw if he needed ammo. "Not as bad as the guys farther forward," the weary paratrooper answered. "Take it to them."

To continue the momentum of his company, Connolly sent them into position beyond TF Black's perimeter, which now measured barely fifty meters across. The fresh Sky Soldiers advanced boldly, spraying the jungle in front of them with M16 and M60 fire. The NVA started a fighting withdrawal.

The first member of Charlie, 4/503d, Lieutenant Brown saw was an Asian American NCO. The sergeant asked, "Who's in charge?"

"I am," Brown told him.

"Okay, here's some men. Let's get them in position."

Together, Brown and the NCO reinforced that sector of the perimeter. Brown's RTO, Specialist Linton, with obvious relief, said to him, "Looks like we'll make it, Charlie."

Brown good-naturedly chastised him. "Hey, it's *Lieutenant* Brown."

Once he had his men in position, Connolly sought out McElwain. Still under small-arms fire, Connolly moved in a crouch, staying as low as he could. Around him lay the debris of the fight. Here and there corpses lay in grotesque positions. Nearly all the men of TF Black still fighting seemed to have been wounded more than once. The more seriously wounded lay shoulder to shoulder at the aid station, lost in a maze of bloody bandages and torn limbs.

McElwain briefed Connolly on his situation and then turned over command of the combined force to him. They agreed to break the back of the NVA force by increased use of artillery. Connolly's FO, Lt. Michael Raymond, joined with Lieutenant Elrod to coordinate the artillery fire. Specialist 4th Class Duffy and Private 1st Class Haymes worked with them to call in range adjustments.

By 1530 the NVA fire had slackened enough to allow resupply choppers to drop in much needed water, rations, and ammo. Though the small-arms fire had noticeably decreased—McElwain figured the NVA were running low on ammo, too—there was little reduction in the enemy's mortar fire. Every few minutes the distinctive thunk of a mortar round leaving its tube could be heard. In the few seconds before the round detonated in the perimeter there'd be a mad scramble as everyone dove for cover.

Connolly's first sergeant, thirty-eight-year-old Edward Crook, a 1960 Olympics gold-medal boxer, rapidly dug a shallow hole near the CP. Just as he settled into it, a mortar round came crashing through the trees. Connolly hit the ground near Crook seconds before the round exploded.

Shrapnel tore through a stand of bamboo, spraying Connolly with so much water that he thought he'd been wounded and was bleeding. When he realized he was uninjured, he crawled back to his radio.

The same round sent a piece of shrapnel into Crook's right hand. He looked at the wound in amazement. To Captain Connolly, squatting a few feet away, he protested, "Geez, Captain, it's not fair. I'm in a hole and I get hit. You're not and you don't. It's just not fair!"

By 1545 the enemy fire had diminished to the point where Connolly decided to pull the force back to the more easily defended laager site. At his signal, everyone literally arose as one, going up the hill as a moving perimeter. Those paratroopers who were on the firing line would move in leaps, with one man providing covering fire while the others moved back. When they'd gone twenty meters or so they'd cover the other man's withdrawal.

Lieutenant Cecil's platoon had the worst time. Still in contact with the NVA, they were followed up the slope by the enemy soldiers, who fired at them every few minutes. Cecil's men crawled, snaking through the underbrush, dragging their wounded, returning the enemy's fire whenever they could.

McElwain and Connolly made the difficult decision to leave their dead behind. Carrying them out would only slow the movement and unnecessarily endanger the others.

The wounded of TF Black helped one another as best they could. Sergeant Wooldridge, with his shattered left knee, joined up with another paratrooper whose right foot had been blown off. Leaning on each other, they hobbled up the slope, ignoring the occasional enemy round that slapped into the trees near them.

Sergeant Scharf was rolled onto a poncho and carried uphill by four 4th Battalion Sky Soldiers. They kept telling him he'd be okay.

The artillery FOs called in a wall of howitzer fire behind the moving perimeter to prevent the NVA from following them. It worked. By the time the remnants of the three companies reached the old laager site, enemy fire had ceased.

The able-bodied Sky Soldiers and those with slight wounds took up firing positions around the new position, ready for a renewed assault. It never came.

Other soldiers worked feverishly to cut an LZ so that medevac choppers could get in for the wounded. One of the first helicopters in was Colonel Schumacher's. He darted in, loaded aboard the most seriously wounded, and headed back to Dak To. Only a few more medevacs made it in before darkness halted the activity. Sergeant Scharf made it out that night. Sergeant Wooldridge didn't. He and dozens of others had to spend a pain-wracked night on the hill. Captain McElwain and Lieutenants Brown and Cecil were tagged for evacuation but all three refused to leave.

One of the inbound choppers carried Capt. Thomas Needham, the 1/503d's S-2. He took command of Dog, 1/503d, and, because he was the senior captain, also took over TF Black. McElwain willingly gave up the responsibility; he had enough to do reorganizing his company.

Needham carried explicit orders from Colonel Schumacher regarding the two POWs: They were not to be harmed. His orders were timely. Once the enlisted men had settled in, a number of them began talking about avenging their fallen comrades by murdering the POWs. Only the direct intervention of the officers and NCOs prevented that from happening. Needham put an officer in charge of the prisoners, warning him that it would be his butt if any harm came to them.

The weary paratroopers spent a sleepless night, kept awake by the fear of another attack and the combined roar of artillery fire, mortar rounds, and Spooky gunships ringing the Sky Soldiers' position with a wall of protective fire.

Dawn on 12 November brought orders from Colonel Schumacher for McElwain to recover his dead, police up the battlefield, and get an enemy body count. First, though, McElwain reported his known casualties to Schumacher. TF Black had suffered 20 dead, 154 wounded, and 2 missing in action. Connolly's company had about 30 wounded with no dead.

The rest of the day was spent surveying the battlefield. To McElwain, his former perimeter looked like a garbage dump. Equipment was strewn everywhere. The nighttime artillery barrage not only had torn the landscape askew but had mutilated the bodies of both American and NVA dead. The paratroopers spent the rest of the day picking up the pieces of their buddies, collecting abandoned gear, and looking for the bodies of NVA.

Colonel Schumacher and Captain Sills arrived on the scene early in the morning. To Sills, the survivors of TF Black looked physically and mentally whipped. It was also obvious to him that McElwain was furious with Schumacher for what he felt was Schumacher's slow recognition of the seriousness of his situation. The two exchanged short, curt comments, and then Schumacher left, taking Sills with him.

At the end of the grisly day McElwain called the enemy body count into Schumacher at the TOC. By his estimates the bodies and body parts indicated that between seventy and eighty NVA had died in the fight.

Schumacher exploded with rage when he heard that figure. "Goddamnit, Captain, you lose twenty people and you expect me to accept a body count of seventy! You go back down there tomorrow and find me some bodies."

The next day the members of TF Black, with TF Blue, which had joined them the previous afternoon, spread out across the battlefield searching for more enemy bodies. The sweep extended nearly five hundred meters beyond the actual battle site. The Sky Soldiers discovered many blood trails, some of which led to shallow graves. Then the paratroopers had to perform the gruesome task of digging up the graves and removing the rotting bodies.

When McElwain reported to Schumacher that night that he'd found another forty bodies, the colonel was still not pleased. After listening to him rage for a while McElwain finally spoke out. "Jesus Christ, Colonel, what the hell do you want? My men are out there digging up fucking graves. Tell me what you want. What figure do you want? I'll tell you whatever you want to hear."

The two argued for a while longer, then finally settled on an enemy body count of 175. (McElwain would clash with Schumacher again a few weeks later when he submitted a recommendation for a decoration for Pfc. John Barnes's self-sacrifice. Schumacher refused to endorse the recommendation, telling McElwain and others he didn't think medals were for men "who committed suicide.")

Interrogation of the two POWs revealed that TF Black had fought the 8th and part of the 9th battalions of the NVA 66th Regiment, the same unit that had battered 4/503d a week earlier. Although the Sky Soldiers had undoubtedly inflicted heavier casualties on the enemy than the body count indicated, the 173d had paid a steep price for the damage done to the enemy.

On 13 November Charlie, 4/503d, was lifted off the hilltop and returned to Ben Het to take up security of FSB 12 and conduct road-clearing missions. According to the overall plan devised by General Schweiter and Colonel Powers, Colonel Schumacher's battalion would continue its patrolling. Because Charlie Company mustered only 40 able-bodied men and Dog about 50, Captain Jesmer, with about 110 men in Alpha Company, took command of the 1/503d's field force. Colonel Schumacher ordered Jesmer to head generally southwest, following the retreat of the NVA 66th Regiment. He'd be moving along the Ngok Kring mountain range, crossing Hill 889 while moving toward Hill 882, about three kilometers distant.

While the 1/503d had been policing its battlefield, the 2/503d had found another NVA regiment about four kilometers south-southwest of TF Black. In a vicious two-day fight, the 2/503d, facing its first major contact since 22 June, would end up as battered as its two sister battalions.

CHAPTER 10

BATTLE AT FSB 16

Bitter fighting continued to erupt at locations all around Dak To. While Captain McElwain's TF Black fought for its life, three companies from 3/8th Infantry, 4th Infantry Division, received a heavy mortar barrage at their laager site on the slopes of Hill 724. Beginning at 1307 and lasting for nearly thirty minutes, the enemy mortar shells seemed to pour out of the sky onto the hapless infantrymen. Then, while the paratroopers huddled in their holes, NVA soldiers stormed out of the surrounding jungle. By the time the fight ended at 1903, 18 Americans were dead, 118 wounded. The 4th Infantry Division soldiers claimed 92 dead NVA.

North of Dak To that same 11 November a work party of engineers, protected by Troop C, 2d Squadron, 1st Cavalry, was attacked by the NVA. The engineers lost two dead and eight wounded.

To help pinpoint NVA locations the 173d's LRRPs ran dozens of missions out of the Dak To airstrip. Every day a team was either coming in from a mission or going out on one. Specialist 4th Class Moran's team arrived at Dak To on 7 November, right after the fight for Hill 823. Within twenty-four hours they were being inserted into a small clearing somewhere near Dak To; they rarely knew where they were in relation to Dak To.

The patrol lasted two days. They found no sign of the NVA.

Even though the LRRPs couldn't find the enemy, General Peers's other available intelligence resources reported the continued movement of NVA units throughout the region. The NVA 32d Regiment had progressed westward in its running battles with the 4th Infantry Division. The NVA 24th

Regiment seemed to be holding its blocking position northeast of Dak To where it had occasional clashes with the ARVN.

What worried General Peers most, though, was the movement of the NVA 174th Regiment from its positions northwest of Dak To into the area south of Ben Het. Because the 173d had undoubtedly seriously hurt the NVA 66th Regiment in their series of clashes on and around Hill 823, Peers correctly surmised the NVA 174th had moved south to screen the 66th's withdrawal into Cambodia and to assume their positions on the battlefield. To counter that movement, and to block the route of the NVA 66th Regiment, General Peers directed General Schweiter to move his forces deeper into enemy territory.

General Schweiter and Colonel Powers crisscrossed the AO in their C-and-C choppers, searching for a suitable site from which to make the insertion. Their choices were limited due to the heavy jungle covering the numerous mountain peaks and ridges. By a process of elimination they selected an old fire support site used during Operation Greeley. The new FSB 16 would be on a twin-peaked hill five kilometers southwest of Hill 823 and just two kilometers southeast of Hill 882, the objective of 1/503d. Fire Support Base 16 sat on the west edge of the Dak Klong River valley and just seven kilometers east of the Cambodian border. Possession of this hilltop would give the 173d control of a vast area to the west and to the south.

Air Force F-100s, F-4s, and B-52s pounded the area around the new fire support base all day 10 November and during the early morning hours of 11 November. The combat assault had been scheduled for 0900 on 11 November; however, it was delayed until the afternoon because the Cowboys of the 335th Assault Helicopter Company were busy providing support to TF Black. At 1430 elements of Maj. James R. Steverson's 2/503d began landing at the site. Bravo and Dog companies, the tactical CP personnel, an 81mm mortar section, and a platoon from the 173d Engineer Company were on the ground within thirty minutes. All were pleased the LZ proved to be undefended.

The engineers went to work expanding the LZ for the rest of the battalion's arrival the next day. Before they had accomplished much, NVA lurking in the nearby hills started lobbing rockets and mortars into the LZ. The Sky Soldiers went to ground for the night.

At 0850 the next morning Alpha Company began arriving at the FSB. By 0920 the entire company was on the ground. While the choppers flew off to bring in Charlie Company, Bravo Company and the engineers went to work to prepare the FSB for the arrival of Battery A, 3/319th. While they were so occupied Alpha would push out of the FSB and sweep the high ground to the west clear of any enemy.

Alpha's commander was Capt. Michael J. Kiley, West Point class of 1964. A veteran of an earlier tour with the 1st Cavalry Division, Kiley had commanded Alpha less than two weeks but had already impressed his platoon leaders and the enlisted men with his exceptional leadership ability. Kiley was an aggressive, but not foolhardy, officer who took charge of any situation. He also had a charisma that added to his command presence.

Lieutenant Matt Harrison liked Kiley from the instant he met him. Upon Kiley's arrival Harrison moved up from platoon leader to executive officer. Kiley, however, asked, "Do you mind staying out here with the troops on this next op? They know you and that'll help them get used to me."

Harrison felt both disappointed and flattered. As XO he should be spending most of his time in the rear, safely handling the company's administrative needs. But Kiley had asked for his help, and rumor had it they'd be hitting some heavy stuff in the near future. Harrison's recent field experience would be very valuable.

"Of course I'll stay, Captain," Harrison responded.

Harrison would continue to run his platoon and handle some of the XO's duties until the current operation ended.

Alpha left FSB 16 at 0930 on 12 November. The company's permanent point squad led the way with Harrison's 1st Platoon following. Then came 2d Platoon under 1st Lt. Thomas Remington, Kiley's CP group, Weapons Platoon, and 1st Lt. Joseph Sheridan's 3d Platoon.

Moving with the point squad was a scout dog and its handler. Harrison didn't like using the dogs. As did Captain Jesmer, Alpha, 1/503d, he felt they were too nervous and gave too many false alerts.

Just before 1000, and about four hundred meters west of FSB 16, while ascending a narrow, jungle-covered ridge finger, the scout dog alerted. Sergeant Lance D. Peeples, the point squad leader, ordered the dog released. As the handler reached down to unsnap the leash, the NVA suddenly opened fire. A heavy volume of automatic-weapons and small-arms fire poured into the point squad from just twenty meters to their left. The point squad dove for cover, returning the NVA's fire.

In response to Peeples's call for help, Harrison deployed his platoon along the down slope of the south side of the finger, advancing until he was in line with Peeples's squad. Harrison signaled Peeples to move forward to a piece of higher ground.

The point squad made it less than five meters in the dense jungle before the sharp crack of AK-47s erupted from their right. Peeples went down, badly wounded.

Lieutenant Harrison tried to move forward and to his right in order to link up with the point squad, but the jungle to his left again erupted in a flurry of small-arms fire. Four of Harrison's men fell wounded. The rest took cover while the casualties were treated.

Captain Kiley responded to Harrison's plight by ordering Lieutenant Remington to move up on the right.

A twenty-four-year-old resident of central Florida, Remington had entered the army in June 1966 with an ROTC commission from the University of South Florida. He joined Alpha, 2/503d, as a replacement right after the Battle of the Slopes. He'd been in a couple of brisk firefights while on patrol near Tuy Hoa but nothing compared to this.

When Kiley ordered him to move out and establish a base of fire, Remington responded instantly. His platoon of about thirty men rushed forward, bounding from tree to tree. The farther Remington moved forward the heavier the firing became. Several of his men cried out in pain as NVA bullets plowed into them. Remington had no time to think of them; that was the medic's job. He just wanted to get into position to help Harrison and Peeples.

While Remington moved up, Kiley had Lieutenant Sheridan's 3d Platoon form the rear of his defensive perimeter. Weapons Platoon took up positions around Kiley's CP group.

Once the two forward platoons had settled into position, they laid down a furious base of fire, allowing the point squad to pull back about ten meters. After they'd reached safety Harrison signaled for a cease-fire. The jungle grew quiet.

Kiley, still intent on reaching his objective, now ordered Lieutenant Sheridan to take 3d Platoon forward and continue the advance while the two other platoons provided support. Sheridan, a twenty-four-year-old from Orlando, Florida, who'd been a platoon leader for only a few weeks, started his men out of the perimeter.

They made no more than ten meters when the jungle again exploded. This time, besides small-arms and machine-gun fire, grenades, RPGs, and recoilless-rifle fire shattered the jungle air. Two of Sheridan's men died instantly when a RR shell detonated in the tree behind them. Another six were hit by grenade fragments or small-arms fire.

The enemy fire engulfed the other two platoons, too. Lieutenant Harrison's platoon took several casualties when RPGs and hand grenades exploded with deafening crashes within his platoon. Remington's platoon suffered several more wounded from small-arms fire.

One of Remington's riflemen, Pfc. Manuel Orona, fired off magazines as fast as he could jam them into his M16. It seemed to him NVA fire was coming from everywhere. Orona, a twenty-year-old from Tucson, Arizona, had been in South Vietnam since August. When he'd joined Alpha he'd been teased by other paratroopers, being told he was going to "No Return Alpha." He wasn't sure exactly what that meant until he learned about Alpha's recent history. Only then did he realize that those assigned to Alpha weren't expected to reach their rotation date.

Lying behind a tree, firing clips, and listening to the snap of enemy rounds passing overhead in a constant buzz, Orona started thinking he might not make it. When the fighting intensified he felt the rise of panic. Calm down, he told himself. You don't want to let down your buddies. With that he returned to the battle.

While Lieutenant Harrison directed his platoon in the fight against the invisible NVA, Captain Kiley crept forward to his position. Harrison wasn't surprised to see his CO there. This was just like Kiley; rather than direct the fight from his CP he wanted to be up where the action was. Kiley asked, "What's going on?"

Harrison explained the situation. Then Kiley said, "Pull back."

Harrison ordered his platoon to begin a retrograde movement while Kiley moved off to give the same orders to Sheridan and Remington. Sheridan sent his men back while he stayed behind to recover two of his wounded. Only when assured that all his casualties had been recovered did Sheridan himself pull back.

Remington, too, helped cover his platoon's withdrawal. While he did so, the able-bodied among his platoon helped the wounded. Private 1st Class Orona picked up a wounded man and carried him down the ridge.

At 1053, while Alpha fought its way out of the ambush, Major Steverson ordered Bravo Company to dispatch one platoon to help Alpha. Lieutenant Phillip Bodine's 2d Platoon got the nod from Bravo's skipper, Capt. James P. Rogan.

Bodine and his platoon sergeant, Edward E. Kitchen, had the men moving in minutes. By 1110 they'd covered the two hundred meters separating the two units. Captain Kiley had, by this time, reestablished his company perimeter at its original location. When Bodine's platoon reached him, Kiley had them fill in the perimeter at the rear.

Lieutenant Bodine had just gotten his men into position when Alpha's outposts reported that the NVA were moving along both sides of the ridge finger. To avoid being surrounded and cut off, Kiley immediately ordered everyone to drop back about 150 meters. They all made it safely to the vicinity of a large bomb crater. There Kiley put his platoons in position and had the Weapons Platoon members start cutting an LZ for medevacs.

As Captain Kiley got his company settled down, sentries at Bravo's location, just a hundred or so meters to the east, opened fire when they detected movement within twenty meters of their position. At the sound of firing Rogan came running up to the position.

"Check fire! Hold your damn fire!" he shouted.

Rogan thought his men might be firing on members of Alpha who'd come all the way back to his position. The next few minutes passed quietly, then suddenly a burst of SKS fire erupted from a clump of bamboo just fifteen meters away. Before Rogan could yell the order, the men around him opened up. The enemy's fire increased tremendously. Rogan couldn't believe it—the NVA were between him and Alpha!

With only two platoons, less than sixty men, and unable to call in artillery or air strikes because he wasn't exactly sure where Alpha was located, Rogan was in a tight spot. He'd just started to think in terms of being overrun when the lead elements of Charlie Company came up behind him.

Major Steverson had wisely ordered Capt. Harold J. Kaufman's Charlie Company to reinforce his other two companies. Charlie linked up with Bravo at 1138. Together, the two companies put out a tremendous amount of firepower. In response, the NVA again used RPGs against the Sky Soldiers. Additionally, several B-40 rockets whizzed out of the bamboo to explode with horrendous blasts among the Americans.

One B-40 injured Bravo's first sergeant, Enrique Salas. A hard-as-nails, no-nonsense NCO on his second tour with the 173d, Salas had been with Bravo only a few weeks. Before that he'd been Lieutenant Remington's platoon sergeant in Alpha. Though short in stature, Salas had ruled that platoon with an iron fist. Even Remington stood in awe of him. Many of the young paratroopers would rather have faced a platoon of NVA alone than been on Salas's shit list. He was pure hardcore airborne trooper.

When the firing started at Bravo's forward position, Salas had just begun a C-ration breakfast. He tossed aside his food and raced after Captain Rogan. The first B-40 exploded near him, sending shrapnel into his left arm, left knee, and chin. Bleeding profusely, Salas nonetheless stayed in the fight, refusing to be evacuated until the end of the day.

Alpha Company had a respite of nearly thirty minutes, and then the NVA opened up again. This time only relatively light small-arms fire peppered the company's position—not enough to cause serious problems for the paratroopers but enough to keep away the medevacs.

Two F-100s arrived on station just after noon. Captain Kiley directed them to drop napalm and five-hundred-pound bombs uphill from his position. When they were done Kiley had artillery pound the jungle around him.

Light enemy firing continued sporadically until just after 1400. At 1410 Major Steverson ordered Bravo to move to Alpha's position while Captain Kaufman's Charlie pulled back to the FSB.

When Rogan joined Kiley at 1520, their first priority was the wounded. Able-bodied paratroopers worked frantically to cut down trees and bamboo to allow the lifesaving choppers in. The first medevac arrived at 1550. The dustoffs continued until nightfall, nearly ninety minutes later.

Alpha Company had suffered three KIA and twenty-four wounded, including Captain Kiley and Lieutenant Harrison, who both refused evacuation. Bravo had one man killed and eleven wounded. Captain Kaufman's Charlie Company suffered eight wounded.

At 1600 Kaufman sent out a platoon to sweep the area where they had fought with Bravo. The patrol uncovered five NVA bodies and five abandoned weapons.

Because the firing had completely died down, Lieutenant Harrison sent a squad from his platoon on a water resupply mission to a nearby stream just after 1600. Within ten minutes they were racing back into Alpha's night perimeter, yelling excitedly, "Look what we got! Look what we got!"

Being pulled along by two of the squad was a North Vietnamese soldier. Harrison immediately relayed the news to Captain Kiley and then joined the growing crowd around the POW. To Harrison, the enemy looked younger than his own teenaged soldiers. He appeared frightened, perhaps afraid his captors would execute him. Most impressive to Harrison was the NVA's fresh uniform and the newness of his weapon; it still had traces of Cosmoline on it. Harrison realized that the North Vietnamese Army had a far better supply system than he'd thought possible. This could mean we're in for a hell of a fight, he told himself.

Lieutenant Bodine's platoon was selected to escort the POW back to the FSB for evacuation. Once Bodine got to FSB 16 he turned the POW over to Captain Kaufman for safekeeping. Since Kaufman spoke some Vietnamese, he talked to the POW. In a short time Kaufman learned that the soldier was twenty years old, had been in the military for two years, and belonged to a company in the 4th Battalion, NVA 174th Infantry Regiment. His company and one other had been involved in that day's action. Before Kaufman could learn more, the S-1 people arrived to take the POW back to Dak To.

All remained quiet for the 2/503d's rifle companies through that night until 0430 on 13 November. At that time more than a dozen enemy mortar rounds dropped near both night defensive positions. Other than disturbing the Sky Soldiers' sleep, the rounds caused no damage, since none landed inside either perimeter.

After running clearing patrols the next morning, Alpha and Bravo companies returned to FSB 16, arriving there at about 0845. While their troops loaded up on ammo, rations, and water, Captains Kaufman and Rogan met with Major Steverson and the battalion S-3.

Steverson ordered his two companies to head north out of the fire support base, cross a little valley, and secure the next ridge, only three hundred meters away. Then the companies would turn left to follow that ridge to the west. This maneuver would allow them to reach their objective, an unnumbered hill less than a kilometer away. Steverson expected this move would bypass any other NVA positions west of the fire support base. Once in place his two companies would then act as a blocking force for the 1/503d force coming south from the vicinity of Hill 823. Steverson told the two captains they'd move out as soon as the air strikes and artillery (from FSB 15, since FSB 16 sat too close to the target area) finished prepping the area. The company's weapons platoons would remain at the FSB. Instead of mortars each company would carry a 90mm recoilless rifle; in a direct-fire role the rifles would be far more effective against prepared NVA positions than the mortars. Additional fire support was available in the form of two .50-caliber machine guns and five 81mm and four 4.2-inch mortars emplaced at FSB 16.

While Alpha and Bravo conducted their patrol, Charlie would secure the fire support base. Dog Company would conduct clearing patrols in the immediate area of the FSB.

At 1330 the two companies left the FSB. Rogan's Bravo had the lead, with Lieutenant McDevitt's 3d Platoon on point. Behind McDevitt came Rogan's CP and then the two other rifle platoons. Alpha Company followed Bravo, providing rear security.

By 1450 McDevitt had covered nearly three hundred meters up the ridge finger after making the turn to the west. So far neither he nor his men had seen any sign of the NVA. Then word came from the point man; he'd stumbled onto something. McDevitt went forward. Shortly, he was on the radio to Rogan reporting that his platoon had found five one-gallon cans of U.S.-manufactured CS gas crystals and an equal number of unexploded cluster bombs (from CBUs).

Rogan came back to McDevitt in a few minutes to tell him that Steverson had ordered gas masks on and the CS destroyed. By the time that task had been completed, several of McDevitt's men were ill from exposure to the crystals due to faulty masks. Rogan ordered Lieutenant Bodine's platoon to take over the point.

As Bodine continued up the ridge a sixth sense warned him that the NVA were near. His eyes expertly scanned the jungle for any sign of the enemy; they found none. At the point, the dog handler and his German shepherd, Brutus, moved forward confidently, giving no sign there were any NVA within miles.

Between Bodine and the point man walked Pfc. Mike Nale. He could barely concentrate on the search for NVA. At FSB 16 that morning he'd signed his leave papers for his R and R in Australia. In just a few more days he'd be on his way, out of this mess for a whole week.

Nale's two buddies, Sp4 Steve Varoli and Pfc. Doug Roth, walked nearby. Their eyes, too, constantly swept the terrain, alert for any sign of the NVA.

At 1545 Captain Rogan halted Bodine. He wanted to establish a night laager site. After looking over the area Rogan decided it was too narrow for a two-company position. He told Bodine to continue his trek and then radioed Kaufman to close on Bravo.

Bodine covered about two hundred more meters up the ridge before he found a suitable laager site. He spread out his platoon while he reconnoitered the area. As he did so the point man called out that he'd found two bunkers on the north slope of the ridge. Bodine moved toward that location. Before he reached the point man the jungle suddenly reverberated with the sharp reports of two shots from an AK-47. Second Platoon rushed to cover.

"Look into the trees for snipers," Bodine called out to his paratroopers. While they scanned the treetops Bodine radioed Rogan. He told his CO he wanted to fire the 90mm recoilless rifle into the bunker area. Rogan approved the request. He also told Bodine to secure the north edge of the area; he would send Lieutenant McDevitt's 3d Platoon forward to secure the south edge. First Platoon, under Lt. Paul Gillenwater (West Point class of 1966), would hold down the rear while tying in with Alpha. Neither Captain Rogan nor Captain Kaufman wanted to give the NVA any chance to get between them and separate the two units.

Back in Bodine's platoon Pfc. Charles A. Marshall, the 90mm's gunner, fired one canister round at a suspected NVA bunker. At the same instant that round detonated, the enemy opened fire. From dozens of undetected positions small-arms and automatic-weapons fire tore into the platoon.

While Marshall sighted on a second bunker, Sp4 Jimmy Tice slammed another round into the weapon's breech. Before giving Marshall the all clear signal, Tice yelled at Sp4 Robert L. Ross to check the backblast area. Ross looked at Tice but then fell over backward, shot through the head by an enemy sniper. Before Marshall could recover from the shock of seeing his friend die, a flurry of enemy grenades exploded around the gun. Marshall turned the weapon toward where he thought the grenades had come from and pulled the trigger. Then he crawled to Ross. No sooner had he reached his buddy than small-arms fire dug up the dirt around him. This time the AK-47 fire came from Marshall's rear! Marshall rolled behind Ross's body and, using his M16, fired into the tops of the bamboo plants to the southeast. The damn gooks seem to be everywhere, he thought.

During this exchange Lieutenant Bodine and his RTO had snaked their way toward where the point man had originally spotted the bunkers; no one had seen the paratrooper since the first two sniper rounds. If he lay out there wounded Bodine wanted to get him. The two men went about ten meters in that direction before several heavy bursts of RPD fire drove them back to cover.

Bodine felt warm liquid running down his face. He put his hand to his forehead. It came back covered with blood. He had no idea of when or how he'd been hit. A medic slapped a bandage on the wound.

Then Bodine called for a cease-fire; he couldn't tell how much firing was incoming and how much was outgoing. It took a few minutes for the word to reach all the platoon members, but soon all the firing had stopped. In the lull Bodine decided to look again for the point man.

When he reached the same spot as before, the firing started again, though much heavier in volume. Bodine sought refuge behind a tree. He grabbed the radio's mike from his RTO. As he started to call Rogan, the mike's cord suddenly went taut.

"C'mon, give me some slack," Bodine shouted to his RTO.

When he got no answer he looked around. The RTO lay on his back, blood gushing from a gaping bullet wound in his throat. Unwilling to admit the man was dead, Bodine started to pull him to cover while screaming for a medic.

Something made him look up. In a scene that would haunt him for years, Bodine saw three Chicom grenades arcing toward him across the blue sky. In apparent slow motion, the three deadly missiles tumbled end over end. Bodine tried to crawl into his helmet.

The grenades exploded with an ear-shattering roar. A sharp pain gripped Bodine's left leg. With no time to examine his wound he crawled to the center of his platoon, yelling for everyone to tighten up the perimeter.

The NVA were right behind Bodine. He fired his CAR-15 at them. After four rounds his weapon jammed. Just twenty meters away Bodine could see the NVA darting from tree to tree. Somewhere he found an M16 and fired off a clip at the enemy. That slowed them enough to allow Bodine to scramble for cover with Marshall, Tice, and several others behind a pile of logs.

One of the men, Sp4 Wayne P. Murray, had his M60 propped across the top of a log. It chugged heavily as he fired measured bursts up the ridge. Next to him Pfc. Willie J. Simmons threw grenades. Simmons popped up after one exploded, his M16 at the ready. Before he could squeeze the trigger he took a round between the eyes. Murray reached for him. An NVA round drilled him in the chest. Marshall tried to bandage the wound, but Murray died before he could tear open the medical packet.

To Bodine's left front Private 1st Class Nale had found refuge behind a teak log. All alone, with most of the rest of the company behind him, Nale laid his M16 on top of the log and sprayed the jungle in front of him with fire. He'd gotten off several magazines when he heard someone call for a medic. As he turned to see who'd been hit, a B-40 rocket exploded right behind him.

The deafening blast blew Nale up and over his protective log, dropping him behind a large anthill; blood poured from several large holes in his left arm. He tried to crawl back over the log, but a sniper's round plunked onto the jungle floor next to him. Instead, he pulled himself into a tight ball at the base of the anthill. The earthen mound protected most of his body, but he couldn't get his legs under cover. Several of the sniper's bullets zipped into his position, cutting across the backs of his legs. He couldn't get a clear shot at the sniper without dangerously exposing himself, and he couldn't get up to jump back behind the log. He was trapped.

Not far away Sp4 Steve Varoli saw the blast that tossed Nale over the log. He didn't think his friend could have survived such a blast. Varoli turned to report Nale's death to Pfc. Doug Roth when he felt a sharp blow to his head. He passed out.

B-40 rockets continued to slam into the tiny perimeter. Their distinctive whoosh as they sailed downhill gave the paratroopers ample warning of their arrival, but a large number of Sky Soldiers still fell victim to their blasts.

By this time Lieutenant McDevitt had worked his platoon into positions along the southern edge of the ridge. B-40 rockets occasionally flashed out of the jungle uphill to explode among McDevitt's men. One erupted in a thick stand of bamboo near McDevitt. Sharp slivers of the plant ripped his skin, sending rivulets of blood coursing down his face and arms. The dozens of razorlike cuts hurt like crazy, but there was no turning back for McDevitt. "Go! Go!" he urged his men.

Rogan constantly radioed McDevitt. "Watch for snipers in trees," he warned. McDevitt had his men rake the stands of bamboo from top to bottom with M60 fire. Several times the gunners were rewarded when snipers fell from their perches.

At Lieutenant Bodine's position several B-40 rockets exploded right in front of his protective log. Sure that the blasts must have eliminated the Americans, the NVA charged headlong at the position. To their eternal surprise, Bodine, Tice, and Marshall all popped up from behind the log and mowed them down with sweeping bursts of M16 fire.

By this time Captain Rogan had advanced to within twenty meters of Bodine's position. The jungle was so thick, though, that he couldn't see any of Bodine's men. He tried numerous times to raise Bodine on the radio but had no luck; he had no way of knowing that Bodine's RTO was dead and the spare radio was shot full of holes. Needing to know more about the situation, Rogan yelled forward for Bodine to get on the radio. Instead, Bodine sent a runner back to Rogan.

Specialist Varoli had regained consciousness by this time. An NVA sniper round had hit him right in the helmet. The round shattered, pieces of the slug embedding themselves in his skull. But he didn't have time to worry about himself. Private 1st Class Roth had been hit in the legs six different times. Varoli bandaged him and then reloaded his M60. With Roth spotting targets Varoli blazed away at them.

At one point more than a dozen NVA suddenly burst from cover to charge directly at Varoli and Roth. Disregarding the rounds striking near him, Varoli knelt in the open, the M60 cradled under his arm, a belt of ammo trailing into the dirt beside him.

With a cigarette dangling from his mouth, Varoli swung his machine gun back and forth. "C'mon, you fuckers. I'm ready for you. C'mon!" he yelled.

Varoli continually exposed himself, ignoring the deadly fusillade of fire to cut down the NVA wherever he saw them.

Not far away, Private 1st Class Nale was still pinned down. He had pulled several grenades from his pouch, placing them within reach. If the NVA rushed him he'd take as many of them with him as he could. He wouldn't sell his life cheaply.

But he wouldn't have to. Several members of McDevitt's platoon had now reached his position. While they laid down a base of fire two other men pulled Nale through a small depression under the logs. Rather than seek evacuation because of his wounds, Nale stayed on the firing line. A little later one of his platoon's NCOs, Sergeant Funderburk, finally killed the sniper that had caused Nale so much trouble.

The fight had been raging for nearly an hour with no sign of a letup. Captain Rogan had coordinated the use of artillery and air strikes against the NVA, but the enemy were too close to Bodine's platoon to be affected by ordnance since they couldn't be targeted without endangering U.S. troops. At 1700 Major Steverson and his battalion artillery liaison officer boarded a chopper and flew over the battle site, hoping to be able to bring the artillery in closer. As usually happened in the Central Highlands, though, they found the jungle canopy too thick to give them more than occasional glimpses of the ground.

At FSB 16 the cannoneers of Battery A lowered the muzzles of their 105s as far as possible. They fired point-blank into the neighboring ridge, not more than four hundred meters distant. The .50-caliber machine guns would have added their deadly punch to the fight, but the inability to accurately pinpoint Bravo's position rendered the devastating weapons nearly useless.

The NVA continued to apply heavy pressure on Lieutenant Bodine's forward positions. From distances of less than twenty meters they poured a horrendous volume of fire at the paratroopers. Numerous snipers made any movement a deadly adventure. Every few minutes a B-40 rocket flashed through the jungle to explode on impact with a tree, a bamboo clump, or a human body.

Bodine knew he couldn't hold his forward position much longer; he had too many casualties. He'd have to pull back and tie in more tightly with the rest of the company. He passed the word: "Withdraw. Make sure you get all the wounded." Since all his radios had been destroyed in the fighting, Bodine wanted to find Rogan, advise him of his decision, and receive further instructions.

Bodine rose from his position on the ground. As he started to turn, a sniper's bullet tore into his right buttock. He realized with a start that the NVA were moving in behind him. The vivid memories of the carnage inflicted on Alpha Company in June flashed through Bodine's mind: He had no intention of being caught up in such a massacre.

Ignoring the pain in his hip, Bodine hobbled through the thick jungle, intent on finding Rogan. To his surprise he found his CO just twenty meters to his rear. He hadn't realized how close Rogan was to him.

After hearing Bodine's situation, Rogan concurred with his decision to withdraw. He radioed McDevitt and received his assurance he could safely pull back. Then, as he turned back to Bodine a B-40 rocket exploded against a nearby tree.

Bodine slammed violently into the ground. Shrapnel ripped holes in his back and right arm. Conscious but in great pain, Bodine saw that Rogan's two RTOs and Bravo's senior medic had been killed in the blast. Rogan had received minor shrapnel wounds but was still functioning.

Bodine initially tried to return to his embattled platoon but was too badly wounded to do so. Against his protests someone pulled him to the aid station.

Captain Rogan stripped a radio from the body of one of his RTOs. "November Six," he called to McDevitt, "fall back on me." Before he could repeat the order to Bodine's platoon, McDevitt radioed back that now he couldn't move. The firing was just too heavy and the NVA too close.

In Bodine's absence Sergeant 1st Class Kitchen had taken over the platoon. He crawled up to Private 1st Class Nale's position and asked, "Do you know where the gooks are?"

"Shit yeah, Sarge. The bastards are everywhere," Nale replied.

And they were. They were so close that at one place on the perimeter six dead paratroopers lay on one side of a log. On the other were six dead NVA, one an officer still clutching an M16 he'd snatched from the Americans' side of the log.

Kitchen got word back to Rogan that nearly every man in 2d Platoon was dead or wounded. He had to have help if he were to hold.

Rogan then radioed Captain Kiley. He not only needed Alpha to close up but he needed one of its platoons. Kiley sent Lieutenant Remington's platoon forward to Rogan's position.

When Remington reached Bravo, Rogan had him join with Lieutenant Gillenwater's platoon to push out to the right and restore that flank. Once that was done 2d Platoon's casualties could be recovered.

Though they'd never worked together before, Gillenwater and Remington succeeded in counterattacking beyond Bravo's forwardmost position. Their bold advance startled the NVA, who pulled back up the hill. In this lull McDevitt's

3d Platoon and Bodine's 2d Platoon pulled back to Rogan's position. Most of the wounded were brought out, but the heavy undergrowth meant that several were overlooked.

Private 1st Class Nale was one of those. He spent the night behind his log, throwing grenades at the sounds of marauding NVA rather than firing his rifle and revealing his position.

Even though Alpha and Bravo had joined forces, the NVA continued their efforts to overwhelm the Americans. Taking advantage of the lack of American air and artillery support, the NVA crept down the sides of the ridge finger to harass the Sky Soldiers with small-arms and automatic-weapons fire from all directions. The paratroopers responded by throwing grenades at the NVA. Soon, however, ammo started to run low.

Captain Rogan radioed for an emergency resupply of ammo. It was nearly dark when, at 1845, two Hueys appeared overhead. Under a clear sky, Rogan courageously moved into an open area and signaled the choppers to drop the ammo. As the first chopper did, a flurry of NVA automatic-weapons fire raked the ship. Hydraulic fluid squirted from severed lines. Two crew members were shot. The pilot turned toward Dak To, escorted by the second ship.

Fortunately, the ammo load had dropped right on target. Eager hands quickly snatched up the ammo and grenades and carried them back to the firing line.

With more than two dozen wounded crowded into the center of the perimeter, Rogan knew that he had to get them out to safety and treatment. He requested a dustoff. At 2000 a chopper appeared above the perimeter. As it started its descent the surrounding jungle exploded with NVA automatic-weapons fire. Badly damaged, the medevac limped back to Dak To.

The wounded would have to remain on the ground overnight. Although the medics did their best, several of the wounded died before morning.

The NVA probed the perimeter all night. At dawn's first

light Rogan sent out small patrols to look for missing Americans. Several were found. One Sky Soldier killed an NVA soldier caught rifling the pockets of an unconscious American.

Private 1st Class Nale was rescued when two paratroopers armed with M60s suddenly appeared beside him. While they laid down a base of covering fire he scampered into the perimeter.

Specialist Varoli, lying among the wounded, reacted with surprise when he saw Nale. "You're not dead!" he exclaimed.

"Of course not, you dumb fuck. Do I look like a ghost?" Nale chided his friend.

Nale felt a tremendous sense of euphoria at having survived the vicious fight. With all that he'd seen during the previous eighteen hours he couldn't believe that he'd made it. His R and R to Australia was forgotten; he was just glad to be alive.

Once assured that all the wounded had been recovered, Captains Rogan and Kiley moved their companies nearly three hundred meters east. From this new position, centered on a large bomb crater, the evacuation of the wounded finally began.

Beginning at 0900, and lasting for several hours, medevacs flew in and out of the bomb crater, ferrying the wounded to the security and comfort of the battalion aid stations.

Father Watters flew out to the battle site on one of the first medevac choppers. He knew there were hurt paratroopers out there, and he could help comfort them. Not everyone felt he should go. As Watters boarded a chopper both Father Peters and Sergeant Major Rogiers tried to dissuade him.

"Don't go out there, Charlie," Father Peters begged. "There's still fighting going on. We don't know where the NVA are."

Watters disregarded the warning. "My boys are hurt," he told his two friends. "They need me. I couldn't stay here knowing that. I belong out there."

With that, Watters signaled the pilot that he was ready. As Peters and Rogiers stepped back, the Huey's turbines raced to a scream. The long rotor blades whirled faster and faster. A few minutes later the chopper was gone. Peters never saw his friend again.

Specialist Varoli didn't want to be evacuated, but Captain Rogan took one look at him and ordered him back to FSB 16 for treatment. While he waited for the medevac, Varoli saw Father Watters working with the wounded. The priest moved confidently among the torn paratroopers, calming them with words of assurance. If there was anyone who inspired the Sky Soldiers, Varoli thought, it was Father Watters.

Bravo Company had been badly hurt in the fight. Twenty-one of its members were killed and seventeen wounded; most of the casualties had occurred in Lieutenant Bodine's platoon.

While the medevac operation continued, Dog Company left FSB 16 and joined Alpha and Bravo. Charlie Company, which had fought three small skirmishes with NVA just outside the fire support base that same night, moved onto the FSB to take over security duties.

All during the morning of 14 November, Captain Rogan directed air strikes, artillery fire, and 4.2-inch mortar fire on suspected NVA positions. At 1300 all three companies swept up the ridge, with Bravo in the center, Alpha on the left, and Dog on the right. They pushed through the previous day's battle site and advanced several hundred meters beyond that point before returning to it to set up a night defensive position.

On the sweep the paratroopers found thirty-four NVA bodies and more than twenty enemy weapons. The next day Alpha and Bravo continued searching the area while Dog cut an LZ and loaded up the weapons. Alpha fired on several groups of NVA seen running through the jungle. Bravo captured one badly wounded NVA.

On 16 November Bravo returned to FSB 16 while Charlie replaced it in the field. The three companies continued search-and-destroy operations in the area about fifteen hundred meters southwest of FSB 16 and a thousand meters north of Hill 875.

Three kilometers to the north, elements of the 1/503d continued pushing south, bearing on their objective, Hill 882.

CHAPTER 11

BATTLE AT HILL 882

Correspondents were pouring into Dak To in unprecedented numbers. Word of the brutal battles being fought by the 4th Infantry Division and the 173d Airborne Brigade in the rugged Central Highlands spread rapidly among the reporters and photographers covering the war in South Vietnam. Boarding C-130s and resupply helicopters, some ninety correspondents, male and female, from France, England, Japan, Germany, South Vietnam, and the United States made their way to the Dak To airstrip. From there they descended upon the 4th Infantry Division's Public Information Office demanding to join units in the field where they could get their stories.

And there were plenty of stories to be had.

Some of the less adventurous correspondents who stayed at the Dak To airstrip got a closer look at the war than they may have wanted. On the night of 12 November the NVA launched the first of many rocket attacks on the airstrip. From well-concealed positions in the hills around the American enclave, forty-four missiles were fired. Fortunately, only two Americans were slightly wounded and three vehicles damaged. Sporadic mortar and rocket fire continued to hit the base the next few nights, causing only minor damage.

At 0845 on 15 November the NVA dumped a dozen mortar rounds on the airstrip. This time they were much luckier. Three C-130s received direct hits. One was slightly damaged, but the other two erupted in huge balls of flame. The nearly full fuel tanks on the two transports burned furiously for hours, the intense heat driving off several attempts to douse the fire. Finally, someone decided to just let them burn.

Beginning at 1549 that afternoon, and continuing for two hours, seventy-eight mortar rounds and rockets fell on the airstrip. This time the NVA were even luckier. Several of the rounds landed in the ammunition supply area. Fires broke out, and ordnance started exploding. Soon, nearly the entire ammo storage area was engulfed in roaring flames. Explosion after explosion thundered across the base. Men searched frantically for cover as shrapnel filled the air. Those who found refuge in open trenches faced further peril as flaming debris fell from the sky.

At 1715 a seven-hundred-pound cache of TNT blew up with a tremendous roar. Lieutenant Fred Drysen witnessed the blast. "I thought, Jesus!" he said. "It looked like Charlie had gotten hold of some nuclear weapons."

The towering flames burned through the night, casting a shimmering light across the entire base. The incredible display of exploding pyrotechnics—flares and colored signal rockets—added a festive air to the event for those not endangered by the falling debris. When the fire died down the next morning, it was found that, miraculously, only three Americans and three ARVN had been wounded. However, more than eleven hundred tons of ordnance were destroyed. Replenishment of the ammo would present General Rosson with his biggest logistical headache of the war. Supply depots throughout South Vietnam were scoured for spare ammo. Top priority was given to all ammo-bearing flights inbound to Dak To. Several times in the upcoming weeks the availability of ammo neared the critical stage, but General Rosson's superior ability to get the job done prevented any serious shortages for the troops in the field. With the near-constant enemy contacts being made by the 173d, any lack of ammo supplies could have meant a serious disaster.

On the morning of 15 November 1967, Capt. David Jesmer led his Alpha, 1/503d, southwest from the site of TF Black's battle, venturing farther into the forbidding hills. Since arriving at the scene of Captain McElwain's fight, Alpha had helped scour the surrounding area, searching for any overlooked American casualties as well as NVA dead or wounded.

Once Colonel Schumacher was convinced there was nothing more to be gained by remaining in the area, and under some pressure from deputy brigade commander Col. John J. Powers, he ordered Jesmer to move to Hill 882, about three kilometers to the southwest. Intelligence reports indicated that the NVA were operating in that vicinity. Also, the 2/503d's fight on 12–13 November convinced General Schweiter he was tightening the noose on the NVA.

Behind Alpha Company came Captain Needham's Dog Company with about fifty men. In the trail position was Captain McElwain's Charlie Company with no more than forty men. The first day's march was uneventful, though frequent signs of the enemy were found. Jesmer felt sure he was on the trail of survivors of TF Black's fight.

The next morning Jesmer ordered Lt. Ed Robertson's 2d Platoon to take the point for the move across Hill 889. Progress through the tropical forest was slow as Robertson's men moved in measured leaps, following cloverleafing teams. The accompanying scout dog alerted several times, but no NVA were spotted. Both Jesmer and Robertson began to doubt the effectiveness of the dog.

At 1145 Robertson's point man spotted an NVA soldier moving into position behind a thick stand of bamboo some distance ahead of him. He instantly triggered a burst from his M16. The resulting NVA return fire sent everyone scrambling for cover. AK-47, SKS, and RPD fire shattered the hillside.

Following Jesmer's SOP, Robertson's platoon spread out to the right, as 1st Platoon under Lt. John Robinson took up fighting positions on the left. Lieutenant Larry C. Kennemer's 3d Platoon secured the rear while Lt. David Holland's Weapons Platoon hastily set up 60mm mortars.

The volume of enemy fire surprised Holland. Rounds snapped through the trees, forcing the soldiers to keep their heads down. Soon, though, he had mortar rounds soaring skyward to crash behind the NVA.

Captain Jesmer instantly reported the contact to Schumacher and then requested that air and artillery suppressive fire be laid on the NVA. Within minutes the heavy karump of

105mm shells could be heard in the jungle ahead of Alpha. A short time later jets were overhead adding their five-hundred-pound bombs and napalm canisters to the rain of destruction falling on the enemy.

While waiting for the fast movers, Robertson's platoon continued to take heavy small-arms fire and grenades. Though none of his men had been hit, Robertson was frustrated at his inability to dislodge the NVA.

"Damnit, Captain," he radioed back to Jesmer one time, "the fucking gooks are in trenches and nothing we do gets to them."

At first, Jesmer didn't believe Robertson about the trenches. Then, 1st Sgt. Samuel Duckett got his attention and pointed uphill. Through a break in the bamboo and trees they could see an enemy soldier appear out of a trench and toss grenades at four of Robinson's men lying behind a log.

"I'll be damned," Jesmer said.

In the rear, Captain McElwain wondered what the delay was all about. He'd monitored Jesmer's radio report to Schumacher that he'd been held up by enemy fire, including B-40 rockets, but couldn't hear any rockets. He radioed Jesmer. "Why aren't we attacking?" he asked.

"Too much fire," Jesmer responded. "We'll wait for the heavy stuff to do its job before we attack."

McElwain didn't think the enemy firing seemed that heavy, but he couldn't override Jesmer.

Under the pounding of artillery and aerial bombs, the NVA pulled out, leaving the battlefield at about 1400. Once the firing had ceased, Robertson cautiously pushed his men forward. Within fifteen meters of their positions they came upon the first of the NVA trenches.

As Alpha moved farther into the abandoned NVA position, Jesmer was shocked at what they found. At least three ten-by-ten-by-ten-foot command bunkers were dug fifteen feet into the hillside, with bamboo-reinforced steps leading to their entrances. They had withstood unscathed the blast of the bombs and the napalm. Jesmer's men also found a number of 122mm rocket launchers constructed of bamboo slats.

He now knew where the rockets that had periodically fallen on Hill 823 had originated.

The paratroopers found numerous pools of fresh blood and several blood trails but no bodies. While Jesmer was calling in his findings to Colonel Schumacher, one of his enlisted men ran up to him and said, "Cap'n, come see what we've found."

Jesmer followed the excited paratrooper to a spot just outside the base camp. There a small knot of paratroopers were examining a 12.7mm antiaircraft gun.

"We found it under this tree the bombs knocked down, Captain," one of the sergeants said. "We also found him." The sergeant pointed to the corpse of a North Vietnamese soldier entangled in the branches of the tree.

"I figure he was a sniper killed when a bomb blew this tree down," said the sergeant.

Jesmer agreed. Fortunately, the tree had fallen on the gun, rendering it useless. If it had been used against his force, it could have been devastating. Jesmer called for a chopper to retrieve the weapon before nightfall.

Sergeant Joseph S. Mescan, Alpha's senior medic, had nothing to do since the company had taken no casualties during the fight, so he snapped several photographs of the antiaircraft gun and the men gathered around it. A tough little twenty-two-year-old from Columbia Station, Ohio, Mescan had been a championship wrestler in high school and still had the physique to prove it. A very gung-ho youngster, he'd enlisted in the army in July 1965 hoping to get sent to South Vietnam right away. But that wasn't to be. He spent nearly two years at Fort Bragg before he received his orders to the war. Mescan was assigned to Headquarters Company, 1/503d. He was temporarily attached to whatever line company had a need for a medic for any reason, such as combat loss, R and R, or rotation. As a result, he spent time in several companies but never got to know the men very well. He'd been with Alpha only since it had returned to Dak To and knew only Captain Jesmer and several of the senior NCOs. When he finished taking his pictures, he joined the others from Jesmer's headquarters group in preparing their night positions.

At about this time Jesmer received word from battalion headquarters that his column would be joined that evening, via the resupply choppers, by a number of correspondents. Jesmer didn't object to their presence but did not like the added responsibility of caring for civilian reporters when contact was imminent.

The choppers brought rations, water, ammo, and other supplies out to the 1/503d's position before dark. To Jesmer's surprise nearly a dozen correspondents piled off the Hueys. There was an NBC camera team, several newspaper reporters, a five-man still- and motion-picture team from the Department of the Army Special Projects Office, a photographer and an interviewer from the U.S. Army, Vietnam, Public Information Office, and a free-lance female correspondent.

Jesmer refused to let one correspondent, Jack Laurence of CBS, join his column. He felt that Laurence's reports on America's efforts in South Vietnam did not accurately reflect the truth. So when Jesmer found out that Laurence was among the correspondents, he ordered him back on the chopper.

Jurate Kazickas, a twenty-four-year-old former schoolteacher from New Rochelle, New York, had given up her secure job in the States to report on the war in South Vietnam. Since arriving in-country in spring 1967, she had spent most of her time with the marines fighting below the DMZ. When the fighting there died down around early November, she headed to Dak To.

Kazickas was the first "round-eye" female the Sky Soldiers had seen in months. In those pre-feminist-movement days, the paratroopers, almost to a man, believed the field was no place for a woman. Fighting was a man's job; women didn't belong in a war. But she was there, and there wasn't a thing they could do about it. Most tried to ignore her, very self-conscious about their filthy appearance.

At first light the next day, 17 November, the three companies continued their pursuit of the NVA. Jesmer had concluded that the enemy he'd engaged the previous day were once again nothing more than a stay-behind force ordered to delay his advance while the main unit made good its escape. That meant there was a large group of NVA somewhere ahead of him. He had no doubt he'd hurt them and they were burdened with wounded. He planned to stay hot on their trail until he found them.

Throughout that day Jesmer's column found repeated signs of the fleeing North Vietnamese. Several times they found discarded blood-soaked bandages. It was obvious the enemy was no more than eight hours ahead of the paratroopers. To harass them Jesmer had artillery blast five hundred meters ahead of his route.

For a laager site that night Jesmer selected an LZ his troops had cut in July when they'd been humping that same area. Ahead of them lay the mass of Hill 882. This, too, was familiar to Jesmer, since that was where Alpha Company had been bivouacked when he took it over. There'd been no sign of the NVA then, but Jesmer had a feeling that would not be the case now.

At 0730 on 18 November, Alpha started out of the laager site; Dog Company and Charlie Company followed in that order. Lieutenant Robinson's 1st Platoon had the point. Behind it came 2d Platoon, then Jesmer's command group, Lieutenant Kennemer's 3d Platoon, and finally Lieutenant Holland's Weapons Platoon. Not more than fifty meters behind the latter came Captain Needham's point squad.

Because of the threat of contact, Robinson's platoon screened forward about a hundred meters and then cloverleafed back, sweeping the sides of the ridge they moved along. Once assured the area was clear, Robinson radioed back for the rest of the company to move forward. This accordionlike movement was slow but safe.

About five hundred meters from their laager site the point squad came across a slit trench. Its bottom was covered with bloody bandages, still damp. It was estimated they were only two to three hours old. The enemy had to be close.

Five hundred meters farther, just after noon, the column arrived at the base of a finger leading to the summit of Hill 882. Jesmer put his force into a large perimeter and then summoned Robinson. "Take your platoon to the top of the hill on a recon," Jesmer told him. "If you run into trouble fall back on the rest of the force."

Robinson's platoon started up the finger at about 1315. Thick underbrush and numerous stands of bamboo hampered their progress. While Jesmer waited nervously for a report from Robinson, he was approached by Jurate Kazickas.

"Will we see any enemy today?" she asked.

He told her he thought there was a pretty good chance of that happening. Then 1st Sergeant Duckett approached. The platoon's commo sergeant, a youngster named Sandstrom, had written a poem about Alpha Company. He'd started it in the summer while they were laagered on Hill 882. He'd just finished it the night before; he wanted the captain to read it. Jesmer did so, hastily, and returned it to Duckett. "Very nice," he commented.

Duckett then started telling Jesmer about a strange dream he had had the night before. He'd seen a B-40 rocket flashing over a hill at him. That's all he remembered.

Robinson's platoon, in the meantime, had crested Hill 882 at about 1400. They soon found several strands of commo wire running across the hill. Robinson ordered his platoon into a defensive perimeter. At the same time, he sent his point squad forward to recon the area.

Private 1st Class Steven Suth, an M60 gunner, with his two assistants, Privates 1st Class Brown and Hale, crept out into the jungle. Within meters Suth spotted a sole NVA soldier to the south of the hill, along a trail. Brown fired at the man with his M16. The enemy soldier jumped behind a thick clump of bamboo. Suth stepped forward. He shredded the bamboo with a long burst from his M60. The North Vietnamese tumbled into a ravine.

At the same time that Jesmer heard the firing, Robinson radioed him. "I got commo wire and gooks," he reported.

Some sixth sense warned Jesmer a big fight was coming. He made a decision. "Saddle up," he yelled. "We're going forward."

Alpha, followed by Dog and Charlie, double-timed up the ridge. The path first descended into a shallow ravine and then ascended again. As Jesmer ran up the hill he was startled to see bamboo-reinforced steps cut into the earth. *Jesus, what have we got here?* he thought.

While the rest of the force advanced toward Robinson, he had sent three of his men to find the dead enemy soldier. They couldn't find the corpse but did find a series of bunkers, commo wire running in and out of each one. They followed a strand of wire toward the west.

A short time later they spotted a squad of NVA not thirty meters away. They turned and raced back to the perimeter.

Robinson had just started explaining his situation to the newly arrived Jesmer when the patrol ran into the perimeter. "We got gooks! Gooks!" they yelled.

Everyone dove for cover, some of the Sky Soldiers jumping into fighting holes left over from the summer. Robinson's platoon held the west side of the hill, most of his men being about fifty meters from the rest of the company. Kennemer's men took up positions along the southwest side of the hill; Robertson's platoon covered the southeast side. On the north, at an old LZ, Holland set up his mortars. Across from him, on the other side of the LZ, Charlie and Dog companies went to ground.

And none too soon.

Within a minute after everyone had taken cover, a single shot rang out. Five feet from Suth a paratrooper fell dead, shot in the head.

"Snipers in the trees," someone called.

With that the entire jungle around Alpha Company exploded in a cacophony of sounds. Small-arms and automatic-weapons fire crashed down on the paratroopers. Lieutenant Robinson counted a dozen machine guns firing at him. NVA mortar rounds broke through the trees in their downward flight, to explode with a sharp crash among the paratroopers. The deep bark of a .50-caliber machine gun could be heard above the other explosions.

From his position at the base of a wide tree, Jesmer glanced over at 1st Sergeant Duckett, crouched behind another tree just ten feet away. At that instant a B-40 rocket flashed between the two men and exploded against a tree farther behind them. Jesmer couldn't believe that Duckett's dream had come true.

One of the first casualties in Lieutenant Robinson's platoon was his medic. As the number of wounded mounted rapidly, the plaintive cry, "Medic!" went out.

Near Captain Jesmer's position Sergeant Mescan heard the call. Without a thought for his own safety, the gutsy medic sprang to his feet and ran forward through the jungle. When he reached Robinson's platoon, a rifleman he didn't know pointed to a figure lying in the grass underneath a tree. The fallen Sky Soldier had taken a sniper's round in the head. A large piece of his skull lay alongside his ear, hanging by a thin flap of skin. Mescan could clearly see the man's brain through the opening.

Aware he couldn't treat the man there due to the heavy volume of enemy fire, Mescan slung the casualty over his shoulder and headed back to his former position. At five feet five inches and 130 pounds, Mescan struggled under the weight of a man a good six inches taller and 50 pounds heavier. He stumbled through the heavy foliage, greatly concerned that he might be shot by his own men. That didn't happen, and Mescan soon reached the command group, where other medics had already set up an aid station.

Mescan gently put the piece of skull back in place and then wrapped the man's head in bandages. More casualties were drifting back to the aid station as the firing continued unabated. Mescan busied himself treating the other wounded.

On the firing line Lieutenant Kennemer couldn't believe the boldness of the NVA. In groups as large as thirty they came up the slight slope, bounding from cover to cover. Once they hit the ground their clever camouflage—branches and twigs entwined on their uniforms and helmets—made them nearly impossible to see. Only the blasts of their weapons parting the underbrush revealed their location. Under Kennemer's intrepid leadership 3d Platoon beat off the first wave of attackers.

Snipers continued to take a fearful toll of the paratroopers. From their treetop perches they looked right down on top of the Sky Soldiers. No position seemed safe.

Around Jesmer's position most of the men were firing skyward, trying to hit a sniper who'd caused several casualties. Even the artillery FO, Lt. Sherman E. Watson, had propped himself against a tree where he blazed away with his twelve-gauge shotgun.

"Knock that off, Watson," Jesmer ordered. "Get on the radio and get some artillery in here."

Then Jesmer called for those around him to hold their fire. "You're just wasting ammo. Don't fire unless you've got a target."

The sniper fired again. Sergeant Mescan scanned the treetops. He saw movement and fired a few rounds. He missed. The sniper got off another round, hitting a wounded man. This time Mescan saw the muzzle blast. He fired the rest of his magazine into a treetop seventy-five feet away. Mescan's aim was true. To his immense satisfaction the lifeless sniper fell from his lair. The corpse landed square on the barrel of a machine gunner's M60. ("That scared the shit out of me," the man told Mescan later.)

At Lieutenant Holland's position his mortar men were busy returning sniper fire, too. Holland hadn't fired the mortars yet because, two days earlier, Captain Jesmer had chewed him out for using the weapons before he'd wanted them. So Holland kept himself busy locating snipers for his men. He also made several trips back to Captains Needham and McElwain to make sure they knew where his people were and wouldn't accidentally shoot at them.

From its position behind Alpha, Captain Needham's Dog Company was taking mostly sniper fire. Needham radioed Jesmer several times, offering to come forward to help, but Jesmer vetoed the idea. There was simply too much fire to risk the movement.

Needham had some concerns about the NBC news team with him. He didn't want them hit while he was responsible for their safety. He crawled off to check on them. To his amazement he found they'd taken over an M60 from a wounded Sky Soldier. One correspondent manned the weapon while the other dug a fighting hole. Their participation in the fight was against orders, but Needham didn't worry; he needed all the help he could get.

Snipers harassed Captain McElwain's company, too. Several times Lt. Ed Kelley fired tracer rounds to mark a sniper's nest. Then an M79 grenadier would blow the sniper away.

Both companies took casualties, but the bulk of the enemy fire was still against Alpha.

During one of the brief lulls in the fighting, Lieutenant Holland had crawled among the riflemen gathering up the mortar rounds they carried. When he had a canvas bag filled with them, he started back to his mortars. He passed near Jesmer.

"When are you going to fire your mortars?" the captain asked.

"Right away, Captain," Holland responded.

Within minutes he had his weapons going. The distance to 1st Platoon was so short that the tubes were pointed nearly straight up. The missiles exploded just meters in front of Robinson's men.

By this time, too, air support had arrived on station. Five-hundred-pound bombs and napalm landed within two hundred meters of Alpha's position, but once again their effectiveness was greatly diminished by the heavy jungle. Also, the bomb blasts blew huge clouds of dirt and debris into the air, further reducing the already-poor visibility.

The NVA took advantage of that. Time after time they swarmed out of the jungle, firing their weapons under a covering barrage of rockets, grenades, and mortars. The brunt of their attack fell on Robinson's platoon. Braving the heavy fire, he moved among his men, repositioning them and directing their fire. Despite his brave efforts the NVA pressed to within ten meters of his line. Under their withering fire more of his men were hit. As they worked their way back to the medics, Captain Jesmer sent forward men from Lieutenant Robertson's platoon to fill the gaps. Sergeant Mescan and volunteers from the command group repeatedly crept forward to help the wounded to safety.

Lieutenant Kennemer's platoon had beaten off several

determined human-wave assaults, too. When the NVA closed to within twenty meters, the men responded by throwing grenades into the massed enemy. One of Kennemer's machine gunners knelt right in the open, firing his weapon in long, sweeping bursts, cutting down the enemy while screaming, "C'mon, you motherfuckers. I'm ready for you, you fuckers!" Kennemer had to order him to seek cover.

At about 1530, while firing his rifle from a standing position behind a tree, Kennemer saw a brief flash of light go past his head, and a tremendous explosion threw him viciously to the ground. At first he thought an enemy sniper had dropped a grenade on him from a tree. Then he realized an RPG had hit the tree behind him. Fragments from the grenade blew a huge hole in Kennemer's back. Before the intense pain really registered, two of Kennemer's men pulled him to safety. They tore off his fatigue shirt, wrapped a bandage around his torso, and helped him back to the medics. There Sergeant Mescan took over the officer's care.

In 1st Platoon's area Private 1st Class Suth had repeatedly exposed himself to the enemy's fire to blaze away with his M60. The heavy slugs from his weapon tore through the bamboo, inflicting numerous casualties on the NVA. When Suth's machine gun overheated and jammed, another gunner instantly came forward to take over the position. While he did so Suth helped a wounded buddy back to the medics. Because the medics were overwhelmed with casualties, Suth treated his friend. When he'd done all he could, he picked up a discarded M79 and blazed away at snipers still clinging to the treetops.

Captain Jesmer had been too busy directing the fight, co-ordinating the air support and artillery, and moving men up to replace casualties in Robinson's platoon to think about the correspondents. He was suddenly reminded of them when he felt a tap on his shoulder. When he turned and looked up from his position on the ground, Jurate Kazickas was standing there.

"Captain, are you going to attack now?" she asked innocently.

"Get down," Jesmer barked as he pulled her to the ground. "Go back and help with the wounded."

She did.

In a radio conversation Colonel Schumacher told Jesmer he had no reinforcements to send him. All he could do was offer air support and artillery. For the first time Jesmer worried that his force might not make it. He knew what had happened to other units of the 173d in the fighting around Dak To. He didn't want his company to be overrun. He made up his mind that wouldn't happen.

Since Jesmer and his radioman were lying in an open area, the RTO suggested they move behind some trees. Jesmer said no. They were in a small depression, defiladed from all but sniper fire. Just then a B-40 rocket whizzed overhead. It landed among three men only twenty feet behind Jesmer, near where Mescan knelt beside a casualty.

The blast blew Mescan to the jungle floor. When his ears stopped ringing he sat up. The whole left side of his face felt numb. When his hand came back covered with blood, he thought half his face had been blown off. Then his fingers explored some more. With an overpowering sense of relief he realized the wound had caused no serious damage. Before he could apply a field dressing an anguished cry of pain filled the air.

Just across from him, not more than ten feet away, Sergeant Sandstrom writhed in agony. Both his legs were gone. Next to him lay the mangled corpse of a paratrooper. A third man had been blown about ten feet away. One of his legs was gone.

Mescan crawled on all fours to Sandstrom. While he applied tourniquets to the torn stumps, Sandstrom grabbed his arm. Between gasps he asked, "Will I walk? Will I walk?"

"Sure," Mescan lied. "You'll be up and around in no time." Then he pushed Sandstrom's head down so he couldn't see his wounds. When he'd finished with the tourniquets, several paratroopers helped Mescan carry Sandstrom to the aid station.

After more than two hours of solid fighting, Alpha had suffered more than thirty casualties, nearly one-third of its strength. Lieutenant Robinson's 1st Platoon had only three of its original members remaining unwounded. Even though Captain Jesmer had sent men from his other platoons to replace the casualties in Robinson's platoon, the western portion of his perimeter was still weak. He just didn't have enough men left to fill in the numerous gaps in Robinson's line. He made a decision.

"Lima Six," he radioed Robinson. "Pull back about fifteen to twenty meters. We've got to tighten up the perimeter."

Robinson immediately circulated the order among his platoon. In twos and threes the Sky Soldiers started inching back. While one group moved to a new position, another provided protective covering fire. Then the first group covered the second. In this way 1st Platoon slowly compressed rearward. With one exception.

Shortly before Robinson received Jesmer's order, one of his squad leaders, Sgt. Douglas B. Baum, had been badly wounded and knocked unconscious while manning one of the platoon's forwardmost positions. The heavy enemy fire drove off all rescue attempts. Finally one of the medics, Sp4 Joseph F. Dyer, tried. He timed his dash forward to coincide with a break in the enemy's fire, but it was a setup. When he was halfway to Baum, a sniper opened fire. Dyer fell in a heap, a bullet buried deep in his thigh.

Intent only on saving Baum, Dyer ignored his intense pain and crawled forward. When he reached Baum he dragged the limp form behind a tree, propelling himself backward with his elbows. No sooner had Dyer completed his mission of mercy than the sniper fired again. The brave medic slumped forward, dead.

There was no way Robinson was going to leave Baum in front of the lines. Three different times the gallant officer moved toward Baum. Each time he was hit by enemy fire. Then he called out to Baum.

The sergeant finally opened his eyes. When he saw what Robinson had been trying, he cried out, "For God's sake, Lieutenant, don't come out here. There's a gook machine gun right behind this tree!"

The sniper fired. Fired again. Again. Again.

Sergeant Douglas Baum, twenty years old and one of the most popular members of Alpha, 1/503d, died on the jungle floor, riddled with enemy bullets.

With his perimeter tightened, Captain Jesmer breathed a little easier. All his able-bodied troopers held mutually supporting positions. Enemy fire had slackened to sporadic bursts. Ammo was plentiful since a daring chopper pilot had dropped a load at the old LZ near Lieutenant Holland. Jesmer could at last turn his attention to his wounded. He radioed for medevacs.

Colonel Schumacher came up on the net. "Negative on the dustoff, Alpha Six. We gotta get those civilians out of there," he stated.

Jesmer couldn't believe it. Neither could Capt. Ed Sills, monitoring the fight from the battalion TOC on Hill 823. Placing civilian correspondents ahead of the wounded was absurd. But it was also typical of the command's thinking: A dead correspondent wouldn't look good on one's record. Schumacher repeated his order.

Captain Jesmer was livid. "No way, Six," he yelled. "I've got men who are going to die if they don't get help. We've got to have those medevacs. Now!"

With Jesmer's refusal to allow any correspondents out until his seriously wounded were evacuated, Schumacher had little choice. He ordered the medevacs into Jesmer's LZ.

As it turned out only two choppers made it in before darkness and an increase in enemy fire halted the evacuations. Most of the casualties, and all the correspondents, spent the night on Hill 882.

Sergeant Mescan, assisted by Jurate Kazickas and other volunteers, spent the entire night tending the casualties. There were several whom he did not think would survive until dawn, including Sergeant Sandstrom. Mescan stayed in constant communication with Capt. James R. Griffin, the medical platoon leader. Griffin relayed precise instructions to Mescan, allowing him to keep Sandstrom alive until morning, when he was finally lifted out.

Besides worrying about the wounded in his care, Mescan

also worried that the NVA would overrun them in the night. The pitch-black darkness made it impossible for him to know where the company's lines were. He did know that the number of casualties he was treating meant there weren't more than about sixty men left in Alpha. There were another ninety men from Charlie and Dog companies, but Mescan had no idea where they were.

Captain Jesmer was worried, too. Earlier, he'd moved among the casualties, gathering their ammo and grenades. These he passed out to the men still on the line. He warned them to keep a sharp lookout. He was sure the NVA would attack that night. He knew if they had any idea of just how weak the three companies were, they'd be back.

Fortunately for the Sky Soldiers the NVA didn't know. A couple of enemy soldiers did stumble into Alpha's lines that night—Jesmer thought they were probably lost—but no major attack developed. Too, the combined punch of artillery and the miniguns of Puff the Magic Dragon kept on station all night might have discouraged any NVA attacks.

When dawn came on Sunday, 19 November, the evacuation of the wounded resumed. Those pulled out included Lieutenants Robinson and Kennemer, Sergeant Sandstrom, and Private 1st Class Suth. In all, Alpha Company, 1/503d, lost six men killed and twenty-nine wounded. Charlie and Dog companies suffered only five wounded, although one Dog Company paratrooper died on Sunday when a grenade exploded at his feet after being accidentally pulled from his web gear by a tree branch.

A sweep of the battlefield turned up fifty-one dead NVA. More than a dozen weapons, including three B-40 rocket launchers, were also recovered. Information gleaned from the enemy corpses revealed that Jesmer's foe on Hill 882 had indeed been from the NVA 66th Regiment.

The correspondents left Hill 882 that morning, too. Few of the Sky Soldiers were sorry to see them go.

Colonel Schumacher and Captain Sills came into the LZ late that morning. The three rifle company commanders briefed them on the action and the results. Schumacher ordered them to continue patrolling in the immediate area.

Then he left to return to FSB 12. He'd been on the ground all of fifteen minutes.

At nearly the same time that Alpha, 1/503d, started its fight with the NVA, Dog, 4/503d, also suffered a large number of casualties. Unfortunately, as had happened too often in the past, these were caused by friendly fire.

After its fight on 6 November, Dog had been sent on low-risk road-clearing operations around the Ben Het area. While there, Capt. Robert Crabtree took over the company. A member of West Point's class of 1964, Crabtree had served an earlier tour in South Vietnam. He'd arrived back in South Vietnam on 28 October and had just finished processing into the 173d when Dog, 4/503d, got hit on 6 November. As an experienced captain, Crabtree was picked by Colonel Johnson to take over Dog Company.

Lieutenants Allen and Burton took an instant liking to Crabtree. A friendly, easygoing man, Crabtree impressed the pair with his quiet self-assurance and innate leadership abilities. Crabtree had earned a Purple Heart on his previous tour, contributing to his acceptance in the company. With the macabre humor of men who faced death every day, Allen and Burton joked that they hoped the captain "had better luck this trip."

At 1035 on 18 November 1967, Colonel Johnson ordered Captain Crabtree to take Dog Company and join a mike force three kilometers west of Ben Het and one kilometer north of Highway 512. Earlier that morning the CIDG unit had spotted a squad of NVA. The Special Forces advisers called for reinforcements to help track them down.

Captain Crabtree found the mike force atop a small hill, its members scattered among the trees surrounding an elephant grass–covered clearing. Lieutenant Burton's platoon reached the site first. He joined Crabtree, 1st Sergeant Collins, and several Special Forces NCOs standing in a circle discussing the proposed sweep.

Lieutenant Allen, whose platoon was still climbing the hill, received word to hurry forward and join the command conference. He did so, elbowing his way into the group on

Burton's right. Across from him were Collins and Crabtree, who held a map. The captain was telling the group that Allen's platoon would lead the way down a finger that went in a generally northeast direction from their hilltop.

A short distance behind Crabtree, 1st Lt. Douglas G. Magruder, an FO for Battery A, 3/319th, called in a fire mission. Seconds later, the 105mm shells impacted on the finger, not more than a hundred meters away.

The closeness of the artillery bursts made Allen nervous. He'd been involved in the friendly fire incident on 15 July; he kept one ear tuned to Magruder as he listened to Crabtree's instructions.

Just inside the tree line Sgt. Morrell Woods also listened to Magruder. He thought the artillery rounds were landing close because they were being called in to suppress sniper fire the CIDG had been complaining about.

Magruder asked Sergeant Collins for a firing correction. Collins said, "Right a hundred."

Woods heard Magruder call in, "Left one hundred." He knew that was wrong. He moved to jump in a hole. Then he heard Magruder calling into his radio, "Check fire! Check fire!" Woods returned to his sitting position under the tree.

Allen didn't hear Magruder call the check fire. He was still focused on the FO's one-hundred-meter correction. That seemed too large.

Lieutenant Burton, too, sensed something was wrong. An odd sensation engulfed him. He felt as if he were in a completely uncontrollable situation.

Just then Allen grabbed his shoulder and shoved him to the ground. "Goddamnit, get down!" Allen screamed.

A split second later two artillery rounds hit right behind Crabtree and Collins. The explosion blew Crabtree into the air. He was dead before he landed on Allen. Jagged shards of red-hot shrapnel mortally wounded Magruder and Collins.

When he'd pushed Crabtree's corpse aside and found his glasses, Allen grabbed a radio and called the FDC. "Check fire, redleg! Check fire!" he screamed.

"What happened?" someone radioed back.

"We had a short round. We need choppers."

"How many?"

"All you got," Allen responded. "We got a lot of people hurt."

Then he joined Burton and the others in checking the casualties. Neither Magruder nor Collins lived very long. Sergeant Woods had received a load of shrapnel in his stomach. In all, six Americans and three CIDG were killed; fifteen paratroopers were wounded, as were thirteen CIDG. Two American artillery rounds had caused more friendly casualties in a second that day than the NVA had caused in several hours of fighting.

Once all the casualties were evacuated, Colonel Johnson flew into the clearing. "What happened?" he asked. The two young officers told him.

Johnson ordered them to proceed with their patrol. Burton said no. Dog had had too much, he argued. There were no more than forty men remaining in the company, less than the strength of a platoon. Colonel Johnson finally concurred. He directed them to return to FSB 12. They'd provide security for the fire base until they received a new CO and replacements.

That night the two young officers talked. "You know," said one, "the way things are going I don't think I'm gonna make it outta here."

"I don't think I will either," the other agreed. "There's just too much death."

CHAPTER 12

HILL 875: THE FIRST DAY

While the 1/503d fought its battle on Hill 882, three kilometers due south the 26th Mobile Strike Force (MSF) Company, which was opconned to the 173d, also encountered the NVA. On the south slope of Hill 875 the CIDG unit took several heavy bursts of NVA automatic-weapons fire. Six CIDG and one South Vietnamese Special Forces NCO were wounded in the brief exchange.

Because of the limited capabilities of the CIDG company, its U.S. Special Forces adviser wisely decided not to develop the contact. Instead, he withdrew to the south and radioed word of the contact back to Dak To.

When General Schweiter heard of the encounter, he immediately had his staff prepare an operational order to exploit the situation. From the available information Schweiter decided that the enemy forces on Hill 875 were elements of the NVA 66th Infantry Regiment. His maneuver battalions had been battling the 66th for nearly two weeks now. The Sky Soldiers had been badly bloodied, but so had the 66th. If he closed with the enemy on Hill 875, Schweiter could destroy the NVA 66th Regiment before it slipped out of his grasp into the refuge of Cambodia.

What Schweiter and the other Americans did not know was that elements of the fresh NVA 174th Infantry Regiment held Hill 875. From its previous location northwest of Ben Het, the 174th had slipped south undetected. From its new position the 174th could stop the American advances while the remnants of the NVA 66th and 32d Infantry Regiments, as well as the relatively undamaged 40th Artillery Regiment, pulled back across the Cambodian border. Once that had

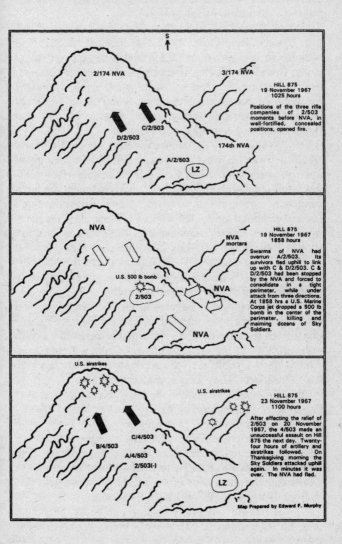

S

2/174 NVA

3/174 NVA

HILL 875
19 November 1967
1025 hours

Positions of the three rifle companies of 2/503 moments before NVA, in well-fortified, concealed positions, opened fire.

D/2/503   C/2/503

174th NVA

A/2/503

LZ

NVA

NVA mortars

U.S. 500 lb bomb

2/503

NVA

NVA

HILL 875
19 November 1967
1858 hours

Swarms of NVA had overrun A/2/503. Its survivors fled uphill to link up with C & D/2/503. C & D/2/503 had been stopped by the NVA and forced to consolidate in a tight perimeter, while under attack from three directions. At 1858 hrs a U.S. Marine Corps jet dropped a 500 lb bomb in the center of the perimeter, killing and maiming dozens of Sky Soldiers.

U.S. airstrikes

U.S. airstrikes

B/4/503   C/4/503

A/4/503

2/503(-)

LZ

HILL 875
23 November 1967
1100 hours

After effecting the relief of 2/503 on 20 November 1967, the 4/503 made an unsuccessful assault on Hill 875 the next day. Twenty-four hours of artillery and airstrikes followed. On Thanksgiving morning the Sky Soldiers attacked uphill again. In minutes it was over. The NVA had fled.

Map Prepared by Edward F. Murphy

occurred the 174th would follow the rest of the NVA 1st Infantry Division into its sanctuaries.

General Schweiter had a unit within a day's march of Hill 875. Since its contact on 12–13 November, the 2/503d had been in the field, pursuing the forces that had chewed up its Bravo Company. Moving in a generally southwest direction the three companies—Alpha, Charlie, and Dog—had searched for signs of the enemy. And they found them. Not only did they discover a number of enemy corpses, but they also found abandoned equipment and weapons.

On 17 November the column made a major discovery. About halfway between FSB 16 and Hill 875 they stumbled upon an abandoned enemy base camp. Capable of supporting a full-strength battalion of one thousand men, the huge camp was carved out of a hillside, hidden beneath a thick canopy of trees. Besides the obvious bivouac sites, the paratroopers also found a number of caves used as hospital rooms. Their floors were littered with bloody bandages and empty medicine bottles. There was no doubt the encampment had recently been occupied. Intelligence experts were choppered in to examine the camp closely.

The three companies laagered at the site that night. The discovery caused a great deal of anxiety among the Sky Soldiers. Even the freshest FNG knew that it meant there were a lot of NVA in the area. Lieutenant Thomas Remington, Alpha, 2/503d, could see the apprehension on the faces of his paratroopers. They were scared; he was, too.

On Saturday, 18 November, the three companies searched the adjacent jungle, looking for any further sign of the enemy. No major discoveries were made.

Early that afternoon Major Steverson flew out to confer with his company commanders. He told them of the MSF contact south of Hill 875. He ordered his three companies to advance up the north slope of the hill. They'd push any NVA in front of them into the waiting CIDG force.

"If you run into any heavy contact, pull back," Steverson told the three officers. "Then we'll bomb the shit out of them."

That sounded pretty good to 1st Lt. Bart O'Leary. He was

not only the junior of the three company commanders but, at twenty-four, the youngest. A native of Portsmouth, New Hampshire, he'd attended Notre Dame for one year before enlisting in the army in early 1964. Two years later he applied for OCS, was accepted, and received his commission in April 1966.

He arrived in South Vietnam in January 1967, just in time to make the Junction City jump as a platoon leader in Alpha, 2/503d. On 9 March he received a leg wound that hospitalized him for several weeks. After a short stint as the assistant battalion S-1, he became the XO of Alpha after the 22 June fight. When Captain Milton was wounded and evacuated, O'Leary stayed on as Capt. Ken Smith's XO. When Smith moved over to the newly formed Dog Company he took O'Leary with him. When Smith left Dog for a brigade staff position, O'Leary took over the company. That was on 22 October 1967.

O'Leary had fought the NVA around FSB 16 and knew what they were capable of doing. In fact, he and Captain Rogan, Bravo, 2/503d, had discussed the NVA's well-known tactic of quickly flanking a unit and working to cut it off. With Steverson's orders to pull back and let the artillery and air destroy the NVA, they wouldn't have to worry about that.

Alpha Company led the way toward Hill 875. After being wounded on 12 November, Capt. Mike Kiley had spent a couple of days at FSB 16 and then returned to his company. At that point he sent his XO, Lt. Matt Harrison, back to FSB 16. Harrison, slightly wounded on 12 November, would get treatment for his injury, which had started to fester in the jungle. Then he would remain at the fire support base, funneling supplies to the field and handling administrative tasks.

At dusk the three companies reached a spot about 750 meters north of Hill 875. Without bothering to dig in they set up a laager site and sent out their OPs. The night passed quietly. Lieutenant O'Leary slept comfortably on his air mattress.

Back in the United States most people focused their thoughts on Thanksgiving, just four days away. The unique American holiday provided its citizens an opportunity to express their gratitude for all their blessings and visit with relatives and friends. The holiday also signaled the traditional start of the Christmas shopping season. When the typical American awoke on the morning of 19 November his thoughts were focused on the three-day workweek and the delicious turkey he'd consume on Thursday.

When the paratroopers of the 2/503d arose that Sunday morning they heard the screams of F-100s roaring out of the morning sky to unload their ordnance across the face of Hill 875. The deep explosions echoed through the valleys. After the planes expended their bombs came the shrill whistle of artillery, instantly followed by the crash of shells on the hillside.

While the companies prepared themselves for the day's march, the indefatigable Father Watters laid out his Mass kit on his portable altar. The priest had been humping with his "boys" since 13 November. The sight of the forty-year-old tirelessly humping through the jungle inspired many a twenty-year-old to continue walking and not complain.

Mass that morning was well attended. There was hardly a man in the three companies who didn't think they'd have some contact before that day was over. Private 1st Class Manuel Orona, Alpha Company, was sure they would. He heard a few of the guys talking about Thanksgiving, but most, like him, were silent with their own thoughts. He took Communion and then, after Mass, double-checked his gear.

Sergeant Steve Welch, Charlie Company, took Communion, too, and he wasn't even Catholic. He just figured he needed all the help he could get. A twenty-year-old from Santa Cruz, California, who'd been in South Vietnam since January 1967, Welch knew all about trying to stack the odds in his favor. He'd fought in every one of Charlie, 2/503d's fights since making the jump on Junction City. Welch had been a member of the ambush patrol sent out by Lieutenant Bodine on 21 June 1967. When the CIDG was shot Welch pulled his body out of the line of fire. He and another paratrooper had tried to save the man, but the enemy round had done too much damage. The next day he helped lead Charlie Company down to Alpha. On 23 June he was among the first to reach the massacre site. The vision of all those bloated and torn American corpses never left him. What he saw convinced him that the NVA were a far more treacherous foe than the VC they'd been used to fighting down south. From then on Welch did anything he could to improve the odds of surviving the rest of his tour.

One Catholic who didn't attend Mass was Welch's best friend, Sp4 Raymond Zaccone. The M60 machine gunner, who'd just turned nineteen three weeks earlier, had grown up in Hagerman, Idaho, graduating from high school in 1966. Three months later, following in an older brother's footsteps, he enlisted in the army, volunteering for airborne training. He arrived in South Vietnam in March 1967.

Zaccone and Welch hit it off right away and became very close. So close, in fact, that Zaccone felt Welch, his squad leader, became overly protective. Zaccone voluntarily transferred to another squad to avoid any conflicts, but the pair still remained close. That's why Zaccone took no offense when Welch asked him why he hadn't attended Mass.

"I've got a funny feeling about this," Zaccone responded. "It's like going to church would be giving myself the last rites. I just feel weird about the whole thing."

Welch agreed. An eerie stillness had descended on the jungle; a silence broken only by the scream of another flight of jets and the explosions of bombs and artillery shells. The usual jungle sounds were absent. All the men seemed nervous, wired real tight, Welch thought. He hoped the fight would be a quick one; he wanted to get out of there as soon as possible.

By 0900 the companies were assembled in preparation for the move up the hill. Overhead, the last of the jets zoomed in, dropping bombs and strafing with their cannons. One spent shell casing dropped through the trees, striking Welch's helmet. The impact scared the hell out of the young sergeant. When he realized what had happened he laughed nervously in relief. Up ahead he could hear the staccato cracks of CBUs dropping on the top of the hill. They sounded good, reassuring.

According to the battle order issued by Capt. Harold J. Kaufman, Charlie Company CO and the senior commander on the ground, his company and Dog Company would lead the attack; Dog would be on the left side of the ridge finger, Charlie on the right. A well-worn trail separated the companies. Each company would advance with two platoons up and one back, with each platoon moving in double columns. Thus, eight columns of paratroopers would ascend the hill.

Captain Kiley's Alpha Company protected the rear. Two of his platoons would advance behind the assault companies, not only maintaining a physical link, but ready to help any of their wounded down the hill to an LZ being cut by the Weapons Platoon. Kiley's remaining platoon would provide rear security.

The formation was the classic two-up-and-one-back assault tactic taught in the classrooms of the Infantry School at Fort Benning since before World War II. Unfortunately, it was essentially useless against the North Vietnamese Army forces fighting in the jungles of South Vietnam's Central Highlands. Probing suspected enemy strong points with small, highly mobile teams of specially trained infantrymen was advocated by realists like Col. William Livsey, G-3 of the 4th Infantry Division, a man with considerable combat experience in the Korean War, where he had witnessed the senseless loss of American soldiers in frontal assaults on well-prepared enemy positions. Once the infantrymen confirmed an enemy presence they would withdraw and leave the destruction of the enemy to artillery and air power. The result would be a lot of dead NVA and only a few dead Americans.

Few among the 173d's commanders endorsed this new tactic. Their "hey-diddle-diddle, right-up-the-middle" attack mentality, drilled into them through countless hours of airborne indoctrination, did not allow for this kind of approach. The 173d's infantry companies would seek the enemy in the same type of formation used since World War I, the same type of attack formation that had proven disastrous before in the Central Highlands.

Alpha Company that Sunday morning mustered about 110 men. Charlie had about the same number; Dog Company fielded only about 80 members. Another 9 or 10 unassigned men moved with each company: a scout dog team, a medical team, the artillery FO and his RTO, a 4.2-inch mortar FO and RTO, and an engineer team. In all, about 330 American soldiers stood ready to move against whatever NVA forces held Hill 875.

The ridge finger they prepared to move along averaged about a hundred meters in width as it sloped gradually uphill to the top of Hill 875. The ridge's east edge fell off sharply; the west side sloped more gently. The hillside was covered with tall trees, frequent stands of bamboo, and dense scrub brush. Toward the top of the hill, the bombardment had torn up the jungle, creating much deadfall and many holes in the thick jungle.

At 0943 the companies started up the hill. No one spoke. The only sounds came from the hundreds of jungle boots striking the ground, equipment clanging, and the occasional crackle of a PRC-25.

Sergeant Welch led the point squad in Charlie. On point was Private 1st Class Quinn. Welch's RTO was Private 1st Class Harmon. Five meters behind Welch's squad came Specialist Zaccone and his assistant gunner, Pfc. Neal Best.

Twenty meters to Welch's left moved Dog Company's point squad. Specialist 4th Class Kenneth Jacobson had the point. Behind him came Sp4 Charles Hinton and the point squad leader, Sgt. Frederick Shipman. Jacobson was to stay even with Zaccone, meaning Welch's squad served as the point for the entire battalion.

Just after the jets had ceased their bombing runs, a small recon squad had scurried up the hill. After a quick look they came back downhill where they met Welch's squad. As Zaccone passed, the recon squad's sergeant pointed to Zaccone's M60. "Watch your ass, Zack. The gooks are up there and they'll be after you."

Zaccone nodded and moved past the recon sergeant. A short distance farther he noticed a large number of leaflets scattered across the ground. He bent and picked one up. In crude English the North Vietnamese pamphlet said something like, "You are here under the orders of your Imperialist

Government. Sit down and hold your weapon over your head. You will not be shot."

The presence of the leaflets scared Zaccone more than their message. They wouldn't be there unless the NVA were nearby. Zaccone felt as if the NVA were watching him. He tucked the leaflet into his pocket. To calm himself he mentally recited a ditty popular among infantrymen in South Vietnam: "Yea, though I walk through the Valley of the Shadow of Death I will fear no evil for I am the meanest motherfucker in the valley."

Welch suddenly whipped his head around. "What'd you say?" he asked.

Zaccone didn't realize he'd spoken aloud. His utterances had frightened Welch. "Nothing. It's nothing," he reassured Welch.

As the advance continued Specialist Jacobson kept getting ahead of Welch. Welch would signal him to slow down. It was hard for the two point teams to maintain their spacing as they advanced through the bomb- and artillery-tangled jungle. About three hundred meters from the crest of Hill 875, Private 1st Class Quinn came to a large clearing torn out of the jungle by the bomb blasts. Mounds of dirt and downed trees littered the landscape. Welch felt uncomfortable. He halted the two companies. Seconds later Private 1st Class Harmon handed him the radio's mike.

"Charlie Six," Welch radioed to Kaufman, about thirty meters behind him. "I don't like what I see up here. I'd like to recon by fire."

Kaufman came back instantly. "Negative. Keep moving."

Welch couldn't believe it. He tried again. "Six, this shit up here makes me nervous. I'd really like to recon by fire."

"I said 'Negative.' Move your men out now."

Zaccone looked at Welch. "This is stupid," he said. "This is fucking crazy."

Welch nodded in agreement. Then he signaled Dog Company's point to move out while Quinn stepped into the clearing. It was just 1030.

Specialist Jacobson walked about ten steps into the clearing. Three shots rang out. At least one hit him square in the head. From ten meters away Welch could see the spray of blood and brains. Zaccone saw it, too, just before he hit the ground. He, and those around him, started putting out rounds. They couldn't see anything, they just fired where they figured the NVA were.

Sergeant Shipman and Specialist Hinton called for a medic. Specialist 4th Class James C. Farley crawled up. As he reached Jacobson he, too, was hit by a rifle shot and killed. Shipman and Hinton still could not locate the source of fire. They just sprayed the other side of the clearing with their own M16 fire.

In Charlie Company's area Zaccone was up on one knee trying to see what was going on. He looked to his left. He was startled to see the brush being mowed down as if by an invisible scythe. He instantly flattened himself on the ground. The flurry of enemy slugs cracked overhead, missing him by inches.

From his prone position Welch couldn't see anything but the AK-47 rounds hitting all around him. The volume of fire amazed him. In eleven months in-country he'd never seen or heard anything like this. The blaze of enemy weapons built to a steady roar.

About this time Quinn was hit. Harmon inched forward and pulled him back out of the line of fire. One of Charlie's medics, Sp4 William T. Hagerty, snaked up beside Welch. Welch told him to move over and treat Quinn. Hagerty apparently misunderstood, for he moved forward. He made only a few feet before he was shot and killed.

Next to Zaccone, Private 1st Class Best took a round in the shoulder. He curled up into a ball, fighting the intense pain.

"Get down the hill," Zaccone told him. "The medics will patch you up."

Through clenched teeth Best mumbled his agreement. After he shucked off his ammo belts, he crawled back down the hill. A short distance later someone from Alpha Company helped him to his feet. Best was taken to the casualty collection point Alpha had established.

Other paratroopers were now making their way to the firing line, taking up positions to fire back against the blistering

NVA attack. The fire of AK-47s was cracking and snapping overhead in a furious roar. Still the Sky Soldiers could not see the enemy bunkers. The NVA were just too well dug in.

From his position near the rear of Dog Company, Lieutenant O'Leary could not see what was happening. His old platoon-leader instincts took over. He had to know what was going on. Taking just one RTO with him, he cautiously advanced. As he neared Shipman's squad the firing grew louder. The small-arms and automatic-weapons fire was now punctuated with the sharp crash of Chicom grenades and RPGs coming from the NVA. A steady stream of wounded filed past O'Leary, painfully making their way to the rear.

As he neared the firing line, O'Leary overheard Captain Kaufman on the radio advising Major Steverson, overhead in his C-and-C chopper, of the contact. O'Leary heard the battalion commander order Kaufman to "move up the hill."

O'Leary was confused. He broke in on the net. "Six, you told us to pull back if we made contact."

Steverson replied, "Go!"

By then the NVA's fire had lulled. O'Leary used the calm to push his lead platoon forward. They made about five more meters before the jungle across from them again exploded in a hail of small-arms fire. The advance halted.

Charlie Company's lead elements had crawled forward a few meters also, but the enemy fire struck them furiously, too. Near Harmon six or eight Chicom grenades plopped down. Miraculously, none went off. Zaccone kept slugs from his M60 flying toward the NVA, but he still couldn't see anything; he was just firing where he thought the NVA were. Welch had picked up an abandoned M79 grenade launcher. He fired a dozen rounds, but they seemed to have no effect on reducing the enemy fire.

With the lead elements pinned down Captain Kaufman once again requested artillery support. This time Steverson agreed. Within minutes the first rounds were crashing into the enemy's positions. Unfortunately, some of the artillery fell short, hitting among the lead elements of both Charlie and Dog companies. At 1117 a check-fire order went out to all supporting batteries. While corrections were radioed to the FDC, the NVA unleashed 57mm recoilless-rifle fire and B-40 rockets on the paratroopers. Chicom grenades continued raining down on the helpless Sky Soldiers.

After more artillery fire came in, this time landing on the enemy's positions, the paratroopers tried to advance again. Some elements made nearly thirty meters uphill before they were forced to the ground by the vicious return fire.

At 1258 four F-100s began making bomb runs against the top of Hill 875. For nearly an hour the jets bombarded and strafed the hill with close-air support. Some of the five-hundred-pound bombs were landing within fifty meters of the paratroopers, their blasts showering the Sky Soldiers with dirt and tree branches.

In order to deceive the NVA Zaccone and those around him would keep their heads up as the jets screamed in on their runs. Only when the bombs, which they could clearly see tumbling from the bellies of the planes, were seconds from impact would they duck down. They hoped their actions would fool the enemy into not ducking, but they weren't sure if it did any good.

When the jets were finished just before 1400, another uphill attack was ordered. In front of Dog Company 1st Sgt. Michael Deeb finally identified the bunker from which the shots came that had killed Jacobson. With several others he bombarded the position with grenades. Then they moved forward, using fire and maneuver techniques. To their surprise rifle fire now struck them from the rear, pinning them down.

Unknown to the paratroopers, tunnels connected many of the enemy positions. Bunkers they thought were destroyed suddenly came alive with new fire. Some Sky Soldiers were being fired on from three directions.

At Charlie Company Welch's and Zaccone's platoon leader, 1st Lt. Peter J. Lantz, had joined them during the air strikes. Both enlisted men liked Lantz and greatly respected him. Yet another member of West Point's class of 1966, Lantz had been featured in the *Newsweek* report on that group along with Lt. Gerald Cecil. Lantz had married while the *Newsweek* reporters tracked him; pictures of his wedding appeared in the magazine. In September, at Tuy Hoa, the members of his 2d Platoon helped the twenty-four-year-old celebrate the birth of his first child.

Now, Lantz ordered his platoon to prepare to attack. On his signal the fifteen or so men remaining under his command started forward. To their left Charlie's 3d Platoon also started moving.

Within ten meters the enemy firing grew so heavy that everyone stopped. Third Platoon's lieutenant had been killed; wounded were crying in agony. Those still able snaked their way to cover, forgetting the attack.

Lieutenant Lantz and Sergeant Welch found themselves well forward of Charlie Company, all alone. Bullets from both sides snapped overhead. Without a word both men turned and raced for the protective tree line. Yelling "Friendlies!" they crashed through the brush to safety.

About this time Zaccone, who had become separated from his buddy Welch as he maneuvered to cover the right flank with his M60, heard the blare of bugles. The sound seemed to be coming from down the ridge finger's slope to the west, in NVA territory.

Lieutenant Joseph Sheridan's 3d Platoon, Alpha Company, had followed Dog Company up Hill 875. Behind Charlie, Lt. Thomas Remington deployed 2d Platoon. Captain Kiley emplaced 1st Platoon around his CP group and the Weapons Platoon.

When the firing started, its intensity startled both Remington and Private 1st Class Orona. Both men were surprised at how quickly the enemy firing built to a deafening crescendo. From their positions about a hundred meters behind Charlie, they could see nothing. No firing was directed at them, but bullets crackled overhead, smashing through the bamboo and smacking into nearby tree trunks.

Within minutes the first of Charlie's wounded appeared in the jungle above Orona. He and others instantly went to their aid. Over the next couple of hours Orona stayed very busy collecting the wounded, helping them to Alpha's aid station, and going back for more. He couldn't believe the number of casualties. Each time he went back up the hill, wounded were sprawled along the trail, sobbing and moaning in pain.

As the casualties mounted Captain Kiley directed his Weapons Platoon to cut an LZ. It had become obvious that there were going to be more wounded than his overworked medics could handle. Some seventy-five meters behind Kiley's CP the members of the Weapons Platoon started clearing trees and brush.

The job of caring for the casualties continued unabated for Sheridan's and Remington's platoons. The cries from Charlie's wounded rose above the pounding and crashing of the artillery shells up the hill. Only the ear-piercing shriek of the F-100s drowned out the wails of the hurt. The cries for help became too much for Remington's medic, Sp4 Olis R. Rigby. He started uphill. Remington yelled after him, "Don't go. I'll need you here."

Rigby ignored him. Up toward the fighting he went, swallowed by the foliage. Remington was angry. Medics were supposed to stay with their units. Now 2d Platoon had no medic. Remington never saw Rigby again.

Construction of the LZ progressed slowly. The jungle was just too thick. At 1300 Kiley radioed the battalion TOC for an LZ kit (chain saws and machetes) and fifty pounds of C-4 explosive. A chopper dropped it in a short time later.

Kiley deployed his 1st Platoon around the LZ to provide protection to the members of the Weapons Platoon. That still left his rear, in the direction where the three companies had laagered the night before, uncovered. Kiley radioed Remington for a squad to cover the vulnerable area.

Remington looked around. Most of his men were busy tending the wounded, but Sp4 James Kelley's squad was near Remington, holding positions behind trees.

"Kelley, take your squad down to the six."

Without a word Kelley led his three men back down the ridge finger. Kiley directed him to set up an OP down the trail.

With Kelley were Sp4 John Steer, Pfc. Anthony Romano, and Pfc. Carlos J. Lozada. Steer knew and liked Lozada. The twenty-one-year-old Lozada had grown up on the tough streets of the Bronx, New York. Like Steer, the Puerto Rican had a wild streak. He frequently rebelled at authority, often finding himself in trouble as a result.

When Sfc. Enrique Salas was Remington's platoon sergeant he thought Lozada had a bad attitude. So, apparently, did Lozada's squad leader. The sergeant came to Salas one day to complain that Lozada was always giving him a hard time, questioning his every order. What could be done?

Salas said, "Look, I'll turn my back. You drop the guy."

The squad leader walked back to Lozada and laid him out with a roundhouse punch. Lozada was no trouble after that.

One man who befriended Lozada was Father Watters. Lozada's daughter had been born in May 1967, one month before he headed to South Vietnam. She was all he talked about. He told all his buddies what he was going to do for her once he got out of the army. He had grand plans for her future. Unfortunately, his pay as a private first class didn't allow him to save much for her future. In fact, he was having a hard time finding money to buy a crib for her. Father Watters heard of Lozada's plight. He pulled Lozada aside one day and offered to loan him the needed money. Lozada couldn't believe it; no one, especially a priest and an officer, had ever treated him so well. Lozada accepted Watters's generosity, mailing the money to his wife.

Now, as the squad moved down the trail, Lozada argued with Kelley over where he should set up his M60. Finally, Kelley moved off to the right, followed by Romano. Steer and Lozada settled in just to the left of the trail. Steer would serve as Lozada's assistant gunner.

After just a few minutes Romano grew nervous. He paced up and down the trail, cursing. "This is stupid," he'd say, "a fucking suicide mission."

Lozada called to him. "Shut the fuck up, will ya? You'll give our position away."

Romano stomped off. Steer never saw him after that.

A few minutes later three quick explosions, probably NVA mortars, erupted near the partially completed LZ. The three men nervously gripped their weapons. Over the sounds of fighting behind them they could hear rustling in the brush down the trail.

Suddenly, camouflaged figures could be seen not twenty meters away darting toward them from tree to tree. "Here they come, Kelley," Lozada said. Then he opened up with his machine gun.

The weapon bucked heavily as the youngster squeezed the trigger in short, measured bursts. Steer guided the belted ammo with one hand while firing his M16 with the other. Across the trail and slightly to their rear, Kelley, too, opened fire.

The NVA were so close the three paratroopers couldn't miss. Lozada's long, sweeping bursts of deadly fire tore into the enemy, but there were more than the three men could handle. The NVA pressed closer to the little squad.

Some of the closer paratroopers in 1st Platoon were calling to the three to escape. Steer hollered back, "We can't. We're pinned down."

Three or four members of 1st Platoon tried to come to the OP's aid, but they ran into a wall of NVA fire. One was hit and the others were pinned down.

As Steer slammed a fresh magazine into his M16, Lozada suddenly cried out, "My gun's jammed!" At the same time, Steer saw a North Vietnamese soldier, his face blackened and his AK-47 wrapped in burlap, duck behind a tree only twenty feet away. He fired a long burst at the man but missed.

With that Lozada cleared his M60. "Pull back," he hollered at Steer. Steer started falling back, enemy bullets whizzing past his head. He slid behind a fallen tree just as a spray of AK-47 fire tore up the tree behind him.

Lozada walked backward up the trail, boldly defying the heavy volume of fire directed at him, firing his M60 from the hip. Back and forth he moved the automatic weapon, spraying the jungle in front of him with lethal fire. The slightly built New Yorker moved behind Steer and dropped to his knees beside him, still firing.

Steer looked to his right. He saw groups of NVA moving past him in the dense jungle. "Get down, Carlos!" he cried as a burst of enemy fire slammed into his back and left arm. The impact spun Steer around to the ground in front of Lozada. He looked up just in time to see his friend take a round in the head. Lozada fell forward over his gun.

While Steer recoiled in shock Kelley suddenly appeared at his side. "Come on, John, we gotta get outta here."

With Kelley prodding him the badly wounded Steer stumbled up the hill through the thick vegetation. Behind the pair the NVA drew closer. Kelley tore grenades off his belt and flipped them behind him to ward off the enemy.

The frantic twosome burst upon Weapons Platoon at the LZ. "The gooks are right behind us," Steer gasped. "You gotta clear out. If you stay here you'll die."

Steer and Kelley barely paused long enough to spread the word; then they continued their flight up the hill. They finally made it to a relatively safe location. While a medic tended to the eighteen-inch rip in his back, Steer could hear the roar of gunfire from Kiley's CP.

At about the same time that Steer and Lozada began their fight, around 1430, Captain Kiley's CP group and 1st Platoon came under a sustained, two-pronged ground attack. Seemingly from nowhere, well-camouflaged NVA suddenly appeared to pour point-blank fire on the paratroopers. A company of NVA attacked Alpha from the rear while another pressed in from along the ridge slope to the west.

Lieutenant Remington could hear the firing below him from Kiley's CP. Distinguishable single shots soon were lost in the roar of small-arms and automatic-weapons fire. Grenades exploded one after another; Remington didn't know whose.

Kiley's voice, panicky but controlled, suddenly came through Remington's radio. "Mike Six. Get everyone you can down here. I need help, now!"

Remington gathered half of his remaining twenty men and headed down the ridge toward Kiley, about a hundred meters away. He never made it.

Halfway to Kiley a vicious blast of enemy fire erupted from Remington's left. A full company of NVA lay in ambush along the down slope on the west side of the ridge finger.

Sergeant Aaron Hervas spun firing, dropping several enemy before he fell in a hail of AK-47 fire. Specialist 4th Class Frank Stokes and Pfc. Ernesto Villareal moved to his aid but were mowed down, too. Specialist 4th Class Bruce M. Benzene flopped behind a tree and killed half a dozen NVA with one spray of M16 fire before he was cut down.

Remington caught an AK-47 slug in the right shoulder. No sooner had he hit the jungle floor than a B-40 rocket detonated against a nearby tree. Red-hot shrapnel tore into his leg. Despite the agonizing pain, the gutsy officer continued fighting. The NVA were mere meters away. Every time one showed himself, Remington fired. He didn't know if he hit anyone, but it was satisfying to shoot.

In the meantime, elements of Lieutenant Sheridan's 3d Platoon had fought their way to Kiley's CP. They found the captain and five others, including his RTO and the company's senior medic, lying dead in a shallow depression. From the evidence it appeared the NVA had simply overrun the command group, killing the paratroopers at point-blank range.

Nearby, they discovered the bodies of a group of wounded who had been awaiting evacuation. They'd never had a chance. All were dead from multiple gunshot wounds. Among them was Pfc. Neal Best.

As Sheridan's people moved back up the hill toward Dog, Lieutenant Remington ordered those still alive around him to make their way to Charlie. Inching along, firing his weapon into the trees behind him, Remington crept up the hill. Finally, at about 1500, he linked up with Charlie. Suffering immeasurable pain, he still managed to direct his remaining dozen men in digging fighting holes. Since they'd dropped their rucksacks in an area now swarming with NVA, the Sky Soldiers used whatever they had—bayonets, helmets, or their bare hands—to scrape shallow holes in the soil.

The enemy firing at Charlie and Dog had continued nearly unabated during Alpha Company's ordeal. The sounds of the fighting to their rear carried to the paratroopers farthest up the hill. They instinctively knew they were surrounded.

With no targets, Sergeant Welch busied himself pulling casualties to cover. One big Polish youngster, naturally nicknamed "Ski," had taken a round in the testicles and right leg. Deep purple blood squirted from his leg with each heartbeat. Welch leaned over to pull him behind a tree when another round struck Ski in the foot. The bullet then passed through Welch's drive-on rag before hitting a nearby paratrooper in the chest. Its path left a white welt down that man's torso before it exited, tearing out the front of his stomach.

Welch placed a field dressing over the man's stomach wound. Then he turned back to Ski. He was too late. The big kid was dead.

Welch defied the odds all that afternoon. People died around him but he remained unharmed. One time he crawled up between two riflemen. Suddenly, the man on his left screamed as an enemy slug tore open his neck. As Welch ducked to avoid the spray of blood the paratrooper on his right was drilled in the forehead. Welch crawled away.

Specialist 4th Class Zaccone narrowly escaped death several times that day, too. Once he was firing his M60 from behind a tree, dueling with a sniper, when an RPG slammed into the tree above him. The explosion tossed him into an open area. As he lay there he heard someone screaming. With a start he realized it was himself. He crawled back behind the tree. Because his foot hurt he asked a nearby paratrooper to look at it. The man told Zaccone there were a number of small shrapnel holes in the leather. Since he wasn't immobile Zaccone ignored the wound.

Later, a medic crawled up looking for wounded. Zaccone told him, "Better get outta here, Doc. The gooks got this place zeroed in."

The medic nodded and crawled off. He made ten feet before he was cut down.

At one point during that long afternoon Zaccone happened to look into the jungle behind him. He saw Father Watters squatting down, tending to a casualty. Watters met Zaccone's gaze. The priest wore a smile across his face that told Zaccone he was completely at peace with himself. Watters waved to Zaccone. He waved back, the gesture giving him strength. Then he returned to the fight.

To those who saw him that day, Father Watters was an inspiring example of coolness under fire. Totally oblivious to the hail of enemy fire, he moved across the battlefield, tending the torn and mangled bodies, giving last rites to the dying. Time after time he advanced to the firing line, pulling the wounded to safety, carrying them to the aid station, and recovering the dead.

At the aid station Specialist 4th Class Steer watched the chaplain work his way through the rows of wounded. The priest had words of comfort for each man. He held the hands of some as they cried from the pain. Others he embraced as they died, unwilling to let them depart this world alone.

After the NVA slammed into Alpha Company, Captain Kaufman realized his attack was going nowhere. He ordered the forward elements of both companies to pull back, forming a tighter perimeter. It meant giving up more than thirty meters of hard-won ground, but Kaufman had no choice. With the move completed Kaufman radioed Steverson for another air strike. At the same time he reported that about three hundred NVA had them surrounded. The jets made their first pass at 1503.

Because the three companies had been fighting without pause for nearly five hours, their ammo was growing critically low. Major Steverson ordered choppers from the 335th Assault Helicopter Company to attempt to drop in pallets of ammo. The first chopper set out from FSB 16 at 1539. At 1552 it returned, still loaded and shot full of holes. As soon as the pilot had neared the perimeter, an astounding volume of enemy fire flew out of the jungle. Hit too many times to count, the Huey shuddered violently as the pilot banked back to the fire support base.

A second chopper load of ammo was sent out at 1617. This time the crew chief managed to kick out one pallet of ammo before the heavy fire forced the chopper away. The pallet crashed into the jungle about twenty meters forward of Charlie's lines and tumbled down the slope.

The paratroopers desperately needed that ammo, so Lieutenant Lantz organized a recovery party. He led them forward of the line. As the enlisted men hauled the heavy crates back to their lines, Lantz provided covering fire, walking backward, shooting left and right, spraying the nearby treetops. He'd nearly made it back to safety when a sniper killed him instantly with one shot.

As the afternoon wore on, the NVA continued to pound the beleaguered Sky Soldiers. Besides small arms, they blasted away at the paratroopers with RPGs, B-40s, and mortars. Though there were periodic lulls in the fighting, they didn't last long. Just as soon as the paratroopers thought they might be safe, the unmistakable thunk of mortar shells leaving their tubes would be heard. Anyone above ground instantly broke for cover, knowing he had but a few seconds to find refuge. Then the shell would crash in, spewing death and destruction.

General Schweiter had been monitoring the fight on Hill 875 all afternoon. It was obvious to him that the 2/503d was in a desperate situation. He immediately gave them priority on all air strikes.

Major Steverson must have realized that he was way over his head in this fight. At 1541 he had his XO, Maj. William Kelly, request from brigade the assistance of the 1st Battalion. Though they were physically close, Colonel Schumacher's companies were in no shape to help anyone. Instead, General Schweiter turned to his reliable 4th Battalion.

At about 1600 Schweiter flew into Colonel Johnson's headquarters at FSB 12. The general hurriedly explained 2/503d's predicament. It was obvious to Johnson that Schweiter was greatly disturbed by the events on Hill 875. Schweiter told Johnson to prepare one of his companies for immediate deployment to FSB 16. Then he flew back to Steverson's TOC.

Captain Ron Leonard's Bravo, 4/503d, had been lifted into FSB 12 at 1125 that morning on a routine rotation of line companies from the field. Thus, it was Bravo that received the orders to prepare for departure.

Leonard had just finished a hot shower and donned fresh fatigues and boots when Colonel Johnson sent word that he wanted to see him. At the TOC Leonard learned of 2/503d's situation. Johnson ordered him to have his company ready to go on five minutes' notice.

Leonard hurried back to his company, where he issued a flurry of orders. It was a good thing he did. A short time later Johnson sent word that Bravo was to go to FSB 16 as soon as the necessary Chinooks arrived at the LZ. They were to provide the security at the FSB that night and be prepared to move to Hill 875 the next day.

All of Bravo, 4/503d, was on FSB 16 by 1715.

Water and food were critically low on Hill 875. Most of the Sky Soldiers had dropped their rucksacks where they had first made contact with the NVA. Those locations were now outside the tight perimeter. Several choppers had tried to drop in fresh supplies, but the heavy volume of enemy fire drove them off before they could hover over the paratroopers. A total of six Hueys from the 335th Assault Helicopter Company had been badly damaged or shot down that afternoon while trying to get to the 2/503d.

Specialist Zaccone and a buddy, driven by the need to get water for the casualties, volunteered to try to get to their rucks, which were now more than fifty meters outside the perimeter. Stealthily, the pair low-crawled across the shattered ground, cautiously picking their way through the deadfall. They reached the rucks unmolested and quickly stripped the packs of the extra canteens.

Once back inside the perimeter Zaccone carried the canteens to the aid station. He found Chaplain Watters. "Here's some water for the wounded, Father," Zaccone told him.

The chaplain smiled at him and said, "Thanks, son."

Once again Zaccone was impressed by the priest's calm demeanor. Though several dozen wounded crowded the aid station, some crying uncontrollably, others screaming, Watters remained composed. His prayers provided strength to those in despair. Just being in his presence comforted Zaccone.

Zaccone moved off to the southwest edge of the perimeter. There he joined three others digging a hole at the base of a tree just over the edge of the slope.

Several dozen meters behind Zaccone, Lieutenant Remington was convinced the NVA would launch a night attack against the weakened companies. If that happened he planned to sell his life dearly. "Don't let it come easy," he advised those near him. "Give 'em hell. Make it costly for the gooks. Make every shot count."

Those who had not yet dug in worked frantically to scrape some protective holes in the ground. The numerous roots made the digging difficult, but the desperate men hacked away at them until they finally cleared a spot.

North Vietnamese mortars, rockets, and RPGs continued to rock the perimeter at regular intervals. Any time someone dared to rise above the ground, his movement brought a flurry of small-arms fire from the NVA.

Artillery from Battery A, 3/319th Artillery, continued to blast the upper reaches of Hill 875. Shell after shell crashed into the hill, tearing up the trees and, the paratroopers hoped, killing the NVA. A heavy pall of smoke and dust hung over the hilltop, obscuring it from view.

The only time the artillery halted was to allow jet fighters to drop their bombs and napalm canisters on the enemy. The fighters screamed in low, generally from east to west on a run perpendicular to 2/503d's line of advance, dropping their ordnance as close as they dared to the perimeter. Some of the napalm burned so near Sergeant Welch he felt the air sucked from his lungs as the oily fire consumed oxygen.

Besides the jets, Puff the Magic Dragon hosed the NVA positions with its minigun fire. The colorful streams of tracers greatly cheered the paratroopers. As darkness grew, Spooky dropped flares over the hill. Their million-candlepower light not only helped those on the ground detect any movement by the NVA but also marked targets for the fast movers.

At about 1830 Captain Kaufman called a meeting of his platoon leaders and sergeants at his CP, adjacent to the aid station. He planned an assault up the hill early the next morning and wanted to ensure that everyone understood his role.

At different locations around Dak To that afternoon numerous members of the 173d Airborne Brigade monitored 2/503d's fight on Hill 875. At FSB 16 Lieutenant Harrison, along with his friend 1st Lt. Robert J. Philbin, Charlie Company's XO, huddled around a radio in the TOC. Those were their buddies up there being chewed up. They belonged with them. Both felt guilty they were safe while their friends died.

Two kilometers north of Hill 875, on Hill 882, Captain Jesmer and his command group of Alpha, 1/503d, also eavesdropped on the radio traffic. Throughout the day the sounds of the 2/503d's fight had drifted over the jungle to Jesmer's force. It was obvious that one hell of a battle was going on. After what 1/503d had suffered over the last week, Jesmer prayed that 2d Battalion would deal the NVA a decisive blow.

At FSB 15 on Hill 823 Capt. Ed Sills monitored 2d Battalion's fight, too. He listened as the FAC who'd been directing the air strikes reported he was getting low on fuel. A short time later a replacement FAC arrived on the scene. The first pilot conveyed to him the strike pattern he'd been running. Sills heard the pilot tell the new FAC to guide on a certain fire burning near the top of Hill 875.

Soon afterward a Marine Corps jet reported on station. He had several five-hundred-pound bombs left. Did the FAC have any use for them?

Indeed he did. The FAC relayed instructions, directing the pilot to drop his bombs on the fire burning near the top of Hill 875. The jet pilot tally-hoed, circled around, and began his run.

Somehow, the pilot misunderstood the FAC's instructions. Instead of making the run in a northeast-to-southwest direction, the pilot bore down on Hill 875 from the north, from directly behind the embattled Sky Soldiers. As he neared the release point he spotted a flare drifting across the face of Hill 875.

Several paratroopers on the ground saw the same flare. It floated lazily just above their position. Suddenly, the shrill scream of the approaching jet caught their attention.

When the pilot reached the release point he toggled the firing switch. From under each wing a five-hundred-pound bomb fell toward Hill 875. The pilot yanked back on the stick, pulling the plane's nose up into a steep climb. A few seconds later he had leveled off and was on his way back to his base at Da Nang with its air-conditioned officers' club, ice-cold beers, hot showers, and clean sheets.

At 1858 those monitoring 2/503d's radio frequencies heard a huge blast. Then the radios fell silent.

CHAPTER 13

RELIEF OF HILL 875

Sergeant Steve Welch and a buddy had just finished scraping a fighting hole in the jungle floor with their helmets when they heard the scream of the incoming jet. Welch instinctively glanced over his left shoulder. As the jet grew in size Welch saw the bombs fall from its wings. He knew something was wrong. The bombs were coming right at him.

"Holy shit!" he yelled. With that he threw his buddy into the hole and piled in on top of him.

Seconds later a tremendous blast rocked the perimeter. The violent concussion tore Welch's helmet from his head and knocked him unconscious.

When he came to and his ears stopped ringing, all Welch could hear were the painful screams of the wounded. Somewhere behind him a man kept crying over and over, "My legs are gone! My legs are gone!"

My God, Welch wondered, what happened?

The first bomb had landed just outside the perimeter. Its blast fortuitously caught a group of North Vietnamese as they prepared to attack the paratroopers. At least twenty-five of them died. The rest scattered.

The second five-hundred-pound bomb landed in the center of the aid station. On the west edge of the position Captain Kaufman squatted in conference with his platoon leaders. The full force of the explosion killed them all. Included among Charlie Company's dead was another member of West Point's class of 1966, 1st Lt. Richard W. Thompson. "Buck" Thompson, among the more popular members of his class, had already been hit three different times as he roamed the firing line during the day, but he had refused to be evacuated. He'd returned to the CP only because Captain Kaufman had finally ordered him to have his wounds treated.

At the east edge of the aid station Lieutenant O'Leary sat with his back against a wide, tall tree just twenty meters from Kaufman's CP. Next to him squatted 1st Sgt. Michael Deeb. Together, the two reviewed Dog Company's casualties. O'Leary had just started to speak when a bright light flashed and he heard a huge explosion.

The next thing O'Leary knew, he was flat on his back, his arms and legs askew. A weight pressed on his chest. He brushed at the object, recoiling in horror when he realized it was an arm and most of a shoulder.

Near him Sergeant Deeb moaned in agony. "I'm hit, Lieutenant. I'm hit."

O'Leary crawled to his first sergeant. In the fading light he could see that Deeb had suffered a massive head wound. He bandaged the NCO as best he could.

As he worked O'Leary saw a soldier stagger past, holding the stump of his left arm with his right hand as he mumbled repeatedly, "Will someone tie off my arm?"

The soldier disappeared behind O'Leary, and he never saw him again.

When O'Leary finished with Deeb he checked himself for wounds. For the first time he realized he had a bad sucking chest wound. To seal the hole he fished his plastic-covered ID card from his wallet and taped it over the wound. Still dazed by the brutal concussion, O'Leary did not yet fully comprehend what had happened. He thought an enemy mortar round had hit near them.

Specialist Steer, after having his wounds treated, spent most of the late afternoon helping the medics and Father Watters in the aid station. Several times Steer saw the priest reenter the aid station after a foray to the front lines, struggling under the dead weight of an unconscious paratrooper, disregarding the enemy rounds cracking and snapping through the woods. The chaplain's unflappable calm even when aiding men with terrible wounds impressed Steer. Time after time Watters spoke soothing words of encouragement to maimed paratroopers, assuring them that help was on the way. Steer saw the priest cradle sobbing youngsters in his arms, holding them until the pain-killing medicine injected by the medics took effect. He wondered if he would ever have the inner strength that Father Watters did to deal with such adversity.

The bomb landed almost beside the valiant priest, killing him instantly.

At about 1800 Specialist Steer had started searching the dead for water and ammo. The ammo he passed out to the able-bodied; the water he carried back to the wounded. The food and water Steer found had to be carefully rationed; everyone was desperately low on both. He hoped that a chopper with supplies would make it through before darkness set in.

A little later an RPG blew up against a tree near where Steer rested. Jagged slivers of metal tore into his foot. He crawled off to find a medic. As he did the bright flash of a flare suddenly bathed the area. In its brilliant light a burst of NVA sniper fire raked the area. Steer slid under a poncho, desperately trying to escape detection. Seconds later the bomb hit.

The next thing Steer knew, he was awakening. His head felt as if it had been squeezed in a vise. Blood poured from his ears, eyes, and mouth. His right leg was folded awkwardly behind him. Dimly, he became aware that the lower part of his right arm was gone; a thick stream of blood flowed from the ragged stump. He swallowed several mouthfuls of salty blood, gagging as he struggled to breathe. "God, don't let me go to hell!" he cried. Then he blacked out again.

Earlier, in Alpha Company's sector, Pfc. Manuel Orona had joined up with another man he did not know to carve a hole in the ground. They took turns hacking at the dirt with knives and then scooping out the loose soil with their canteen cups and helmets. Orona was on his knees taking his turn at digging when the bomb hit. The blast knocked him forward and out.

When he came to, he became aware first of the intense ringing in his ears. A pall of smoke hung in the air. "What happened?" he asked.

When no one answered he turned to his foxhole buddy and recoiled in shock. The soldier's entire right side was gone. Christ, he realized, that could have been me.

Orona was surprised at the quietness of the perimeter. He fought off a rush of panic when he thought he might be the only Sky Soldier left alive. Then, before he could dwell on his situation, the quiet was shattered by the plaintive cries and moans of the many wounded. Knowing only that some tragedy had befallen his battalion, but not yet comprehending exactly what, Orona picked up his rifle and crawled off to help the injured.

The first man he came to sat propped up against a tree, an odd stare in his eyes. Both his legs were gone. "Are you all right?" Orona asked.

"Go away," the man answered in a weak voice. "I'm gonna die. Go help someone else."

Orona next found a youngster whose back had been badly torn by shrapnel. "You got any water?" the young soldier asked.

Orona had to tell him no.

"Then leave me alone. I gotta have water."

Orona spent the next hour or so crawling from casualty to casualty, doing what he could to ease their agony. Some were too badly wounded to help; Orona bypassed them to help others. Everyone he saw begged for water; he had none to give. He just promised them he'd bring it to them when he found some.

Another paratrooper who responded quickly despite his own wounds and the carnage was Lieutenant Remington. He'd been fairly groggy most of the afternoon after a medic injected him with morphine, but he still managed to help the remaining members of his platoon secure a section of the perimeter. When the bomb hit, Remington took additional shrapnel in his exposed left arm and leg; the concussion also shattered both his eardrums.

When he recovered from his shock, Remington knew instinctively what had happened. He also knew he had to stop any further bombing. Painfully making his way toward the CP, he crawled across shattered jungle debris. As he neared the bomb site corpses and mangled body parts increased in number. Remington crawled over them intent only on finding a working radio. At Charlie Company's CP the bodies were stacked so deep he had to tug and pull at them to look for a radio. The first two he dug up were ruined. Finally, he found one that worked.

"No more fucking planes. Please no more planes," he pleaded into the mike. "You're killing us up here. Stop it."

Remington reached Lt. Mike Coffas, an artillery officer at the FDC; the radio he'd found had belonged to an FO. In a halting voice Remington told Coffas of the disaster on Hill 875; his message at 1912 was the first word the 2/503d TOC had of the errant bomb. Coffas quickly passed the word of the disaster to the battalion staff.

Major Steverson nearly fell apart when he heard the news. In less than a week his battalion had been all but destroyed. He immediately ordered a halt to further air strikes. Then he radioed the bad news to General Schweiter.

At FSB 12 Colonel Johnson received word that General Schweiter was coming to see him for the third time that day. After his initial visit to advise Johnson of the need for preparing to move to the assistance of 2/503d, the general had returned ninety minutes later to say that the situation had quieted down. Fourth Battalion probably wouldn't be needed, Schweiter told Johnson. His troopers could stand down.

Now, at about 1945, Schweiter's chopper settled onto the FSB's LZ. The general was visibly distraught. In a voice filled with intense emotion Schweiter told Johnson what had happened. Then he said, "Jim, you'll have to get your people to that hill. Get them there as fast as you can."

Then Schweiter returned to his chopper and flew off.

Johnson immediately began planning the move with his staff. Captain Leonard's Bravo Company was already at FSB 16; they'd be the first to head toward Hill 875. Captain Muldoon's Alpha Company would be lifted from FSB 12 at first light. As soon as they assembled at FSB 16 they'd follow Bravo to Hill 875. Charlie Company would come next.

The colonel issued a flurry of orders. Chinooks were ordered up to provide the necessary lift for the companies. Because of the difficulty encountered in resupplying the 2/503d by helicopter, Johnson ordered his S-4 to round up extra ammo, medicine, water, and rations. Each man in the three relieving companies would have to carry a double load in order to resupply 2d Battalion. Since his companies would be moving through jungle swarming with NVA and would have to march alone, Johnson arranged for the artillery liaison officer to provide a moving wall of artillery fire to surround each company as it moved to Hill 875.

After reviewing his maps Johnson realized that the only feasible overland route for his companies was the same one 2d Battalion had taken. He summoned Connolly and Muldoon to the TOC. He reviewed the operation with them in great detail. He wanted to be sure they understood every phase of the movement. When he finished, Johnson dismissed them to prepare their companies.

On FSB 16 Captain Leonard received word of the relief effort over the radio. Everyone in Bravo was eager to help their fellow paratroopers, but it was too late at night to begin the movement. Besides, a very real danger existed that the fire support base might be hit that night. Second Battalion needed Bravo as security. Captain Leonard set his platoons into position and then conferred with his platoon leaders about the next day's mission.

On Hill 875, more 2d Battalion paratroopers were recovering from the shock of the bomb. In small groups, sometimes singly, sometimes in pairs, the Sky Soldiers reestablished their perimeter against an expected enemy attack. And none too soon. Private 1st Class Orona was tending another casualty when someone called out, "Here they come again!"

Orona scrambled to the edge of the perimeter, where he joined another soldier in setting up an M60. While Orona fed in belts of ammo, the gunner fired into the surrounding jungle. RPGs flashed out of the foliage, exploding behind them.

Orona could see the muzzle blasts of AK-47s as the NVA dashed toward them. When he could, Orona threw grenades in front of his position. In the flashes of their explosions he could see enemy soldiers silhouetted in the jungle.

Several times Orona crept off to find more ammo. He pulled belts of M60 ammo off corpses and returned to the gunner. The action continued for another fifteen minutes before the NVA withdrew. Orona and the gunner manned the position throughout the night, ever vigilant for another probe. None came.

Specialist Steer lapsed into and out of consciousness all night long. Around him men moaned and screamed in agony. He called for a medic, but no one came; the bomb had killed nearly all the medics. Finally, during one lucid moment, Steer crawled off into a clump of bushes. Convinced the NVA would soon be swarming over the area, he pulled two corpses over his own body to conceal himself. To his immense relief one of the bodies still had a full canteen on its belt. Steer removed it and eagerly gulped the brackish liquid. Then he passed out again.

With three others from Charlie Company, Specialist Zaccone had dug a hole on the down slope of the ridge finger's west side. Although they were only thirty meters from the company CP, they were not wounded by the bomb due to their defiladed position. The concussion, however, shook them badly, and it was some time before they regained their senses.

The first thing Zaccone heard were the same screams Welch heard. Somewhere behind him a frantic voice screamed, "My legs are gone! My legs are gone! Mom, my legs!"

Zaccone had no idea what to do except stay alive. He, too, thought the NVA would rush their position, so he laid grenades within easy reach, checked to make sure his M60 was loaded, and prepared for the attack. Then one of his foxhole buddies whispered that he had a problem. A nude corpse hung in the tree above him, caught in its branches. Together they tried to pull the body from the tree but could not dislodge it. Because they didn't want to reveal their position to any lurking NVA by making too much noise, they finally decided to leave the body there until morning. The other paratrooper spent the night with the corpse's legs dangling along each side of his head.

After Zaccone settled back into his position, he listened to the continued cries of the wounded. He wondered how many others besides his little group were still alive. He figured his buddy Steve Welch had been killed. He'd miss him. Welch was a great guy. Zaccone only hoped that Welch had died painlessly.

Not thirty meters away Sergeant Welch mourned the loss of Ray Zaccone. Because Zaccone reminded him of his younger brother, also named Ray, Welch had grown very close to him. Now that Zaccone was apparently gone, Welch vowed never to get that close to another soldier again.

By this time Welch had accepted the inevitability of his own death. No doubt the NVA would soon come out of the night, killing the battalion's survivors as they had Alpha Company's in June. Welch felt no inner peace after acknowledging his impending demise. His major concern was how his parents would react to his being killed in action. He hoped they would learn he'd gone down fighting, because he planned to take a lot of NVA with him.

A short time later the sound of NVA could be heard moving through the jungle at the base of the slope below Charlie Company. Rather than reveal their location by firing their weapons, Zaccone and the others threw grenades at the noises. After the explosions Zaccone heard an enemy soldier crying. A Vietnamese voice yelled something, apparently a warning to keep quiet. The crying continued. Zaccone heaved another grenade. The crying stopped.

Sergeant Welch heard the NVA moving around, too. He threw grenades down the slope. A North Vietnamese started screaming, "*Chieu hoi!*" Welch and those around him unloosed more grenades. Finally, the noises stopped.

Of the sixteen company officers who'd started up Hill 875, eight were now dead and the other eight wounded, most rather severely. First Lieutenant Joseph Sheridan of Alpha was one of the few with only minor wounds. His platoon CP had been protected from the major effects of the bomb's blast. From his position across the ridge finger from Remington, he took control of Alpha.

Platoon Sergeant Peter Krawtzow was the ranking survivor in Charlie Company. He immediately began reorganizing the remnants of the company. Krawtzow moved through his sector of the perimeter, determining who from Charlie was still alive. He didn't put many names on his list.

It took some time for Lieutenant O'Leary to fully regain his senses. As he did, the extent of the damage caused by the misaimed bomb became more apparent. No matter where he looked, all he could see were piles of bodies and body parts. Few paratroopers were moving. Those who did stumbled and staggered about in a zombielike trance. O'Leary could not hear the screams of the wounded because the bomb's concussion had blown both his eardrums; he was almost totally deaf.

Slowly, O'Leary pieced together what had happened. As soon as he learned that Captain Kaufman had been killed, O'Leary realized he was the senior surviving officer. Despite his injuries O'Leary immediately stepped into the leadership role. After turning over command of Dog Company to its other remaining officer, 1st Lt. Bryan McDonough, O'Leary took charge of the entire force. His initial priorities were to ensure that the perimeter was still secure, care for the wounded, and communicate with headquarters. O'Leary rounded up several NCOs and had them check the perimeter. When they reported back they had to shout directly into O'Leary's ear in order for him to hear them. To protect what was left of 2d Battalion, O'Leary called in suppressive artillery fire on the slope above them and along each side of the finger. Soon the 105mm shells were ripping into the jungle all around the battalion.

Unfortunately, one gun was firing a little too low. Several of its shells barely cleared the treetops above Sergeant Welch before detonating. Sergeant Krawtzow repeatedly yelled "Check fire!" into his radio, but no one acknowledged his warning.

Then a shell landed among the forward elements of Dog Company. At least one more paratrooper died and four were wounded by the friendly fire. O'Leary pleaded into the radio, "We've had enough help for the night. Put that fire away from us. If I need it any closer I'll call it."

Someone at the FDC finally got the message. The battery's shells started impacting farther up the hill, hurting the NVA, not the Americans.

Surprisingly, the NVA made no further serious attempts to overrun the battalion's perimeter. All of the surviving Sky Soldiers fully expected them to come that night, but they never did. Why is a mystery. Perhaps they had no real idea of how badly hurt the battalion was and how weak they were. No doubt, too, the NVA defenders of Hill 875, though well dug in, had suffered heavy casualties from the near-constant bombardment from artillery and air strikes. Plus, those who knew the NVA's tactics knew they frequently used a trapped unit as bait to lure in more U.S. troops.

First light on 20 November witnessed a flurry of activity at FSB 16. Captain Leonard had the three platoon leaders and ninety-six enlisted men of Bravo Company ready to go by 0700. Each Sky Soldier carried a minimum of six hundred rounds for his M16, five to ten fragmentation grenades, two smoke grenades, a round for the 60mm mortars, and several spare canteens. The M60 gunners had more than two thousand belted rounds wrapped around their bodies. Grenadiers carried at least fifty rounds of both high explosive and shotgun ammo for their M79s. The medics toted as many spare medical supplies as they could. Sergeant Riley's Weapons Platoon carried two 60mm mortars and seventy rounds of ammo for them.

At 0745 Leonard sent several clearing patrols out from the base to check for any lurking NVA. While they were out Colonel Johnson arrived from FSB 12 to brief Leonard before he moved to Hill 875.

"From what we can tell," Johnson told Leonard, "several hundred enemy soldiers hold Hill 875. The S-2 thinks there are more out there waiting for you. I'll keep the artillery around you as you move, but watch out for an ambush.

"Muldoon will be here soon and I'll have him on his way

behind you as soon as I can. Connolly's also coming in as soon as we can get the choppers for the lift. If you do get hit, help won't be far away."

Johnson then headed back to FSB 12 to get his other companies going.

Based on what he knew, Leonard decided to swing wide and approach Hill 875 from the northwest. The NVA would probably be expecting a relief force to take a more direct route from the base; Leonard's detour might avoid an ambush.

Bravo Company would move in a diamond formation. On point Leonard put Lieutenant Lindseth's 3d Platoon. Lieutenant Larry Moore's 1st Platoon took the right flank position and Lieutenant Proffitt's 2d Platoon held the left. Sergeant Riley's Weapons Platoon secured the rear. Leonard's CP moved in the middle of the formation.

Sergeant Leo Hill led Bravo out of FSB 16 at 0937. Still considered the best point man in the company, Hill had Specialist 4th Class Diaz on his left and Private 1st Class Quillen on his right. Moving in an arrowhead formation, Hill stayed about a hundred meters in front of the rest of his platoon. During the platoon briefing Lindseth had told Hill that the point team was expendable; if they were hit they couldn't expect to be rescued. Getting to the hill was more important than saving the point team. Neither Hill nor the others were happy about that, but they knew there wasn't anything they could do.

Hill headed almost due west from FSB 16. At first he traveled along well-used trails running through a grassy area punctuated by thick stands of bamboo and scrub brush. Occasionally, he lost sight of either Diaz or Quillen in the tall grass, but they always reappeared back in the open. Every few hundred meters Hill would pause. After checking his compass he'd turn and signal to his platoon sergeant, Sfc. William L. Cates. Cates would respond with a reassuring wave and Hill would continue.

From time to time Lieutenant Lindseth moved up to Hill's position. They'd confer for a few minutes; then Lindseth would return to his platoon to radio a progress report to Leonard.

The promised artillery provided a curtain of red-hot steel fragments around the small force. Impacting at a distance of several hundred meters from Bravo, the barrage undoubtedly discouraged any NVA from harassing the relief force.

Moving as rapidly as caution allowed, Bravo proceeded toward Hill 875. By 1115 they were about eleven hundred meters west of FSB 16. Here, Hill turned to the southwest, toward the hill.

On Hill 875, just before dawn, several RPGs flew out of the surrounding jungle to explode in Charlie Company's lines. Fifteen minutes later Dog Company reported movement in the jungle on the slope above them. They called in some artillery. The movement stopped.

Lieutenant O'Leary radioed the TOC at 0638 requesting that an LZ kit be dropped in. He had to get the wounded out; that was now his major priority. He'd already assigned some able-bodied men to the task of cutting an LZ. They worked in an area about halfway between the battalion's perimeter and where Alpha Company had started an LZ the day before. The workers were protected from direct fire from the NVA by the lay of the land. However, mortar fire could still reach them, and did. Also, any helicopter approaching the LZ would be under observation by the NVA and subject to all kinds of gunfire.

The chopper bringing in the LZ kit found that out the hard way. At 0818 it hovered over the hillside. As the crew chief prepared to push the equipment out the door, a fusillade of automatic-weapons fire peppered the ship. The crew chief fell, badly wounded. The pilot quickly ascended to a safe altitude before flying back to FSB 16. The paratroopers cutting the LZ would have to make due with what they had.

After the RPGs hit Charlie Company's sector that morning, only an occasional sniper's round bothered the paratroopers. Sergeant Welch decided it would be safe enough to move about to find Zaccone's body. He pulled back into the tree line and started searching.

At about the same time Zaccone went looking for Welch. Earlier, Sergeant Krawtzow had confirmed that his friend was dead. He crawled out of his fighting hole to search for Welch's body.

When the two young warriors found each other a short while later they hugged in uncontrolled joy.

"I thought you were dead."

"Not me, you SOB. I thought you'd bought it."

"No way. Those fucking gooks can't kill me."

The friends spent the rest of the day together, either helping wounded to the new aid station set up just behind the old one or manning the edge of the perimeter, waiting for an attack that never came.

Daylight revealed the full extent of the damage done by the errant American bomb. Where Captain Kaufman had established his CP there was now only a deep bomb crater. Bodies and pieces of bodies were scattered everywhere. Arms, legs, heads, and other parts of the human anatomy littered the ground. Private 1st Class Orona reacted with stunned horror when he found a limbless torso hanging in the tree above him. Lieutenant O'Leary had Sky Soldiers begin the loathsome task of separating the living from the dead. The wounded were gathered at a new casualty collection point just downhill from the original. There was precious little first-aid treatment to give them; nearly all medical supplies had been stripped from the dead and that still wasn't enough. More than eighty men were wounded badly enough to be brought to the aid station. Of these, forty-eight merited immediate evacuation. But choppers still couldn't get in.

The exact number of dead was not yet known. Based on preliminary information he received from the new company commanders, O'Leary estimated that close to eighty Sky Soldiers had lost their lives either in the fighting going up the hill or in the bomb blast.

Major Steverson, though he'd been over Hill 875 in his chopper several times and had communicated frequently with Lieutenant O'Leary, still did not really understand just how desperate the situation was. Even while Bravo, 4/503d, headed to the rescue of his battalion, Steverson radioed O'Leary to ask if he could bring the artillery in even closer.

O'Leary responded with an emphatic "No!"

Steverson then wanted to spray the jungle around the perimeter with machine-gun fire from helicopter gunships. Again O'Leary said no. Helicopters could not get near Hill 875 without being mercilessly attacked by enemy automatic weapons. The paratroopers were the bait, the rescuers the trophies.

Finally, after being asked several more times by Steverson, O'Leary agreed that if the gunships made their passes from east to west only (he wanted no aircraft of any kind coming in from behind him again), they might help. At about 0940 some gunships approached Hill 875 and, sure enough, received an incredible amount of enemy fire. It came not only from Hill 875, but from nearby ridges, too. The gunships departed, full of holes.

Earlier that morning Steverson had organized a provisional command group under his XO, Maj. William H. Kelly. Consisting of the XOs of Alpha and Charlie—Lts. Matt Harrison and Robert J. Philbin, respectively—the command group was to go to Hill 875, reorganize the elements, evacuate the wounded, and "exploit the tactical situation."

At first Steverson wanted the group to reach Hill 875 via overland march. Permission for that was denied by the brigade S-2. Then Steverson put the three men on a Huey. Accompanied by two gunships, they'd fight their way onto the hill.

As Harrison took his seat aboard the chopper, its pilot told him the situation at Hill 875 was "not very good." According to the pilot, several of the Cowboys' choppers had already been damaged beyond repair by enemy fire that morning.

A few minutes later Harrison's Huey approached the hill. Flying at treetop height, the two gunships were just ahead of the slick. With one firing left, the other right, they cut a path toward the original LZ. The door gunner yelled a warning to his passengers, "We won't be stopping long!"

About then the slick shuddered as it caught a burst of NVA

machine-gun fire in its tail boom. The pilot didn't wait. He pulled into a tight right-hand turn and headed back to FSB 16.

Still determined to get his men onto the hill and gain control of the situation, Steverson hatched another plan to deliver the command group to Hill 875. When Lieutenant Harrison heard the details, he reacted with stunned disbelief. Surely there had been a mistake. He and Philbin were being sent to a certain death. But there was no mistake: Harrison and Philbin were to be lowered into the perimeter by sling from a hovering helicopter.

An obedient, dedicated soldier to the end, Harrison climbed aboard the chopper. He'd be dead in the next fifteen minutes, he realized. How anyone could expect the two officers to survive a descent via a sling from a stationary target when fast-moving gunships had been getting hit left and right for two days was beyond Harrison's ability to comprehend.

While he fastened the straps of the sling about his body, Harrison saw a nearby group of photographers taking pictures of him. This is the last picture my parents will see of me, he said to himself. He only hoped that he would not do anything to shame or embarrass them.

Harrison sat passively at the edge of the ship's open doorway, his feet on the landing strut. Surprisingly, he felt calm. He'd accepted his death. This is what soldiers are paid to do: Die for their country. He was about to earn his pay.

Then, just before lift-off, Major Kelly walked up. "We're not going to do this. Get off the chopper," he said. Harrison nearly collapsed with relief.

For the paratroopers trapped on Hill 875, 20 November passed with agonizing slowness. With no water available, the day's increasing heat seemed worse than it actually was. And there was no food for anyone. All the Sky Soldiers were hungry and thirsty. But the wounded suffered most. Hysterical screams for water rose from the hill all day long. Pain-killing morphine injected the previous day had worn off; men cried, screamed, and begged for relief from their pain and suffering. But there was no relief available.

Except for sporadic sniper fire, most of the enemy fire

directed at 2d Battalion during the day came from their mortars. The weary Sky Soldiers would hear the distinctive thunk of the round leaving its tube. That meant they had five to six seconds to find cover before the round hit. Many didn't make it.

Private 1st Class Orona spent the second day wondering when he'd be hit. With all the ordnance going off around him, he knew it was simply a matter of time before enemy metal tore into his flesh. If he were going to die, he hoped the end would come quickly. In the meantime, Orona wanted to get his licks in.

He picked up a discarded M79 grenade launcher, scrounged up a bag full of loose rounds, and crept uphill to reinforce the perimeter. Once he got there another paratrooper pointed out a target. "I can't see anything," Orona noted.

"Fuck it, man. They're there. Just fuckin' fire."

Orona did. He pumped round after round up the hill, never knowing whether he hit anything other than trees and bamboo, but feeling very good.

Meanwhile, the men working on the LZ were making better progress than O'Leary could have hoped for. Several chain saws discarded by Alpha's Weapons Platoon during the initial attack were recovered and put to good use. Although the LZ crew frequently had to duck mortar shells and sniper fire, by 1400 a one-ship LZ was nearly complete.

By 1300 Bravo, 4/503d, had closed to within seventeen hundred meters of Hill 875. Though they had not been molested during their trek, it had not been uneventful. The column passed through several abandoned NVA base camps. In one they discovered four freshly killed NVA soldiers. Various body parts amidst a pile of bloody bandages were also uncovered, giving evidence of the casualties the NVA had incurred. At another base camp more than a dozen mortar rounds were found lying around. Captain Leonard halted his company momentarily so the rounds could be destroyed. Then he signaled to Lindseth to get his platoon going.

Considerable activity and change had occurred at FSB 16

since Bravo, 4/503d, departed. Captain Muldoon's Alpha, 4/503d, arrived via Chinook about two hours after Leonard headed out. With little delay Muldoon formed the 110 men of his company into a marching formation and set off after Bravo. Captain Connolly's Charlie Company arrived on the heels of Alpha. He, too, quickly formed up his 100 men and set off for Hill 875.

With the arrival of three companies from 4th Battalion, General Schweiter turned over control of FSB 16 to Colonel Johnson. In addition to securing the relief of 2/503d, Johnson would also assume command of its personnel on the hill. On Schweiter's orders Major Steverson, his staff, and most of the remaining 2/503d members left FSB 16 beginning at 1538 and moved to FSB 12. Among those from 2/503d who remained at FSB 16 were Major Kelly and Lieutenants Harrison and Philbin. All three were determined to get to Hill 875.

Bravo Company, 4/503d, made radio contact with Lieutenant O'Leary at 1420. Captain Leonard advised O'Leary that he expected to make physical contact within the next two hours.

Word of the impending arrival of the 4/503d force spread rapidly among the 2/503d paratroopers. A tremendous sense of relief engulfed everyone. They wouldn't die on this god-forsaken hill; they hadn't been forgotten.

Lieutenant Remington nearly cried when someone whispered the good news to him. All around him he could hear the buzz of excitement as his Sky Soldiers realized that their ordeal was nearly over. I just might live after all, Remington told himself. Suddenly concerned about his future, Remington slipped his helmet from his head. He carefully placed it over his groin. If I do get out, he reasoned, I might want to have kids someday so I better protect the family jewels.

Shortly after 1600 Sergeant Hill reached the base of Hill 875. He paused briefly until Sergeant Cates came into view behind him. Then he started up the hill.

Not twenty minutes later Hill came upon bamboo-reinforced steps cut into the hillside. This is definitely a bad sign, he thought. Not much farther on, he came across an American body. A young paratrooper lay next to his M60 and a pile of spent cartridges. Hill didn't know it, but he'd found Carlos Lozada's remains.

Soon more bodies, both American and North Vietnamese, were found. There seemed to be an awful lot of them. Lieutenant Lindseth, now moving with Hill, estimated that at least twenty dead paratroopers littered the jungle floor. Christ, he wondered, is anyone alive?

The path up Hill 875 steepened noticeably for Bravo. Also, damage to the jungle from ordnance became apparent as the men stepped over fallen tree trunks and jumped bomb craters torn out of the jungle floor.

As Sergeant Hill continued uphill he grew increasingly nervous. He feared that jittery sentries from 2/503d might mistake him for an NVA. If only he knew where their lines were. Then he smelled gunpowder. Soon, the thick foliage forced him to crawl on all fours. Suddenly, the jungle in front of him opened onto a large clearing. Hill called softly, "Fourth Batt coming in."

Three helmeted heads popped up from a hole a few meters in front of Hill. The grimy faces stared blankly at him.

"Where's your company?" Hill asked.

"Ain't no company left," one of them answered.

Hill crawled up to them, distributing his extra water and rations.

"We sure are glad to see you," one of the paratroopers remarked. "We were starting to think we were goners."

"Where's your CP?" Hill asked.

The youngster pointed over his shoulder. "Up there. But be careful, there's all kinda fucking gooks up that way."

Hill moved toward the CP. He couldn't believe the destruction. Bodies were everywhere; most were horribly torn. He saw a pair of boots, perfectly laced up, standing neatly side by side, completely empty. He came upon one wounded man, half of whose buttocks had been blown away. Hill knelt to give him water. "Don't worry," he assured the man. "The whole 4th Battalion's behind me. You'll be okay."

As Hill crossed the perimeter, other members of Bravo

followed. Lieutenant Lindseth was only a short distance behind Hill. He directed his medics to tend to the wounded and
then moved to the far side of the perimeter. There he took up
a position behind a large fallen log. Not forty meters in front
of him the NVA opened fire from their bunkers. Lindseth
couldn't get above the log to fire back, so he just stayed put.

As Lindseth's platoon members took up positions at the
front of the line, Lieutenant Proffitt's tied in on the left;
Lieutenant Moore's were on the right.

The carnage shocked Proffitt. Trees were down everywhere.
Dead paratroopers were scattered where they had fallen. The
survivors from 2d Battalion seemed dazed, shocked. Proffitt
was reminded of pictures he'd seen of shell-shocked combatants from World War II and the Korean War. It was all very
grisly.

When Captain Leonard entered 2d Battalion's position, he
immediately joined Lieutenant O'Leary. Word of the linkup
reached Colonel Johnson at 1700. O'Leary, though greatly
relieved by the reinforcements, couldn't help but wonder if
they weren't all in the same desperate situation. Putting
aside his concerns O'Leary briefed Leonard on what he
knew about the disposition of the 2d Battalion men and then
turned over command to him.

Once Bravo, 4/503d, arrived on Hill 875, Major Kelly decided that it was time for another try at getting his little command group in. He rounded up a Huey, loaded Harrison and
Philbin aboard, and took off just before 1800.

A few minutes later the Huey hovered ten feet over the
LZ; the pilot couldn't get any lower because of his vulnerability to enemy fire. Harrison looked out the door. He
couldn't believe it. Below him were dozens of stumps, most
pointing jaggedly toward him.

Harrison turned and started to say to Kelly, "I don't
think . . ." when he felt a hand shove against his back. He
tumbled downward, fortunately missing the stumps. The
door gunner had pushed him out of the chopper. Seconds
later Kelly and Philbin leapt earthward.

While Harrison and Philbin went to find what was left of

their companies, Kelly ordered the chopper to stay put. Some 2/503d members were carrying casualties to the LZ. With no enemy fire directed at him at that moment, the pilot descended to just above the stumps. Five severely wounded paratroopers were loaded up. Then the chopper lifted off.

Lieutenant Harrison found little unit cohesion as he moved about the perimeter. Paratroopers were in position without regard to any real coordination of effort. Most, he noticed, seemed unable to comprehend the simplest of commands. They had suffered too much to be an effective force.

Harrison realized that he'd found Tom Remington when a crumpled form asked in a familiar voice, "Matt, how ya doing?"

Harrison could barely reply. He didn't see how Remington could be alive. With dried blood caked around his ears and nearly a half dozen holes in his body, Remington should have been dead.

"You got any water, Matt?" Remington asked weakly.

"Sure, Tommy. All you need."

While Remington drank the welcome fluid, Major Kelly went by. He was running around, yelling at the paratroopers to get up. Most stared numbly back at him. Kelly was getting madder by the minute. "C'mon, goddamnit!" he yelled at one small group. "Get up and get on the line."

Several of the men responded—slowly to be sure—but they moved toward the perimeter. One paratrooper didn't move. Kelly berated him. "What's the matter with you, trooper? You too good to fight or are you just too scared?"

When that didn't affect the man, Kelly reached down and shook his shoulder. He recoiled. The man was dead. Kelly moved on, yelling and swearing at any reluctant paratroopers.

Harrison spent the time remaining before dark trying to find out how many people were left in Alpha. It was dangerous work, for most movement brought a burst of AK-47 or machine-gun fire from the NVA. Harrison could plainly see the muzzle blasts farther up the hill. Then several enemy mortar rounds fell in the perimeter. Their sharp explosions were immediately followed by new cries of pain. God, how long can the slaughter continue? he wondered.

When he'd finished his count Harrison had been able to identify twenty-five members of Alpha still on their feet. Only two were NCOs.

Alpha, 4/503d, arrived on the hill at 2100. Their trek had been uneventful. Captain Muldoon had fully expected to be hit after it got dark, but there had been no evidence at all of the enemy. In fact, the first sign Muldoon had of the fighting on Hill 875 came when he stumbled across the bodies of Captain Kiley and his command group. He saw a few more bodies; then they were in the perimeter. Muldoon pushed his people out past the positions held by 2/503d on the left, or east, side of the hill.

One hour and twenty minutes after Muldoon arrived, Captain Connolly's Charlie, 4/503d, came up Hill 875. Most of Charlie's movement had occurred after dark, making the paratroopers very nervous. Private 1st Class Tauss gave the radio mike to Connolly at one point so the captain could ask Colonel Johnson for permission to dig in for the night at their current position. Johnson denied the request. "You've got to get to Hill 875 tonight," he told Connolly. Though anxious about moving through enemy territory at night, Connolly pushed on.

Sergeant Ray Bull had to hang onto the pack straps of the man in front of him to avoid getting lost in the dark. Specialist 4th Class Jake Duffy had to hang onto the man in front of him, too. He couldn't understand how the point man could tell where he was going in the dark. He must have a sixth sense, Duffy finally decided. As they neared Hill 875 some of the paratroopers from 4/503d already on the hill periodically fired their weapons to guide Charlie in.

By the time Charlie reached the base of Hill 875, Spooky was overhead, dropping flares near the hill's crest, providing some light for them to see by. Suddenly, Duffy stumbled over a dead body. "Shit!" he cursed.

His RTO, Pfc. Darryl Haymes, said, "Christ, there's gook bodies all over the place."

Duffy peered into the flare-lighted jungle. "I'm afraid they aren't gooks," he announced.

He was right. Dead Americans lay everywhere. This was worse than what he'd seen at the 11 November fight. It had to have been one hell of a battle, he told himself.

A few minutes later Charlie, 4/503d, entered the new perimeter. Connolly set his men into position along the hill's west edge. Together, Duffy and Haymes scraped a narrow, full-length slit trench in the ground, then lay down in it. Not far away Private 1st Class Tauss hunted for a place to sleep. For him, it was too much effort to dig in. He finally spotted a log and lay behind it, protected from enemy fire.

By midnight the relief force was firmly established on Hill 875. No more enemy fire came at the paratroopers for the rest of the night. The only sounds to punctuate the stillness of the jungle were the continued screams and moans of the wounded.

CHAPTER 14

HILL 875:
THE FINAL DAYS

While the 173d's maneuver battalions had been tangling with the NVA's 66th and 174th regiments south of Ben Het and west of the Dak Klong River, other elements of the I Field Force had not been idle. On 18 November at Hill 1416, a high peak northeast of Tan Canh, the ARVN 3/42d Infantry found the NVA 24th Infantry Regiment in well dug-in positions. Unable to dislodge the enemy forces alone, the 3/42d was reinforced by the ARVN 2d and 3d Airborne battalions. A 4th Infantry Division 155mm howitzer battery joined two ARVN 105mm batteries in pounding Hill 1416 for most of the morning of 19 November.

With the ARVN 3/42d Infantry in blocking positions to the west, the two ARVN airborne battalions came at the hill from the north and south. Vicious, brutal, close-in fighting raged for the rest of the day and into the night. The ARVN paratroopers threw the NVA off Hill 1416 on 20 November, but at a heavy cost: Sixty-six South Vietnamese died and more than 290 were wounded. The ARVN reported an enemy body count of 248. As a result of the fight, the NVA 24th Infantry Regiment was finished as an effective fighting force. Its survivors snuck away to the north before heading west to refuge in Laos.

The area around Hill 1338, south of Dak To, continued to be hotly contested. The 4th Infantry Division's 3/12th Infantry suffered fifteen wounded on 18 November in a brisk firefight west of the hill. U.S. artillery, called in to blast the NVA's positions, caused two additional friendly casualties.

Far to the south, near Hill 530, east of the Dak Klong, Dog

Company, 1/8th Infantry, engaged a good-sized NVA force for more than an hour on 19 November. They suffered four killed and five wounded, while killing four NVA.

That same day, about four kilometers west of Hill 1338, elements of the 3/12th Infantry were attacked by the enemy. After driving them off, the infantrymen were subjected to a vicious mortar barrage as they dug in for the night. In all, they lost four dead and seven wounded. Eighteen NVA bodies were counted on the battlefield.

Despite these intense contacts, the main focus of Generals Rosson, Peers, and Schweiter continued to be the two battalions of the 173d Airborne Brigade locked in mortal combat on the dusty hilltop just six kilometers from the Cambodian border.

Dawn on Tuesday, 21 November, revealed a scene on Hill 875 that no survivor of that battle could ever forget. The enormous amounts of ordnance expended by both forces had turned the once-lush tropical jungle into a scarred and torn landscape. Most trees had been stripped of their branches, which now covered the ground in piles two to three feet deep. Trunks of fallen trees lay helter-skelter across the hill, providing fighting positions and cover for Americans and North Vietnamese alike. Those trees not knocked down stood starkly denuded against the blue sky, vivid reminders of man's destructive power.

The paratroopers' perimeter resembled a garbage dump of war. Everywhere one looked lay abandoned weapons, helmets, rucksacks, clothing, canteens, and empty ration containers. Nearly every square foot of ground was covered with debris. Hanging over the perimeter was a horrible smell: the smell of death. The acrid odor of decaying and rotting flesh combined with the smells of vomit, feces, urine, blood, gunpowder, and napalm etched itself permanently into the memories of those who were on Hill 875.

And everywhere were bodies and parts of bodies. The five-hundred-pound bomb had flung human remains all across the hill. Though some effort had been made to gather the casualties, many of the paratroopers killed or injured over the past two days still lay where they had fallen. The sight sickened many of the hardened veterans.

When Private 1st Class Tauss awoke that morning he found that the log next to which he'd sought protection the night before was actually a dead paratrooper. He moved away with a shudder.

Lieutenant Lindseth had a similar experience. He'd taken a position behind a large log. Near him lay a 2d Battalion paratrooper partially covered with a poncho. During the night the man suffered repeated bouts of coughing and hacking. Lindseth attributed it to the cold night air. When morning came, and the coughing continued, Lindseth called for a medic. The medic pulled aside the poncho to reveal that the Sky Soldier had no legs. The man died a short time later.

As soon as it was light enough to see, Captain Connolly sent Sergeant Bull's squad on a clearing patrol. Bull made about thirty meters outside the perimeter, carefully stepping over bodies and loose ordnance, when he heard the frantic cry, "Incoming!" He and his men hit the dirt.

The first NVA mortar shells dropped into the compact perimeter at 0655. While everyone frantically scrambled for cover, the enemy 60mm and 82mm mortars slammed into the paratroopers. For the next two hours, at fifteen- to twenty-minute intervals, five- and six-round volleys fell on the crowded hillside. With several men jammed into each fighting hole, most mortar bursts caused multiple deaths and injuries.

Once the first mortar barrage ended, Sergeant Bull and the men in his squad scrambled back inside the perimeter. Bull felt great relief. His brief foray outside the friendly perimeter had scared him. He had sensed that the NVA were nearby in concealed positions, just waiting for him to move farther from the perimeter. In a way, Bull realized, the enemy mortar barrage had saved his life.

Specialist 4th Class Duffy and Private 1st Class Haymes lay crouched under some fallen trees, trying to get a fix on the enemy mortar positions. They could clearly hear the sounds of shells leaving their tubes, which seemed to be emplaced on a hill to the west. Duffy would shoot a compass azimuth toward the sound and then give the coordinates to Haymes. By the time the 4.2-inch mortar shells impacted, however, the North Vietnamese had moved. Soon mortars from a new position came in and Duffy would repeat the process.

The enemy mortar attacks that day killed five Americans and wounded forty-seven.

Despite the mortars, the first priority was the evacuation of the wounded. Colonel Johnson, now in command of all forces on Hill 875, directed that a new, larger LZ be cut. Captain Leonard found a site farther down the hill, out of the direct line of fire. After pulling the 2d Battalion survivors off the firing line, Leonard, operating as the overall ground commander, put some of them to work clearing the LZ while others gathered up and treated the wounded.

A 4th Battalion medic found Sp4 John Steer about mid-morning. "Don't worry, you'll be okay," the man assured Steer. "They can put that arm back on."

Steer knew that was bullshit, but he appreciated the sentiment. After being bandaged, he was carried away on a poncho to await evacuation.

Lieutenant Remington had been given morphine by a 4th Battalion medic on Monday evening. Most of the night and the following morning passed in a blur for him. But at least he knew now he'd live.

Lieutenant O'Leary, too, had been treated by 4th Battalion medics. After he'd briefed Captain Leonard on the situation, he was removed to the aid station. His first sergeant, Mike Deeb, lay nearby, his head heavily swathed in bandages. O'Leary prayed he'd survive.

The task of identifying the 2/503d's dead fell on the companies' executive officers. Both Lieutenants Philbin and Harrison carried company rosters with them. When the enemy firing permitted, they moved about the perimeter, turning over corpses, checking dog tags, and making the appropriate notes on their rosters.

Harrison worked his way down the hill to where Alpha Company had been overrun. Nothing he'd witnessed so far in the war, including the carnage of 22 June, prepared him for what he saw. Bodies lay everywhere. He found Captain Kiley and his command group where the swarming NVA had gunned them down at point-blank range. It was obvious that Kiley had tried to organize a hasty defense, but there had simply been too many NVA.

Nearby, Harrison found the bodies of the Weapons Platoon members who'd been overrun. Farther down the hill he found Lozada. The plucky paratrooper lay where he had fallen, his M60 beside him. Already Harrison had heard of Lozada's remarkable courage in holding off the advancing NVA and warning the others of the approaching danger.

Although the new LZ itself was defiladed from any direct NVA fire, helicopters would still be exposed to fire as they arrived and departed. To suppress the enemy's fire, Captain Leonard coordinated artillery barrages and air strikes against the top of Hill 875 and other nearby hilltops.

While all this activity occurred, Colonel Johnson had been in constant radio contact with Captain Leonard. At 0900 Johnson told Leonard to be ready to attack Hill 875 at 1100. Alpha would move down off the ridge finger along its east side and attack from that direction. Captain Connolly's Charlie would go up the hill along the right half of the finger, while Bravo would attack on the left half. In the intervening two hours Hill 875 would continue to be pounded by jets and artillery.

At about 1000 several helicopters hovered over the perimeter to drop in much-needed supplies. While enemy fire tore into the choppers, their brave crew members kicked out rations, water (in long rubber bladders that the paratroopers called "elephant rubbers"), ammo, and weapons. Besides several 81mm mortars and their shells, flamethrowers and LAAWs came in. They would be used against the enemy's bunkers. Because none of the junior enlisted men knew how to use the LAAWs, the company commanders issued them to the NCOs. The flamethrowers couldn't be used because they arrived without the strikers necessary to ignite their flammable mixture. Leonard thought that maybe the fuel could be pumped into enemy bunkers and then ignited by a grenade.

Then, with everyone nervously awaiting the order to go, the attack was postponed. The LZ had not yet been completed. Since Colonel Johnson didn't want to start the assault until all the previously wounded had been evacuated, he told Captain Leonard to wait. The intervening time was put to good use, though. Ten F-100s and two F-4Cs dropped fifteen more tons of high-explosive bombs and seven more tons of napalm on the top of Hill 875. Few of the Sky Soldiers expected any NVA to have lived through that horrible morning bombardment.

Sporadic enemy mortar attacks delayed completion of the LZ until 1415. At 1430 the first dustoff came in. It picked up seven of the most seriously wounded and headed out. More medevacs headed in to carry the casualties to safety.

At 1505 Captain Leonard gave the order, "Attack!"

The advancing paratroopers were forced to go up and over the tangle of fallen logs, silhouetting themselves against the sky, making them perfect targets for the NVA. And the North Vietnamese responded with a horrifying barrage of small-arms and automatic-weapons fire, Chicoms, RPGs, B-40 rockets, and mortars.

Lieutenant Proffitt's 2d Platoon, with twenty men, held the left flank of Bravo's advancing line. Before they'd made ten feet an enemy mortar shell exploded among them, killing two. The terrain 2d Platoon moved over was less tangled than other areas, allowing them to use fire and maneuver techniques to move toward the first enemy-held bunker line. As Proffitt's Sky Soldiers sought cover behind upright trees, enemy snipers from farther up the hill took them under fire, hitting several men. So much enemy lead filled the air that Proffitt thought the bullets would chew right through the tree he had taken refuge behind. He crouched lower, wishing he could crawl into his helmet.

In the center of Bravo's line, Lieutenant Lindseth had just eighteen men in 3d Platoon. Sergeant Hill moved at the front of Lindseth's platoon, a medic on his left, an engineer to his right. They ran forward perhaps twenty feet before the enemy bunkers above them unleashed a blistering hail of fire. Two men behind Hill died in the fusillade. Duck-walking, crawling, and jumping over logs, Hill and his two companions advanced about another ten feet, firing their weapons at the invisible enemy.

Hill turned to yell at the men off to his right to slow down; he thought they were moving too fast and getting ahead of the others. They didn't hear him due to the incredible volume of noise. Hill started to yell again, but just then an enemy mortar shell exploded right in front of the engineer. All three men went down in the blast. As Hill regained his senses he felt blood running from his neck and leg. He pulled his drive-on rag free and wrapped it around his neck wound, stanching the flow. A few feet away the engineer lay on his stomach, moaning loudly. To Hill's left the medic slowly sat up, both legs jutting in front of him at odd angles.

"Doc, you okay?" Hill called out.

"I got two broken legs" came the answer.

Hill snaked forward to the engineer and turned him over. Something rolled to the ground from a gaping hole in the engineer's trousers. In horror Hill realized it was the man's penis. Hill carefully picked it up and stuck it back in the engineer's pants. He didn't want him to see it and become hysterical. He also hoped that the doctors at an evacuation hospital might be able to reattach it. He rolled the engineer back over onto his stomach, then crawled over to the medic.

Hill put dressings on the medic's wounds, then the medic bandaged the quarter-sized hole on the back of Hill's neck and the wound in his leg. When he'd finished Hill said, "I'll crawl back downhill and get some help."

A short distance down the hill Sergeant Hill found Captain Leonard. "Sir, I got two wounded right up there that need help bad."

"I'll send some medics," Leonard responded. "Now get your ass on the ground. You're on your way out of here."

Lieutenant Lindseth had taken refuge behind a log. Enemy bullets beat a steady tattoo on it as they tore into the wood. Around him B-40 rockets skimmed along just inches above the ground, exploding with deadly effectiveness among the

crowded Sky Soldiers. He spotted an NVA bunker camouflaged with leaves and branches. Braving the intense fire, he
left his position to crawl toward it. The bunker's firing slit
measured barely twelve inches in length. Lindseth shoved in
four grenades. They erupted in a crashing roar. Suddenly,
three Chicoms flew out of the bunker, landing just in front
of him. He flipped himself out of the way. None of the
grenades went off.

Just as he finished congratulating himself on his good fortune, two more enemy grenades landed nearby. Lindseth
curled into a tight ball. The two Chicoms blew up in quick
succession. Amazingly, Lindseth escaped injury.

Now thoroughly angry, Lindseth slid back downhill. He
collected an armful of LAAWs and made his way back to the
bunker. He fired six of the bazookalike weapons point-blank
at the bunker. The shells erupted unsuccessfully against the
well-built position.

Unable to continue his platoon's advance, Lindseth stayed
behind a log for the rest of the afternoon, directing artillery
fire against enemy bunkers. Others around him fired back,
but the enemy fire was just too heavy for them to aim effectively.

At one point a new lieutenant from another company
whom Lindseth did not know well dropped in beside him.

"We gotta attack," the new arrival said.

"Don't try it," Lindseth warned. "You'll be killed."

Ignoring Lindseth's admonition, the lieutenant slid over
the log, firing his M16. He made all of ten feet before he was
cut down in a flurry of small-arms fire.

On Bravo's right flank Lt. Larry Moore's 1st Platoon, with
thirty-six men, ran into heavy firing from snipers farther up
the hill. As they slowly pushed forward, response from the
enemy bunkers increased in intensity. Soon, the platoon was
nearly engulfed with NVA automatic-weapons fire. Moore's
paratroopers sought protection behind whatever cover was
available: small trees, logs, or dirt mounds. When Moore finally spotted an enemy bunker, he turned and called for his
platoon to take it under fire. To his surprise, only a dozen
paratroopers had come this far forward with him.

While they fired, NVA from other concealed positions started sending B-40 rockets into 1st Platoon. Moore called for his RTO, but the youth was riddled by a burst of RPD fire as he dashed to Moore. Seconds later Moore heard the distinctive swoosh of an incoming B-40. He desperately tried to twist from its path but didn't make it. The rocket's explosion wounded him and several others. First Platoon's attack halted.

Charlie Company moved on Bravo's right, or west, flank. As Captain Connolly got his company into position, he was concerned about the narrowness of the ridge finger. There simply wasn't enough room for the two companies to operate effectively. In fact, his right flank platoon actually moved along the downward slope of the finger. There they would not only be exposed to NVA fire from nearby hills, but they'd be unable to help if the other platoons ran into trouble.

And they did run into trouble. The enemy bunkers were all mutually supporting, preventing any bold flanking attacks. The enemy positions had to be taken straight on. As had Bravo's paratroopers, Charlie's found the tangled jungle growth to be a major impediment to their advance. Unable to move over the logs due to the constant streams of hot lead snapping over their heads, Charlie's members unleashed a barrage of hand grenades at suspected enemy positions. The explosions were comforting but had little effect on the well-constructed enemy bunkers.

Private 1st Class Tauss stayed with Connolly throughout the assault. As the brave captain repeatedly exposed himself to enemy fire to dash between his platoons, encouraging the men to attack, Tauss moved beside him, frequently wishing that Connolly wasn't so bold. In response to Colonel Johnson's radioed inquiries, Tauss, while dodging around and ducking bullets, kept him informed of Charlie's progress or lack of it.

Connolly wished Johnson was on the ground, guiding the attack from there rather than from a Huey a thousand feet above the hill. As far as Connolly was concerned, the battalion commander couldn't really understand how the battle was progressing unless he participated at ground level.

Despite the heavy enemy fire, Connolly's men continued to push forward. One of Charlie's platoon leaders, 1st Lt. Tracy Murrey, spotted an NVA machine-gun nest. Yelling for a nearby squad to cover him, Murrey pulled the pin on a grenade. With the deadly missile clamped in one hand and a .45-caliber pistol in the other, Murrey attacked the position head-on. He made it about halfway before being cut down by a burst of enemy fire. His leaderless platoon faltered in its attack.

Not far away, Sergeant Bull dove for cover as B-40 rockets skimmed in along the ground. They seemed to be coming from every direction, making it hard to dodge one without jumping in front of another. Bull finally gave up. He just burrowed down under some twisted undergrowth and hoped a rocket wouldn't find him.

Specialist 4th Class Duffy called in dozens of volleys of 4.2-inch mortars, trying to suppress the NVA's fire, but without much success. Most of the enemy bunkers were covered with several feet of dirt and additional overhead cover. The shells just couldn't penetrate that much protection. In other places the ground was so soft after being churned up by tons of U.S. explosives that the shells failed to detonate upon impact. But Duffy kept calling in missions, walking the shells back and forth in front of Charlie Company, hoping he was doing some damage to the NVA.

Because of the narrowness of the spur leading to the crest of Hill 875, Alpha Company moved down the east side of the ridge finger and advanced to the south before turning and starting up the steep eastern face of the hill. The company had suffered heavily in the morning mortar attacks, losing several killed and fifteen wounded, including 1st Platoon's leader, 1st Lt. Rudolph Bejarano. First Lieutenant Mercer O. Vandenberg came over from Weapons Platoon to replace Bejarano, leaving Sfc. Thomas W. Thornton in command of the mortars.

Captain Muldoon put Lieutenant Denny's 3d Platoon on the left; Lieutenant Wolfe's 2d Platoon took the center and Lieutenant Vandenberg held the right. When Muldoon received word from Colonel Johnson to move out, he relayed the word to his platoon leaders.

Initially, Alpha made good progress. Because of the steep terrain the NVA weren't expecting an attack from that direction. When they discovered the paratroopers, all hell broke loose. First, small-arms fire crackled sporadically from higher on the hill. A few minutes later the heavy cough of RPDs added to the din. Next, the NVA began rolling hand grenades downhill. Then mortar shells rained from the sky, dozens of them at once.

Most of the shells landed with devastating accuracy in 1st Platoon. Lieutenant Vandenberg fell, badly wounded in the stomach. Around him, nearly a dozen of his men fell, too. As soon as Muldoon learned of Vandenberg's injuries, he dispatched a medic and his XO, 1st Lt. Thomas J. Tarpley, to 1st Platoon. While the medic patched up the wounded, Tarpley reorganized the remaining six to eight men.

In the meantime, Denny's and Wolfe's platoons had overcome stiff resistance to advance more than halfway up the hill. In 3d Platoon, Plt. Sgt. Joseph F. Decanto and M60 gunner Sp4 John H. Deatherage crept up on one bunker and knocked it out. But a sudden increase in the enemy's automatic-weapons fire drove them to ground. Others sought cover, too. Alpha's attack halted.

Then, 1st Sgt. Irwin Frazier jumped up, yelled, "Follow me!" and went after a key enemy bunker firing diagonally across Alpha's front. While machine gunner Pfc. Dennis Adams pumped rounds at the bunker's narrow firing slit, Frazier crept close enough to toss in a grenade. With that bunker gone the advance continued.

Moving behind 3d Platoon, Muldoon couldn't believe the number of NVA grenades coming at him. Chicoms hit all around his command group, most rolling farther down the slope before exploding. Some of the missiles actually hit him, his RTOs, and those around them before bouncing away. Soon, their luck ran out; both RTOs were hit by shrapnel. Amazingly, no enemy metal found Muldoon.

By 1700 Lieutenant Denny's platoon, clawing, fighting, bleeding, and dying, had neared the top. Denny was crouched in the bottom of an NVA trench he'd just captured, lobbing grenades back and forth with the North Vietnamese in the next trench line. Wolfe's platoon was not far behind Denny's, and Tarpley, who'd been joined by 1st Sergeant Frazier, had brought the few men remaining in his platoon nearly as far up the hill as Denny.

Muldoon began to think that he might just make it all the way to the top. If only he didn't lose too many more men, they might do it.

Then Muldoon got a radio message from Colonel Johnson. "Pull back," Johnson ordered.

Muldoon was incredulous. They'd been fighting for nearly two hours and, now, as they neared their objective, they were being called back. It wasn't right. He radioed Johnson that he wanted to keep on going.

Johnson said no. Bravo's attack had ground to a halt under the vicious NVA fire. With less resistance but no support along its left flank, Charlie Company could not advance, either. Johnson ordered all three companies to return to their jump-off position.

Muldoon still didn't want to do it; giving up terrain his men had died for when they were so close to achieving victory seemed grossly unfair. He felt that if Johnson had been on the ground to see how close they were to punching through the NVA's line he wouldn't have issued the withdrawal order (Captain Connolly, too, believed they were close and that Johnson didn't understand that from his chopper). But Muldoon had no choice. Johnson's orders were clear. Muldoon passed the order to his platoon leaders.

Lieutenant Denny argued against the recall, too. Tarpley did, also. They were within meters of being atop Hill 875.

"Orders are orders," Muldoon told them. "Begin disengaging. Account for everyone. We don't want to leave any of the wounded out there."

Reluctantly, Denny, Tarpley, and Wolfe began the retrograde movement. On the north slope of Hill 875 Bravo and Charlie companies started inching back, too. By 1800 all three companies had linked up at their former position, forming a protective perimeter.

The aborted attack had been very costly. Lieutenant Moore's 1st Platoon of Bravo Company suffered seven killed and fifteen wounded, reducing it to fourteen effectives. Lind-seth's platoon had just nine able-bodied men left. Proffitt's platoon had a few more. Alpha Company lost seven killed and fifty-seven wounded. Charlie Company had lost about twenty-five men.

Members of 2d Battalion not assigned to security duty around the LZ followed 4/503d's assault companies, helping evacuate their wounded. Sergeant Welch and Specialist Zac-cone were among those assisting 4th Battalion's casualties. Dodging bullets, braving exploding grenades and mortar shells, the pair edged forward to reach the casualties, pulled them out of the line of fire, and carried them to the waiting medics. They made a dozen trips before the attack ended. Those casualties too badly wounded to return to the firing line after treatment were gathered near the new aid station established adjacent to the LZ.

A few choppers made it in after dark to evacuate the more seriously wounded. Most of the casualties, though, had to spend a long cold night on Hill 875. Their crying and moan-ing drowned out most other sounds.

Wednesday, 22 November, was mortar day on Hill 875. Beginning just after first light the NVA began dropping mor-tar shells into the Sky Soldiers' perimeter with alarming pre-cision. As they had before, the NVA gunners would loose a barrage of a half-dozen rounds and then move the tubes. As long as an hour might pass before the fear-generating cry "Incoming!" reverberated again across the perimeter. Those unlucky enough to be caught above ground dashed madly about seeking cover.

Most of the men spent the day under cover, huddled at the bottom of their holes. They'd eat in the hole, throwing the empty ration cans outside to add to the growing litter piles. They'd defecate and urinate in their helmets, spilling those contents onto the ground, too. Few Sky Soldiers were bold enough to perform these bodily functions in the open. Some-times, even staying in your hole was not safe.

Private 1st Class Orona was crawling to a new position when he heard his name called. He turned to find himself face-to-face with an old buddy from basic training and jump school. They talked for a few minutes, bringing each other up-to-date on dead or wounded friends, before someone screamed, "Incoming!" Orona hurriedly low-crawled back to his own hole.

When the barrage ended Orona snaked back to his friend's hole to finish their conversation, only to find his buddy dead. A mortar shell had landed right in his hole. He never knew what hit him.

Lieutenant Proffitt spent time moving among his platoon's positions, making sure that everyone was as secure as possible. He'd just finished conferring with Sergeant 1st Class Wiggins when he heard the warning of incoming mortars. Proffitt hurried to his own hole. Seconds after he crawled into it the mortars struck. Proffitt came through the attack unharmed, but his PRC-25 wasn't so lucky. He'd left it above ground along the edge of his hole. When the mortars stopped Proffitt found his radio riddled with shrapnel. Thank God he'd made it to cover, he told himself.

In Charlie Company Specialist Duffy, as he had the day before, tried to pinpoint the enemy mortars' location by sound, but he wasn't having too much luck. By plotting the presumed locations of the NVA tubes on their maps, Duffy and Private 1st Class Haymes tried to anticipate the enemy's next relocation but without success. For the two mortar FOs it was a very frustrating ordeal.

Captain Muldoon watched helplessly, and with growing anger, as the mortars inflicted numerous additional casualties among his already-battered men. All three of his remaining officers had been hit by fragments; rare was the enlisted man not hit at least once by flying metal.

Muldoon himself took several pieces of jagged shrapnel in his chest from a mortar burst. The impact sent him flying in one direction, his helmet, radio, and rifle in others. The wounds maddened Muldoon more than hurt him. He raced around, gathering his gear. With that done he stormed off toward the jungle, nearly making it past the perimeter before one of his privates stopped him.

"Where ya going, sir?" the youngster asked solicitously.

"I'm tired of this shit. I'm gonna go get those little fuckers," Muldoon announced, shaking his rifle toward the dense jungle.

"Sir, you don't really want to do that, do you, sir?"

Muldoon looked around him. Several nearby soldiers were looking at him. "No," he said after brief reflection. "I guess I don't."

Then he returned to his bunker, still mad but in control of himself.

Some of the Sky Soldiers were forced to spend most of their time above ground. The huge amounts of ordnance shot back and forth inevitably meant that some of it did not detonate. The live rounds had to be destroyed lest they cause friendly casualties. That dangerous task fell to the engineers attached to each rifle company.

Nineteen-year-old Sp4 James Coleman had just joined Charlie, 4/503d, in October. Though initially trained as an engineer, Coleman had spent the previous eighteen months as a parachute rigger at Fort Campbell. His assignment as an explosive ordnance demolition man caught him by surprise. He tried to explain this to the CO of the 173d Engineer Company but to no avail. The captain unceremoniously told him to get his "ass out to the field."

As an FNG Coleman was totally unprepared for the carnage on Hill 875. He thought there was just a platoon cut off, not three companies. The large number of casualties stunned him. He couldn't believe there could be that many dead and wounded in one place.

Part of Coleman's responsibilities included collecting all unexploded ordnance and detonating it. He had to check each corpse for any live ammo; that was a gruesome task. When he'd collected a load of unexploded grenades, he'd pass them out. Enemy grenades he found were piled at the base of a tree and blown up with C-4 explosives.

On 22 November many of the NVA's mortar shells didn't go off, either due to faulty mechanisms or because they'd landed in soft dirt. Coleman would hear the call, "Engineer up!" He'd have to leave his hole, crawl to where the shell was, and disarm it or carry it away. All day long he kept wishing he'd paid more attention in explosive ordnance disposal class.

Originally, the 4/503d was scheduled to launch another attack against Hill 875 beginning at 1000 Wednesday. Earlier that morning General Schweiter choppered in to FSB 16 to confer with Colonel Johnson about the situation on Hill 875. The two talked for only a few minutes before several NVA rockets hit just short of the landing pad. Schweiter had to leave. As he boarded his C-and-C chopper he told Johnson, "The decision to attack is yours." Then he was gone.

Johnson met with his staff at the TOC. After putting together a plan of attack the battalion commander flew to Hill 875. In a shallow depression not far from the front line, Johnson met with Muldoon, Leonard, and Connolly.

Johnson told his three captains that General Schweiter had left the decision to take Hill 875 to them. Someone had to take the hill, he told them. Either they or the 4th Infantry Division would do it. Since they were already there, Johnson felt they should do it. Did they have any problem with that?

None of them did. (In fact, Connolly was surprised that Johnson gave them any option.) As far as they were concerned, they'd take the hill or they'd all die trying. Johnson nodded his approval; he'd really expected nothing less. Then the four began planning and coordinating the attack.

All agreed that the final attack would come the next day. The rest of Wednesday would be used to subject the top of Hill 875 to one of the most severe bombardments yet witnessed in the war. Every available howitzer and jet plane would be turned loose on the hill. A constant pounding by artillery shells, five-hundred- and seven-hundred-fifty-pound bombs, and canisters of napalm would create havoc among the defenders. The barrages would continue right up to H hour, 1100 on 23 November.

Bravo Company would advance up the left half of the ridge finger; Charlie would take the right. The badly weakened Alpha Company would advance behind them, ready to go wherever the need was greatest. Behind Alpha, members of 2d Battalion would follow, once again in charge of aiding the wounded.

Reinforcements had been made available, Johnson said. Two companies from the 4th Infantry Division would attack up the north slope of Hill 875. The coordinated assaults would squeeze the NVA in a vise, destroying them, the battalion commander predicted.

Was there anything else they needed? Johnson asked as he prepared to depart.

Captain Leonard said yes. He needed more 60mm mortar ammo. Plus, he wanted the battalion executive officer, Maj. Richard M. Scott, to come out. The 2d Battalion XO, Major Kelly, was still on the hill running around being a pain in the ass. Would Johnson get rid of him? Johnson would.

When the battalion commander left, the three captains returned to their units. Captain Leonard voluntarily moved to the very forward edge of the perimeter. From that advanced and exposed position he coordinated the artillery barrages and air strikes for the rest of the day.

During the morning hours of 22 November the LZ was expanded so two choppers could be on the ground at one time. It took the balance of the day for the rest of the wounded from the two battalions to be evacuated, with the last casualties from the previous day's fight not pulled out until early afternoon. Then, when there were no more fresh wounded from mortar attacks to evacuate, the extraction of the dead began. There were many of them, so many that the 173d had to obtain extra body bags from the 4th Infantry Division's quartermaster.

Such a large number of helicopters were trying to get in and out of the LZ that some coordination was needed to relieve the congestion. Colonel Johnson ordered the S-3 (Air), 1st Lt. Peyton Ligon, and his chief NCO, SSgt. William Chenault, to go to Hill 875 and establish control of the LZ.

Ligon had no easy time getting onto the hill. On his chopper's approach the Huey in front of them was driven off by heavy fire. In response, the pilot of Ligon's aircraft overtorqued the machine as he tried to break off his approach. It crash-landed about a kilometer southeast of Hill 875.

Unhurt, Ligon and the crew took up defensive positions around the downed Huey. A short time later Colonel Johnson's Huey swooped down, picked them all up, and took them to Dak To. There Ligon boarded another chopper and finally completed his journey.

Once on the ground Ligon and Chenault immediately went to work prioritizing the loads. First consideration was given to getting any wounded out, then to supplies coming in, and finally to removing the dead.

Ligon functioned as an air traffic controller, issuing precise landing instructions to incoming choppers when they were about two kilometers out. Throughout the day sporadic mortar rounds landed on the LZ, damaging helicopters and wounding men. Nearly every chopper landing or taking off took small-arms fire from NVA farther up Hill 875 or on nearby hills. Ligon had the paratroopers positioned around the LZ put out suppressive fire, but it did little good, since they didn't know where the NVA were.

Correspondents by the score were clamoring to get to Hill 875. Dak To was the biggest story in South Vietnam that fall, and the correspondents wanted to go where the action was. The 173d's public information officer and his staff went to extraordinary lengths to accommodate the numerous correspondents, but some of the reporters wouldn't wait for permission to board a chopper.

On FSB 16, MSgt. Larry Okendo, filling in for Sgt. Maj. Ted Arthurs while he was on R and R, oversaw the loading of choppers with supplies bound for the hill. When two reporters boarded a Huey without authorization, Okendo explained why they had to debark. When they refused Okendo cocked his M16, aimed it at the two civilians, and threatened to shoot them unless they got off. They got off.

About the same time, at the LZ on Hill 875, Sergeant Chenault radioed Captain Muldoon (the former S-3 [Air]). "I've got a problem, sir," Chenault said. "Can you help?"

When he arrived at the LZ Muldoon found Chenault

confronted by three correspondents. They'd come in on an earlier chopper and now that they had their stories they wanted to leave. Chenault had refused to let them board a chopper since he still had wounded to get out. The reporters were demanding seats.

Muldoon looked at the three civilians. It was obvious they were scared. He patiently explained that they would not be flown off Hill 875 until all the wounded had been evacuated. Then he turned to Chenault and, in a loud voice, told him, "If any reporter tries to board a chopper without your permission, shoot him in the leg. Then they can be boarded."

Even Colonel Partain had problems with correspondents. At the main airstrip at Dak To, a group of reporters badgered him for a ride to Hill 875. Partain told them that rations and ammo had first priority; he couldn't spare any space for reporters. As soon as he could, he promised them, he'd get them out to the hill.

Later, when he had room on two Hueys, Partain told the reporters they could board. "But," he said, "since the choppers will be evacuating wounded on their return trips, anyone who does go out to the hill will have to spend the night there." No one took Partain up on his offer.

Captain Ken Smith hitched a ride out to Hill 875 on Wednesday. He had just returned from his R and R in Hawaii when his old battalion went up the hill. Reports of the devastation filled Smith with dread. He knew so many of the men; from Father Watters to Bart O'Leary. And now they were dead or badly wounded. Though Smith knew it was a soldier's plight to lose friends, it was still hard to take.

Smith was particularly anxious for news of his friend and former first sergeant, Mike Deeb. He'd heard that Deeb had been badly wounded but could get no more information on him. Smith checked the names of the Sky Soldiers who'd passed through the medical company but did not find Deeb's name. Then Smith heard that Deeb was still on the hill, unable to be medevaced because of heavy enemy fire.

I'll get him out, Smith told himself. He wasn't about to let Deeb linger in pain. So he hitched a ride on an outgoing Huey. When he set foot on the hill Smith was not at all prepared for what he saw. It was a scene out of hell. Mass confusion reigned. Choppers were flying in and out; walking wounded were staggering about looking for medics or dustoffs; equipment lay absolutely everywhere; correspondents wandered about trying to interview battle participants; and, amidst all the hustle and bustle, the NVA tossed in occasional mortars or bursts of automatic-weapons fire.

Smith spent the better part of the day searching for Deeb. He not only checked the wounded but looked among the growing stacks of dead, too. When he'd almost despaired of finding his friend, he finally ran into someone who assured him that Deeb had been medevaced earlier. Smith then rejoined the brigade staff at Dak To.

Captain Joseph Grosso, the battalion doctor, volunteered to set up an aid station on Hill 875 on Wednesday. Accompanied by a corpsman nicknamed Pee Wee, Grosso loaded a chopper with saline solution, albumin, and other basic medical supplies. When they arrived at the LZ, Grosso and Pee Wee jumped off, unloaded their supplies, and set up an aid station and triage point adjacent to the LZ.

The next few hours passed rapidly as Grosso worked on scores of wounded, patching them up, preparing them for the next stop on the medical evacuation route. Some he couldn't help. They had to be passed by in order to treat those who had a better chance of living.

When the wounded had been cared for, Grosso helped in picking up the dead. To him it seemed as if they were everywhere. He found some dead paratroopers still slumped over their weapons, frozen in rigor mortis. Grosso also helped collect body parts from around the area where the bomb had hit. This was grisly, sickening work, sorting through the offal trying to find enough of a body to render a positive identification, but, of course, it had to be done.

Father Peters flew out to Hill 875 from FSB 16 as soon as there was space on a chopper. As it had others, the carnage on the hill shocked the priest. He couldn't afford to dwell on the destruction, though. Too many men needed his help. Working side by side with the medics, Father Peters helped casualties to the aid station, administered medication, carried stretchers to waiting choppers, and, most importantly, provided spiritual comfort to the Sky Soldiers.

Once the casualties had been evacuated, Father Peters turned his attention to the dead. Regardless of the religious preference stamped on their dog tags, the priest administered the Roman Catholic church's last rites to every corpse. He was busy for some time.

When Major Scott arrived on the hill, Master Sergeant Okendo accompanied him in his role as acting battalion sergeant major. The physical damage on Hill 875 reminded Okendo of some artillery-blasted hills he'd viewed in South Korea. That was to be expected. More shocking, though, was the human damage. Okendo could not believe the piles of dead; they were stacked four and five high, waiting for the evacuation of the wounded to end so they could be flown to the morgue at Dak To. Many of the 2d Battalion survivors Okendo saw were still in shock; a few sobbed uncontrollably. In twenty-five years in the paratroopers he'd never seen anything approaching this.

While Major Scott busied himself overseeing preparations for the next day's assault, Okendo circulated among the enlisted men. His calm demeanor reassured the soldiers, convinced them they'd be victorious. He helped them get their equipment squared away for the next day's battle, making sure they had enough ammo, water, and rations. Okendo also used his extensive combat experience to instruct the squad leaders on the tactics to use the next day.

Dawn on Thursday, 23 November, brought with it much anticipation and excitement. The Sky Soldiers of 4/503d knew they were going up the hill that day. They had to take it; there was no other way. For most of them the hill had assumed a personality of its own. Dark, gloomy, and malevolent, Hill 875 had become an enemy itself. As intimidating and dangerous as it was, none of the Sky Soldiers doubted they'd defeat it. But they knew it would be a fight to the death.

Specialist 4th Class Duffy didn't expect to survive the day. For him it was do-or-die time. As he looked around he didn't see many paratroopers left. If they weren't able to take the hill on this attempt, they wouldn't have enough strength left to try again. Then the NVA would overrun them for sure.

Once again, as on Tuesday, the morning hours prior to the attack were devoted to pounding the summit of Hill 875 with all available artillery and air. Captain Leonard again coordinated the strikes from his position near the front of the perimeter. Between 0939 and 1015, five F-100s delivered four tons of high explosives, three tons of napalm, and twenty-four hundred rounds of 20mm cannon fire onto Hill 875. Leonard reported that the bombs were right on target.

At the rear of the perimeter Father Peters set up his altar on a stack of empty C-ration boxes. Sky Soldiers of all faiths gathered around to hear the Mass. Father Peters distributed Communion to all who wanted it; many non-Catholics participated in the sacrament. Then the priest moved among the paratroopers positioned on the line, giving them Communion.

At 1100 Captain Leonard spoke into his radio. A preparatory barrage of 81mm mortar shells from the three companies' weapons crashed down in front of Bravo and Charlie. When the shelling ended Leonard looked at Lieutenant Lindseth and said, "Let's go."

Lindseth repeated the words to his platoon. Then he jumped up from his crouching position and ran uphill. Much to his surprise only desultory enemy fire greeted his charge. What are the gooks up to? he wondered.

Thirty meters from his jump-off spot Lindseth saw his first enemy bunker. Unhesitatingly, the young officer jumped right into the hole. Crumpled at its bottom lay a wounded North Vietnamese soldier. Lindseth poked him with his rifle barrel. The NVA was unconscious. Lindseth leapt from the bunker and continued his attack.

Around him other Bravo paratroopers raced across the torn ground. Screaming and yelling as loud as they could, they charged headlong toward the enemy.

"Geronimo!"

"Airborne!"

"Die, you fuckers!"

"All the way!"

The epithets and obscenities rose to a crescendo, nearly drowning out the bursts of M16 and M60 fire from the paratroopers.

On the right Captain Connolly urged his men to keep in line with Bravo. He didn't want the two companies to get out of sync, exposing one's flanks or rear to the enemy's fire. Whenever he saw one of his platoons slowing down, he yelled at them to keep up the pace.

Right behind the assault companies came Captain Muldoon's Alpha Company. Alert for any bypassed enemy soldiers who could fire into Bravo's or Charlie's rear, Alpha's Sky Soldiers carefully searched each bunker and trench. Everyone now knew the NVA had underground tunnels connecting many of their bunkers, so even a destroyed bunker had to be carefully approached lest a marauding NVA had snuck back into it.

Behind Alpha came members of 2d Battalion again functioning as litter bearers for the wounded. Lieutenant Harrison led about two dozen members of Alpha, 2/503d. Originally, there had been no plans to include 2d Battalion in the final assault. But Harrison successfully argued that the battalion had earned a role in the final attack.

Captain Grosso moved with Harrison. With no more casualties to treat at the LZ, the doctor felt that he could do the most good by being with the troops.

By the time the lead paratroopers covered the first fifty meters, NVA mortar shells started dropping among them. Sharp blasts sent hot metal zinging across the hillside.

One round landed right behind Connolly. He went to his knees, his ears ringing from the explosion. Blood ran from several shrapnel wounds. Ignoring them, Connolly arose. "Go! Go!" he yelled. Those paratroopers who'd sought cover came out and continued the charge.

Another mortar round landed right between Sergeant Bull and three others. Bull flew through the air, landing in a heap. When he'd gathered his senses he found he'd taken shrapnel in both legs, his right arm, and his jaw. A medic crawled up, looked at Bull, and started crying. Bull, surprised that he didn't feel more pain, crawled over to his buddies. One was dead, the other two were wounded. Bull patched them up; then, together, the three started downhill. Someone from 2d Battalion guided them to waiting medics.

Captain Grosso took a load of shrapnel up and down his back from another mortar burst. Though the fragments didn't nick any major blood vessels, they did damage several nerves. Howling in pain, Grosso writhed on the ground. Lieutenant Harrison called forward some stretcher bearers and got the doctor headed toward the rear.

Seventy-five meters in front of Grosso and Harrison, Lieutenant Proffitt urged his few remaining men forward. Dashing from cover to cover, crouching behind logs, firing his M16 in long, sweeping bursts, Proffitt closed in on Hill 875's summit. By the time he'd covered half the distance, Proffitt had begun to realize that only intermittent enemy rifle fire and scattered mortar rounds hampered his progress. Could it be possible, he wondered, that the NVA were gone? Or were they simply holding their fire, drawing the paratroopers into an elaborate trap?

The same thoughts occurred to Colonel Johnson. From his chopper circling above the hill, Johnson could see the dark green–clad figures of his battalion rushing up the hillside. To his surprise, enemy resistance appeared minimal; only the occasional burst of an enemy mortar round seemed to be holding them back. Radio reports from his company commanders confirmed his feelings.

Captain Leonard couldn't believe the good progress Bravo was making. At the beginning of the attack most of his Sky Soldiers had advanced cautiously, using classic fire and maneuver techniques. As they realized the enemy's resistance was practically nonexistent, they became bolder, running upright, yelling and screaming. "C'mon, you mother-fuckers! Come out and fight," one youngster yelled as he darted past Leonard.

Concerned that his men were becoming careless, Leonard urged caution. "Toss grenades in those bunkers," he ordered. "There might be gooks hiding in there."

To others he warned, "Don't just jump in those holes. They could be booby-trapped. Use grenades there, too."

At the forefront of the attack, Lieutenant Lindseth neared the summit. He was practically running now. He couldn't believe how close he was to the top. Ignoring the enemy mortars, he raced upward, jumped over a log, and was there—on top of Hill 875. In just twenty minutes Lindseth had completed an attack that had stalled two battalions for four days. Behind him other members of Bravo fanned out across the summit. Feeling relieved at his good fortune, but still fearful of a mortar attack, Lindseth found the deepest hole and jumped in.

Not far from Lindseth, Sergeant 1st Class Cates, his platoon sergeant, saw the officer and a few others reach the top. As Master Sergeant Okendo and Major Scott moved past him, Cates smiled broadly. "Looks like we made it, Okie," he said, patting Okendo on the back.

"Yeah, we're on top," Okendo said.

"Shit, we took this fucking hill!" Scott exclaimed.

Okendo and Scott moved on, eager to join the others at the top. Cates, who carried a twenty-pound satchel charge slung across his back, joined a nearby group of six other soldiers.

Fifteen steps past Cates, Okendo heard the unmistakable thunk of an NVA mortar round leaving its tube. He and Scott dove headfirst into a nearby bunker. Seconds later a huge double explosion rocked the hillside.

The enemy shell landed right at Cates's feet, setting off the satchel charge he carried. The resulting blast vaporized Cates, killed five men near him, and tossed a sixth violently into the air. The latter landed, badly wounded, near Okendo.

Reacting instantly, Okendo pulled the casualty into his hole. "Medic!" he screamed. "Medic up!" A medic materialized, patched the man up, and, with the help of a few others, carried him downhill.

A few minutes later an enemy rifle round ripped into Captain Leonard's left leg, entering and exiting cleanly, spinning him around and down. Brushing away a medic's attempts to dress the wound—Leonard would not be denied this victory—he bounded up and limped on. Soon he joined Lindseth and the earlier arrivals at the top. Behind him others came, hooting and hollering in celebration of their success.

Right behind Bravo the first of Charlie Company's paratroopers reached the summit. There was a lot of backslapping, whooping, and tears. Specialist 4th Class Duffy had called in mortars as he advanced, putting the rounds as close as thirty meters from the front line. Now as he crossed onto the top he jubilantly radioed his FDC, "We made it! We're here!"

Private 1st Class Tauss was surprised to find himself suddenly on top of Hill 875. He'd been so busy handling the radio for Connolly that he really hadn't paid attention to where he was. As he stood alongside Connolly, Tauss felt pleased at being fully upright for the first time in days. All around him the bald hilltop vividly displayed the effects of the pounding it had taken. It looked like a landscape out of Hades.

The victory celebration was short-lived. In anticipation of an expected counterattack the three captains put their men into defensive positions. While they did so Johnson's helicopter landed. The colonel and Specialist 4th Class Jones hopped off. Johnson moved among the jubilant paratroopers, congratulating them on their success. Then the colonel moved down the hill to view the enemy positions.

The enemy's network of trenches and bunkers impressed Johnson. The trenches were deep enough for a soldier to walk upright and still not be exposed to fire. Spaced along the back wall of the trench were small caves into which men could crawl to escape bombardments. Connecting tunnels linked many of the bunkers and trenches. Some bunkers had as much as six feet of overhead cover; others had been dug among the roots of wide trees, gaining both cover and concealment.

The main thing missing on the top of Hill 875 was enemy corpses. Only a few dozen were found in and around the top of the hill. Once again, the NVA had successfully eluded a decisive battle. Somehow, despite a near-constant pounding by artillery and aircraft, the NVA had managed to slip off Hill 875, taking their wounded and most of their dead with them. The paratroopers were denied the satisfaction of viewing the results of their victory.

Intelligence gleaned from the few corpses and discarded documents confirmed that the paratroopers had fought the NVA 2d Battalion, 174th Infantry. Holding positions on nearby hills were members of the regiment's 3d Battalion.

Shortly after Colonel Johnson landed, the point team for the 1/12th Infantry companies crossed onto the top of Hill 875. The movement of the two companies up the north face of the hill had been completely uneventful. In fact, the only casualties they'd incurred had come the previous day when an errant Huey strafed their column, wounding nine. As they entered the paratroopers' lines the infantrymen, too, began taking up defensive positions.

An LZ was blasted along the top of the hill. Casualties could be evacuated right from the summit. Between medevacs, C-and-C choppers brought in the brass. General Schweiter arrived, visited briefly with Johnson, and flew off. Sergeant Major Rogiers came in, prepared to join in any remaining fighting. "Where do you want me?" he asked Okendo.

"Just find a hole, Sergeant Major," Okendo answered.

But a counterattack never materialized.

Once it became apparent that the enemy had relinquished control of Hill 875, the paratroopers went to work policing up the battlefield. While some enlarged a clearing along the crest for a larger LZ, others fanned out across the hill searching for any American bodies. They found many of them from the first day's fight. Lieutenant Harrison recovered the badly charred corpse of his classmate, Peter Lantz. Private 1st Class Tauss found the head and shoulders of a Sky Soldier blown apart by artillery. Others found similarly gruesome remains, some so badly decomposed that they had to be shoveled into body bags.

Additional doctors and medics had been called in. Once the hill was secure the medical teams established a clearing station near the new LZ. There they treated the wounded.

One of them was Captain Leonard; he was soon on his way
to Pleiku for treatment of his leg wound. Lieutenant Lindseth took command of Bravo.

Captain Connolly also left Hill 875 early that afternoon.
Not for medical treatment, though. He was a candidate for
the job of aide to General Rosson and had an interview with
the senior officer. Connolly did not want the job and thus
was not disappointed when he was not selected.

Beginning at 1630 Chinooks touched down on Hill 875 to
evacuate the remaining members of 2/503d. It didn't take
many of the transport helicopters to complete the task. Not
more than eighteen members of Charlie, 2/503d, joined
Sergeant Welch and Specialist Zaccone aboard their helicopter. In Alpha Company Lieutenant Harrison commanded
about two dozen survivors. Lieutenant McDonough had about
the same in Dog.

The Chinooks carried the Sky Soldiers to FSB 12. When
they'd debarked many of the paratroopers were confused by
the apparent indifference to their ordeal. A passing sergeant
major accosted Private 1st Class Orona and told him to get in
a chow line for Thanksgiving dinner.

Geez, Thanksgiving, Orona thought. He hadn't realized it.
But he had no stomach for turkey. He wandered off until he
located the bunker where he and his buddies had spent their
last night at the FSB. Now he was the only one left. Why, he
didn't know. He only knew he was lonely and felt very sad.

Colonel Johnson had Thanksgiving dinner flown out to Hill
875. In the waning light of 23 November the battle-weary
paratroopers of 4/503d lined up in front of steaming insulated
containers to have turkey and the trimmings dropped in their
mess kits. Most of the men eagerly partook of the meal. A
few refused to eat; though they had much to be thankful for,
they were in no mood to participate in the normally festive
dinner.

The next day was spent patrolling the area around Hill
875. Numerous enemy bodies were found, but not more than
a hundred. These were buried in a mass grave on Hill 875.

It took several days for the casualty figures for the battle for
Hill 875 to be determined. After all personnel had been ac-

counted for, the 173d Airborne Brigade released the following statistics: 2/503d lost 87 men killed in action, 130 wounded, and 3 missing; 4/503d suffered 28 killed, 123 wounded, and 4 missing.

On 25 November 1967, 4/503d was helicoptered off Hill 875. While the 1/12th Infantry maintained a presence around the hill, the Sky Soldiers moved to Dak To for reorganization.

CHAPTER 15

AFTERMATH

General Westmoreland was not present in South Vietnam during most of the fighting around Dak To. He'd been summoned home by President Johnson on 15 November to help sell the war to the American public and press. Growing domestic dissent over Johnson's policies in Southeast Asia, culminating with thirty-five thousand protesters marching on the Pentagon in October, prompted the visit. Johnson wanted Westmoreland to extol the positive aspects of the war to as wide an audience as possible. Coming as it did on the heels of the savage fighting around Con Thien and Loc Ninh, and while the slaughter of young paratroopers continued on Hill 875, Westmoreland's visit did little to assuage the concerns of many Americans.

In his most important appearance, at Washington's National Press Club on 21 November, Westmoreland gave a very optimistic appraisal of the war. Referring directly to the fighting around Dak To, Westmoreland told his audience: ". . . the enemy may be operating from the delusion that political pressure [in the United States] combined with the tactical defeat of a major unit might force the U.S. to throw in the towel."

Westmoreland went on to state that the war in South Vietnam was in what he termed the "Third Phase." In this phase, according to Westmoreland, the United States would not only continue to destroy the enemy but would also increase efforts to build up South Vietnamese forces. Then, once the ARVN was capable of assuming more responsibility for the war, American troops, in Phase Four, could begin to return home.

Westmoreland was always very careful to avoid providing

the media with any exact prediction for when Phase Four might commence. He did, however, estimate that withdrawal of American forces might begin "within two years or less." Although his estimate ultimately proved to be very accurate, the withdrawals began for reasons far different from those envisioned by Westmoreland.

During the press conference a reporter asked Westmoreland if he thought ". . . that the battle of Dak To is the beginning or the end of anything particular for the enemy?"

"I think it's the beginning of a great defeat for the enemy," the general responded confidently.

Upon his return to South Vietnam on 29 November, Westmoreland was briefed by Generals Rosson, Peers, and Schweiter on the fighting around Dak To. Although he agreed that the 4th Infantry Division, 173d Airborne Brigade, and their attached units had blunted Giap's plan to annihilate a major American unit, Westmoreland expressed shock at the extent of U.S. casualties incurred in so doing.

In all, 376 Americans were killed in action, or listed as missing–presumed dead, in the fighting around Dak To. Another 1,441 were wounded.

The 173d Airborne Brigade lost 208 men killed and 645 wounded during these fights. On 1 November 1967, 5,228 officers and men were on the rolls of the 173d Airborne Brigade's assigned and attached units. About 3,200 of them deployed to Dak To. Twenty-seven percent of them became casualties during the battles. Losses among the individual rifle companies were even more severe.

The twelve rifle companies of the 173d that deployed to Dak To averaged 125 officers and men each at the start of the campaign. Since at least 90 percent of the brigade's casualties occurred in their ranks, the rifle companies suffered 51 percent losses in just one month! And about 60 of the dead paratroopers—29 percent—were killed by friendly fire! No wonder General Westmoreland was shocked.

Westmoreland queried General Rosson on how such horrific casualties could have been avoided. Without more extensive use of artillery and air support, Rosson replied, they could not.

North Vietnamese dead were reported as 1,644 by body count. Because a high enemy body count reflected favorably on unit commanders, these figures are suspect. In his memoirs, Westmoreland says that 1,400 enemy died, though he cites no source for the figure. General Rosson is particularly skeptical of these figures. By his estimates the NVA lost no more than 1,000 men around Dak To.

Regardless of the exact figures, it was undeniable that the North Vietnamese Army had been dealt a severe blow. Three regiments of its 1st Infantry Division—the 32d, 66th, and 174th—sat out the winter-spring offensive in Cambodia, licking their wounds and absorbing replacements. Only the NVA 24th Regiment was able to take the field in the January 1968 offensive.

With the attacks on Dak To now halted, General Westmoreland turned his attention northward. Intelligence sources indicated that the NVA planned to overrun the isolated marine combat base at Khe Sanh. They hoped this would result in a decisive defeat for the Americans, on the same scale as their victory at Dien Bien Phu against the French in 1953. Westmoreland planned to meet the enemy in the hills around Khe Sanh and deal them a blow that would effectively end their military operations in South Vietnam and lead, ultimately, to a truce.

The capture of Hill 875 ended, for all practical purposes, the fighting around Dak To for the 173d. There were minor skirmishes with small bands of fleeing NVA, but these were relatively brief firefights. The 1/503d continued patrolling in the vicinity of Hill 882, finding occasional signs of the enemy but making no major contact.

The 2/503d and 4/503d spent the last days of November absorbing replacements and training them by taking them on patrols around the FSBs. To the chagrin and anger of the paratroopers, most of the incoming infantrymen were nonairborne-qualified "legs." A major shortage of airborne personnel necessitated the use of regular infantrymen. Their assignment would be temporary, lasting only until parachute-trained replacements were available. Many of the Sky Soldiers initially treated the legs with derision and contempt. Not only did they feel themselves to be superior to the legs, they found the deployment of line infantry troops to be insulting to the memories of their fallen airborne buddies. But as the paratroopers got to know the regular infantrymen, some of the hostility abated and lifelong friendships developed.

The final ground combat in the battle for Dak To came on 30 November. The previous evening Sp4 Irvin Moran's LRRP team had been inserted into the jungle near the junction of the Laotian, Cambodian, and South Vietnamese borders. They passed that night uneventfully. The next morning the team set out on patrol. They crossed numerous trails but saw no enemy. At approximately 0930 Moran and the team leader, Sp4 Nick Brooks, were paralleling a well-used trail about twenty meters ahead of the rest of the team. Sensing something, the pair crept noiselessly to the trail's edge. Then the silence was abruptly broken by a burst of M16 fire.

Three enemy soldiers—one, an older veteran covered with jungle sores, leading two apparently freshly arrived soldiers—had come down the trail. Spotting one of the LRRPs, the older soldier raised his AK-47. Before he could pull the trigger, though, Sp4 Robert Noel, from Colorado Springs, jumped up and loosed a burst of M16 fire. All three NVA soldiers fell.

Moran and Brooks instantly dashed toward the sound of firing. One of the enemy soldiers moved. Brooks sprayed him with M16 fire. He didn't move again.

"Get their weapons and let's go," Brooks urged. "There's probably other gooks nearby."

Within minutes the five men were scrambling down a steep slope toward a PZ. The RTO kept calling "Timber!" the code word for an immediate extraction, into his radio. When they reached the site, they detected movement on their flanks. Brooks called for gunships to strafe around them. Then a slick appeared, hovering overhead, dangling ropes. Moran and two others tied themselves to the ropes and were hoisted out of the jungle, twisting and turning a hundred feet below the chopper. From his aerial position Moran could see the NVA closing on Brooks's position.

But Brooks realized the enemy did not know exactly

where he and his RTO were located. So they wisely held their fire. A few minutes later another slick arrived on station, trailing its ropes. The two LRRPs quickly tied themselves in and signaled for extraction.

"We were about thirty feet off the ground when all hell broke loose," Brooks later said. "We fired at the NVA while dangling from the ropes, but the gunships are what saved us. They did a great job."

A few minutes later Brooks and his RTO joined their three teammates at a nearby 4th Infantry Division FSB.

That night, in an apparent final act of defiance, the NVA pounded FSB 12 with a heavy 82mm mortar and 122mm rocket attack. From 1835 to 1945 nearly twenty-five missiles landed in the perimeter. One paratrooper was killed and nine were wounded as a result of the bombardment.

At midnight on 1 December 1967 General Rosson declared the battle for Dak To over. The MACV issued a press release lauding the great victory at Dak To, but General Rosson and the surviving participants knew better. Sure, the Americans had driven the North Vietnamese from the region, but the NVA had not been defeated; they'd be back someday. The Americans controlled some strategic hilltops, but they would soon depart, returning the hills to the jungle and the enemy.

And General Rosson knew that the 173d had been hit very hard. In conversations with Westmoreland, Rosson recommended that the brigade, especially the 2/503d and 4/503d, be given a chance to refurbish, take in replacements, reorganize, and train. Westmoreland concurred. The three battalions were assigned light patrol activities around their fire support bases. By mid-December all three battalions had departed Dak To: The 1/503d and 2/503d moved to Kontum in a task force commanded by Colonel Powers, and the 4/503d and the brigade headquarters returned to Tuy Hoa to aid the 3/503d in Operation Bolling. Elements of the 2/503d went to Ban Me Thuot in early January to strengthen that garrison against anticipated VC attacks.

Before they departed Dak To, the Sky Soldiers conducted their traditional "boots" ceremony. In an emotion-filled tribute to their fallen comrades, the paratroopers held a memorial service with a pair of jump boots placed in rank to represent each fallen paratrooper. Few Sky Soldiers were unaffected by the sight of hundreds of boots arranged in neat rows; none have ever forgotten the ceremony.

In recognition of the outstanding valor displayed by the members of the 173d Airborne Brigade (Separate) during the battles around Dak To, Secretary of the Army Clifford Alexander awarded the brigade the coveted Presidential Unit Citation. This is the equivalent of awarding each Sky Soldier the DSC.

After the Dak To battles the 173d Airborne Brigade never again operated as a complete unit. For the first six months of 1968 its four maneuver battalions served in different parts of South Vietnam. The 4/503d remained near Tuy Hoa where, during the Tet Offensive, its companies, particularly Dog, fought several pitched battles against the VC and NVA. At Ban Me Thuot during Tet the 2/503d also experienced bitter combat.

When General Westmoreland left South Vietnam in June 1968 to become the army's chief of staff, his successor, Gen. Creighton Abrams, quickly adopted a different strategy for conducting the war. Rather than battalion-sized operations, smaller company-sized sweeps became the norm. As efforts intensified to place increasingly larger shares of the combat burden on South Vietnamese units, American units retreated to large fire support bases from which they sent forth daily patrols and nightly ambushes.

For most of the rest of the war the 173d operated in Binh Dinh Province, a key rice-producing region long dominated by the VC. The Sky Soldiers' main missions were to provide military security to selected hamlets and improve the combat capabilities of the local defense forces. To do so, the paratroopers were organized into small advisory teams that trained the local forces in various combat skills.

By spring 1971 most American military units had been withdrawn from South Vietnam. Beginning in April 1971 the 173d started redeploying back to Fort Campbell, Kentucky. By 25 August 1971 the movement was complete. With more than six years in the war zone, the 173d held the record for service in South Vietnam. During that time 1,748 Sky Soldiers gave their lives supporting America's policy in South Vietnam; more than 8,700 were wounded.

In ceremonies at Fort Campbell on 14 January 1972, the 173d Airborne Brigade was deactivated.

In June 2000, in order to meet theater rapid response force requirements, the 173d Airborne Brigade was reactivated at Vicenzo, Italy. The brigade once again welcomed into its ranks newly qualified paratroopers as well as seasoned, experienced veterans, both of whom were ready to meet the many and the varied challenges of a modern world.

Three years later, on March 26, 2003, following the United States' invasion of Iraq, in the largest combat parachute jump since World War II, over 1,000 members of the brigade jumped into Kirkuk, Iraq; the rest of the brigade followed by transport plane. The brigade remained deployed in Iraq until the fall of 2003.

One-and-one-half years later, in February 2005, the entire brigade deployed to Afghanistan for a 14-month tour.

Upon its return to Italy in late spring 2006, the Department of the Army redesignated the brigade the 173d Airborne Brigade Combat Team with six battalions stationed at various locations throughout Germany and Italy. From those bases the members of the 173d are ready to deploy wherever the global war on terrorism may demand.

After any engagement as vicious and as prolonged as the fight for Hill 875, questions will be raised over the need for the battle. Was the fight for Hill 875 worth it?

General Westmoreland's stated strategy for defeating the enemy in South Vietnam was attrition, plain and simple. Kill enough of them that they will be unable to absorb any more losses, and they will eventually give up. Thus, Westmoreland launched his multibattalion search-and-destroy operations, the goals of which were "find, fix, and destroy" the enemy.

Unlike earlier wars, where battles were fought for key

road junctions, bridges, towns, seaports, and so forth, no
such objectives existed in South Vietnam. American troops
were, instead, sent to where the enemy was believed to be,
and they sought him out and killed him. When the fight
ended, the Americans moved on.

Not everyone agreed with the attrition strategy. Colonel
John Powers, the deputy brigade commander, wondered
even before the battle had ended what was being accomplished. He knew Hill 875 would soon be back in the hands
of the NVA and some Americans would have to take it all
over again. He hoped it would not be the Sky Soldiers.

Lieutenant Colonel Johnson felt much the same way. He
was glad the fight ended with Americans victorious but wondered, So what? Now we'll just walk off the damn hill. His
battalion lost a lot of people in the Dak To fighting. Each and
every man's death pained Johnson deeply, but he felt that the
deaths among the senior NCO ranks had been particularly
devastating. The loss of these seasoned veterans, many with
more than fifteen years of service, would hurt the army for a
long time.

Even as loyal an enlisted man as 1st Sergeant Crook asked
whether it was worth taking Hill 875. He answered no to his
own question. As far as he was concerned, every plane in
South Vietnam should have been used to blow Hill 875 off
the map.

Master Sergeant Okendo felt empty when he came off
Hill 875. There were too many dead, too many wounded.
But despite his feelings, he had been impressed that so many
of the young paratroopers, having experienced the worst
that war had to offer, still displayed the will to fight. A large
number of them wanted to charge right after the NVA, even
if it meant crossing into Cambodia. They were disappointed
when they couldn't continue after the battered enemy and
finish them off.

Lieutenant Al Lindseth thought the whole battle was a
waste. He agreed with 1st Sergeant Crook's plan for con-
quering the hill. Lindseth was also very skeptical of any enemy body counts reported for Hill 875. He was the first man
to make it all the way up and he saw no more than ten dead

NVA. His most impressive memory of the fight was the incredible courage demonstrated by the Sky Soldiers during his three days on the hill. With only a few exceptions they bravely did their duty without hesitation. That was the essence of a well-disciplined army.

The majority of the Sky Soldiers accepted the fact that they were fighting on Hill 875 because that's where the enemy was. Even if they had been offered the chance to leave the hill, few of them would have accepted. Too many of their buddies had been killed or wounded fighting on the hill. To walk away from Hill 875 would have diminished the importance of their sacrifices. The paratroopers' esprit de corps, elitism, and personal pride would not permit that.

In the context of Westmoreland's strategy, then, the fight for Hill 875, with its attendant losses, was worth it. There was never any thought of holding the hill once the enemy had been driven from it. It was just one more place where the enemy could be killed.

APPENDIX A

ROLL CALL

James B. Adamson (4th Infantry Division) retired from the army as a three-star general. He died in Jupiter, Florida, in January 2003.

Robert Allen (D/4/503) left South Vietnam in May 1968. A University of Oklahoma graduate, he is married with five children and runs his own flooring company. He lives in Oklahoma City. He holds the ARCOM w/V and ARCOM.

Ted Arthurs (4/503) retired from the army in 1973. He then worked in Saudi Arabia for ten years. Today, he is retired and lives with his wife in Destin, Florida. He earned a SS for Hill 823 and another for the fight at Cemetery Hill near Tuy Hoa on 31 January 1968. He is the author of a book of short stories about his experiences in the army and the many fascinating characters he encountered.

Jerry M. Babb (B/4/503) later served as the sergeant major of the 2/503 before he left South Vietnam in August 1968. He returned in April 1969 to serve a second tour with the 2/505th Airborne Infantry. He retired in September 1972 having made 748 parachute jumps in his twenty-year career. He died in October 2005. He had earned the BS w/V w/OLC, BS w/4 OLC, AM w/8 OLC, PH w/OLC, and ARCOM w/2 OLC.

Thomas H. Baird (D/4/503) spent eight months at Walter Reed Hospital recovering from his wounds. In 1971 he returned to South Vietnam as an adviser to Vietnamese forces. He later earned his master's degree from Kansas State University, was an instructor at the Command and General Staff College at Fort Leavenworth, Kansas, and commanded a mechanized battalion at Fort Polk, Louisiana. He retired from the army in 1981 as a lieutenant colonel. He then joined the family building supply company in New Jersey. Retired, he lives with his wife in Haddonfield, New Jersey. He earned the BS w/V, AM w/V, and PH.

He still has the pistol Lieutenant Burton removed from the dead NVA officer.

George Baldridge (A & B/4/503) extended his tour and remained in South Vietnam until October 1968. He stayed in the army until 1979, when he was diagnosed with multiple sclerosis. He died in February 1997.

John Barnes (C/1/503) was posthumously awarded the Medal of Honor, despite Colonel Schumacher's objections, on 4 November 1969. He is buried at Brookdale Cemetery, Dedham, Massachusetts.

Phillip Bodine (B & C/2/503) spent two months in the hospital being treated for his wounds, which still cause him pain. He then successfully completed helicopter pilot school and returned to South Vietnam in July 1969 as a Cobra gunship pilot. In September 1981, while serving as an aide to Gen. Frederick J. Kroesen, he was wounded again when terrorists fired an RPG-7 rocket into Kroesen's staff car near Heidelberg, Germany. He retired in 1986 as a lieutenant colonel. Married, he is an administrator for a large Atlanta law firm and resides in Fayetteville, Georgia. Among his decorations are the SS w/OLC, BS w/V w/2 OLC, BS w/OLC, PH w/OLC, DFC w/2 OLC, AM w/V w/OLC, and ARCOM.

Anthony Brangaitis (D/4/503) received an early discharge in March 1968 following his father's death. A retired New York City Police Department narcotics officer, he lives with his wife in Massapequa, New York. He holds the PH w/OLC.

Charles D. Brown (C/1/503) returned to South Vietnam in 1970 as a helicopter pilot. He retired in 1985 as a lieutenant colonel. He has since been employed in the aerospace industry. He holds the BS w/V, BS w/OLC, PH, and AM.

Ray Bull (C/4/503) spent several weeks in the hospital and then returned to his company. Discharged in 1969, he went to work for the U.S. Postal Service. He retired in 2004 and lives with his wife in Yuba City, California. He holds the BS and PH.

Michael D. Burton (D/4/503) fought at Cemetery Hill near Tuy Hoa in January 1968 and left South Vietnam in May 1968. In January 1971 he returned to South Vietnam and became a company commander in the Americal Division. During a patrol in 1971 he was wounded by a booby trap and lost his eyesight. He later became a regional manager for the Virginia Department for the Visually Handicapped. Now retired, he lives with his wife in Buchanan, Virginia. He holds the SS, BS w/V w/2 OLC, ARCOM w/V w/OLC, and PH w/OLC.

Gerald Cecil (C1/503) earned the DSC for his outstanding valor on 11 November 1967. He remained in the army until 1984, when he converted to reserve status. He retired as a colonel in 1996. Married with three children and four grandchildren, he teaches American history at Lexington Community College in Lexington, Kentucky, is a civilian aide to the secretary of the army, and runs the family farm near Winchester, Kentucky. Besides the DSC, he holds the LOM, MSM, BS w/V, PH, AM, and ARCOM.

James Coleman (C/4/503) remained in South Vietnam until he was WIA in November 1968. Discharged the following month, he reenlisted in April 1970 and returned to South Vietnam for a second tour, remaining there until December 1971. He holds the SS, BS, and PH w/2 OLC.

William J. Connolly (C/4/503) rotated from South Vietnam in December 1967. He remained in the army and retired as a colonel in 1993. After eight years with the Panama Canal Commission, he is now a vice president for a major government contracting firm. Among his awards are the SS w/OLC, BS w/V, PH, and ARCOM.

Edward Crook (C/4/503) left South Vietnam in June 1968. He retired as a sergeant major in 1980. He then went to work for the U.S. Postal Service in Columbus, Georgia. He died in August 2005. He had earned the SS, BS w/V, and PH w/OLC.

John R. Deane, Jr. (173d Airborne Brigade) later commanded the 82d Airborne Division and the Army Material Command. He retired as a four-star general on 31 January 1977. He divides his time between homes in South Carolina and Maine.

Michael J. Deeb (A & D/2/503) retired from the army and lives in Macon, Georgia.

John M. Deems (D/4/503) rotated from South Vietnam in December 1967. He returned for a second tour with the highly classified Studies and Observation Group in 1970. He retired in 1986 as a lieutenant colonel. He was then employed in the aerospace industry. He earned the BS w/V w/2 OLC and ARCOM w/V.

Jerry Draper (B/1/503) remained in the army and retired as a colonel in 1993. He then worked as an auditor for the Commonwealth of Pennsylvania for five years. Now completely retired, he resides in Mechanicsburg, Pennsylvania.

James R. Duffy (C & D/4/503) extended his tour in South Vietnam, remaining with the 173d until December 1968. He is self-employed in the plumbing business and lives in Scituate,

Massachusetts. He retired as a captain from the Massachusetts National Guard. He holds the BS w/V, ARCOM, and AM.

Darryl Fitch (C/1/503) took his discharge in May 1968. He resides in Sun City West, Arizona.

Joseph X. Grosso (173d Support Battalion) spent two months in Walter Reed Hospital and then finished his service in Philadelphia, where he was discharged in July 1968. He lives in Woodcliff Lake, New Jersey, and is a practicing psychiatrist. He holds the SS, BS w/V, and PH.

Matthew C. Harrison (A & C/2/503) returned to South Vietnam in November 1968 and served with the 25th Infantry Division, including duty as Major General Williamson's aide. He retired from the army in 1986 as a lieutenant colonel. Today he is self-employed as a business consultant, helping troubled companies return to profitability. He lives with his wife in Greenwich, Connecticut. He holds the SS, BS w/V, the BS w/3 OLC, AM, and PH w/OLC.

Darryl Haymes (C/4/503) extended his tour for six months and served with D/4/503. He was discharged in September 1969. Employed as a sea urchin diver, he lives in Fort Bragg, California. He holds the ARCOM w/OLC.

Leo E. Hill (B/4/503) spent two months in the hospital and returned to his company. He finished his tour and was discharged in 1968. He went to work for the Ford foundry plant in Brookpark, Ohio, and retired from there in 2002. He and his wife divide their time between their homes in Westlake, Ohio, and Myrtle Beach, South Carolina. He holds the BS w/V, BS, PH, and AM.

Charles J. Holland (LRRPs) was posthumously awarded the DSC.

David S. Holland (A/1/503) served in South Vietnam until April 1969. He then earned a law degree, an MBA, and a doctorate in international business. He lives with his family in Alexandria, Virginia. As an army reserve colonel he was called to active duty during the first gulf war. He has written two books on his experiences in South Vietnam. He holds the BS w/2 OLC.

Lawrence Jackley (4/503) retired from the army as a colonel in 1980. He later earned his master's degree in M.I.S. He resides in Alexandria, Virginia, where he is active in community and church projects. He holds the SS, BS w/V, and AM w/V.

John ("Mike") Jeakle (B/4/503) left South Vietnam in June 1968. He entered college while working for a major computer firm. He later formed several companies, sold them, and retired at an early age. He resides in Ohio. He holds the BS w/V and ARCOM w/V.

David G. Jesmer (A/1/503) received the SS for his gallantry on Hill 882. He served a second tour in South Vietnam as an adviser with the legendary John Paul Vann. He retired as a lieutenant colonel. He holds the BS.

James H. Johnson (4/503) earned the DSC during the heavy fighting at Cemetery Hill near Tuy Hoa on 30–31 January 1968. The next month he became the 173d's XO. He rotated from South Vietnam in July 1968. He received his first star in November 1972 and his second in 1980. He commanded the 2d Infantry Division in South Korea from July 1981 until August 1983. He retired in 1985 and lives in Murrells Inlet, South Carolina. In addition to the DSC, he holds the DSM, DSS, SS, LOM, BS, and AM.

Stanley Jones (4/503) left South Vietnam in April 1968. He later joined an army reserve unit and earned his wings as a helicopter pilot. He remained in the reserves until 1975. He resided in Phoenix, Arizona, where he ran an automotive salvage company. He died in 2004.

Daniel Jordan (A/4/503) was posthumously awarded the DSC.

Edward Kelley (C/1/503) was WIA in March 1968 while commanding a 4.2-inch mortar platoon. After release from a stateside hospital, he took helicopter training, returning to South Vietnam in 1971 as a Cobra gunship pilot. He retired in 1983 as a CWO. He lives in Fernandina Beach, Florida, where he is a teacher.

Thomas A. Kelly (1/503) retired from the army in May 1978 as a master sergeant. Retired from the U.S. Postal Service he lives in Lakeland, Florida. He holds the BS w/3 OLC and the AM.

Larry Kennemer (A/1/503) spent three weeks in the hospital and then was reassigned to the 101st Airborne Division. He fought with them at the battle for Hue during the Tet Offensive. He later spent thirty months in Southeast Asia as a member of the Special Forces and the highly classified Studies and Observation Group. He left the army in 1971. A widower, he lives in San Antonio, Texas, where he is in the construction business. He holds the BS w/2 OLC and PH w/OLC.

Stanley R. Larsen (1FF) retired on 1 October 1972 as a lieutenant general after being involved in the courts-martial of the antiwar mutineers at the Presidio in San Francisco, California. He died in an automobile accident in November 2000. He held the DSC for heroism in World War II.

Ronald R. Leonard (C/2/503 and B/4/503) received the DSC for his repeated acts of personal gallantry and outstanding leadership during the fight for Hill 875. He returned to South Vietnam in 1971 as an adviser in the II Corps area. He retired from the army in August 1991 as a colonel. He resides in Fairfax Station, Virginia. He also holds the SS, BS w/V, and PH w/OLC.

Peyton Ligon (B/4/503) received the SS for his heroism in the 10 July 1967 fight. He left South Vietnam in June 1968, returning three years later for another tour. Married and the father of two daughters, he retired as a colonel in July 1983. He currently resides in Hoover, Alabama, where he is employed as a regional sales director. Besides the SS he holds the LOM, BS w/V w/3 OLC, BS, and PH.

Alfred A. Lindseth (B/4/503) received the SS for his gallantry in action on Hill 875. He finished his tour in June 1968 and two years later left the army. After graduating from Harvard Law School, he joined an Atlanta law firm where he is now a senior partner specializing in education law. He resides in Atlanta with his wife.

William J. Livsey (4th Infantry Division) retired as a four-star general. He lives in Fayetteville, Georgia.

Carlos Lozada (A/2/503) was posthumously awarded the Medal of Honor on 18 November 1969. He is buried at Long Island National Cemetery, New York.

Jerald Lytle (B/4/503) left South Vietnam and the army in April 1968. He reenlisted in November 1969 and rejoined the 173d in South Vietnam. After being discharged a second time, he earned a degree in criminal justice. He was a criminal investigator for the Crow Creek Sioux tribe in South Dakota.

C. Allen McDevitt (B/2/503) left South Vietnam in July 1968, completed his service, returned to school, and earned two graduate degrees. Married with four children, he is an executive in the forest products industry. He resides in Lake Oswego, Oregon. He holds the SS, BS w/V, BS, PH, AM, and ARCOM.

Thomas McElwain (C/1/503) was awarded the SS for his gallantry in action on 11 November 1967. He served a second tour in South Vietnam as an adviser. He retired from the army in 1978 as a major. He later earned two master's degrees, taught school, and was a general contractor in El Paso, Texas. He is now retired and lives in Henderson, Nevada. In addition to the SS, he earned the BS w/V w/2 OLC, PH, AM, and ARCOM.

Don Martindale (C & D/1/503) was WIA on 10 November 1967. He spent two months in the hospital and was reassigned stateside. After the Tet Offensive began in January 1968 he was ordered to return to South Vietnam as a member of the 82d Airborne Division. He was discharged in May 1968. He then went to work for General Motors in Warren, Michigan.

Joseph S. Mescan (A/1/503) earned a BS for his rescue of the casualty on Hill 822. He completed his tour in July 1968. He was self-employed as a realtor and auctioneer in Columbia Station, Ohio.

David H. Milton (A/2/503) spent fifteen months in the hospital and had fifteen major operations. Despite his massive wounds, he returned to South Vietnam in September 1968 to serve as a brigade S-2 with the 1st Cavalry Division. He retired in 1982 as a lieutenant colonel due to complications from his wounds. He later founded the Hilton Head Island Tanning Secret Lotion Company in Hilton Head, South Carolina. He holds the SS w/OLC, BS w/V w/4 OLC, LOM, AM w/10 OLC, and PH w/2 OLC.

Irvin W. Moran (LRRPs) extended his tour in South Vietnam for two months, until April 1968, in order to get an early out, since he'd have less than ninety days remaining on his enlistment at that time. He later earned a degree in criminal justice and went to work for the Bureau of Alcohol, Tobacco, and Firearms.

James J. Muldoon (A/4/503) served a second tour in South Vietnam in 1972–1973. He retired as a colonel in 1990. He holds the BS w/V, PH, and AM w/2 OLC.

Michael Nale (B/2/503) never did get his R and R. Instead, he spent a month in the hospital and returned to his company. He fought during the opening phase of the Tet Offensive, finally leaving South Vietnam in January 1968. After more surgery for his injuries, he was discharged in October 1968. A postman, he has two children and lives in Florence, Alabama. He earned the PH w/OLC and ARCOM w/V.

Thomas Needham (S-2, 1/503 & D/1/503) was WIA in March 1968. He returned to South Vietnam and the 173d Airborne Brigade in May 1969 and remained with them until the unit returned to the United States in August 1971. Promoted to brigadier general in 1990, he organized and commanded the Joint Task Force Full Accounting in Hawaii, which is responsible for determining the fate of MIAs/POWs in Southeast Asia. He later served as deputy commanding general for the 18th Airborne Corps at Fort Bragg, North Carolina. He retired as a major general and resides in Exeter, New Hampshire. Among his decorations, he holds the BS w/V and PH w/OLC for service with the 173d.

William Nichols (A/2/503) left South Vietnam in February 1968. He later operated a Snap-On Tool dealership in Pennsylvania. He holds the ARCOM w/V.

Lawrence Okendo (B/4/503) left active duty in 1968. He then served in the army reserves, eventually retiring as a sergeant major. He later served as the honorary sergeant major to the 503d Infantry, then part of the 2d Infantry Division in Korea. He lives in Payson, Arizona. He holds the SS w/2 OLC, BS w/V w/3 OLC, PH w/2 OLC, AM, and ARCOM. He is one of only 281 men to have earned the coveted Combat Infantryman's Badge in three wars.

Bartholomew O'Leary (A & D/2/503) spent sixteen months in the hospital recovering from his wounds. He married his nurse, and they have one son. O'Leary remained in the army, retiring in 1989 as a lieutenant colonel. He now lives in Orange Park, Florida. He earned the SS for Hill 875 and also holds the BS w/V w/OLC, and PH w/OLC.

Manuel Orona (A/2/503) completed his tour in August 1968. He returned to South Vietnam for a second tour a year later and served with B/2/503. He was WIA in August 1969 and spent four months in the hospital. He was discharged in January 1970. He later went to work for the Southern Pacific Railroad and lived in Tucson, Arizona. He holds the BS w/V w/3 OLC, BS, PH, ARCOM w/V, ARCOM w/2 OLC, and AM.

Arturo Ortiz (C/4/503) left South Vietnam in April 1968 and was dischargd in May 1968. He later worked for the U.S. Postal Service and lived in Venice, California.

Phillip Owens (B/4/503) needed two years in army hospitals to recover from his wounds. He didn't lose his left arm, but was still left 80 percent disabled. He holds the BS w/V, PH w/2 OLC, and ARCOM w/V w/OLC.

Edward A. Partain (2/503 and 173d Airborne Brigade) left South Vietnam in December 1967 as a result of injuries received during a helicopter crash on 22 June 1967. After promotion to colonel in 1968, he attended the prestigious War College. He received his first star in June 1973 and then learned to fly helicopters. After receiving his second star in 1977, he commanded the 1st Infantry Division. As a lieutenant general he commanded the Fifth Army before retiring in 1985. Among his numerous decorations and awards are the DSM, SS, DSS, LOM, DFC, PH, AM w/4 OLC, and ARCOM.

Richard E. Patterson (A/2/503) spent one year in army hospitals recovering from his many wounds before being discharged in June

1968. Permanently disabled, he went to work for the Disabled American Veterans Organization. He received the BS w/V for his valor on 22 June 1967 and holds the PH.

Roy V. Peters (173d Support Battalion) served a second tour in South Vietnam from 1969–1970 as a division chaplain, 25th Infantry Division. He retired as a colonel in 1986. He is pastor emeritus at Saints Peter and Paul Parish in Honolulu, Hawaii. Among his decorations are the LOM w/2 OLC, BS w/V w/ OLC, PH, AM, and ARCOM.

Alan Phillips (A/4/503) earned a SS for the 10 July fight (exactly twenty-four years earlier his father had earned a Navy Cross during the invasion of Sicily). The father of four, he and his wife live in Brussels, Belgium. Among his decorations are the LOM w/2 OLC, BS w/V w/5 OLC, PH, AM, and ARCOM.

John J. Powers (173d Airborne Brigade) retired from the army in 1975. In addition to the DSC he earned during the Korean War, he holds the LOM, BS, PH w/2 OLC, and AM w/7 OLC. He lives in Ponte Vedra Beach, Florida.

Hugh M. Proffitt (B/4/503) was WIA in March 1968, earning a SS and PH. Hospitalized in the United States, he returned to South Vietnam to serve as an adviser with the ARVN 1st Infantry Division during the Laotian invasion. He left the army in 1972. He was living in Hutchinson, Kansas. He holds the BS w/V.

Thomas Remington (A/2/503) spent eight months in hospitals before being assigned to Fort Belvoir, Virginia. While there he received an early discharge to attend Florida State University Law School. Graduated in 1970, he is a judge in Fort Walton Beach, Florida. He holds the SS, BS w/V w/2 OLC, PH w/OLC, and AM.

James P. Rogan (B/2/503) was killed in action in February 1968.

Vincent Rogiers (2/503 & 173d Airborne Brigade) left South Vietnam in June 1968. He then served as sergeant major of the U.S. Military Academy. He retired in 1979 and worked for the city of Columbus, Georgia, before retiring again ten years later. He holds the BS w/V w/2 OLC, AM, and ARCOM w/V.

William B. Rosson (1FF), a recipient of the DSC for World War II heroism, retired from the army as a four-star general. He lived in Salem, Virginia, until his death in December 2004.

Enrique Salas (A & B/2/503) returned to Bravo, 2/503, after several weeks in the hospital. He left South Vietnam in June 1968. In 1972 he retired as a first sergeant. Married with six children, ten grandchildren, and one great-grandchild, he lives in Columbus,

Georgia. He holds the BS w/V w/2 OLC, BS w/3 OLC, PH w/OLC, AM, and ARCOM w/2 OLC.

Philip H. Scharf (C/1/503) spent three months in the hospital before returning to his unit, where he was promoted to staff sergeant and served as a platoon sergeant. Discharged in 1968, he lives in Wisconsin and is in the commercial swimming pool construction business.

David Schumacher (1/503) could not be located.

Leo H. Schweiter (173d Airborne Brigade) died of lung cancer in 1972.

Daniel Severson (B/4/503) spent a year in the hospital recovering from his wounds. He retired from the army in 1988 as a lieutenant colonel. He is a high school principal and football coach in Shushan, New York. In 2004 he was inducted into the College Football Hall of Fame as a Distinguished American. In addition to the DSC, he earned the BS w/V w/3 OLC, PH w/OLC, AM, and ARCOM w/V.

Edward Sills (S-3, 1/503) completed his tour in South Vietnam in June 1968. He remained in the army and retired as a full colonel in 1988.

Kenneth Smith (A & D/2/503, S-3, 2/503) left South Vietnam in March 1968. He returned in June 1971 for a tour with the Americal Division, the last major combat unit to depart South Vietnam. He remained in the army and retired in 2003 as a colonel. Today he is employed by the Diplomatic Security Service of the U.S. Department of State. He holds the BS w/V for his service with the 173d.

John Steer (A/2/503) spent seven months in hospitals recovering from his wounds. Medically discharged in July 1968, he sank into a world of alcohol and drugs, trying to cope with his pain, both physical and mental. In 1973 he became a born-again Christian. Today he is a nondenominational minister and a well-known religious and veterans' advocate speaker and inspirational author. Originally told that Carlos Lozada and he had been recommended for the DSC, Steer was later advised that since there were no witnesses to the action, his award had been downgraded to the SS. He also holds the BS w/V, PH w/OLC, and ARCOM.

James R. Steverson (2/503) retired from the army as a colonel. He refused to be interviewed for this book.

Steven E. Suth (A/1/503) remained in the army.

Gerhard Tauss (C/4/503) extended his tour and remained in South Vietnam until his discharge in June 1968. He earned his degree in engineering and worked as a project manager. He holds the BS w/OLC, ARCOM, and AM.

Steven F. Varoli (B/2/503) rotated from South Vietnam in April 1968. He was discharged in September 1969. He holds the BS, PH w/OLC, AM, and ARCOM w/V. He was in the air-conditioning business.

H. Glenn Watson (2/503) was WIA in July 1967 and evacuated from South Vietnam. He retired in 1984 as a brigadier general. He lives in Belington, West Virginia.

Charles J. Watters (173d Support Battalion) posthumously received the Medal of Honor on 4 November 1969. He is buried at Arlington National Cemetery.

Steven Welch (C/2/503) survived the Dak To fighting unscathed only to be accidentally shot in the back in January 1968 by a FNG the night before he was leaving South Vietnam for the United States. He was actually shaking hands with his buddy Ray Zaccone when he was shot. He spent one month in Letterman Hospital and was then assigned to Fort Ord, California. He was discharged in June 1969. Married, he has two daughters and two granddaughters and lives and works in Santa Cruz, California. He holds the BS.

William C. Westmoreland (MACV) served as army chief of staff for four years and retired to Charleston, South Carolina, in 1972. He died in July 2005.

Ellis W. Williamson (173d Airborne Brigade) returned to South Vietnam in 1968 after assignments as the commanding general of Fort Polk, Louisiana, and Fort Benning, Georgia, to command the 25th Infantry Division. He later served as an adviser to the shah of Iran. He retired on 1 January 1974 as a major general. He lives in Arlington, Virginia.

Morrell J. Woods (D/4/503) spent three weeks in the hospital before returning to his company. He was WIA again on 30 January 1968 during the fighting for Cemetery Hill. Discharged in August 1969, he returned to Arkansas, where he operated a hunting and fishing resort in the Ozarks until he retired. He holds the BS w/V and PH w/OLC.

Robert E. Wooldridge (C/1/503) spent one month in the hospital before rejoining his company. He left South Vietnam in December 1967, receiving his discharge one year later. He returned to Newton, Iowa, and was employed at the local Maytag plant until his retirement. He and his wife raised two children. He held the BS w/V w1/OLC, BS, and PH. "Sergeant Opie" died in April 2004.

Raymond Zaccone (C/2/503) completed his first tour in South
Vietnam in March 1968. He returned one year later and again
served with the 173d. A power plant mechanic for the Idaho
Power Company, he is married and lives in Halfway, Oregon. He
holds the BS, ARCOM, and PH.

APPENDIX B

THE 503d IN WORLD WAR II

The 503d Infantry Regiment (Airborne) came into existence on 24 February 1942 at Fort Benning, Georgia, as the 503d Parachute Infantry Regiment. Originally, the unit had been designated the 503d Parachute Battalion, one of the first three airborne units organized in the U.S. Army.

In the early days of World War II, American military leaders recognized the need for new methods of warfare. German dictator Adolf Hitler had used a variety of new techniques to complete his conquest of the European continent. Among the innovations was the delivery of highly trained shock troops behind enemy lines via parachutes.

This bold offensive tactic captured the attention of several imaginative, forward-looking U.S. Army officers. Under their guidance the army formed a parachute test platoon, commanded by 1st Lt. William T. Ryder, at Fort Benning in July 1940 with volunteers from the 29th Infantry Regiment. Following seven weeks of rudimentary training the test platoon made its first jump on 19 August 1941. It was successful, and, though there were many rough spots to overcome, the army knew it had a powerful new tool to help the United States achieve battlefield victories. Accordingly, in November 1940 the 501st Parachute Battalion was formed at Fort Benning. Additional airborne battalions, including the 503d, soon followed.

Eventually, sixteen airborne regiments were formed during World War II. The first full airborne division, the 82d, was organized on 15 August 1942 at Fort Bragg, North Carolina. In just two years the army's airborne forces had grown from a single test parachute platoon to a full airborne division, with four more to follow. It was truly one of the most remarkable metamorphoses in American military history.

One month after activation, the 503d Parachute Infantry Regiment

(PIR) moved to Fort Bragg for intensified combat training. Once judged combat-ready, the 503d boarded a troop train bound for Camp Stoneman, California. There the regiment began its final preparations for overseas movement. On 19 October 1942 the regiment, less its 2d Battalion (which became the 2/509th PIR and fought in the European theater with the 82d Airborne Division), boarded a troopship for the long voyage to Australia. The *Paula Laut* initially sailed south from San Francisco to Panama. There the 501st Parachute Battalion boarded the ship. It then became the new 2d Battalion, 503d Parachute Infantry Regiment.

Forty-two days after leaving Panama, the *Paula Laut* docked in northern Queensland, Australia. The paratroopers eagerly debarked from the rusty Dutch freighter, anxious to have their feet once again on solid, dry land. For the next eight months the 503d continued its training preparatory to its first combat mission.

While the 503d trained in Australia, other units of the army and the U.S. Marine Corps slugged it out with Japanese forces in the upper Solomon Islands, north and east of Australia. At the same time, Gen. Douglas MacArthur continued his drive to retake the Philippine Islands. His main route lay via the island of New Guinea. MacArthur's tactics involved leapfrogging along the coast of New Guinea, bypassing locations where the Japanese were strong in order to land forces where the enemy was weak.

Early in May 1943 MacArthur decided to assault the Lae-Salamaua area of New Guinea, at the base of the Huon Peninsula. Possession of Lae would ensure control of the strategically vital peninsula on New Guinea's eastern end.

MacArthur planned to isolate Lae using amphibious, parachute, and air-landed troops. He would send troops ashore east of Lae who would then turn west to attack the Japanese defenders. In the meantime, an American parachute regiment would drop on Nadzab, west of Lae, and seize the airfield there. Once in control of the airfield they would hold it open while an Australian infantry division arrived via transport plane. The Aussies would then drive east to hit Lae from the west. The American parachute regiment selected to drop onto the Nadzab airfield was the 503d.

Three weeks before the scheduled jump on 5 September 1943, the 503d was flown from Australia to Port Moresby, on New Guinea's south coast. Two weeks later the regimental commander, Col. Kenneth H. Kinsler, briefed his battalion commanders on their individual missions. Lieutenant Colonel John W. Britton's 1/503d would jump directly onto the airfield and clear it of enemy soldiers.

The 2/503d under Lt. Col. George M. Jones would drop north of the field to provide flank protection for Britton's battalion. Lieutenant Colonel John J. Tolson's 3/503d would land east of Nadzab where they could blunt any Japanese attack from Lae, twenty-two miles away.

The predawn takeoff on 5 September was delayed by heavy fog and rain. Not until 0830 that day were the paratroopers able to get airborne, at last on their way to combat.

At 1022, at an altitude of just four hundred feet over the Nadzab airfield, the first paratrooper of the 503d to make a combat jump stepped out of his C-47 transport plane. Four minutes and thirty seconds later the entire regiment was on the ground. But they were not organized. Most of the paratroopers found themselves lost in razor sharp ten- to twelve-foot-high *kunai* grass. Fortunately, the Japanese, facing pressure from the Allied troops landed east of Lae, had withdrawn from the area, posing no threat to the paratroopers. Over the next few hours the paratroopers floundered around seeking escape from the high grass. Not until early afternoon had most of them assembled around the airstrip. Once there the paratroopers and a detachment of Australian engineers began preparing the airfield for the arrival of the reinforcements. All the remainder of that day and the morning of 6 September were spent getting the airstrip ready for the Australian 7th Infantry Division. The arrival of the Aussie infantrymen went smoothly. As soon as they landed, the Australians headed east toward Lae and the Japanese.

During the final battle for Lae on 15 September, some fleeing Japanese units ran into Colonel Tolson's 3d Battalion, still holding its positions east of Nadzab. A brisk firefight ensued, during which eight paratroopers died and twelve were wounded. The Japanese were forced to detour, withdrawing into the hills north of Lae where they disappeared.

Two days later, the 503d left Nadzab and returned to Port Moresby. Though only a limited number of paratroopers had actually experienced combat, the regiment was blooded. It could proudly boast of both a successful jump and an operation.

A few weeks after its return to Port Moresby, a personal tragedy struck the 503d. One day, for unknown reasons, Colonel Kinsler walked into the jungle adjacent to his regiment's bivouac and killed himself. Lieutenant Colonel Jones, recently promoted from command of 2/503d to regimental executive officer, took over the regiment.

In January 1944 the 503d returned to its base camp in Queensland. There its members underwent additional rugged combat training interrupted by occasional weekend passes into the friendly city of Brisbane. They remained in Australia until April when they returned to New Guinea and established a new camp at Dobodura. The paratroopers spent five weeks at "Dobo" before moving to Hollandia, at the center of New Guinea's north coast. There they took on the mission of mopping up isolated pockets of Japanese troops left behind by General MacArthur's leapfrog amphibious operations along the island's north coast.

In mid-May 1944 MacArthur leapt farther along New Guinea's north coast, taking the offshore island of Wakde. Next on the target list was the island of Biak. Lying 180 miles northwest of Wakde, Biak not only held three excellent Japanese airfields, but also guarded Geelvink Bay where the U.S. Navy would stage for the impending assault on New Guinea's western Vogelkop Peninsula.

On 27 May 1944 two regiments of army infantry landed on Biak. Though the island's main airfield fell by 7 June, the fierce resistance displayed by the Japanese slowed the capture of the island. A third army regiment was thrown into the fight before Biak finally fell. The ability of the Japanese on Biak to fight so hard for so long puzzled the Americans, until they learned from a Japanese POW that reinforcements had been snuck in nightly from the island of Noemfoor, eighty miles to the southwest. MacArthur decided to seize Noemfoor.

Noemfoor is roughly egg-shaped, measuring fourteen miles long and eleven miles wide. Most of the island's northern half is relatively flat. The southern half is dotted with hills reaching to 650 feet above sea level. Dense jungle covers nearly every square foot of Noemfoor except for some stretches of tropical beach on the north coast. MacArthur's intelligence office estimated some 3,250 Japanese combat soldiers held the island.

Assault troops of the 158th Regimental Combat Team hit the beaches on Noemfoor's northwest coast at 0800, 2 July. Initially, enemy resistance was nearly nonexistent. Within the first hour the soldiers had captured the main airfield, Kamiri, and the strategic ridgeline behind it. A short time later, following a small skirmish, a captured Japanese soldier revealed to his interrogators that more than six thousand of his comrades actually held the island.

Alarmed at this significant change in the enemy's strength, the 158th's commander asked that reinforcements be sent immediately. As MacArthur's reserve force, the 503d was notified they would be making a parachute jump at Kamiri. There was little time for preparation. They'd be going in the very next day, 3 July.

Colonel Jones selected the 1/503d, under Maj. Cameron Knox, to make the initial jump. The battalion, and Colonel Jones, boarded C-47s at Hollandia at the crack of dawn on 3 July. At 0630 the transport planes took off, bound for Noemfoor.

At 1000, twin columns of C-47s appeared over Kamiri. From a planned altitude of four hundred feet the paratroopers leapt from the planes, Colonel Jones jumping first.

Unfortunately, due to faulty altimeters, Jones's plane and one other were actually only 175 feet above the ground. Jones's parachute had barely opened when he slammed hard onto the crushed-coral runway. Only his steel helmet kept him from suffering a shattered skull. As it was he had a severe headache for the next week. Around the stunned commander, other paratroopers from his plane crashed into the runway.

Some paratroopers who jumped from planes flown at the proper altitude had their own problems. Scores of amphibious assault vehicles had inadvertently been left parked along the runway. As Jones watched in horror dozens of his paratroopers collided with the parked vehicles. In all, 72 of the battalion's 739 paratroopers were injured badly enough to require evacuation; among them was Major Knox.

On 4 July, Maj. John Erickson's 3/503d dropped on Kamiri starting at 0955. This time the amphibious vehicles had been moved well back into the jungle. Still, fifty-six paratroopers suffered injuries upon landing on the runway—an 8 percent casualty rate. The injured included a number of key personnel. Besides Major Knox, the regiment lost three company commanders, the regimental communications officer, a number of platoon leaders, and several senior sergeants.

Rather than risk further nonbattle injuries, Colonel Jones recommended that his remaining battalion, 2/503d under Lt. Col. John Britton, be brought in by sea. The suggestion was approved. Britton's unit landed safely on 10 July.

Regrettably, it was later learned that the Japanese prisoner was either misinformed or deliberately lying; in actuality less than twenty-five hundred of his comrades were on Noemfoor. The urgency with which the 503d was dispatched, and the resulting high injuries, were unnecessary.

On 11 July Colonel Jones learned that his regiment would be responsible for clearing the rugged southern half of Noemfoor of the enemy. For the rest of July and well into August the paratroopers chased the Japanese through the thick jungle. Combat in the jungle-clad terrain was characterized by a series of brief but violent fire-fights between platoon-sized units, foreshadowing the fights the 503d would experience in South Vietnam twenty-three years later.

One such contact occurred on 23 July. Company D, 2/503d, collided with a Japanese force near a small village along the south coast. One platoon was cut off and in danger of being overrun. Sergeant Roy E. Eubanks was ordered to take his squad to their relief. Moving at the head of his men, he maneuvered to within yards of the Japanese positions before their vicious fire drove his squad to ground. Eubanks then took two men and crept forward another fifteen yards. Intense machine-gun fire halted them again. Eubanks grabbed a Browning automatic rifle (BAR) from one of his men, stood up in full view of the enemy, and launched a singlehanded charge right into their position.

Halfway there he was knocked down by a burst of rifle fire that also rendered his BAR useless. Undaunted, Eubanks staggered back to his feet and, bleeding profusely, continued his charge. Swinging the BAR as a club, Eubanks killed four Japanese before another burst of fire killed him.

The gallant charge by Eubanks not only broke the back of the Japanese defense, allowing the trapped platoon to escape, but brought him the first Medal of Honor earned by a member of the 503d.

Despite such courage it was not until 17 August that the paratroopers were able to eliminate the Japanese in the southern half of Noemfoor. Two weeks later the island was officially declared secure. The fight for Noemfoor cost the 503d 60 dead and 303 wounded in action.

While bivouacked at Kamiri in September, the 503d was reinforced by two units, the 462d Parachute Field Artillery Battalion and the 161st Parachute Engineer Battalion. With these additions the regiment changed its name to the 503d Parachute Regimental Combat Team (RCT), a designation it retained for the balance of the war. The 503d RCT stayed on Noemfoor until mid-November when it was shipped to Leyte, again to act as MacArthur's reserve.

General MacArthur's long-anticipated return to the Philippine Islands he'd been forced to leave in April 1942 came on 20 October 1944, when U.S. troops landed on the northeast coast of Leyte. Weeks of bitter fighting followed before the island fell on 25 December 1944.

To tighten the noose around the Japanese holding the rest of the

Philippines, MacArthur landed on the north shore of Luzon Island on 9 January 1945. The main prize in the Philippines, the capital city of Manila, lay 110 miles to the south.

Enemy resistance was surprisingly light as MacArthur's divisions crossed the high plains of northern Luzon bound for Manila. The first U.S. troops entered the city on 4 February 1945. However, the battle for Manila would prove to be one of the costliest in World War II. City block by city block, the tenacious Japanese defenders stubbornly resisted the brave American attackers. No less than four full infantry divisions were committed to the battle to wrest Manila from the Japanese.

The brutal street fighting in Manila still raged on 16 February 1945 when the 503d RCT took off from Mindoro Island to launch one of the most daring and unconventional parachute assaults attempted during World War II—a combat drop on tiny Corregidor Island.

Situated at the mouth of Manila Bay, Corregidor held both strategic and symbolic significance. Diehard Japanese defenders on Corregidor shelled each U.S. Navy ship that sailed past it into and out of Manila Bay. Until the numerous artillery pieces on the rocky island were silenced, no naval vessel would be safe.

Perhaps more importantly, though, Corregidor had been General MacArthur's headquarters for his defense of the Philippines during the early days of World War II. From deep within the concrete-lined tunnels dug into Malinta Hill at the center of the tadpole-shaped island, MacArthur had directed the defense of Bataan Peninsula for nearly three months. Finally, though, the lack of supplies and reinforcements forced Bataan to surrender on 9 April 1942.

Some four thousand valiant Americans continued to hold out on Corregidor. When President Franklin D. Roosevelt ordered MacArthur to escape to Australia, he reluctantly complied, turning over command to Gen. Jonathan M. Wainwright. Inspired by Wainwright's indomitable courage, the island's defenders held out for another month. On 6 May 1942, following a brutal twenty-four-hour bombardment that buried alive in rock slides many of the defenders, Wainwright complied with the Japanese commander's surrender demands.

Now, three years later, MacArthur prepared to turn the table on his foes. His staff prepared a plan to attack "The Rock" on 16 February with three battalions. Two of those battalions would come from Colonel Jones's 503d RCT. Once the two airborne units dropped on Corregidor, the 3d Battalion, 34th Infantry Regiment, 24th Infantry Division, would make an amphibious assault on the south side of Corregidor at the base of Malinta Hill. The two forces would then link up to complete the capture of the fortress.

Colonel Jones welcomed the opportunity for the jump. His regiment had originally been sent to Leyte as a reserve unit, missing all the action of that campaign. On 15 December 1944 they made an amphibious assault on Mindoro but met no opposition. Since then they'd been waiting on Mindoro for the call to combat.

As soon as Jones received his mission he immediately began studying the tiny island and making plans for the drop and subsequent ground attacks. Aerial photos and an aerial reconnaissance of Corregidor revealed a three-and-a-half-mile-long island with a bulbous head and a long, narrow tail. At its widest point at the head Corregidor stretches but one and a half miles.

The island's head, at the western side, reaches 550 feet above sea level. Prewar American soldiers dubbed this portion of Corregidor Topside. Several large military barracks sat nearly in the middle of Topside. Directly to the south of the barracks was a large (325 by 250 yard) parade ground. Adjacent to the parade ground's eastern edge lay a nine-hole golf course.

As Corregidor continues east the terrain slopes gradually downward to a small plateau called Middleside. Then the ground drops sharply some three hundred feet to the narrowest part of the island, known as Bottomside. Here the island is but three hundred yards across.

To the east of Bottomside, Malinta Hill rises to 390 feet. Beyond Malinta Hill the tadpole's tail continues eastward until it takes a sharp turn south at Monkey Point before petering out about a half mile farther on. At Monkey Point, in the days before World War II, U.S. Army engineers had carved an airfield in the rocky ground. A series of manmade storage tunnels also penetrated the area.

After carefully reviewing his options, Colonel Jones, who had been designated overall commander of the invasion forces, put together the plan of attack. On the morning of 16 February 1945, the 3/503d, commanded by newly promoted Lt. Col. John Erickson, would jump onto Topside, with the parade ground and golf course as the drop zone (DZ). With the infantrymen would be Company C, 161st Parachute Engineer Battalion, and Battery D, 462d Parachute Field Artillery Battalion.

Erickson had two missions: Secure and hold both DZs for use that afternoon by Maj. Lawson B. Caskey's 2/503d and other supporting paratroopers, and secure that portion of Topside overlooking the landing beaches of the 3/34th.

On 17 February Jones's remaining battalion, 1/503d led by Maj. Robert Woods, and the final battery of artillery, would jump onto Topside. Once all the paratroopers were on the ground they would drive east toward Malinta Hill, link up with 3/34th, and then the airborne and straight-leg infantry would continue the attack east until the island was cleared of Japanese.

At 0830 on D day the C-47s carrying Colonel Jones and Colonel Erickson's battalion approached Corregidor from the south. Because the drop zones were tiny, each plane would be over them for just six seconds—time for only six paratroopers to jump from each plane. The columns of planes would then circle back and make successive passes over the island until all the paratroopers had jumped.

Colonel Erickson hit the silk first. From an altitude of five hundred feet he and the other airborne infantrymen started down to Corregidor. Some of the paratroopers drifted too far south, crashing onto the rocks bordering Topside, but most landed safely. One who didn't was Colonel Jones. He slammed into a tree that had been badly shattered by an artillery shell. A long splinter tore into Jones's leg, embedding itself deep in his thigh. Though he could barely stand the pain, Jones pulled the splinter from his flesh, bandaged the wound, then limped off to establish his command post.

The Japanese, though completely surprised by the airborne assault, did not remain idle long. They fired on descending paratroopers and attacked those already on the ground. Heavy fighting broke out at scattered locations as the paratroopers floated down. Between injuries suffered in the jump and casualties from enemy contact, the first wave suffered nearly 25 percent casualties.

While the paratroopers still rained down from the morning sky, the amphibious force left their embarkation point on Bataan. Covered by the paratroopers above them on Topside, the first four waves of infantrymen landed unopposed. The fifth wave took fire from a previously quiet Japanese machine gun but, amazingly, incurred no casualties. As suddenly as it had started, the machine gun ceased firing. The fifth wave landed without further incident, joining up with the earlier waves. Already they had captured Malinta Hill with minimal casualties.

Major Jones's second wave of paratroopers began jumping from their planes at 1240. Jones had considered cancelling the airborne assault by 2/503d, but since he still anticipated a Japanese counterattack he elected to continue as planned.

With the Japanese defenders alerted to the invasion of their fortress, Colonel Caskey's battalion received more enemy fire than the first paratroopers. Still, by the time the last member of 2/503d had touched down, Jones had more than two thousand members of his RCT with him. Fifty had been shot and killed as they descended. Another eight had died when their parachutes carried them over the sides of Topside to be smashed on the rocks five hundred feet below. Two hundred ten paratroopers had been put out of action due to wounds or jump-related injuries. Though his combat effectives were accordingly reduced, Jones had not incurred the 50 percent casualties he had predicted in his original planning.

So far the air-amphibious assault of Corregidor had been far more successful than anticipated. Colonel Jones was pleased with the performance of both his paratroopers and the infantry, casualties were much lighter than anticipated, and the Americans had a firm hold on the site of General MacArthur's former headquarters. This was only the beginning, however. More than five thousand Japanese troops still occupied the tunnels of Corregidor. They were determined to drive the Americans off the rocky island, or die trying.

For the balance of D day the paratroopers busied themselves clearing Topside of Japanese. Colonel Erickson's 3/503d concentrated on the northern half of Topside while Major Caskey's 2/503d worked the southern half. Few Japanese were found, but those discovered were felled by quick but deadly bursts of fire from the airborne soldiers' weapons. By the time D day drew to a close, Colonel Jones felt that he had firm control of Topside. He sent a message to Maj. Robert Woods, CO of 1/503d, cancelling the planned 17 February airborne drop of Woods's battalion, and the last battery of the 462d Artillery. Instead, the final contingent of the invasion force would fly to an airfield near Subic Bay, transfer to landing craft, and come ashore across the same beaches the 3/34th had assaulted.

From this change of orders Major Woods drew the proper conclusion that the landing beaches were secure. However, as the 1/503d approached the beaches south of Malinta Hill on 17 February, two Japanese machine guns opened fire on their landing craft. Though the enemy fire was of short duration, six paratroopers died. No further enemy activity impeded the landing. The men of the 1/503d climbed trails to Topside and took up positions as regimental reserve.

The first organized Japanese resistance on Corregidor came just before midnight on 17 February. About fifty screaming, howling Japanese swarmed out of the night. They fell on Company K,

3/34th, sitting atop Malinta Hill. Because they had to charge up a barren, steep slope, the Japanese were easily repulsed by the well dug-in soldiers.

Another, stronger force of Japanese hit Malinta Hill at 0300 on 18 February. This fight raged until the early afternoon. For a time it appeared as if the Japanese might succeed in their effort. Only the massed firepower of the American rifle company prevented that success. Sixty-eight Americans were killed or wounded in the fight; 150 Japanese bodies dotted the hillside.

On Topside, the paratroopers of the 503d RCT listened anxiously to the fierce fighting below them. Most were thankful they were not ensconced on Malinta Hill fighting the Japanese. By the time the next twenty-four hours had passed, however, a large number of these same paratroopers would be dead. Below Topside, in a network of deep-running tunnels, some six hundred Japanese prepared for their own banzai attack.

At 0600 on 19 February, the paratroopers of the 503d were finishing breakfast, shaving, or preparing for a relatively quiet day on Topside. Suddenly, the terrifying chant of hundreds of Japanese erupted from the thickly wooded area just west of the parade ground. While the stunned paratroopers stood there, the chanting changed to screams of "Banzai! Banzai! Banzai!" Then, a moving wall of howling Japanese charged into the open from behind Topside's buildings. Before many paratroopers could react, the Japanese had swarmed over them, hacking them to bits with their swords and knives.

The platoon of paratroopers closest to the attackers disappeared under the weight of the Japanese. The rest of the paratroopers dove for their foxholes and weapons. In a short time the morning air crackled with bursts of M1 rifle and BAR fire. Japanese began falling, but the survivors charged on.

The fighting evolved into hand-to-hand combat as the paratroopers groped at close quarters with the fanatical Japanese. Bayonets and pistols replaced rifles and machine guns as distances narrowed. Small clumps of combatants fought to the death while the Japanese drove on.

Somehow, the beleaguered paratroopers halted the banzai charge. Intrepid Americans willingly risked their lives to stop the Japanese. Finally, it ended. Nearly five hundred dead Japanese lay scattered along the parade ground. Surprisingly, casualties among the 503d were relatively light: thirty-three dead and seventy-five wounded.

Japanese survivors of the frenzied banzai charge continued running east. The paratroopers organized reaction forces to hunt them down. Rather than surrender, almost all the Japanese fought to the death. From small caves and ravines the Japanese engaged their pursuers. They kept fighting until killed by the paratroopers. It would take more than two days before all the Japanese were slain.

In the midst of these mopping-up operations the men of the 503d were unwitting witnesses to yet another desperate attempt by the Japanese to throw the Americans off the island. Unknown to the members of the 3/34th atop Malinta Hill, about two thousand Japanese were trapped beneath them in Malinta Tunnel. The intense preinvasion bombardment had caused massive landslides, sealing the entrances to the tunnel network. Entrapped with the Japanese were tons of ammunition, bombs, and other assorted pyrotechnics.

The leaders of the trapped Japanese concocted a plan that would not only bring them a glorious death, but would also kill many of the hated Americans. They would use a few hundred pounds of TNT to blow a hole in one of the blocked tunnel entrances. Then they'd rush out in a massive banzai charge, killing every American they saw.

At 2230 on 20 February, a tremendous explosion erupted inside Malinta Hill. It was of such huge proportions that many of the American soldiers felt that the entire hill actually moved. Tremendous balls of flame shot out of the tunnel entrance, lighting the night. Rocks, dirt, trees, and other debris flew everywhere. Several large fissures opened in the sides of Malinta Hill, causing more landslides.

On Topside the bewildered paratroopers looked down on the tunnel's entrance, which still belched flame and smoke. What was going on?

The Japanese had miscalculated the effects of their controlled explosion. The backblast from the initial detonation had blown deep into the tunnel, touching off the tons of other explosives stored there. The resulting blast killed nearly fifteen hundred of the assembled Japanese. Only about five hundred, staged in a side tunnel, survived the eruption. When the smoke cleared, most of these snuck out of the tunnel and eventually made their way to the island's tail, there to await the advancing Americans.

And the paratroopers weren't far behind. By D day plus 8, Colonel Jones felt the situation on the main part of Corregidor was stable enough to commence operations against the island's tail. On 24 February Major Woods's 1/503d led the advance eastward.

The paratroopers' ground attack went well. By that afternoon more than a hundred Japanese had been killed. Resistance stiffened at nightfall and the paratroopers dug in. A short time later a brief but violent banzai charge hit Major Woods's battalion. The paratroopers beat off the attackers, losing twenty-one wounded and three killed. One of the dead was Major Woods.

The paratroopers pushed the Japanese eastward into an ever smaller area over the next two days. The fighting was at close quarters as the enemy fought from behind nearly every rock, from in the trees, ravines, caves, and anywhere else that cover was available. The Japanese soldiers had to be rooted out one-by-one in a fight to the death. As they had at Noemfoor, the airborne infantrymen of the 503d RCT were engaged in a brutal no-holds-barred battle with a fanatical foe.

Major John N. Davis had taken command of 1/503d after Woods's death. His battalion continued leading the advance eastward. By the morning of 26 February they were at Monkey Point, overlooking the airfield. The Americans did not know of the extensive tunnel network that permeated Monkey Point. They also did not know that tons of explosive ordnance were stored in these tunnels, too.

At noon on 26 February the Japanese blew up Monkey Point. If possible, this eruption was more powerful than the one that rocked Malinta Hill. Major Davis was catapulted through the air, fortunately landing without serious injury. A thirty-five-ton Sherman tank was tossed about like a child's toy; all inside died. Boulders, rocks, and pieces of human beings flew through the air; some rocks sailed as far as Topside.

American casualties were severe; 52 paratroopers died and 140 were wounded. An estimated 150 Japanese died in the tunnel.

Colonel Jones rushed medics forward from his other battalions to help with the casualties. As soon as the situation was under control he pushed Colonel Erickson's 3/503d through the damaged 1/503d to continue the pursuit of the enemy.

Slowly, cautiously, the paratroopers fought their way down Corregidor's tail. Using small-arms fire and grenades the paratroopers killed the Japanese wherever they could find them. The fighting continued for several more days, but Colonel Jones declared organized resistance ended as of 27 February 1945.

Japanese losses, by actual body count, numbered 4,500 killed; only 20 were taken prisoner. The rest were assumed blown to bits in the two massive explosions.

American casualties totalled 1,005; of these 455 had been killed in action.

General MacArthur returned to Corregidor on 2 March 1945. Demonstrating his natural flair for the dramatic, MacArthur arrived the same way he'd departed three years earlier—by PT boat, Jones escorted MacArthur around Topside, pointing out sites of fierce battles. Then the two men moved to the parade ground.

In front of the assembled survivors of the 503d RCT and 3d Battalion, 34th Infantry, Colonel Jones saluted his commander, then said, "Sir, I present you Fortress Corregidor."

MacArthur returned the salute, then addressed the assembled soldiers. He congratulated them on their courage and their victory. Then, his voice filled with emotion, MacArthur observed, "I see the old flagpole still stands. Have the troops hoist the colors to its peak and let no enemy ever haul them down." At that, a paratrooper color guard rapidly raised the Stars and Stripes to the top of the flagpole.

One week later the 503d RCT departed Corregidor. They returned to Mindoro for several weeks of recuperation, training, and the absorption of replacements.

On 25 March the 503d was alerted for its fourth combat jump of World War II. The 40th Infantry Division was scheduled to land on Negros Island, in the south central Philippines, on 28 March. American intelligence estimated that some forty thousand Japanese held the island. Though most of them were former members of the Japanese air force, untrained in infantry tactics, they still represented a formidable foe. If they proved too much for the 40th, the paratroopers would jump in as quick-reaction reinforcements.

The 40th Infantry Division made a successful landing and quickly pushed the Japanese into the center of the island. When it became apparent that an airborne assault would not be required, Colonel Jones's 503d RCT came ashore via amphibious vehicles. Attached to the 40th, the 503d fought as regular infantry across the jungle-clad mountain ranges of Negros.

The paratroopers dug out, as they had so many times before, the stubborn defenders using tried-and-true small-unit tactics. These same tactics would still be in use twenty years later when the sons of World War II veterans fought the Viet Cong and North Vietnamese.

But that was two decades in the future. Through April, May, and June, the paratroopers chased the Japanese on Negros. Organized resistance on the island was declared over on 10 June 1945. From that point the paratroopers were engaged in routine patrols hunting down small bands of Japanese.

The hunting was still going on when the war ended in August. To the utter amazement of the paratroopers, some six thousand Japanese came out of the Negros mountains over the next few months to surrender and return to Japan.

The 503d Regimental Combat Team sailed from the Philippines for the United States in early December 1945. On Christmas Day 1945, at Camp Anza, California, the 503d RCT was deactivated.

Thirteen years would pass before the 503d was reactivated. Then it was designated the 503d Infantry Regiment (Airborne) and assigned to the 2d Airborne Battle Group on Okinawa.

ACKNOWLEDGMENTS

This book is the result of the efforts of a large number of people. I had the distinct pleasure of interviewing more than eighty men for this project—men who, with just one exception, unselfishly searched the darkest recesses of their minds for memories of this period of their lives. Oftentimes the memories they found were not only long forgotten but painful. Despite the stress of reliving their wartime experiences, these men unhesitatingly responded to my request for help. Whether in a personal interview, by telephone, or by mail, these heroic veterans of the fighting around Dak To shared their recollections with me, a total stranger, because they felt that their story needed to be told.

In addition to giving their stories, most of the veterans provided photographs of themselves and their buddies, as well as letters, diaries, official reports, and the names, addresses, and telephone numbers of other 173d veterans whom they felt I should speak with. Without their unflagging support this book could not have been written.

Among the many men who helped me on this project I would like to extend special thanks to Col. Kenneth Smith, U.S. Army, and Sgt. Maj. Larry Okendo, U.S. Army (Ret.). Because Colonel Smith was then the secretary of the International Society of the 173d Airborne Brigade, he was one of the first veterans I contacted from the 173d. From the time of our initial meeting he was absolutely outstanding in his support of my project. He believed in it from the start and offered guidance and assistance whenever I needed it. In addition, he steered me toward many other 173d veterans from this time period who helped me understand the events of 1967 and their roles in them.

As I interviewed veterans of the 173d many told me I had to talk to "Okie." He's the one, they said, who can really help you. Not only had he served at Dak To, but he had written his own privately published book on the battles around Dak To and knew a lot about what was going on then. After hearing about the legendary Larry Okendo a dozen times, I contacted him at his home in Long Beach, California. From the instant I met this rugged veteran of three wars I knew I had found the man who could help me understand the ins and outs of life in an airborne unit.

Retired Sergeant Major Okendo has conducted research on the 173d and its fights in South Vietnam for years, collecting huge quantities of material. Without hesitation he offered me complete access to his files and agreed to help me in whatever way he could. Sergeant Major Okendo was also instrumental in putting me in touch with several senior officers whose perspective added immeasurably to my comprehension of this time period.

Both Colonel Smith and Sergeant Major Okendo agreed to review a draft of the manuscript. Their uncompromising assistance in helping me accurately portray this time period of the war in South Vietnam was invaluable. Thanks to both of you for all your help.

The other veterans of the 173d Airborne Brigade, 4th Infantry Division, and other units involved in these battles whom I interviewed and to whom I owe a major thank-you are: Lt. Gen. James B. Adamson (Ret.); Robert Allen; Ted G. Arthurs; Jerry M. Babb; Thomas H. Baird; George T. Baldridge; Phillip E. Bodine; Anthony Brangaitis; Charles D. Brown; Ray Bull; Michael D. Burton; Gerald T. Cecil; James Coleman; Col. William J. Connolly; Edward Crook; Gen. John R. Deane, Jr. (Ret.); John M. Deems; Col. Jerry Draper; James R. Duffy; Darryl Fitch; Dr. Joseph X. Grosso; Matthew C. Harrison; Darryl Haymes; Leo E. Hill; David S. Holland; Lawrence Jackley; John Jeakle; David G. Jesmer; Maj. Gen. James H. Johnson (Ret.); Stanley Jones; Edward Kelley; Thomas A. Kelly; Larry C. Kennemer; Lt. Gen. Stanley R. Larsen (Ret.); Ronald R. Leonard; Col. Peyton Ligon; Alfred A. Lindseth; Gen. William Livsey (Ret.); Jerald Lytle; C. Allen McDevitt; Thomas McElwain; Donald Martindale; Joseph S. Mescan; David H. Milton; Irvin W. Moran; James J. Muldoon; Michael Nale; Brig. Gen. Thomas Needham; William Nichols; Bartholomew O'Leary; Manuel Orona; Arturo Ortiz; Phillip Owens; Lt. Gen. Edward A. Partain (Ret.); Richard E. Patterson; Fr. Roy V. Peters; Alan Phillips; John J. Powers; Hugh M. Proffitt; Thomas Remington; Vincent Rogiers; Gen. William B. Rosson (Ret.); Enrique Salas; Philip H. Scharf; Daniel Severson; Edward Sills; John Steer; Sfc. Steven E. Suth; Gerhard Tauss; Steven F. Varoli; Brig. Gen. H.

Glenn Watson (Ret.); Steven Welch; Gen. William C. Westmoreland (Ret); Maj. Gen. Ellis W. Williamson (Ret.); Morrell J. Woods; Robert E. Wooldridge; and Raymond Zaccone.

In addition, Brig. Gen. Frank Akers, U.S. Army, provided valuable insight into the life and command style of Brig. Gen. Leo Schweiter. Retired army Lt. Col. George L. MacGarrigle, historian at the Department of the Army's Center of Military History, rendered help in locating key documents relating to the 2/503d's fight on Hill 875.

My editor at Presidio Press, Bob Tate, believed in this project from the start, encouraged me to pursue it, and tirelessly responded to my many questions.

Most importantly, I must thank my wife, Kay, who willingly gave of her rare spare time to type repeated drafts of the manuscript. She spotted my mistakes and offered suggestions to improve the book.

Despite controversy over their role on the battlefields of South Vietnam, eroding support at home for their sacrifices, and unclear objectives, the Sky Soldiers fought their country's war to the best of their ability, serving courageously and heroically against tremendous odds. Rarely has the United States Army fielded a more intrepid combat unit.

I have been privileged to serve as the recorder of the stories of these brave paratroopers who served their country so well. These men have put their trust in me to tell their story honestly and accurately. With their help, I believe I have achieved that objective. To them I say, AIRBORNE ALL THE WAY!

GLOSSARY

AK-47: Standard NVA assault rifle; Russian manufacture, 7.62mm, magazine-fed, shoulder-fired, automatic rifle.

Alpha: Phonetic designation of the letter *A*.

AM: Air Medal, awarded for both combat heroism and meritorious service.

AO: Area of operations; specifically designated geographical area where a given unit will perform its mission.

ARCOM: Army Commendation Medal; awarded for both combat heroism and meritorious service.

ARVN: Army of the Republic of Vietnam; South Vietnam's military force.

B-40: Russian-manufactured antitank rocket launcher; usually used against American infantry.

Blue Line: River on a map.

Bravo: Phonetic designation of the letter *B*.

BS: Bronze Star; army's fourth highest award, given for both combat heroism and meritorious service.

CA: Combat assault, usually by helicopter.

CAR-15: Modified version of the M16, usually carried by officers.

CBU: Cluster bomb unit; aerial bomb containing dozens of smaller, hand grenade–sized bombs.

C and C: Command-and-control helicopter; used by battalion and higher commanders to oversee a battlefield, usually at altitudes greater than 1,500 feet above ground level.

Captain: Commissioned officer rank above lieutenant; normally in command of a company.

Charlie: Phonetic designation of the letter *C*; also slang for the enemy.

Cherry: A military person new to South Vietnam.

Chicom: Chinese Communist; usually refers to hand grenades.

Chieu hoi: Vietnamese for "Open Arms," a surrender program for NVA or VC; an enemy soldier who surrenders.

Chopper: Helicopter.

CIDG: Civilian Irregular Defense Group; a Special Forces–led, CIA-sponsored force of indigenous personnel.

Claymore: Antipersonnel mines carried by infantry that spew out seven hundred steel balls in a sixty-degree arc fifty meters distant.

Colonel: Commissioned officer rank below general; usually in command of a brigade or holds a senior staff position at division or a higher headquarters.

Company: Infantry unit consisting of three or four platoons, normally commanded by a captain; in Vietnam, companies rarely mustered more than 125 to 130 men in the field.

CP: Command post; location of a unit's commander.

CS: Tear gas.

DDS: Defense Distinguished Service Medal; Defense Department's highest meritorious service award.

DEROS: Date of estimated return from overseas; when a military person can expect to return to the continental United States.

DFC: Distinguished Flying Cross, awarded for both combat heroism and meritorious service.

Dog: Phonetic designation of the letter *D*.

Drive-on rag: A towel, usually green in color, worn around the neck to absorb sweat while humping and to cushion rucksack weight.

DSC: Distinguished Service Cross; army's second highest combat award.

DSM: Distinguished Service Medal; army's highest meritorious service award.

DSS: Defense Superior Service medal; Defense Department's second highest meritorious service award.

Dustoff: Medical evacuation Huey.

EM: Enlisted man.

FAC: Forward air controller; airborne spotter for air strikes.

FDC: Fire direction center; controls artillery battery fire.

Field force: The U.S. Army equivalent of a tactical corps; use of the term *corps* by ARVN forced the U.S. Army to adopt this term to avoid confusion.

Fire team: Basic infantry maneuvering unit; usually consists of three to five riflemen.

1st Sgt: First sergeant; the rank below sergeant major; usually the senior enlisted man in a rifle company.

FNG: Fucking new guy; see **Cherry** above.

FO: Forward observer; usually provided by an artillery battery or a mortar battery to an infantry unit to adjust the fire of the battery via radio from actual observations.

FSB: Fire support base; location of one or more batteries of artillery, secured by infantry; provides on-demand artillery fire for infantry units in the field; usually very mobile.

G-1: Personnel officer at division or higher level.

G-2: Intelligence officer at division or higher level.

G-3: Operations officer at division or higher level.

G-4: Logistics officer at division or higher level.

Grunt: The term used throughout South Vietnam during the war to identify a line infantryman; origin of term is unclear but believed to refer to the sound he made when lifting an eighty-pound pack on his back prior to moving out.

H and I: Harassment and interdiction; random artillery rounds fired, usually at night, in an attempt to catch marauding NVA and VC by surprise.

Hooch: South Vietnamese dwelling; usually made of thatched straw.

Hotel: Phonetic term to designate a unit's medical corpsman.

Huey: Bell UH-1, and later models, of the utility helicopter that was the workhorse in the Vietnam War.

Hump: Soldier's slang term for patrols, especially in the field.

KIA: Killed in action.

Kilo: Phonetic term to designate a radio telephone operator (RTO).

Klick: One kilometer.

LAAW: Light, antitank assault weapon. A one-use only 66mm shoulder-fired weapon; replaced WWII and Korean War bazooka. Used in South Vietnam to attack enemy bunkers.

Leg: Short for "straight leg," a derisive term used by paratroopers to describe a nonairborne-qualified infantryman.

Lieutenant: Lowest commissioned officer rank; usually commands a platoon.

Lieutenant Colonel: Commissioned officer rank above major; usually serves in a staff position at brigade or division level or in command of a battalion.

Lima: Phonetic term to designate 1st Platoon.

LOM: Legion of Merit medal; awarded for meritorious service.

LP: Listening post; set out by anys unit when it establishes a base of operation, regardless of duration; usually two- or three-man teams set up twenty-five to one hundred meters from the unit site to provide advance warning of an enemy attack.

LRRP: Long-range reconnaissance patrol.

LZ: Landing zone; site of a helicopter landing area.

M16: The basic weapon of the U.S. infantryman; 5.56mm semiautomatic, magazine-fed, shoulder-fired, plastic-stock rifle.

M60: U.S. light machine gun; 7.62mm, belt fed, shoulder or tripod fired; team consists of gunner, assistant gunner, and ammo bearer. Usually two M60s per infantry platoon.

M79: 40mm grenade launcher; resembles sawed-off shotgun.

MACV: Military Assistance Command, Vietnam; the highest U.S. command authority in Vietnam.

Major: Commissioned officer rank above captain; normally serves at a battalion staff level or as executive officer of a battalion.

Medevac: Medical evacuation, especially when performed by a Huey for a casualty in the field.

MH: Medal of Honor; highest combat award.

MIA: Missing in action.

Mike: Phonetic term to designate 2d Platoon.

Mike force: A CIDG unit.

MP: Military police.

MSM: Meritorious Service Medal.

Navy Cross: Navy's second-highest combat award.

NCO: Noncommissioned officer; any of the enlisted ranks of sergeant and above.

Net: Radio frequency.

November: Phonetic term to designate 3d Platoon.

NVA: North Vietnamese Army; regular army troops fighting in South Vietnam.

OCS: Officer candidate school.

OLC: Oak Leaf Cluster; small bronze device mounted on medal's ribbon to denote additional awards of that medal.

OP: Observation post.

Opcon (v): Operational control.

Oscar: Phonetic term to designate Weapons Platoon.

Pfc: Private 1st class; the enlisted rank above private.

PH: Purple Heart medal; awarded for wounds received in combat and, posthumously, to those killed in action.

Platoon: Infantry unit consisting of three or four squads; smallest unit normally commanded by a commissioned officer; during the Vietnam War platoons rarely mustered more than twenty-five to thirty men in the field.

PRC-25: Backpack FM radio; used at nearly all levels of command for communications.

PTSD: Posttraumatic stress disorder.

Puff the Magic Dragon: C-47 aircraft equipped with three 7.62mm machine guns capable of firing 5,400 rounds per minute.

Pvt: Private; the lowest enlisted rank.

PZ: Pickup zone.

RPD: Russian-manufactured light machine gun, 7.62mm, comparable to the U.S. M60.

RPG: Russian-manufactured 82mm antitank rocket; used primarily as an antipersonnel weapon against American infantry; larger than the B-40.

RR: Recoilless rifle.

R and R: Rest and recuperation; each man assigned to a one-year tour in South Vietnam was entitled to one week's R and R, at government expense, at one of numerous Pacific Rim cities. Some men also received in-country R and Rs at one of several recreational sites established by the military in South Vietnam.

RTO: Radio telephone operator.

S-1: Personnel officer at battalion or brigade level.

S-2: Intelligence officer at battalion or brigade level.

S-3: Operations officer at battalion or brigade level.

S-4: Logistics/supply officer at battalion or brigade level.

Satchel Charge: Cloth-covered explosive package usually containing twenty pounds of TNT.

Sfc: Sergeant first class; the NCO rank above staff sergeant; usually holds position of platoon sergeant.

Sgt: Sergeant; the lowest noncommissioned rank; usually holds position of fire team leader.

Sgt. Maj.: Sergeant major; the highest enlisted rank; usually the senior enlisted man in a unit, battalion and higher.

Six: Radio term for a unit commander.

SKS: Russian-manufactured NVA carbine.

Slick: Unarmed Huey, especially a troop-carrying Huey.

Snoopy: Same as Puff the Magic Dragon, above.

SOP: Standing operating procedure.

Sp4: Specialist 4th class; enlisted rank above Pfc.

Sp5: Specialist 5th class; enlisted rank above Sp4; holds same pay grade as a sergeant.

Spooky: C-47 transport plane equipped to drop flares, especially over a combat area.

Squad: Infantry unit consisting of two or three rifle teams; usually commanded by a sergeant.

SS: Silver Star; third highest combat award.

SSgt: Staff sergeant; the NCO rank above sergeant; usually holds position of a squad leader.

TAC CP: Tactical command post.

TOC: Tactical operations center; manned by the S-3 and his staff during operations of the unit; battalion commander and/or brigade commander usually here, too, during operations.

V: A device worn on the ribbon of certain decorations to indicate that it was earned for combat valor rather than meritorious service.

VC: Victor Charlie; insurgent indigenous forces in South Vietnam.

Whiskey: Phonetic term to indicate wounded in action.

WIA: Wounded in action.

WO: Warrant officer; a military grade between enlisted men and commissioned officers.

XO: Executive officer; assistant unit commander, usually at company and higher levels.

BIBLIOGRAPHY

Atkinson, Rick. *The Long Gray Line*. Boston: Houghton Mifflin Co., 1989.

Berry, F. Clifton. *Sky Soldiers*. New York: Bantam Books, 1987.

Casey, Michael, et al. *The Army at War*. Boston: Boston Publishing Co., 1987.

Cash, John A., John Albright, and Allan W. Sandstrum. *Seven Fire-fights in Vietnam*. Washington, DC: U.S. Government Printing Office, 1985.

Devlin, Gerard M. *Paratrooper!* New York: St. Martin's Press, 1983.

Dougan, Clark, and Stephen Weiss. *The American Experience in Vietnam*. Boston: Boston Publishing Co., 1988.

Doyle, Edward, et al. *America Takes Over*. Boston: Boston Publishing Co., 1982.

Flanagan, E. M., Jr. *Corregidor*. Novato, CA: Presidio Press, 1988.

Maitland, Terrence, et al. *A Contagion of War*. Boston: Boston Publishing Co., 1983.

Rogers, Bernard W., Lt. Gen. *Cedar Falls-Junction City: A Turning Point*. Washington, DC: U.S. Government Printing Office, 1974.

Scruggs, Jan C., and Joel L. Swerdlow. *To Heal a Nation*. New York: Harper & Row Publishers, 1985.

Stanton, Shelby L. *Anatomy of a Division*. Novato, CA: Presidio Press, 1987.

———. *Order of Battle, U.S. Army, World War II*. Novato, CA: Presidio Press, 1984.

———. *The Rise and Fall of an American Army*. Novato, CA: Presidio Press, 1985.

———. *Vietnam Order of Battle*. Washington, DC: U.S. News Books, 1981.

Tolson, John J., Lt. Gen. *Airmobility 1961–1971*. Washington, DC: Department of the Army, 1973.

Westmoreland, William C. *A Soldier Reports*. Garden City, NY:
    Doubleday & Co., Inc., 1976.

In addition to the above published works, various issues of the following news magazines and newspapers were consulted:

   Life
   Look
   Newsweek
   The Arizona Republic
   The Los Angeles Times
   The New York Times
   Time

Invaluable as references were the Quarterly Lessons Learned reports filed by the 173d Airborne Brigade in 1967 and the various
combat after-action reports issued by specific units of the 173d for
their particular actions.

Index